Debtor Protection in American and European Union Bankruptcy Law: A Comparative Analysis of Automatic Stay

by
Dimitris Liakopoulos[1]

[1] Dimitris Liakopoulos is Professor of international law, European Union law and criminal and procedural law in various Universities in US and Europe. Attorney at Law a New York and Bruxelles. ORCID ID: 0000-0002-1048-6468. The present work is updated until July 2019.

Debtor Protection in American and European Union Bankruptcy Law: A Comparative Analysis of Automatic Stay

by

Dimitris Liakopoulos

W. B. Sheridan Law Books
Academica Press
Washington – London

Library of Congress Cataloging-in-Publication Data

Names: Liakopoulos, Dēmētrēs I., author.
Title: Debtor protection in American and European Union bankruptcy law : a comparative analysis of automatic stay / Dimitris Liakopoulos.
Description: Washington : Academica Press, 2019. | Includes bibliographical references and index. | Summary: "This is a legal study of debtor protection law in the U.S. and EU legal systems"-- Provided by publisher.
Identifiers: LCCN 2019035647 | ISBN 9781680532036 (hardcover)
Subjects: LCSH: Automatic stays in bankruptcy--United States. | Automatic stays in bankruptcy--European Union countries.
Classification: LCC K1379 .L53 2019 | DDC 346.2407/8--dc23
LC record available at https://lccn.loc.gov/2019035647

Dedicated to Sofia and Irene

CONTENTS

METHODOLOGY

The present study aims to analyze in depth the automatic stay in US bankruptcy law, in order to verify if and within what borders today's equality can be said to be justified. The survey will proceed in order to identify the exact source and the actual legal nature which will have different repercussions in terms of operational protection, especially with regard to the hypothesis of its violation, and then to examine the functional and application profiles of the same, with special regard to the repercussions that its operativity expounds on the procedural level. The analysis carried out will allow to verify that, to the detriment of the impression that can be matured prima facie, of a much more rigid and guaranteeing protection mechanism, the automatic stay present, vice versa, aspects of flexibility and with it of derogability to competition rules, completely inedited and unknown in the domestic reality.

In the second part we dedicate this part of our work to the study and exposure of US federal bankruptcy criminal system, paying particular attention to the crime figures that are closer to those contained in the American bankruptcy law, in order to grasp similarities and differences.

In the third part of the present survey a lack in the discipline is evident starting from 1997, at both international and regional level, studies and enacted normative instruments have been carried out, questions of private international law and of procedural law or of substantive law relating to a situation bordering on the subject of this work. The financial crisis recalled the necessity and importance of a coordinated crisis resolution mechanism for large financial conglomerates that the authorities of the States involved can use. We can define, the lack of discipline in the field of cross-border insolvency and especially in the banking sector, as a cumbersome gap, which strikes, in particular, considering that, starting from 1997, at both international and regional level, studies have been carried out and legislative instruments have been issued that deal with questions of private international law and of procedural law or of substantive law relating to cases in line with that which is the subject of this work.

The present work is based on an original research that has tried to make an analysis of the criminal system of protection of the debtor in moments of business crisis by comparing legal sources both from the American system and from the European one. The sources used are in the American penal system and from the European Union that reaches the international private law of the Union.

PART 1

Analysis of automatic stay in the American bankruptcy system. Procedural aspects and jurisprudential evolution.

1.Introduction

The overall North American insolvency regulation is subdivided between the Title 11 of the United States Code, that is the US bankruptcy Code (Bankruptcy Code) containing the regulations of a substantial nature of the matter, and the subsequent Title 28, dedicated to "judiciary and judicial procedure", which, together with the Federal Rules of Bankruptcy Procedures issued by the Supreme Court of the United States, completes this apparatus with some essential procedural and proceedings provisions[2]. The Bankruptcy Code, in force since 1978, is divided into nine Chapters, all originally numbered using only odd numbers, in order to allow future expansions of the legislation (the only exception, in fact, is represented by Chapter 12, inserted with an amendment of 1986)[3]. In particular, Chapters 1, 3 and 5 constitute the so-called universal chapters, i.e. those containing norms destined to be applied in all the remaining chapters of the law, namely, Chapters 7, 9, 11, 12, 13 and 15, called operative chapters as they contain the discipline of different procedures regulated by the Bankruptcy Code[4]. Specifically, Chapter 7 regulates the liquidation procedure, corresponding, for its essentially liquidatory vocation, but open to all types of debtors, except for some limited exceptions; within this procedure the

[2]M.A. FREY, S. K. SWINSON, Introduction to bankruptcy law, Cengage Learning, New York, 2013.

[3]M.A. FREY, S. K. SWINSON, Introduction to bankruptcy law, op. cit.

[4]Section 109 of Bankruptcy Code, "Who may be a debtor", which is stated that: "(...) A person may be a debtor under chapter 7 of this title only if such person is not (1) a railroad; (2) a domestic insurance company, bank (...) (3) (A) a foreign insurance company, engaged in such business in the United States; or (B) a foreign bank (...) that has a branch or agency (...) in the United States (...)". M.A. FREY, S. K. SWINSON, Introduction to bankruptcy law, op. cit.

appointment of a trustee is mandatory. The subsequent Chapter 11 regulates the reorganization procedure, which has always been the subject of attention as it is recognized as an inspiring discipline of negotiation solutions[5], on all the preventive arrangement. This is a procedure that tends to promote recovery even if the possibility that the plan presented by the debtor has the object of liquidation of its activities and that is accessible, approximately, to the same subjects to whom the liquidation procedure is reserved is not excluded; during the procedure, the debtor generally maintains the administration and the availability of his assets (debtor in possession), but it is possible that the court proceeds to appoint a trustee when it deems it opportune. The liquidation and reorganization procedures, as required by section 303 of the Bankruptcy Code, are the only ones to be initiated not only through a voluntary at the request of the debtor himself but also through an involuntary petition after request made by the creditors. The remaining procedures, in addition to being accessible exclusively through the presentation of a voluntary petition, are rehabilitation procedures designed for the benefit of certain categories of debtors, expressly defined by law. First of all, there is the adjustment of debts of a municipality procedure referred to in Chapter 9, which is a recovery instrument intended for public bodies[6]. At Chapter 12 we find the procedure of adjustment of debts of a family farmer or fisherman with regular annual income, always of a sanitary nature, and dedicated to those who operate an agricultural enterprise; following the presentation of petition, which must follow the filing of the recovery plan, the debtor maintains the administration and the availability of his assets, as well as the business of the company (debtor in possession), but the appointment of the trustee is made in any case it is necessary in order to collect the future income of the debtor and redistribute it among the creditors[7]. Chapter 13 regulates the adjustment of debts of an individual with regular income procedure, vaguely similar to our procedures for the composition of the over-indebtedness crisis, as it is prepared for the benefit of debtor (natural person) in order to settle his failure, presenting to creditors a plan

---

[5]M.A. FREY, S. K. SWINSON, Introduction to bankruptcy law, op. cit.
[6]M.A. FREY, S. K. SWINSON, Introduction to bankruptcy law, op. cit.
[7]M.A. FREY, S. K. SWINSON, Introduction to bankruptcy law, op. cit.

to which satisfaction may also be contributed to future income; the debtor, in particular, maintains the availability of his assets (debtor in possession), while the appointment of the trustee will be functional to the control of the correct execution of the plan and the distribution of the sums collected by creditors[8]. Finally, Chapter 15 encompasses the rules dictated in terms of cross-border insolvency (so-called crossborder cases). Coming to the automatic stay, as we have already anticipated, it constitutes a phenomenon operating ex lege, triggered automatically by the submission of an application for admission to a bankruptcy procedure, by virtue of which, from that moment, it is inhibited to creditors the fulfillment of a substantially all-encompassing series of initiatives, judicial or extrajudicial, against the debtor[9]. It is governed by Section 362 of Bankruptcy Code[10], placed in Chapter 3, i.e. one of the so-called universal chapters, and as such intended to find application in all operational chapters: This means, in other words, that the deposit of a petition for access to one of the procedures referred to in Chapters 7, 11 (in these cases, of course, even an involuntary petition), 9, 12 or 13[11], always produces an automatic stay in accordance with the aforementioned standard. In the course of the discussion, therefore, we will speak generically of automatic stay, with indistinct regarding its operativeness in all the procedures governed by the Bankruptcy Code, obviously saved the adaptations that are necessary by virtue of the peculiar aspects of the different disciplines (think, in particular, to the figure of the trustee, to whom the so-called debtor in possession must generally be replaced in the recovery procedures), as well as any differential features that the automatic stay can know in a given procedure (as happens, for example, in proceedings governed by Chapters 12 and 13 where the figure of the so-called codebtor stay is found)[12].

---

[8]M.A. FREY, S. K. SWINSON, Introduction to bankruptcy law, op. cit.
[9]M.A. FREY, S. K. SWINSON, Introduction to bankruptcy law, op. cit.
[10]M.A. FREY, S. K. SWINSON, Introduction to bankruptcy law, op. cit.
[11]I. RAMSAY, Personal insolvency in the 21st century. A comparative analysis of the US and Europe, Hart Publishing, oxford & Oregon, Portland, 2017.
[12]M.A. FREY, S. K. SWINSON, Introduction to bankruptcy law, op. cit.

2.Beneficiaries of the protective effect: The debtor.

Variously disseminated among the eight numbers identifying the initiatives specifically precluded to creditors[13], the beneficiaries of the protection offered by the automatic stay are identified by subsection (a) of Section 362 of the Bankruptcy Code in three distinct entities, namely "the debtor", "the summer property"[14], as well as "the property of the debtor": Both the initiatives personally addressed to the debtor, and those relating to his personal assets, i.e. the bankruptcy one, are therefore subject to the protective efficacy under examination[15].

If this three-dimensional subjective efficacy of the automatic stay finds correspondence, in the process dimension, in the traditional distinction, peculiar to the American system, between proceedings in rem and in personam the first, a dispute concerning certain goods or status, the second , established against a specific person, on the other, and more generally, is also justified by the objectives pursued by the institution: If the debtor, thanks to the institution in comment, is sheltered from aggressive initiatives coming from its creditors, including, of course, attempts to establish pre-emptive rights over his personal assets, it becomes essential to protect, at the same time, the assets merged into

---

[13]S.V. KELLEY, Ginsberg & Martin on bankruptcy, Wolters Kluwer, New York, 2018, par. 3.01[C]. D. G. EPSTEIN, Bankruptcy and related law in a nutshell, West Academic Publishing, Minnesota, 2013, pp. 47. L. B. BARTELL, Visualizing bankruptcy, Lexis Nexis, New York, 2011, pp. 76ss. W.D. WARREN, D.J. BUSSEL, D.A. SKEEL, JR., Bankruptcy, Foundation Press, New York, 2015, pp. 178ss. F. R. KENNEDY, Automatic stays under the new bankruptcy law, in Michigan Journal of Law Reform, 12, 1978, pp. 12ss. S. PARSONS, Consumer bankruptcy law in focus, Wolters Kluwer, New York, 2016. I. RAMSAY, Personal insolvency in the 21st century. A comparative analysis of the US and Europe, Hart Publishing, Oxford & Oregon, Portland, 2017.

[14]H. CRISTENSEN, International estate planning, LexisNexis, New York, 2013. BARTELL, L.B., Staying the serial filer interpreting the new exploding stay provisions of § 362(c)(3) of the Bankruptcy Code, in American Bankruptcy Law Journal, 82, 2008, pp. 224ss

[15]D. G. EPSTEIN, Bankruptcy and related law in a nutshell, op. cit. It seems opportune to remember that the protective efficacy, in relation to the three subjective entities, is configured differently according to the moment in which the claimed claim arose whether it is a matter of claims that arose before or after the date of filing of the petition. On this point, it is essential to understand the link between the automatic stay and the adjacent institutes of discharge and fresh start.

bankruptcy assets, to ensure that the relative liquidation and distribution periods between bankruptcy creditors occur in orderly and coordinated way before the bankruptcy court[16].

The first subject to benefit from the injunction commanded by Section 362 is therefore the debtor, that is, the person who has submitted an application for admission to one of the bankruptcy procedures governed by the Bankruptcy Code, or that it was the recipient: May therefore be an individual or collective entrepreneur, subject to a procedure liquidation, pursuant to Chapter 7 of the law, or reorganization, pursuant to Chapter 11 below; a family farmer or a fisherman with regular annual income, or an individual with regular income involved in a debt restructuring procedure, pursuant to Chapters 12 and 13 respectively of the US bankruptcy law[17].

It should also be noted in advance that the law, with reference to certain categories of debtors, to the detriment of which specific limitations are placed on the possibility of submitting a second application for admission to one of the aforementioned procedures, establishes the inoperativity of the automatic stay: Since the exclusion of protective effects is provided only with regard to a specific creditor initiative of this issue, in compliance with the sedes materiae chosen by the US legislator, we will talk about exceptions to the objective scope of operation of the automatic stay[18].

All the out-of-court initiatives, as well as the proceedings in personam, which have as a recipient this subject and the exceptions expressly dictated by subsection (b), are therefore impeded by the operation of the automatic stay. Suffice it to mention here only that this discipline, with particular regard to judicial initiatives, is justified by the need to ensure that the satisfaction of the claims arising against the debtor prior to the petition is filed before the bankruptcy court, as part of the procedure initiated. The suspension under review is exactly aimed at preventing the creditor from taking initiatives in a different place from that

---

[16]A.N. RESNICK, H.J. SOMMER, Collier on bankruptcy, ed. Mathew Bender, New York, 2013 § 362.02. D.G. EPSTEIN, Bankruptcy and related law in a nutshell, op. cit. 68ss. I. RAMSAY, Personal insolvency in the 21st century. A comparative analysis of the US and Europe, op. cit.

[17]D. G. EPSTEIN, Bankruptcy and related law in a nutshell, op. cit.

[18]M.A. FREY, S. K. SWINSON, Introduction to bankruptcy law, op. cit.

of the forum concursus, which would clearly entail an uneconomic multiplication of times, costs, as well as an inefficient management of the procedure[19].

3.Exceptional nature of Section 362 of the Bankruptcy Code. Possibility of recourse in an integrative way to Section 105 (a) of the Bankruptcy Code.

If the automatic stay is suitable to provide direct and immediate protection to the debtor who has requested admission to one of the procedures prepared by the Bankruptcy Code, of this protection, naturally, will not be able to enjoy other subjects, i.e. third parties. In particular, in the silence of the law on this point, all those third parties who, despite being in bonis, are connected to the debtor by some juridical relationship[20] cannot avail themselves of it.

This is the case of admission to a bankruptcy procedure of a partnership since no provision provides for this event to achieve automatic submission to the proceedings of general partners, i.e. the members without limitation of the same, the stay which is to benefit the corporate body may not extend to such shareholders, who will therefore remain exposed to credit initiatives within the limits of their responsibility.

Another hypothesis is constituted by the guarantors of the debtor, against which the creditors of the latter remain free to proceed, without being subject to any foreclosure.

The statement just completed, namely that the protection offered by automatic stay would only concern the immediate debtor, since the protective effects connected to it cannot be achieved, in the absence of a regulatory provision to that effect, to benefit third parties, has not,

---

[19]A.N. RESNICK, H.J. SOMMER, Collier on bankruptcy, op. cit., § 362.03[3][d]. W.R. NORTON, JR., Norton bankruptcy law and practice, Thomson Reuters, New York, 2018 § 36:4. D. R. COWANS, Cowans bankruptcy law and practice, West Group, Minnesota, 1989, pp. 469ss. W. D. WARREN, D. J. BUSSEL, D. A. SKEEL, JR., Bankruptcy, op. cit. pp. 203ss. D.G. EPSTEIN, Bankruptcy and related law in a nutshell, op. cit. op. cit. I. RAMSAY, Personal insolvency in the 21st century. A comparative analysis of the US and Europe, op. cit.

[20]D. G. EPSTEIN, Bankruptcy and related law in a nutshell, op. cit. I. RAMSAY, Personal insolvency in the 21st century. A comparative analysis of the US and Europe, op. cit.

however, absolute value, knowing temperaments expressly dictated by law, as well as the possibility of being overtaken by judicial means.

As for the former, the reference is to sections 1201 and 1301 of the Bankruptcy Code, which, entitled "Stay of action against co-debtor" dictate a particular discipline with regard to the recovery procedures of adjustments of a family farmer or fisherman with regular annual income (Chapter 12) and adjustment of debts of an individual with regular income (Chapter 13)[21]. Both the aforementioned provisions, in fact, provide that the automatic stay that the law reconnects to the filing of a petition for admission to one of the aforementioned procedures also occurs in respect of the individual intended solely as a natural person who is co-obliged or guarantor of the debtor with regard to a consumer debt of the same, i.e. a debt it has contracted for personal, family, or domestic reasons, and provided that the assumption of this guarantee did not take place within the ordinary course of affairs of the same condemaker[22]. The ratio of these provisions lies, obviously as well as in a logic of stimulus for consumption, in the need to avoid that the debtor is subjected to those indirect pressures deriving from the initiatives that could in any case be exercised by creditors towards relatives or people otherwise bound to the same by emotional ties, and who presumably have committed themselves to guarantee the fulfillment of the aforementioned obligations[23].

---

[21]D. G. EPSTEIN, Bankruptcy and related law in a nutshell, op. cit. I. RAMSAY, Personal insolvency in the 21st century. A comparative analysis of the US and Europe, op. cit.

[22]A.N. RESNICK, H.J. SOMMER, Collier on bankruptcy, op. cit., D.G. EPSTEIN, Bankruptcy and related law in a nutshell, op. cit. J. F. MURPHY, The automatic stay in bankruptcy, in Cleveland State Law Review, 1986, 34, 1986, pp. 569ss.

[23]This aspect would also be suitable to dispel any doubts as to the constitutionality of the aforementioned discipline. The codebtor stay, in fact, is a functional institution, in the first instance, to the protection of the principal debtor, while the protection of the coobbliged subject or guarantor degrades to a merely secondary consequence in pursuing this purpose: With this it is excluded that an illegitimate discrimination has been introduced, deriving from having extended the suspensive effect under review to a person who does not hold the status of debtor under the Bankruptcy Code. On the discipline in question, see: A. N. RESNICK, H. J. SOMMER, Coller on bankruptcy, op. cit., §§ 1201.01, 1301.01, 1301.02 e 1301.04. S.V. KELLEY, Ginsberg & Martin on bankruptcy, Wolters Kluwer, New York, 2018, § 3.03[B]; W. R. NORTON, JR., Norton bankruptcy law and practice, op. cit.; M. A. FREY, S. K. SWINSON, Introduction to bankruptcy law, Cengage Learning, New York, 2013, pp. 395, 464ss. D. G. EPSTEIN, Bankruptcy and related law in a nutshell, op. cit. L. B. BARTELL, Visualizing bankruptcy, ed. LexisNexis, New York, 2011, pp. 77ss. I. RAMSAY, Personal insolvency in the 21st century. A comparative analysis of the US and

Apart from the two hypotheses mentioned, no provision of the Bankruptcy Code provides for the operation of the automatic stay beyond the subjective boundaries set by Section 362[24].

In this regard, it is appropriate to mention the practice established in some courts, where, in order to overcome the rigidity of the legislative provision, we proceeded to apply analogically Section 362 for the benefit of third parties in the presence of unusual circumstances: The latter would occur, in particular, when there is a sort of identification between the debtor and the third party, such that the negative consequences affecting the latter's legal sphere end up. In fact, the former would be jeopardized, with the consequent re-emergence of the eadem ratio of protection of the interests of the procedure underlying the ordinary operation of the automatic stay[25].

Today's institute is the result of a slow and progressive process of regulatory acceptance of judicial powers of an equitable nature, finally culminating in the configuration of an automatic production protective mechanism, where such automatic operation is explained by the establishment of a legal presumption about the existence of an injury to the proceedings in the absence of a protective instrument. In other words, the automatic stay places its beneficiary in a position of absolute advantage, exempting it from the burden of proving the existence of the ordinary assumptions necessary for the ruling of an injunction, being the existence of the same alleged iuris tantum: An exceptional procedural advantage, justified solely by the established protection requirements

---

Europe, op. cit.

[24]B. L. ZARETSKY, Co-debtor stays in chapter 11 bankruptcy, in Cornell Law Review, 73, 1988, pp. 214ss.

[25]This practice, to be precise, has been established starting from the A.H. Robins Co. v. Piccinin case, 788 F.2d (1986), which identified the mentioned unusual circumstances in the hypothesis of identification between the debtor and a third party convicted in an extrafiscal judgment, such that the first can be said to be the real recipient of the sentence that will be issued therein: This is the case, for example, of the third party who claims against the debtor the right to a total indemnity for any negative consequences deriving from the outcome of the extrajudicial judgment, so that it is also appropriate to apply comparison of the protection offered by the automatic stay. In particular see: D.R. COWANS, Cowans bankruptcy law and practice op. cit., pp. 470ss. D. G. BAIRD, The elements of bankruptcy, Foundation Press, New York, 2010, pp. 195ss. O. COUWENBERG, S. J. LUBBEN, Essential corporate bankruptcy law, in European Business Organization Law Review, 16, 2015, pp. 42ss.

mentioned above, and which is reflected in the equally exceptional nature of the rule contained in section 362 of the Bankruptcy Code. It therefore follows that it is impossible to apply this provision analogously to persons other than those to whom the legislator has expressly decided to grant such an advantage, while it is still possible, on the contrary, to extensive interpretation, in order to ensure the widest possible protection for the debtor and the other entities identified therein.

This is not intended to leave an unbridgeable gap in the system, whenever we are faced with situations in which, in fact, it seems appropriate to intervene to protect even third parties, but in some way related to the debtor. With regard to these situations, the solution that seems to us to be more appropriate to the instruments offered by the equitable powers recognized to the bankruptcy court by Section 105 (a) of the Bankruptcy Code: And it is precisely this possibility of judicial exemption of the other hypothesis of temperament to the general rule of the subjective limits of effectiveness of the protection referred to. The aforementioned law, in particular, recognizes to the bankruptcy court the power to issue the measures that are necessary or opportune in order to achieve the aims of the procedure. It is a power, of an equitable nature, equivalent to that dictated by Section 2a (15) in the framework of the Bankruptcy Act of 1898. On the basis of this provision, it is commonly accepted that tribunal's power to pronounce, on the basis of a discretionary assessment, measures of an inhibitory nature having or, as far as it is concerned, recipients different from the requirements of section 362, where the conditions traditionally required for the pronouncement of an injunction[26] are met: In this way, therefore, third parties are guaranteed the

[26]That is, as is constantly stated in the case law on bankruptcy [for all, see the case In King Eagle Picher Industries, Inc., 963, F.2d 855 (1992), 858]: a) The application on the merits; b) the probability, for the individual or the bankruptcy mass, of suffering irreparable damage in the absence of the required provision; c) that the prejudice, that the bankruptcy procedure would suffer in the absence of the junction, is greater than that which should be borne by the third recipient of the same so that the comparative valuation of the interests at stake is to the advantage of the former; d) the consideration, finally, of instances of public interest, in particular with regard to the type of judicial action that is aimed at suspending. For these notions see: A.N. RESNICK, H.J. SOMMER, Collier on bankruptcy, op. cit., §105.03[1]; S. V. KELLEY, Ginsberg & Martin on bankruptcy, op. cit., § 3.02[B]. D.G. EPSTEIN, Bankruptcy and related law in a nutshell, op. cit., pp. 48ss. I. RAMSAY, Personal insolvency in the 21st century. A comparative analysis of the US and Europe, op.

possibility to receive, where appropriate and necessary, adequate protection in the face of possible aggressive actions by creditors of the principal debtor, but this possibility remains subordinate to the ordinary discipline, and therefore to the prior demonstration by the same of the injury to which they would be exposed, without the possibility of benefiting from the exceptional advantage configured by the presumption contained in section 362, which is the basis for the automatic production of the stay[27].

With regard to guarantors, shareholders with unlimited liability of debtor, the concession of injunction based on Section 105 (a) therefore becomes opportune in cases where the creditorial initiatives against them are suitable to affect the results of the bankruptcy proceedings, given, in particular, the possibility for the latter to avail itself of the economic and financial resources made available by these categories of contributors (think of the case in which a reorganization plan prepared in the context of a reorganization procedure provides for the intervention of third parties as the determining factor for the positive outcome of the proposal): These resources would clearly be distracted by this destination in the event that the condemaker should engage elsewhere to deal with the dispute established against him[28].

It is legitimate to ask, at this point, what is the right element to establish the jurisdiction of the bankruptcy court to pronounce provisions with an inhibitory content in favor of third parties with respect to the

---

cit.

[27]For a restrictive reading, guided by the ubi lex voluit principle dixit, ubi noluit tacuit, and as such contrary to any possibility of providing stays in favor of third parties, as this would betray the will expressed by the Congress, but read the summary of M.D. LEAL, The power of the bankruptcy court: section 105, in South Texas Law Review, 29, 1988, pp. 515ss.

[28]A.N. RESNICK, H.J. SOMMER, Collier on bankruptcy, op. ult. cit., § 105.04[1]; S. V. KELLEY, Ginsberg & Martin on bankruptcy, op. cit., § 3.03[C][2]. D. R. COWANS, Norton bankruptcy law and practice, op. cit. W. D. WARREN, D. J. BUSSEL, D. A. SKEEL, JR., Bankruptcy, op. cit., pp. 204ss. D. G. BAIRD, The elements of bankruptcy, op. cit. P. A. MURPHY, E. E. SAGERMAN, D. NEIER, Creditor's rights in bankruptcy, ed. Thomson Reuters, New York, 2017. D.G. EPSTEIN, Bankruptcy and related law in a nutshell, op. cit. J. F. MURPHY, The automatic stay in bankruptcy, op. cit., pp. 571ss, with specific regard to the reorganization procedure governed by Chapter 11. For further details see: B. L. ZARETSKY, Co-debtor stays in chapter 11 bankruptcy, op. cit., pp. 274ss. I. RAMSAY, Personal insolvency in the 21st century. A comparative analysis of the US and Europe, op. cit.

procedure. Recalling what has been said with regard to the Bankruptcy Act of 1898[29], and based on the criterion of custody legislation, although understood in a broad sense and therefore suitable to understand the assets owned by the debtor wherever located, it is clear that in such conditions, the decision to suspend the benefit it would be included among the powers of the court. The faculty of which now is the subject, in fact, is due to one of the main innovations of the current bankruptcy law, that is to say to the broader jurisdiction which, as we have already mentioned, Section 1334 (b) of Title 28 of the United States Code grants to district courts and, thus, to bankruptcy courts for the district: A jurisdiction, that is, suitable to include all civil proceedings that arise within the Bankruptcy Code, or that derive or are otherwise related to cases in this area arising[30]. Among the civil proceedings connected to a procedure governed by the bankruptcy law, in particular, jurisprudence peacefully encompasses judgments whose outcome may be apt to cause prejudice to the bankrupt active mass[31]: Where the stay request in favor of the condemaker is justified by the possibility, in case of suspension of the creditorial initiatives against the same, to make an essential contribution to the procedure, the bankruptcy court can therefore affirm its jurisdiction and pronounce the equitable provision offered by Section 105 (a)[32].

4.Permissive and required joinder of parties. Automatic stay and reviews with plurality of parts

Speaking of the effectiveness of automatic stay towards third parties for the particular importance that it assumes in the present survey, the question about the impact exerted by the protective effects in question on the judgments with plurality of parts (so-called joinder of parties), one

[29]D.G. EPSTEIN, Bankruptcy and related law in a nutshell, op. cit.

[30]In re Pacor, Inc., 743 F.2d 984 (1984), 994. For further details see: M.L. COOK, Bankruptcy litigation manual, Wolters Kluwer, New York, 2015. R.F. BRUDE, Reorganizations under Chapter 11 of the bankruptcy code, Law Journal Press, New York, 2018. G.W. NEWTON, R. LIGUERMAN, Bankruptcy and insolvency taxation, Wiley & Sons, New York, 2012, pp. 528ss.

[31]B.L. ZARETSKY, Co-debtor stays in chapter 11 bankruptcy, op. cit., pp. 222ss.

[32]D.G. EPSTEIN, Bankruptcy and related law in a nutshell, op. cit., I. RAMSAY, Personal insolvency in the 21st century. A comparative analysis of the US and Europe, op. cit.

of which, of course, is the debtor who has requested admission to one of the procedures governed by the Bankruptcy Code.

Even the civil procedural law of the United States knows, in the context of a discipline regulating the subjectively complex causes flexible and geared to ensure, as a primary objective, the economy of judgments, the distinction between optional and necessary joinder of parties, so the investigation will have to proceed by analyzing the two cases in detail. Since, however, and as we will see better, the suspension offered by Section 362 of the Bankruptcy Code concerns only the judgments established against the debtor, the hypothesis to be taken into consideration is precisely that of the passive joinders (so-called joinder of defendants)[33].

Among the subjectively complex cases, the permissive joinder of defendants is governed by rule 20 (a) (2) of the Federal Rules of Civil Procedure, which the establishment of this type of joinder allows the occurrence of two cumulative circumstances: First of all, that the plaintiff's right arising from one and the same legal fact is asserted in respect of several persons, in solidarity, or in a subordinate manner, and, secondly, that the dispute concerns a question of fact or common law to all defendants.

Since it is characterized, naturally, by the separability of the subjective cumulation, and therefore by the possibility that each co-plaintiff is sued separately, the slope of a permissive joinder of defendants does not matter particular criticality when the automatic stay with the co-plaintiff debtor takes place, inasmuch as the suspensive efficacy connected to it can affect exclusively the juridical sphere of the latter: Thus, the judge can proceed to remove this subject from the judgment, or to separate the case between him and the actor[34], while the original process it will be able to continue with the other optional litigation in bonis. The latter, therefore, will not benefit from the suspensive effects in question, nor will they be

---

[33]D.G. EPSTEIN, Bankruptcy and related law in a nutshell, op. cit.

[34]The text affirmed that: "Persons (...) may be joined in one action as defendants if: (A) any right to relief is asserted against them jointly, severally, or in the alternative with respect to or arising out of the same transaction, occurrence, or series of transactions or occurrences; and (B) any question of law or fact common to all defendants will arise in the action".

affected by this in a reflexive way[35], as the judgment regarding the same will in any case continue.

The possibility, however, for the same, to ask the bankruptcy court for an appropriate suspension of the judgment also against them, pursuant to the aforementioned Section 105 (a) of the Bankruptcy Code: This request can be grounded, for example, in the prejudice that the automatic stay produces towards them, given the consequent impossibility of proposing incident questions, cross claim against the debtor[36], or the non-participation of the latter to the so-called discovery, that is, the process aimed at making edite all the parts of the evidence available to the other parties, and to acquire the instructing elements that may prove useful[37], or again the opportunity to suspend the judgment also against the litigation in bonis can reconnect with the need to prevent a multiplication of judgments, and the consequent diseconomies[38]. It should be noted that, in

---

[35]It is not necessary, therefore, that all matters are common, but the commonality of a single question is also sufficient, which, moreover, does not necessarily have to be challenged, so that any admission or non contestation, by one of the defendants, about the existence of the fact based on the common question is not impeding the possibility of establishing the litisconsort; the only limits, in addition to the conditions described above, concern compliance with the rules on subject matter, jurisdiction and venue (i.e. territorial jurisdiction). In this topic see: G.C. HAZARD, JR., J. LEUBSDORF, D.L. BASSETT, Civil procedure, Foundation Press, New York, 2011, pp. 557ss. L.L. TEPLY, R.U. WHITTEN, Civil procedure, Carolina Academic Press, 2013, pp. 727ss.See, in this regard, the rule 21 of the Federal Rules of Civil Procedure, pursuant to which the court, at the request of the party or office can, at any time, and where conditions exist, expel a party from the judgment, or arrange for the separation of one of the cumulative causes.

[36]D.R. COWANS, Cowans bankruptcy law and practice, op. cit., 471; P.A. MURPHY, E.E. SAGERMAN, D. NEIER, Creditors' rights in bankruptcy, op. cit., pp. 178ss. A.N. RESNICK, Bankruptcy law, West Group, St. Paul Minnesota, 2002, pp. 70ss. D. G. EPSTEIN, Bankruptcy and related law in a nutshell, op. cit., pp. 71ss. J.F. MURPHY, The automatic stay in bankruptcy, op. cit., pp. 570ss. The typical hypothesis of optional passive jointer is represented by the hypothesis of several subjects co-obliged for the same obligation, of contractual origin or for illicit fact.

[37]The cross claim institution is governed by rule 13 (g) of the Federal Rules of Civil Procedure, and consists of the claim that a party can assert against a jointer, "if the claim arises out of the transaction or occurrence that is the subject matter of the original action or of a counterclaim, or if the claim relates to any property that is the subject matter of the original action": In argument see: L. L. TEPLY, R. U. WHITTEN, Civil procedure, op. cit., pp. 665ss. G. C. HAZARD, JR., J. LEUBSDORF, D. L. BASSETT, Civil procedure, op. cit., pp. 254ss.

[38]This is the argument spent in the well known Lynch v. Johns Manville Sales Corp. case, 710 F.2d 1194 (1983), 1199, where an application for compensation for non pecuniary damage had been filed against several asbestos producers. Following the requests for

this circumstance, the inhibitory provision becomes opportune, pursuant to Section 105 (a), in order to ensure that the achievement of purposes of the procedure does not entail iniquity to the detriment of other subjects: A justification, therefore, different from the protection needs analyzed above, with regard to the obligors of the debtor.

The situation is different in the case in which, in the context of extra-food judgment, there is a necessary (passive) joinder, that is a required (or compulsory) joinder of parties, between the debtor and one or more performing subjects. The institute is governed by the previous rule 19 of the Federal Rules of Civil Procedure, where it is provided that, if possible, the joinder must be established when three circumstances are envisaged, as an alternative: As far as it is concerned, the first hypothesis envisaged, i.e. the fact that, in the absence of a joinder, the court cannot grant full protection to the plaintiff towards the present parties[39].

If it is ascertained that a required party has not been mentioned, the court must order the integration of the adversarial against the same: If this, however, proves to be not feasible and is taking into account this eventuality that the present statement "if possible" in the text of the law, the court must determine whether, in "equity and good conscience", the action may in any case continue with regard to the parties present only or must be closed with a pronouncement of dismissal.

It is precisely in this duplicity of the possible developments of the controversy that the further subdivision is inserted, peculiar to the

---

admission to a reorganization procedure, with consequent production of the automatic stay for the benefit of only two defendants, the other litigates in bonis requested the ruling of a suspension provision pursuant to section. 105 (a) in order, in fact, to avoid the fragmentation of judgments: The court however, rejected the request, noting that predominant, with respect to this value, were the interests of the plaintiffs, and in particular the fact that many of them and some crucial witnesses were on the verge of dying, so it was necessary to proceed urgently.

[39]Only this hypothesis, in fact, appears applicable to the hypothesis of necessary litigation, while the other conditions are obviously dedicated to the active situation, which occur when the jointer claims a right relating to the subject of the dispute, such that a decision taken in his absence it is likely to affect or prevent the possibility, for this subject, to adequately protect his situation, or to leave one of the parties present, evidently agreed, exposed to the risk of having to respond several times to the obligation assumed by virtue of a same obligatory relationship, with a multiplication of judgments; on this rule, see L.L. TEPLY, R.U. WHITTEN, Civil procedure, op. cit., pp. 710ss. J.H. FRIEDENTHAL, M.K. KANE, A.R. MILLER, Civil procedure, op. cit., pp. 355ss.

American and unknown order that doctrine and jurisprudence have identified within the general category of required parties: There is distinguished, in fact, between necessary parties, that is to say those that must be included in the case, but whose non joinder[40] is justified and does not entail the closure of judgment, and indispensable parties, i.e. those whose participation is so essential for the resolution of the dispute that it is impossible to quote them in court, the case cannot be continued. The regulation of the effects produced by the original or subsequent failure to establish the necessary litigation does not therefore imply US procedural law, i.e. the extinction of the trial or the inexistence of the sentence that is nevertheless pronounced, even if the contradictory is not integrated. The absent part is only necessary, in fact, it is quite possible, even in the face of its non-participation in the trial, to continue the judgment if the court discretely assesses that it is possible to make a decision usefully and fairly even between the two parties present[41]; where, on the contrary, the part is indispensable, the judge must opt for the admissibility of the proceedings, and then order the closure[42].

If a party carries necessary or indispensable qualification, however, it is not a matter predetermined by the law, which is rather limited, with rule 19 (b), to dictate to the judge some guiding criteria, suitable to assist him in an evaluation that remains however discretionary, to be carried out case by case; he will have to consider, in particular: If a judgment rendered in the absence of the qualified party as required may prejudice the latter or the other parts of the judgment; if this prejudice can be adequately avoided by means of appropriate provisions that he himself may adopt; if the protection accorded to a contradictory that is not complete is in any case adequate and satisfactory for the parties present; finally, if the plaintiff can in any case obtain adequate alternative

---

[40]That is, in fact, the impossibility of integrating the adversarial against a party, to be considered required pursuant to rule 19: for everyone, G.C. HAZARD, JR., J. LEUBSDORF, D. L. BASSETT, Civil procedure, op. cit., pp. 244ss.

[41]G.C. HAZARD, JR., J. LEUBSDORF, D.L. BASSETT, Civil procedure, op. cit., pp. 283ss. J.H. FRIEDENTHAL, M.K. KANE, A.R. MILLER, Civil procedure, op. cit.

[42]G.C. HAZARD, JR., J. LEUBSDORF, D.L. BASSETT, Civil procedure, op. cit., pp. 285ss. J.H. FRIEDENTHAL, M.K. KANE, A.R. MILLER, Civil procedure, op. cit. pp. 356ss.

protection if the judgment is closed for non joinder[43]. Only if, at the end of this assessment, it appears clear to the court that it is in no way possible to avoid the aforementioned prejudices arising from the definition of the non-compliant or incompatible dispute, the absent part will be declared indispensable, and it will be closed rite of judgment[44].

Once the examination of the general discipline of the required joinder of parties has been completed, we can once again turn our attention to the interrelations between the same and the supervised automatic stay.

If the debtor is a subject with the qualification of required defendant, so that it is necessary to integrate the adversarial with the same, it is therefore necessary to first assess whether such integration is possible: For this purpose, it is clear that the protection offered by automatic stay is extended to prevent any judicial initiative that can be carried out against the same, including his summons in the trial, to be established or already pending. The automatic stay, in other words, constitutes precisely a case of impossibility of integrating the adversarial against the debtor required defendant. This data leads us to the next question, ie the need to check whether this subject is a necessary or an indispensable party, and therefore if its failure to assume the quality of a party does not prevent the prosecution of the proceedings against the parties present, or if leads to a ruling of dismissal: The investigation, of course, will be carried out evaluating the factors dictated by rule 19 (b), and may result in a dismissal decision against all parties to the possibility of establishing the dispute against all the indispensable defendants when the protective effect in favor

---

[43]The norm it's the following: "If a person who is required to be joined if feasible cannot be joined, the court must determine whether, in equity and good conscience, the action should proceed among the existing parties or should be dismissed. The factors for the court to consider include: (1) The extent to which a judgment rendered in the person's absence might prejudice that person or the existing parties; (2) the extent to which any prejudice could be lessened or avoided by: (A) Protective provisions in the judgment; (B) shaping the relief; or (C) other measures; (3) whether a judgment rendered in the person's absence would be adequate; and (4) whether the plaintiff would have an adequate remedy if the action were dismissed for non joinder". See in argument: L. L. TEPLY, R. U. WHITTEN, Civil procedure, op. cit.; J. H. FRIEDENTHAL, M. K. KANE, A. R. MILLER, Civil procedure, op. cit., pp. 362ss. For a pure valorization of the public interest to avoid a multiplication of judgments, G. C. HAZARD, JR., J. LEUBSDORF, D. L. BASSETT, Civil procedure, op. cit., pp. 286ss.

[44]G.C. HAZARD, JR., J. LEUBSDORF, D.L. BASSETT, Civil procedure, op. cit., pp. 292ss. L.L. TEPLY, R.U. WHITTEN, Civil procedure, op. cit.

of the debtor has ceased in the establishment or continuation of the judgment with regard to the parts already established. In any case, the automatic stay intervened to protect the debtor required defendant prevents the implementation of the necessary litigation against the same.

In the hypothesis, vice versa, in which the necessary litigation has already been established, before the petition was filed, against the debtor, it is necessary to assess the consequences, on the pending judgment, of the injunction in favor of this subject.

The solution of the problem is quite easy for the eventuality in which the debtor is a merely necessary joinder: Since, in this case, the investigation carried out pursuant to rule 19 (b) led to qualify the debtor in terms of the subject whose non-participation in the proceedings does not prevent the prosecution of the process against the other passive litigates in bonis, the scenario will not be dissimilar to what was seen with regard to the permissive joinder of defendants. The suspensive effect produced by the automatic stay, therefore, will only affect the legal sphere of the debtor, who will be expelled from the trial, whose prosecution will remain possible in respect of the other joinders, save the possibility for the latter to request an injunction to senses of Section 105 (a) of the Bankruptcy Code.

More marked criticalities, vice versa, emerge in the case in which, at the end of the analysis carried out in accordance with the aforementioned rule 19 (b), the judge finds that the debtor is an indispensable party: In this case, the law requires inescapably that the adversarial is also extended to this subject, under penalty of closing the process. Now, in the case we are dealing with, the dispute had been established prior to the petition being filed, and the debtor had also been properly sued for taking on the role of party; the automatic stay in relation to this subject, however, implies that the judgment cannot be continued against him: In this case, unlike what is seen with regard to the case of necessary party, the debtor's exclusion from the court reveals a very uneconomic solution, as well as contra legem, since, as mentioned, the failure to assume the quality of a party by a qualified person as indispensable involves the issuing of a dismissal provision[45]. It follows,

[45]J.H. FRIEDENTHAL, M.K. KANE, A.R. MILLER, Civil procedure, op. cit., pp. 356ss.

therefore, that the possible paths are two: There is, first of all, the possibility for the actor to request a measure of relief from the automatic stay aimed at allowing him the prosecution of the judgment against the debtor and, therefore, of all the necessary litigations; secondly, it is correctly argued that the inseparability of the dispute imposes, obviously, that the operation of the automatic stay incurred to the advantage of the necessary joinder debtor, can achieve the suspension of the process also in favor of the other joinders, in order to guarantee that the dispute can be summarized, in relation to everyone, before the bankruptcy court, or resumed, in an extra-bankruptcy venue, only once the suspensive efficacy intervened in favor of the debtor has ceased. In this regard, however, it should be noted that the jurisprudence is used to base such suspension on that analogical application of Section 362 in favor of third parties, justified by the appeal of unusual circumstances, which would be integrated, to be precise, by a sort of identification, which is implemented on a procedural level, between the debtor and the other necessary litigation, to be considered as entities inextricably connected[46]. We have already had the opportunity to express our opinion on the orientation described above. The exceptional nature of the rule contained in the section cited, which places in favor of the applicant the admission to one of the procedures governed by the Bankruptcy Code a relative legal presumption, only justified by the particular situation in which the subject in favor of which it is placed, is opposed to the possibility of its application to subjects other than the debtor himself, so that, even in this case, it appears preferable to resort to the injunction obtainable through the powers conferred on the bankruptcy court by Section 105 (a)[47]. In the present case, moreover, it is reasonable to consider that among the requisites envisaged for the granting of such a measure, the court will also assess the possible negative consequences deriving from the dismissal decision of the subjectively complex request.

5.(Follows) Bankruptcy assets.

The second category, among the beneficiaries of protective effects

[46]See the case: Oklahoma federated gold and numismatics, Inc. v. Michael W. Blodgett, F.3d 136 (1994), 141ss.

[47]J.H. FRIEDENTHAL, M.K. KANE, A.R. MILLER, Civil procedure, op. cit., pp. 356ss.

produced by automatic stay is represented, as mentioned, by the bankruptcy mass, that is, to put it in the words used by Section 362, "the summer property"[48]: It is, of course, composed of debtor's assets that will be used to satisfy creditors, as part of the bankruptcy proceeding initiated. This entity finds specific discipline in Section 541 of the Bankruptcy Code, where is prescribed that with the filing of a petition for the opening of one of the procedures governed by Chapters 7, 11, 12 or 13 of the law, the creation of summer property is established[49]. First of all, it includes, pursuant to subsection (a) of the aforementioned law, all the interests of a legal or equitable nature in property[50] of which the debtor is the holder at the start of the procedure, wherever they are and by whomever they are possessed: They, in other words, from the moment of filing the petition flow into the bankruptcy mass. The rule is therefore suitable to include all types of subjective legal situations of advantage and not only, therefore, the existing property rights of the debtor, exercisable on tangible or intangible assets, as well as the claims that may be brought to trial[51]; this

---

[48]See in argument: A.N. RESNICK, H.J. SOMMER, Colliers on bankruptcy, op. cit., 5, § 541.01. S.V. KELLEY, Ginsberg & Martin on bankruptcy, op. cit., § 3.03[C][2]. B.A. BLUM, Bankruptcy and debtor/creditor, Aspen Publishers, The Hague, 2010, pp. 292ss. M.A. FREY, S.K. SWINSON, Introduction to bankruptcy law, op. cit., pp. 236ss. W.D. WARREN, D. J. BUSSEL, D. A. SKEEL, JR., Bankruptcy, op. cit., pp. 29ss. D.G. BAIRD, The elements of bankruptcy, op. cit., pp. 95ss. D.G. EPSTEIN, Bankruptcy and related law in a nutshell, op. cit., pp. 92ss. R.A. JOHNSON, M.C. O'LEARY, Automatic stay provisions of the bankruptcy act of 1978, in New Mexico Law Review, 13, 1983, pp. 604ss. I. RAMSAY, Personal insolvency in the 21st century. A comparative analysis of the US and Europe, op. cit. R.W. RIEHL, Property of the estate, in Bankruptcy Developments Journal, 1, 1984, pp. 332ss. G. ORLANDI, Property of the estate: section 541, in Bankruptcy Developments Journal, 3, 1986, pp. 342ss. S.C. GIESER, Property of the estate: section 541(a)(1), in Bankruptcy Development Journal, 4, 1987. O. COUWENBERG, S. J. LUBBEN, Essential corporate bankruptcy law, op. cit.

[49]S.V. KELLEY, Ginsberg & Martin on bankruptcy, op. cit., § 5.01[A]; W. D. WARREN, D. J. BUSSEL, D. A. SKEEL, JR., Bankruptcy, op. cit., pp. 29ss. L.B. BARTELL, Visualizing bankruptcy, op. cit., pp. 65ss.

[50]The term "interest" means a very large legal category suitable to include any right, claim, title, portion, quota or participation in a good or right, or the good or right; to be precise, it is suitable to indicate, from time to time, a right in general or a share of it, a legal interest, a right subject to condition or term, an acquired right, an expectation of law or fact, a status or other subjective legal situation, as well as an obligation related to a specific good, which finds its origin in the common law or in the equity.

[51]It is debated whether a situation of mere possession including those corresponding to imprisonment can be traced back to the category of interests, thus converging in the summer: in this sense majority jurisprudence seems to be oriented (In case of international

general and substantially all-encompassing provision, inter alia, include the community property interests of debtor and spouse, increases and profits of bankruptcy property, as well as any interest in property that the summer subsequently purchases at the beginning of the procedure[52]. Particular mention also deserves the interests in property that the trustee recovers from bankruptcy assets thanks to the exercise of his turnover or avoiding powers. In the first case, these are assets on which the debtor has a subjective legal situation of advantage and that find, on the date of the start of the bankruptcy proceedings, in the possession of third parties, so that, with the opening of the procedure, the mass becomes the holder in respect of such subjects of a right to their return[53]; in the second case, vice versa, there is an act of exercise by the trustee of powers aimed at recovering the bankruptcy mass of assets, rights or other subjective situations that have been object of the deeds of provision before or after the petition has been filed[54].

A particular discipline, vice versa, is dictated with regard to contingencies: The assets and rights that the debtor acquires after the petition is filed, as well as the gains deriving from the services rendered by him in the period subsequent to that moment, in fact, generally converge in the summer, being functional to guarantee the fresh start, that is the possibility of establishing new legal relationships from the day

---

home design, Inc., 28 BR 584 (1983), 586); for a summary of the question, in doctrine, R.W. RIEHL, Property of the estate, op. cit., pp. 332ss. G. ORLANDI, Property of the estate: section 541, op. cit., pp. 353ss.; contra, W.D. WARREN, D.J. BUSSEL, D.A. SKEEL, JR., Bankruptcy, op. cit., pp. 35ss.

[52]H. CRISTENSEN, International estate planning, op. cit.

[53]A.N. RESNICK, H.J. SOMMER, Collier on bankruptcy, op. cit., § 541.02; S.V. KELLEY, Ginsberg & Martin on bankruptcy, op. cit., § 5.01[B]. R. W. RIEHL, Property of the estate, op. cit., pp. 338ss. R.A. JOHNSON, M.C. O'LEARY, Automatic stay provisions of the bankruptcy act of 1978, op. cit., pp. 605ss. H.B. PICKARD, The new bankruptcy code, part II: the interests of secured creditors under the new bankruptcy code, in Memphis State University Law Review, 10, 1980, pp. 210, 220ss. C. GIESER, Property of the estate: section 541(a)(1), op. cit., pp. 124ss.

[54]The mentioned turnover powers are governed by section 542 of the Bankruptcy Code, where it is provided that any subject including the same debtor who is in possession, custody or control of assets or rights over which the summer holds an interest, must return them in kind or equivalent to the trustee, i.e. the due insights. See: L.B. BARTELL, Visualizing bankruptcy, op. cit. pp. 70ss. W.D. WARREN, D. J. BUSSEL, D.A. SKEEL, JR., Bankruptcy, op. cit., pp. 36ss. H.B. PICKARD, The new bankruptcy code, part II: The interests of secured creditors under the new bankruptcy code, op. cit., pp. 223ss.

following the request for admission to a bankruptcy procedure[55]; however, if this is true for the liquidation proceeding established pursuant to Chapter 7, this does not apply to the reorganization procedures governed by subsequent Chapters 11, 12 and 13, where such acquisitions, with regard to the debtor, are property of the summer, to be allocated to the implementation of the recovery plan, and as such protected by the automatic stay specifically designed to protect the summer[56].

An interesting criticality related to the definition of what constitutes property of the summer, in the silence of the law on the subject, is represented by the fate of the arguable property, that is to say goods or rights, in relation to which, at the time the petition was presented, the existence of an interest in the debtor is uncertain: This, with all the evidence, acquires fundamental importance for the present purposes, because debtor, of a determined subjective legal situation, relevant as it is

[55]And we will see, in the next section of this chapter, what this actually entails. Suffice it to anticipate that, against the debtor and his personal assets, the automatic stay exerts its exclusive effect only against bankruptcy creditors, so that, as far as we are concerned, in the liquidation procedure the third parties who undertake new legal relations with the debtor, in the period following the petition, will be free to act on the contingent emerged, as mentioned, in the "property of the debtor", however freed, thanks to the discharge, by the residual claims of bankruptcy creditors , consistently with the objective of guaranteeing this subject the immediate fresh start. On the contrary, in the reorganization procedures referred to in Chapters 11, 12 and 13, the automatic stay placed to protect bankruptcy assets is effective both with regard to bankruptcy loans and those arising after the petition was filed: therefore, since the contingencies flow into the summer, they will be unassailable even for third parties with whom the debtor decides to undertake new legal relations after the application for admission to one of the aforementioned procedures, with the aim of ensuring that contingencies are also allocated to execution of the plan. The provisions of reference, with regard to the reorganization Chapters, are, respectively, sections 1115 (a), 1207 (a) and 1306 (a). In argument see: S. V. KELLEY, Ginsberg & Martin on bankruptcy, op. cit., § 5.03; B. A. BLUM, Bankruptcy and debtor/creditor, op. cit., pp. 296ss. W. D. WARREN, D. J. BUSSEL, D. A. SKEEL, JR., Bankruptcy, op. cit., pp. 29, 35ss. M. A. FREY, S. K. SWINSON, Introduction to bankruptcy law op. cit., pp. 239ss. L. B. BARTELL, Visualizing bankruptcy, op. cit., pp. 67ss. For the section 1306, see also: A. N. RESNICK, H. J. SOMMER, Collier on bankruptcy,op. cit., 8, § 1306.02[2] e [3]. T. E. RAY, Postpetition claims and the automatic stay in chapter 13, in ABI Journal 19, 2000, pp. 12ss.

[56]A further exception, then, concerns the interests in property that the debtor purchases in the 180 days following the petition's deposit: in particular, pursuant to the aforementioned Section. 541, regardless of the type of procedure initiated, the assets that, in this time frame, the debtor purchases by inheritance or tied, by virtue of a division agreement with the spouse or divorce, or as a beneficiary of life insurance for everyone, S. V. KELLEY, Ginsberg & Martin on bankruptcy, op. cit., op. cit., § 5.03[B].

suitable to flow into the summer as a result of the application for admission to a bankruptcy procedure, follows or less its subjection, to the protection offered by the automatic stay to the bankruptcy mass, and therefore in the last instance, the possibility for the creditor who, in the thesis, denies the belonging of the good or the right to the debtor and therefore the subsequent confluence in the bankruptcy mass, to act enforceably on the same, without the burden of requesting liberation in advance from the stay, or without the risk of incurring a violation of the prohibition imposed by Section 362[57]. In such cases, the recognition of the ownership of an interest in property by the debtor constitutes a question prejudicial to the subsequent belonging of the same to the bankruptcy mass, and therefore to the subjection to the benefit that the automatic stay offers to the summer. It is clear that in order to proceed to any initiative that involves problems relating to the operation of automatic stay, the preliminary question must be resolved, that is to say, the question concerning the original existence of the subjective legal situation of advantage for the debtor. Such problematic has found solution, in US jurisprudence, through a shared valorization of one, between the fundamental finality pursued by the normative, that is the requirement to assure an equal distribution of the bankruptcy assets among the creditors, objective that would obviously be frustrated where allowed to only one of them to satisfy an asset whose membership of the debtor, and therefore the mass, is still to be ascertained: This argument has thus led to the affirmation of a presumption of belonging of the arguable property to the debtor, so that itself, flowing into the summer, can fully benefit from the automatic stay. It can be said, therefore, that this institution is called upon to perform, in the circumstances, a function similar to that of a judicial seizure, that is, the custody of the good or right during the time necessary to ascertain its ownership; it follows that the creditor who wants to demonstrate its extraneousness to debtor assets, consequently, to the bankruptcy mass, in order to freely act in an executive way on the same, will therefore be charged with the prior request for release from the automatic stay: The

[57]See, In re Chesnut, 422 F.3d 298 (2005). In re Levenstein, 371 B.R. (2007). For further details see. O. BERTRAND, F. LUMINEAU, Partners in crime. The effects of diversity on the longevity of cartels, in Academy of Management Journal, 59 (3), 2015.

decision about the existence of a given interest in property by the debtor cannot in any way be left to the unilateral initiative of the creditor[58].

In conclusion, the summer constitutes a separate asset, of which the debtor loses his property, while the trustee assumes its substantial and procedural representation. As an autonomous entity, Section 362 therefore considers the bankruptcy mass as the automatic stay beneficiary, in order to prevent creditor initiatives aimed at obtaining the satisfaction of the related claims outside the specific procedure, to be carried out in insolvency proceedings, before the bankruptcy court[59].

6.(Follows) Debtor's personal assets.

Beneficiary of protective effects is debtor's personal assets, represented by the set of property interests that, for some reason, do not merge into the bankruptcy mass.

Debtor's fresh start must start on the day the petition is filed. The law, in order to ensure this purpose, must provide for the mechanisms that allow the immediate restoration of a personal, autonomous and separate asset as soon as possible, in order to satisfy bankruptcy creditors, functional to its return to the market, and removed, for this purpose, from the aggressive initiatives of these subjects, both during the competition procedure, in fact, the automatic stay, and subsequently to its closure, thanks to the discharge.

First of all, the "property of the debtor" is the contingencies, i.e. the assets, rights and gains that the debtor acquires after the date of submission of the application for admission to the liquidation procedure governed by Chapter 765. As mentioned, in fact, as part of the conservative procedures referred to in Chapters 11, 12 and 13, these assets flow into the bankruptcy mass, as they are necessary and functional to implement the prepared recovery plan[60].

---

[58]On the problem of arguable property D. B. LANGEHENNIG, S. MANZ, To infinity and beyond: exploring the reach of the automatic stay, in ABI Journal, 30, 2011, pp. 36ss.

[59]Save, in conservative procedures, the possibility for true constituent the rule, that the debtor is left in possession of his assets (debtor in possession). For further details see: S. V. KELLEY, Ginsberg & Martin on bankruptcy, op. cit., § 5.01[B][2] e [3]. G. ORLANDI, Property of the estate: section 541, op. cit.; H. B. PICKARD, The new bankruptcy code, part II: the interests of secured creditors under the new bankruptcy code, cit., pp. 222ss.

[60]S. V. KELLEY, Ginsberg & Martin on bankruptcy, op. cit., D. G. EPSTEIN, Bankruptcy

Secondly, two categories of interest in property must be considered, which, although initially merged with the summer, can later cease to be part of this separate asset, going to (re) converge into the personal one of the debtor.

The reference, above all, is to the powers Section 554 of the Bankruptcy Code acknowledges the trustee to abandon a certain property of the summer to resort to two alternative circumstances, that is excessively burdensome for the bankruptcy mass, or when its value, and consequent benefit for the procedure, is of irrelevant entity[61]. The described power of abandonment of the trustee, however, is by law subject to certain limits and cautions. Pursuant to rule 6007 (a) of the Federal Rules of Bankruptcy Procedures, such subject must in fact previously communicate its intention to creditors, who are legitimized to present opposition in the next fourteen days; in the presence of oppositions, a hearing will take place before the bankruptcy court, in the contradictory of the parties, at the end of which the permissive measure of abandonment will be pronounced; in the absence of oppositions, presumed consent of creditors, the trustee may vice versa proceed even without judicial authorization[62].

In the event that the trustee remains inert, however, it may also be a party, interested in that, to request the court to issue a provision that obliges the person to exercise. Article 42, second paragraph, with regard to assets occurring during the procedure, the faculty of the trustee is also provided, upon authorization by the creditors' committee, to renounce their acquisition, if the costs to be incurred for the purchase and storage are higher than the their presumable realization value[63]; and art. 104 ter, penultimate paragraph, where it is envisaged that the trustee, upon authorization of creditors' committee, may not acquire assets or waive the liquidation of one or more assets, if the liquidation activity appears

---

and related law in a nutshell, op. cit. I. RAMSAY, Personal insolvency in the 21st century. A comparative analysis of the US and Europe, op. cit.

[61]See what has been said in the previous paragraph, with regard to the rules contained in sections 1115 (a), 1207 (a) and 1306 (a) of the Bankruptcy Code.

[62]Read the Section 554 of the Bankruptcy Code which, for the part that interests us, provides that “the trustee may abandon any property of the estate that is burdensome to the estate or that is of inconsequential value and benefit to the estate (...)”.

[63]D.G. EPSTEIN, Bankruptcy and related law in a nutshell, op. cit.

manifestly not convenient (in this case, these assets will be freely credible by creditors through enforcement or precautionary actions). Also in this case, only in case of opposition of the trustee will open a contentious parenthesis before the bankruptcy court[64]. The abandonment of a property that is part of the summer implies, of course, that it ceases to belong to the bankruptcy mass: This also implies that the protective effects that the automatic stay specifically predisposed with regard to the "summer property", with respect to this asset, are less[65]. However, in the absolute majority of cases, this property is destined to (re) flow into the debtor's assets. This will happen when that subject was the owner of the related interest already in the pre-petition filing, and therefore already before the confluence in the summer; where this occurs, obviously, the property abandoned by the trustee and (re) merged into debtor's personal assets, will receive the protection to that entity specifically granted by the automatic stay.

The second category of property that can flow into debtor's personal assets consists of the so-called exempt property, represented by assets that can be excluded from bankruptcy and thus removed from insolvency execution[66]; in particular, pursuant to section 522 (b) of the Bankruptcy Code, the debtor is granted the right to choose whether to avail of the exemptions granted by the law of his state or those granted by federal legislation, provided for by subsection (d)[67]. However, it should be pointed out that exempt property is not removed from the bankruptcy mass ex lege, since, at the time of petition, it also flows into the summer: It is the debtor who, by initiative taken during the procedure, can declare

---

[64]S.V. KELLEY, Ginsberg & Martin on bankruptcy, op. cit., § 5.06[A]; M.A. FREY, S. K. SWINSON, Introduction to bankruptcy law, op. cit., 255ss.

[65]S.V. KELLEY, Ginsberg & Martin on bankruptcy, op. cit., L.B. BARTELL, Visualizing bankruptcy, op. cit. pp. 74ss. M. A. FREY, S. K. SWINSON, Introduction to bankruptcy law op. cit., pp. 256ss. A further hypothesis of abandonment, governed by the letter (c) of section 554, is represented by the eventuality in which the trustee fails to administer the property interests belonging to the summer, so implicitly showing a lack of interest in the same: in this case, they will reemerge into the debtor's personal assets: again, S. V. KELLEY, Ginsberg & Martin on bankruptcy, op. cit., § 5.06[B][1].

[66]S.V. KELLEY, Ginsberg & Martin on bankruptcy, op. cit., L.B. BARTELL, Visualizing bankruptcy, op. cit. pp. 74ss. M. A. FREY, S. K. SWINSON, Introduction to bankruptcy law, op. cit., pp. 256ss.

[67]W.D. WARREN, D. J. BUSSEL, D. A. SKEEL, JR., Bankruptcy, op. cit., pp. 42ss.

to avail of an exemption, which must be approved by the judicial authority, upon the possible resolution of the oppositions submitted by the interested parties. The exempt property, of course, from the bankruptcy mass will flow into debtor's personal assets, with the same repercussions, as regards the automatic stay regime, which suffer the goods abandoned by the trustee[68].

7.Subjects that suffer the effects of automatic stay

Once the examination of protected beneficiaries offered by the automatic stay has been exhausted, the analysis concerning the subjective effectiveness of this institute must be concluded with a review of the subjects that, on the contrary, this inhibition must undergo. As this provision operates, as well as in accordance with the law, in personam[69], the recipients of the command, and possibly the consequences deriving from its violation, will be individually and individually the persons eligible to fall within the application of Section 362 of the Bankruptcy Code.

In this regard, the last cited provision specifies that the automatic stay produces its own inhibitory efficacy towards "all entities". For the exact delimitation of subjects considered by this general and potentially all-encompassing phrase, it is necessary, then, to make reference to the previous Section 101 general rule containing a series of definitions of terms variously used in the text of law, where, at number (15), it is stated that "the term" entity "includes person, estate, trust, governmental unit, and United States trustee"[70].

---

[68]A.N. RESNICK, H.J. SOMMER, Collier on bankruptcy, op. cit., S.V. KELLEY, Ginsberg & Martin on bankruptcy, op. cit., § 5.01[B]. L. B. BARTELL, Visualizing bankruptcy, op. cit., M.A. FREY, S.K. SWINSON, Introduction to bankruptcy law op. cit., pp. 241ss. D.G. EPSTEIN, Bankruptcy and related law in a nutshell, op. cit. pp. 89ss. H.B. PICKARD, The new bankruptcy code, part II: the interests of secured creditors under the new bankruptcy code, op. cit., pp. 228ss. Interested parties, and as such entitled to propose opposition, are creditors, persons who claim an interest on the property in question, or the trustee.

[69]Even with regard to this discipline, therefore, there are numerous differences between the Bankruptcy Code and the Italian bankruptcy law. What eliminates the bankruptcy is above all the automaticity of the exclusion proper to our system by virtue of which the assets identified therein, with the exception of the sub. b), that constitute the main differential with respect to the US discipline.

[70]A.N. RESNICK, H. J. SOMMER, Collier on bankruptcy, op. cit., 3, § 362.03. B.A.

The provision therefore appears suitable to subject to inhibition a wide range of subjects, both private and public: Physical and legal persons, companies[71], associations and government units of all kinds[72].

First, interested in automatic stay will be all potential subjects who can claim against the debtor: The latter, to be exact, is a suitable term to include any right to a payment against the debtor, regardless by the fact that such right is determined or indeterminate, liquid or illiquid, expired or at term, pure or conditioned, controversial or non-controversial, unsecured or guaranteed, originating in the law or in the equity[73].

It should be noted that in order to fall within the application of the law it is not necessary to hold a claim, i.e. to hold creditors qualification of automatic stay beneficiary, although this is, of course, the most relevant hypothesis. In fact, Section 362 refers generically to the concept of entity, without requiring additional requirements, so that to see blocked their aggressive initiatives will not, evidently, only the holders of a claim. In order to establish whether a subject, belonging to the vast category reported by the law, is subjected to automatic stay, even if he is not entitled to payment towards the debtor, it is therefore necessary to refer to the objective scope of effectiveness of the institute that goes far beyond the sole initiatives concerning a right to credit, that is to verify what initiative, this subject, is intended to put in place against the debtor, regardless of the reason that legitimizes it.

It follows that, even if it is not the holder of a claim, the loaner who demands the return of the property of which the borrower, by virtue of a loan contract, has the integral subjective legal situation, will be

---

BLUM, Bankruptcy and debtor/creditor, op. cit., pp. 244ss.

[71] Read, in addition to what has been said, the section 101 (27), where it is specified that "governmental unit" should be understood "United States; State; Commonwealth; District; Territory; municipality; foreign state; department, agency, or instrumentality of the United States (...), a State, a Commonwealth, a District, a Territory, a municipality, or a foreign state; or other foreign or domestic government (...)".

[72]H. B. PICKARD, The new bankruptcy code, part I: a review of some of the significant changes in bankruptcy law, op. cit.

[73]D. R. COWANS, Cowans bankruptcy law and practice, op. cit., pp. 459ss. D. G. EPSTEIN, Bankruptcy and related law in a nutshell, op. cit., pp. 65ss. I. RAMSAY, Personal insolvency in the 21st century. A comparative analysis of the US and Europe, op. cit.

subjected to the automatic stay, an interest in debtor's property[74] at the time the petition was filed, and thus merged into bankruptcy estate[75]. The same will apply, a fortiori, to the initiatives that can be experienced by the lessor towards the debtor tenant: Even in such circumstances the automatic stay prevents the former from dissolving the lease contract stipulated with the latter, or re-entering the premises, and the same will apply in the hypothesis in which the landlord notifies the tenant of a cancellation, with the effect of causing the termination of the sublease contract between the tenant and the subleasing debtor[76]. The question, more generally, concerns all cases in which the performing party decides to withdraw from a contract after the counterpart submits an application for admission to a bankruptcy procedure, using a contractual clause that expressly attributes to the performing party the right of withdrawal. The deliberate exercise of this right is precluded in the automatic stay. In this eventuality, however, US doctrine and jurisprudence have deemed it appropriate to reconcile the conflicting values of parties contractual autonomy and those underlying the insolvency law, allowing the performing party to demonstrate that the exercise of the right of withdrawal is completely independent of the subsequent request by the counterparty for admission to a bankruptcy procedure, and therefore would have acted in this sense even in the absence of such event. Only the positive outcome of such proof can the performing party obtain a provision for the release of the injunction, which it will allow to proceed in the will to dissolve from the contractual relationship, while at the same time the voluntary withdrawals caused exclusively by the overthrow of a petition[77] remain precluded in the automatic stay.

---

[74]This foreclosure is justified because, as will be seen, by virtue of section 362 (a) (3), all acts aimed at exercising powers of control over assets converged during the summer are forbidden by the automatic stay. On this case, see S.V. KELLEY, Ginsberg & Martin on bankruptcy, op. cit., § 3.01[C], note 93. D.R. COWANS, Cowans bankruptcy law and practice, op. cit., pp. 493ss. D.G. BAIRD, The elements of bankruptcy, op. cit., pp. 191ss. O. COUWENBERG, S. J. LUBBEN, Essential corporate bankruptcy law, op. cit.

[75]D.R. COWANS, Cowans bankruptcy law and practice, op. cit., pp. 459ss. H.B. PICKARD, The new bankruptcy code, part II: The interests of secured creditors under the new bankruptcy code, op. cit., pp. 222ss..

[76]In this sense see: In re 48th Street Steakhouse, Inc., 835 F.2d 427 (1987), 430ss.

[77]A fortiori, therefore, the clauses of automatic termination of the contract in the event of unexpected presentation of a petition are ineffective with regard to the procedure. On the subject see: D.G. BAIRD, The elements of bankruptcy, op. cit., pp. 193ss. P. A. MURPHY,

Another subject affected by the pre-exclusive effectiveness produced by the automatic stay, and of which it seems appropriate to mention, is then the judicial authority, as an entity fit to fall into the category of governmental units: The reference, of course, is exclusively to the authorities different from the bankruptcy court and, also in this case, reference should be made to the analysis of the objective efficacy of the automatic stay in order to understand the exact scope of the current disobedience against these subjects[78].

A doubt, finally, can legitimately arise on the suitability of the institution to inhibit even the debtor himself, thus precluding to him or the trustee, the initiatives, especially of a judicial nature, that from the same can be assumed: And this, as the term "person" which, one remembers, is one of the entities subjected to the preclusive effects in the speech, is certainly abstractly suitable to also include that subject.

Apart from the literal argument, namely the fact that Section 362 of the Bankruptcy Code, in identifying the individual actions precluded by the automatic stay, systematically refers to the debtor as a passive subject of the initiatives taken by other entities, there is also a systematic argument in support of the exclusion, here supported, of the debtor, from the list of recipients of the injunction in comment. The reference is to subsection (a) of the aforementioned provision, where, after the enumeration of the series of judicial and extrajudicial documents, precluded to all the entities mentioned above, a special provision concerning the proceedings before the tax court, with which it is prevented from commencing or continuing. In the US legal system, tax assessments can be established exclusively upon taxpayer's appeal, if the debtor were precluded from carrying out judicial or extrajudicial initiatives, generally, by means of his reorganization of the entities, there would have been no need to provide for a special discipline concerning tax proceedings. This provision, on the contrary indicates that the general rule is in the sense of the normal

---

E. E. SAGERMAN, D. NEIER, Creditor's rights in bankruptcy op. cit., pp. 187ss. In jurisprudence see: In re M.J. & K. Co., Inc., 161 B.R. 586 (1993), 591ss. O. COUWENBERG, S. J. LUBBEN, Essential corporate bankruptcy law, op. cit.

[78]W.R. NORTON, JR., Norton bankruptcy law and practice, op. cit., § 36:5; but in jurisprudence there are no judgments that deny the referability of the judicial authority to the entities affected by the automatic stay. For example, see: In re Willard, 15 B.R. 898 (1981).

freedom of action of the debtor or trustee, and that the foreclosure of tax judgments is to be considered an exception to this rule[79].

What has just been said introduces us, however, to some interesting issues connected with the freedom of action in court for which the debtor or the trustee enjoys, even during the course of the procedure: Think, for example, of the hypothesis in which judicial initiative legitimately initiated by the debtor, the defendant in bonis is the proprietor, with regard to the first, of a counterclaim, i.e. a counter-claim, whose proposition, if admitted, would obviously risk circumventing the prohibitions imposed by the automatic stay; or, furthermore, the operation of the automatic stay towards the appeals judgments promoted by the debtor, especially if in the previous degree he had assumed the role of the defendant: On these issues we will return right in the course of the next Section, dedicated to the objective scope of operation of the institution, that is, of the individual initiatives that the protective efficacy accorded by Section 362 of the Bankruptcy Code specifically precludes[80].

8.The objective effectiveness of automatic stay...the protective effect. Possibility of recourse in an integrative way to the section 105 (a) of the Bankruptcy Code.

The formulation of the provision in question is, however, absolutely redundant. Often, in fact, the same case is suitable to be included in the application of several rules, connotated, therefore, from a mutual overlap: A clear sign, this, of the concern, too much warned by the legislature, to offer the debtor the widest protection possible.

The actions precluded by the mentioned eight numbers, it is worth pointing out, are to be considered mandatory: as a consequence of what was observed in the course of the previous Section regarding the

---

[79]D.R. COWANS, Cowans bankruptcy law and practice, op. cit., pp. 468ss. in general, on the subtraction of the debtor to the preclusive effects of the automatic stay, see also J. F. MURPHY, The automatic stay in bankruptcy, op. cit.

[80]D. G. EPSTEIN, Bankruptcy and related law in a nutshell, op. cit. I. RAMSAY, Personal insolvency in the 21st century. A comparative analysis of the US and Europe, op. cit. I. RAMSAY, Personal insolvency in the 21st century. A comparative analysis of the US and Europe, op. cit.

exceptional nature that must be recognized to the norm contained in Section 362[81]. Also with regard to the objective scope of effectiveness of the automatic stay, it is necessary to conclude that the special discipline in question, of accentuated favor for its beneficiaries, can explain its effects only in relation to the cases expressly contemplated therein. Only with regard to these behaviors, the legislator has held the danger of prejudice that exists in the procedure and justified in the codification of the rebuttable presumption linked to the automatic operation of the stay. It follows, therefore, that in the very remote eventuality given the multiplicity and versatility of the cases considered by the provision in which an initiative is not explicitly contemplated in Section 362, the latter rule cannot be the subject of analogical interpretation in order to make even this activity fall within the application of automatic stay. The fact that an initiative, as not contemplated by Section 362, is not subjected to automatic stay, does not mean however that the beneficiary entities of such protection, in the course of a bankruptcy procedure, are unavoidably condemned to suffer it: As at this point will already be clear, it only means, in fact, that these subjects they cannot avail themselves of the procedural advantage inherent in the discipline in question, and therefore of the legislative position of a legal presumption to which the automatic operation of the suspension is reconnected; it follows, therefore, that the possibility remains, for the debtor or trustee, to ask the bankruptcy court to pronounce an injunction order, in the exercise of equitable powers of injunction to that authority conferred by the aforementioned Section 105 (a) of the Bankruptcy Code, upon demonstration of the relative conditions[82].

Both these phenomena, if on the one hand are an expression of the

---

[81]B.A. BLUM, Bankruptcy and debtor/creditor, op. cit., pp. 247ss. D.G. BAIRD, The elements of bankruptcy, op. cit., pp. 195ss. P. A. MURPHY, E.E. SAGERMAN, D. NEIER, Creditors' rights in bankruptcy, op. cit., pp. 189ss. O. COUWENBERG, S. J. LUBBEN, Essential corporate bankruptcy law, op. cit.

[82]The reference is to the section 362 (a) (1), pursuant to which an application for admission to one of the procedures envisaged by Bankruptcy Code "operates as a stay, applicable to all entities, of (...) the commencement or continuation, including the issuance or employment of process, of a judicial, administrative, or other action or proceeding against the debtor that was or could have been commenced before the commencement of the case under this title, or to recover a claim against a debtor that arose before the commencement of the case under this title".

suitability of equity remedies to face the most different protection needs, as well as being an integrative instrument with respect to the written law, on the other they sound as further confirmation of the equitable roots of the overall discipline object of the present study, and of the persistent relevance of that process of progressive refinement.

9.(Follows) Suspensions set up to protect the debtor.

Among the beneficiaries of protection offered by the automatic stay, the initiatives that Section 362 precludes against the debtor who has submitted or has been the subject of an application for admission to one of the procedures governed by the Bankruptcy Code, are: (1) The beginning (or continuation) of a proceeding that could have been (or is been) started before the beginning of the bankruptcy proceedings, or rather that it is aimed at recovering a credit which arose prior to that moment; (2) execution of a sentence obtained before the start of the bankruptcy proceedings; (6) any act aimed at recovering or collecting a credit that arose prior to the start of the bankruptcy proceedings; (7) compensation for mutual claims arising in an earlier period at the beginning of the procedure; (8) the commencement or prosecution of a judgment before the U.S tax court concerning debtor tax debts.

The injunction imposed by the provision in question is of broad applicative scope, as it is suitable to include all types of judicial, administrative, or other proceedings, which may be instituted or already instituted against the debtor at the date of petition, with the exception of those expressly excluded by the following subsection (b)[83].

The first data that emerges from the mere reading of the law, and which particularly attracts attention as it represents an important differential between the legislation in question, consists of the fact that the provision does not identify any specific type of proceedings affected by the prohibition rather, it merely requires that they present, as a minimum

[83]A.N. RESNICK, H. J. SOMMER, Collier on bankruptcy, op. cit., § 362.03[3]. W. R. NORTON, JR., Norton bankruptcy law and practice, op. cit., § 36:5. D.G. EPSTEIN, Bankruptcy and related law in a nutshell, op. cit., pp. 46ss. F. R. KENNEDY, Automatic stays under the new bankruptcy law, op. cit.

requirement, that of being established “against the debtor”: Regardless, then, from further specifications, except to reserve an autonomous mention to those concerning a right of credit for the importance that they cover[84]. Thus, for example, judgments aimed at obtaining a declaratory judgment similar to our actions of mere assessment will be precluded, since they are aimed at obtaining from the judge the determination of legal certainty with regard to a situation subject to dispute, those of executive nature, the so-called eviction proceedings, i.e. eviction proceedings, and even divorce judgments, at least in the part in which they are intended to divide the marital patrimony, and not with regard to the sole provision for the dissolution of the bond[85]. Neither the field of proceedings affected by the law must be restricted to those of a judicial nature. In fact, not only all types of civil litigation, regardless of the stage or degree of dispute, including any incidental sub-procedures, and state or federal jurisdiction to decide on it, also the procedures of an administrative nature and the alternative dispute resolution, arbitration and mediation, are subject to the automatic stay[86].

---

[84]The declaratory judgments are counted in the context of the preventive adjudication, defined as negative with respect to the so-called. remedial adjudication, by which the aim is to obtain a sentence for damages or for an injunction: in other words, actions which can be carried out to obtain only an assessment of a specific legal situation and to avoid future disputes or injuries, without a command being issued against the unsuccessful party. In argument see: S.L. BRAY, Preventive adjudication, in University of Chicago Law Review, 77, 2010, pp. 1276ss., of which the following definition can be reported: “Generally speaking, in remedial adjudication, a plaintiff seeks damages or an injunction to correct past harm; in preventive adjudication, a plaintiff seeks only a declaration and does so to avoid future harm”.

[85]D. R. COWANS, Cowans bankruptcy law and practice, op. cit., pp. 489ss. L.B. BARTELL, Visualizing bankruptcy, op. cit., pp. 77ss. See also the opinion of: D.G. EPSTEIN, Bankruptcy and related law in a nutshell, op. cit., pp. 70ss., according to which it would be necessary, in a systematic interpretation, that the proceeding against the debtor consists in an initiative aimed at creating new responsibilities for this subject, or reducing bankruptcy assets, or aimed at affecting the financial situation of the same .

[86]B. BARTELL, Visualizing bankruptcy, op. cit., pp. 76ss. P.A. MURPHY, E.E. SAGERMAN, D. NEIER, Creditor's rights in bankruptcy op. cit., pp. 185ss. A.N. RESNICK, Bankruptcy law manual, West Press, Minnesota, 2002, pp. 67ss. D.G. EPSTEIN, Bankruptcy and related law in a nutshell, op. cit., pp. 70ss. F. R. KENNEDY, Automatic stays under the new bankruptcy law, op. cit., pp. 13ss. R.A. JOHNSON, M.C. O’LEARY, Automatic stay provisions of the bankruptcy act of 1978, op. cit., pp. 606ss. A.N. RESNICK, H.J. SOMMER, Collier on bankruptcy, op. cit., § 362.03[3][b]. S.V. KELLEY, Ginsberg & Martin on bankruptcy, op. cit., § 3.01[C]. W.R. NORTON, JR.,

A second datum which can be deduced from the letter of the law, concerns the delimitation of the precluded procedures, carried out with regard to the time in which the claim, which by means of them (or is meant to be) valid, has arisen. In other words, circumscribing the scope of the procedures subjected to the automatic stay to those already begun, or which could have been initiated prior to the petition, the legislator subjected to the prohibition the only claims that arose prior to the time of the request for admission to a bankruptcy procedure, i.e. those that can and must find their orderly satisfaction. The requirement is reiterated in relation to proceedings concerning loans, with regard to which, to be precise, reference must be made to the moment in which the obligation arises not to that, necessarily later, in which it becomes payable, with the consequence that they will be to be considered included in the scope of the injunction also the proceedings concerning receivables not yet due, illiquid or subject to suspensory condition[87]. On the other hand, the proceedings instituted against the debtor for claims arising after the petition were not subject to the preclusive effects of the automatic stay[88]: This reflects, on the one hand, the vocation of any insolvency procedure to act as a vehicle for the satisfaction of the holders of receivables arose prior to their opening and, secondly, the need to ensure the debtor the immediate fresh start, and therefore the possibility for the subject to immediately entertain new

---

Norton bankruptcy law and practice, op. cit. In jurisprudence see: In re R. S. Pinellas Motel Partnership, 2 B.R. 113 (1979), 117ss. S. PARSONS, Consumer bankruptcy law in focus, op. cit.

[87]A.N. RESNICK, H. J. SOMMER, Collier on bankruptcy, op. cit., § 362.03[3][a]. S.V. KELLEY, Ginsberg & Martin on bankruptcy, op. cit., § 3.01[C][1]. D.R. COWANS, Cowans bankruptcy law and practice, op. cit., pp. 492ss. B.A. BLUM, Bankruptcy and debtor/creditor, op. cit., pp. 247ss. D.G. EPSTEIN, Bankruptcy and related law in a nutshell, op. cit., F.R. KENNEDY, Automatic stays under the new bankruptcy law, op. cit. S. PARSONS, Consumer bankruptcy law in focus, contra see from the jurisprudence the: In re M. Frenville Co., Inc. case, 744 F.2d 332 (1984), 337ss.

[88]As far as concerns the interests, in US law there is the fundamental rule according to which the same, generally, do not start in the time between the deposit of the petition and the moment in which the creditor receives satisfaction of his pecuniary claim. This is derived from sect. 502 (b) (2), where it is envisaged that the bankruptcy court admits to the debtor the credit for the amount for which it is insinuated, except for the extent to which "such claim is for in matured interest", i.e. interests that have not yet matured at the time of petition filing. On this point, see: B.A. BLUM, Bankruptcy and debtor/creditor, op. cit., pp. 452ss.

relationships with third parties, who they must be free to act, if necessary, against the first[89]. To conclude on the subject of the requisites that must possess the claim claimed against the debtor in order to submit to automatic stay, it should be noted that does not note that the same may or may not benefit from the discharge[90]: In any case, in fact, it is aspiring credits to find satisfaction within the competition.

The specific rationale underlying this provision appears to be immediately evident, to which reference has already been made in the course of the discussion, that is, in addition to the usual protective petitions of the debtor against harassing initiatives, the opportunity to channel all the investigative and executive proceedings, against him, before the bankruptcy court, so as to ensure efficient management of the procedure and an orderly satisfaction of bankruptcy creditors; it follows, with all evidence, that the proceedings concerned by the automatic stay will be only those incardinated (or incardinable) in the ordinary courts, while no preclusive effect will affect the judgments established at the bankruptcy court[91].

With regard to the proceedings still to be established, the pre-exclusive effect imposed by Section 362 therefore implies that the person authorized to do so is precluded from initiating any judicial action against the debtor: As expressly prescribed by the law, subject to the prohibition in question are also issuance or employment acts of process, that is, the obligations, governed by rule 4 of the Federal Rules of Civil Procedure,

---

[89]However, it will be precluded to post reconciliation creditors to find satisfaction of their claims in bankruptcy assets, since this is reserved for the satisfaction of bankruptcy creditors, as can be seen in the following numbers (3) and (4), while, as discussed in section 5, they will obviously be able to satisfy themselves on the debtor's personal assets. See in argument: A. N. RESNICK, H. J. SOMMER, Collier on bankruptcy, op. cit., § 362.03[3][c]. F. R. KENNEDY, Automatic stays under the new bankruptcy law, op. cit., pp. 12ss. J. F. MURPHY, The automatic stay in bankruptcy, op. cit., pp. 573ss. S. PARSONS, Consumer bankruptcy law in focus, op. cit.

[90]A.N. RESNICK, H.J. SOMMER, Collier on bankruptcy, op. cit., § 362.03[3]. W.R. NORTON, JR., Norton bankruptcy law and practice, op. cit., D.G. EPSTEIN, Bankruptcy and related law in a nutshell, op. cit., pp. 70ss. I. RAMSAY, Personal insolvency in the 21st century. A comparative analysis of the US and Europe, op. cit.

[91]D.G. EPSTEIN, Bankruptcy and related law in a nutshell, op. cit. pp. 69ss. D.G. EPSTEIN, Bankruptcy and related law in a nutshell, op. cit. pp. 74ss. J. F. MURPHY, The automatic stay in bankruptcy, op. cit., pp. 588ss. I. RAMSAY, Personal insolvency in the 21st century. A comparative analysis of the US and Europe, op. cit.

with which the Registrar, after verifying the regularity of the documentation presented by the plaintiff, returns the introductory act (complaint) to this last to provide service to the defendant (defendant)[92].

In the case of proceedings already pending, towards the debtor, at the time of petition filing, the operation of automatic stay implies, on the contrary, the birth of the entity subject to the prohibition of taking any further initiative in procedural: And this, as already known, in a legal and automatic way, that is by virtue of the mere fact of the filing of the application for admission to a bankruptcy procedure, and without it being necessary, by the court or the office, to issue any provision or take specific initiatives.

The effectiveness of the instrument is assured, downstream, by the incisiveness of the consequences reconnected with its violation, such, as will be seen, to entail (in a broad sense) the ineffectiveness[93] of the activities that are carried out despite the operation of prohibition, and regardless of the effective knowledge of the automatic stay in charge of the agent subject of additional sanctions against the violator in case of violation perpetrated in the awareness of the operation of the ban, so that the achievement of the result prescribed by law is in every guaranteed case.

On the other hand, it is clear that, in both cases, the actual operation of the inhibitory is left to the initiative of the entity subject to it, i.e. the fact that the same respects the prohibition to start or continue the procedure against the debtor that arises by virtue of the supervised automatic stay. This happens because, wanting to finally give development to the conclusions reached when analyzing the juridical nature of the institute in comment, the automatic operation of the stay reconnects the onset of the obligations typically descended from a prohibitory injunction, that is, certain duties of conduct supplemented by the prohibition on carrying out certain activities in the present case the beginning or continuation of a judgment, under penalty of being subject to certain sanctions.

The stated principle, while placing itself in the same way in the two cases here taken into consideration, nevertheless implies that there are

---

[92]D.G. EPSTEIN, Bankruptcy and related law in a nutshell, op. cit. I. RAMSAY, Personal insolvency in the 21st century. A comparative analysis of the US and Europe, op. cit.
[93]A.N. RESNICK, H. J. SOMMER, Collier on bankruptcy, op. cit., § 362.03[3][b].

different duties that concretely arise for the recipient entities of the junction, functional to the obedience to the command contained in it: Prohibition to start and prohibition to continue, in other words, require, in order to be respected, the fulfillment of different activities. If, in the hypothesis of procedure still to begin, it will be sufficient, to fulfill this duty, a mere omissive conduct of its addressee, who refrains, that is, from taking any initiative suitable to initiate proceedings against the debtor, in case of proceedings already pending to this subject, something more is required: Even in the silence of Section 362 on this point, i.e. certain "positive" activation duties arise in relation to the person receiving the injunction in order to ensure that the judgment against the debtor is not continued, and that therefore the result pursued by the automatic stay is concretely implemented. Specifically, this subject will have the obligation to notify the court where the proceedings are pending the fact of deposit the petition and the consequent need to stop the trial, as well as to take any other initiative suitable to ensure the non-prosecution[94]; the non-fulfillment of these duties, even though consisting in a mere omissive conduct, is not therefore suitable to ensure that the pending judgment is actually arrested or, if preferred, determines the risk that it continues, and therefore entails an infringement of the automatic stay which are subject to certain penalties for the entity in question.

Here we can see a significant difference between the American system: It is known, in fact, that pursuant to art. 43, third sub-paragraph l. of bankruptcy, the opening of the bankruptcy determines the automatic interruption of the process, detectable ex officio by judge also following the simple acquisition of the news, in any way, of the failure; within the Bankruptcy Code, on the contrary, the non-prosecution of the pending judgment is left to the activation, in this sense, of the debtor's counterparty, as stated, that in the absence of such "upstream" activation the deeds will be affections, "downstream", from ineffectiveness (broadly speaking).

Among the entities subject to the foreclosure effectiveness in

---

[94]A.N. RESNICK, H.J. SOMMER, Collier on bankruptcy, op. cit., § 362.03[3]. S.V. KELLEY, Ginsberg & Martin on bankruptcy, op. cit., § 3.01[C]. the initiatives, preliminary to the arrest of the pending proceedings, are therefore subtracted from the preclusive effects deriving from the automatic stay: D.G. EPSTEIN, Bankruptcy and related law in a nutshell, op. cit., in jurisprudence see: Eskanos & Adler, P.C. v. Leetien, 309 F.3d 1210, 1214 (2002).

comment, there is also the same court before which it hangs, or it can be incardinated a judgment against the debtor: In this case, the automatic stay involves the onset of a ban, to charged with the judicial body, to assume or continue the proceedings, so that its potestas iudicandi is, in fact, suspended. The point now deserves further study given the differences that obviously exist between this situation and that concerning an entity of different nature, in particular a creditor or a third party. We refer, in particular, to the hypothesis in which the proceeding is already pending. Here, unlike what we have just seen, it is to be excluded that the court has any positive duty of activation aimed at ensuring the effective suspension of judgment, as this duty can arise only on those who are in the condition to fulfill: That is, that he has become aware of the deposit of the petition and that, as a counterpart in a judgment instituted against the debtor, he is called to ensure that prosecution is prevented[95]. In the absence of such an initiative, therefore, the only consequences arising from the prosecution of the judgment will concern (in a broad sense) the ineffectiveness of the activities performed by the court: While the other sanctions resulting from the failure to comply with the prohibition contained in the injunction will fall, in the existence of relative assumptions, only by debtor's counterpart, the only person who may be aware of petition's presentation and, as such, must take the necessary steps[96]. Secondly, with regard to the deeds that

---

[95]See, Maritime Elec. Co. Inc. v. United Jersey Bank, 959 F.2d 1194 (1991), 1206, which is affirmed that: "Once triggered by a debtor's bankruptcy petition, the automatic stay suspends any non bankruptcy court's authority to continue judicial proceedings then pending against the debtor. This is so because § 362's stay is mandatory and "applicable to all entities", including state and federal courts (...)". For further details see: W.R. NORTON, JR., Norton bankruptcy law and practice op. cit.

[96]In this regard, it should be noted that the news of the deposit of the petition may also come from the same debtor, and therefore by virtue of this initiative will suspend the judgment; however, in practice this happens very rarely, given that this subject is aware of the fact that any initiative made in violation of the automatic stay will still be affected by ineffectiveness (in a broad sense), with the consequence that the activation burden is in fact to always fall on the entity subjected to this prohibition. As regards, conversely, the knowledge that the entity affected by the injunction has automatic stay, it is ensured by the notice referred to in sect. 342, analytically governed by the Official Form 9 ("Notice of commencement of case under the Bankruptcy Code, meeting of creditors, and deadlines") that, in addition to setting the deadline for submission of applications for admission to the state of the court and the date of the relative hearing, informs creditors of the entry into force of the automatic stay.

can be performed by the court, the so-called ministerial acts are generally excluded from the applicative scope of the automatic stay, that is to say those acts of a merely bureaucratic nature, performed by the chancellery, which do not in any way involve the exercise of decision-making or judicial powers: The typical example is represented by the simple registration by the Registry of a sentence previously pronounced by the court. Because of the expansive vocation of the automatic stay institute, the definition of ministerial act is also constructed in restrictive terms, so as to limit the number of actions that escape the inhibition only to acts that actually constitute purely bureaucratic obligations[97].

Furthermore, the prohibition to continue a pending proceeding is interpreted in such a restrictive sense as to preclude even the possibility of obtaining a dismissal from the insolvency court of the pending request against the debtor: An objective which, with the comminatory of an automatic suspension, the institute in question intends to pursue is, in fact, the maintenance of the status quo, which even such a ruling, with all evidence, would change; the expression "continuation", in other words, is interpreted in such a broad sense as to include any change or occurrence during the trial, including the rejection of the request made against the debtor[98]. This principle has an interesting development in the field of injunctions: In the event that, at the time of filing the petition, the debtor is subject to a prohibitory injunction that prohibits the completion of certain activities, in fact, the maintenance of the status quo implies that the debtor remains obliged to respect the behavior also commanded in the force of the automatic stay[99]; and, of course, in case of violation by the

[97]A.N. RESNICK, H.J. SOMMER, Collier on bankruptcy, op. cit., § 362.03[3][e]. W.R. NORTON, JR., Norton bankruptcy law and practice, op. cit. D. R. COWANS, Cowans bankruptcy law and practice, op. cit., pp. 494ss. See also the case: Rexnord Holdings Inc. v. Bidermann, 21 F.3d 522 (1994), 527ss.

[98]D.R. COWANS, Cowans bankruptcy law and practice, op. cit., pp. 492ss. A.N. RESNICK,Bankruptcy law manual, op. cit., pp. 68 and note 2. D.G. EPSTEIN, Bankruptcy and related law in a nutshell, op. cit., pp. 72ss. In jurisprudence see: In re Westwood Lumbert, Inc., 113 B.R. 684 (1990), 686ss. contra, in case the dismissal ruling is based on "jurisdictional grounds", MTGLQ Investors, L.P. v. Guire, 286 F. Supp. 2d 561 (2003), 563.

[99]S.V. KELLEY, Ginsberg & Martin on bankruptcy, op. cit., B.A. BLUM, Bankruptcy and debtor/creditor, op. cit., pp. 248ss. In jurisprudence Dominic's Rest. of Dayton, Inc. v. Mantia, 683 F.3d 757 (2012), 760ss.

same perpetrated, the counterparty will remain free to take action to obtain a contempt order against the same, given that the offense by which said provision takes place occurred after the submission of the application for admission to the insolvency procedure, while the contrary option would, of course, allow the debtor to continue undisturbed in his illicit conduct.

The subject who, as a result of the automatic stay, sees his trial initiatives inhibited, is faced with a triple alternative. Firstly, of course, he can assert his claim within the bankruptcy proceedings initiated, insinuating himself to the relative passive status (i.e. providing for the so-called removal, that is to say the translation of the judgment already established in ordinary session at the bankruptcy court); in this case, where a proceeding concerning the claim conveyed in the bankruptcy proceedings is already pending, before an ordinary court, it may be resumed (or, in the case of previous removal, another may be established for the recovery of the residual), after the closing of the bankruptcy proceedings, unless the discharge in favor of the debtor intervenes, eventuality in which, obviously, this possibility will be forever precluded; in any case, as already mentioned, the ruling of a dismissal order will be prevented, as a procedure. Secondly, this subject may request a release provision, in order to start or continue the proceedings against the debtor while pending the bankruptcy proceedings. Finally, he can simply limit himself to awaiting the closure of the procedure, in order to start or resume, only at that moment, the proceedings against the debtor: Except, again, that a measure of discharge has not intervened in favor of the latter[100].

Implicit, in the reasoning just carried out, is the regime that is subjected to the procedure that, for the automatic stay, cannot be continued. It is, to be precise, a mere suspension, a conclusion made clear by the possibility, for the subject affected by the injunction, to resume his initiative once that has ceased for the closure of the procedure, or for the granting of a relief provision, both from the exclusion of the possibility of issuing different measures (such as a ruling of dismissal), implying an equally different outcome of the pending judgment.

The circumstance according to which a sufficient requisite for a

---

[100]R.A. JOHNSON, M.C. O'LEARY, Automatic stay provisions of the bankruptcy act of 1978, op. cit., pp. 617ss.

proceeding falls within the scope of the automatic stay as per number (1) of Section 362 is that it is a "against the debtor" procedure, on the contrary, it leads one to believe that the judgments established or instigated by the debtor are, on the contrary, removed from the prohibition in question, and therefore freely activated or pursued[101]. This consideration leads us to some critical issues, arising precisely in the case in which the debtor, after the presentation of a petition, begins or continues a judgment against a third party. It is, in particular, the question about defensive initiatives that, in the vigor of the automatic stay, they remain feasible by the latter in which a particular relief is assumed by the possibility of proposing a counterclaim, that is a counterclaim inherent to the fate of the appeal judgments. Let's therefore analyze separately the problems just outlined.

The first, of the anticipated cases, therefore concerns the eventuality in which the debtor, after the deposit of the petition, starts or proceeds proceedings against another person, evidently affected by the automatic stay: The initiatives assumed by the latter could in fact be affected of the foreclosures deriving from the inhibitory intervention. It is appropriate, at this point, to remember what activities the defendant can perform within the judgment: They are governed by rule 8 of the Federal Rules of Civil Procedure[102], where they are classified according to the increasing incisiveness they exert on the activities carried out by the actress. First of all, in the context of defenses we find, in particular, denials, with which the defendant confines himself to denying the existence of one or more facts annexed by the plaintiff, thereby making

---

[101]Naturally, in order for this to be possible, it must be judicial powers of action that have not merged in the summer, in which case, evidently, the legitimacy to act passes through the trustee; but also to want to hypothesize the persistence, in the name of the debtor, of a supplementary procedural legitimation, this initiative would in any case be bound to be prevented by the norm contained in the following number (3) of the section 362 (a) which, as will be better seen, precludes any act intended to exercise control over bankruptcy assets, see: D.G. EPSTEIN, Bankruptcy and related law in a nutshell, op. cit., pp. 75ss.

[102]The denials can be general or specific, depending on their suitability to deny the existence of all the facts enclosed by the actor, or only some (differentiating, thus, from our concepts of generic and specific, functional dispute, as known, to identify an effective dispute). The denials are opposed to the admissions, which bind the defendant to believe in reality, during the trial, the existence of the fact that it was the object, at the same time freeing the actor from the burden of proving it.

them controversial[103]; secondly, there are affirmative defenses, with which the defendant, rather than simply denying the existence of the facts enclosed by the plaintiff, encloses one or more facts that are extinctive, impedimental or modifying the right claimed by that subject[104]. Finally, the defendant can propose a counterclaim against the debtor: This initiative is governed by the subsequent rule 13, and represents a counterclaim that the defendant in turn asserts against the plaintiff, in the context of the judgment established by them; the counterclaim, in particular, may be compulsory, if there is a charge for the defendant to propose it within the judgment already pending, under penalty of the definitive loss of the possibility to assert the claim in a subsequent, independent judgment, or permissive, if such activity, on the contrary, is a mere faculty[105]. In evaluating the consequences that the automatic stay occurred on these activities, it is interesting to start from the reconstruction offered by a part of the American doctrine and jurisprudence that usually distinguishes between merely defensive initiatives (defensive or responsive actions, i.e. the denials referred to it has been said), that they would escape to the preclusive effectiveness in speech, and viceversa offensive initiatives (affirmative defenses and counterclaims), that for their aggressive nature in regard to the debtor would be the opposite impeded by the automatic stay[106].

---

[103]J.H. FRIEDENTHAL, M. K. KANE, A. R. MILLER, Civil procedure, op. cit., pp. 302ss.

[104] The rule mentioned in subsection (c) (1) contains a list, to be considered non exhaustive, of possible affirmative defenses, among which we can mention the existence of an arbitration agreement, the thing judged, or the payment. They must be contained in the answer that the defendant presents to the plaintiff's complaint, even if some courts have argued in favor of the possibility of the official recognition of any of them, especially that relating to the res judicata. In argument see: J.H. FRIEDENTHAL, M.K. KANE, A.R. MILLER, op. cit., 308ss.

[105]The cases of compulsory counterclaim occur, in accordance with rule 13 (a), when the claim claimed by the defendant arises from the same report as the subject of the claim proposed by the plaintiff: in any other case and, therefore, also the lack of connection , the counterclaim is merely permissive, pursuant to the following letter (b). Unlike what happens in European law, therefore, the connection between the right asserted in reconciliation and the one set for the purpose of the application is not a condition of admissibility of the institution.

[106]G.C. HAZARD, JR., J. LEUBSDORF, D.L. BASSETT, Civil procedure, op. cit., pp. 252ss. J.H. FRIEDENTHAL, M.K. KANE, A.R. MILLER, Civil procedure, op. cit., pp. 368ss. L.L. TEPLY, R.U. WHITTEN, Civil procedure, op. cit., pp. 662ss. J.E. KENNEDY, Counterclaims under Federal rule 13, in Houston Law Review, 11, 1974, pp. 255ss.

The solution is only partially shared. The problem, however, must be set differently, that is always on the premise in the need to find, in the range of defensive activities mentioned above, a possible activity of the third that can be suitable to be included in the type of initiatives precluded by number (1) here considered, as it is suitable to initiate or continue proceedings against the debtor[107]. First of all, therefore, since we are moving in the context of an already pending procedure instituted by the debtor, it does not appear possible to conduct, by the defendant, similar to the prosecution of a judgment against the first subject mentioned, who actor's clothes; this also means that the defendant will not be prevented from reactivating the proceedings instituted by the debtor who for any reason has been arrested, since, in fact, it would still be the judgment instituted by the debtor. It follows, therefore, that the only conceivable initiative as prohibited in the present case is that of the defendant who, in the context of an already pending proceedings initiated by the debtor, performs an activity corresponding to the initiation of a proceeding against the latter. In conclusion, the activity prohibited by the automatic stay will be the initiative by which a claim is made against the debtor, which would be autonomously activated in another judgment and which, apparently, would be destined to be inhibited under exam. From this, in the first instance, the free actability of the defendant, of defensive or responsive actions against the debtor, with which, in fact, the third party does not assert against this subject a claim that could be placed subject to an independent procedure, and therefore does not "start" a new judgment against the same.

On the other hand, the case typically appropriate to fall within the application of the automatic stay will be the proposition of a counter claim against the debtor, by definition aimed at asserting, against the latter, a claim by the agreed, and therefore, in a sense, to initiate a new proceeding against the beneficiary of the injunction; in this regard, however, the

---

[107]W.R. NORTON, JR., Norton bankruptcy law and practice op. cit. D.G. EPSTEIN, Bankruptcy and related law in a nutshell, op. cit., pp. 75ss. V.C. DURRER II, K. D. JAIMEZ, Competing bankruptcies: what defenses survive the automatic stay?, in ABI Journal, 30, 2011, pp. 52, 74ss. See also the case: In re Financial News Network Inc., 158 B.R. 570 (1993). I. RAMSAY, Personal insolvency in the 21st century. A comparative analysis of the US and Europe, op. cit.

requirement to operate the protection referred to in number (1), referred to above, must be supplemented by the other requirement of a temporal nature, concerning the moment in which the claim claimed against the debtor arises. The proposability of a counterclaim, in conclusion, will be precluded only in the hypothesis in which the claim conveyed by the defendant arose in the period prior to petition's date, given the need to submit it to the bankruptcy court freely available will remain those relating to claims arising after that time[108]. However, it must be received with regard to affirmative defenses: The latter constitute allegations of facts other than those annexed by the plaintiff, which are useful for obtaining the rejection of plaintiff's claim, and which, therefore, from the point of view that interests us here, are in no way differentiated from the defensive or responsive actions; in other words, there is no claim against the debtor/plaintiff, which is capable of constituting the object of an autonomous proceeding against that person, and such as to lead the said initiative into the actions precluded by the prohibition in comment[109].

The solution accepted by certain American literature cannot, of course, be perplexing: If applied, in fact, it can lead to the situation for which, for example, a person sued by the debtor for the sentence to pay a credit cannot oppose to the latter the prescription exception (the affirmative defense represented by the beginning of a statute of

---

[108]And, since the automatic stay prevents the proposition of the counterclaim in the ordinary judgment, but not the presentation of the application for admission of the credit to the competition, it is to be excluded that in this case operates, where it is compulsory counterclaim, the aforementioned its repetition: an aspect, this, that could perhaps prove useful also in the current debate about the identification of the exact source (if, in particular, it is to be recognized in the res judicata or in other principles) of this foreclosure.

[109]Especially since, in fact, there is no lack in US jurisprudence aligned with the interpretative solution proposed by us, and therefore prohibit the sole proposition of counterclaims: see in this regard the case, In re Merrick, 175 B.R. 333 (1994), 338, which is affirmed that: "(...) Given this freedom for the debtor or the trustee to prosecute the debtor's claims, an equitable principle of fairness requires a defendant to be allowed to defend himself from the attack without imposing on him a gratuitous impediment in dealing with an adversary who suffers no correlative constraint. The automatic stay should not tie the hands of a defendant while plaintiff debtor is given free rein to litigate (...) Though this paragraph will include chooses in action and claims by the debtor against others, it is not intended to expand debtor's rights against others more than they exist at the commencement of the case (...)".

limitations), with evident impairment of his right of defense[110]. This questionable position can, however, be better understood if only the attempt is made to delve more deeply into the functioning of the North American system: A system, that is, where the need to offer the debtor the most extensive and timely protection possible a completely central role. This datum, together with the pre-ordination of automatic stay to the preservation of the status quo, can perhaps better clarify the drasticity of the interpretative choice described: With the petition filing it is necessary to guarantee the maximum protection to the debtor from the initiatives of others; and to rebalance a situation in any case characterized by a strong favor debitoris. The possibility remains for third parties to request a release from the automatic stay in order to proceed with their own initiatives (and, in the example above formulated, in order to validly oppose the compensation exception)[111].

These few lines offer us some indications to outline, as a working hypothesis, a comparison between the protection offered and the illustrated US discipline: If, in fact, a first and superficial approach to the latter, by virtue of its much more extensive application areas[112], appears to be characterized by greater rigidity than the first. The interpretation and practical application of these institutions show the flexibility of such legislation to left the creditors to overcome the bans imposed by the law and obtain its disuse. This aspect, also reflects the nature of injunction, therefore precautionary, of the automatic stay. The urgency of protecting the debtor from the aggressive initiatives of others imposes, as mentioned, an immediate and generalized inhibition, which nevertheless faces justified reasons that at a later stage give way to the established and prevailing interests of creditors. The solution just illustrated, which the

---

[110]J.F. MURPHY, The automatic stay in bankruptcy, op. cit.; in jurisprudence see: Koolik v. Markowitz, 40 F.3d 567 (1994), 568.
[111]In re Financial News Network Inc., 572.
[112]F. VAZQUEZ, Modification of automatic stay to permit litigation to proceed remains possible, in ABI Journal, 27, 2008, pp. 34ss. In re The SCO Group Inc., 395 B.R. 852 (2007), 857, where the court identifies, among the circumstances to be assessed for the grant of a provision of release from the automatic stay that inhibits the prosecution of a trial against the debtor, the reasonable probability of accepting the reasons claimed by the creditor, see: D.G. EPSTEIN, Bankruptcy and related law in a nutshell, op. cit., pp. 75ss. A.N. RESNICK, Bankruptcy law manual, op. cit.

affirmative defenses wants in any case precluded in the automatic stay, it seems easier to understand. This also avoid the establishment of a specific litigation, aimed at issuing an injunction to release from the injunction, whose positive outcome, most of the time, can only appear obvious, otherwise, the risk compromising defendant's right of defense.

A contiguous but different matter from that just analyzed is the one concerning the fate of the counterclaim promoted by the debtor/defendant, towards his/her creditor/actor, and in the context of a procedure established by them. In fact, in such circumstances the main judgment promoted by the creditor must stop, by virtue of the operativity of the automatic stay; however nothing is found, in the law, about the fate of the counter claim promoted by the debtor. The prevailing interpretation is in the sense of allowing the continuation of the counterclaim proposed by the debtor, even if the main action, promoted by the creditor, is suspended from the automatic stay: In other words, the autonomy between the main cause is enhanced the one introduced through the counterclaim, so that the automatic stay intervened is refracted only on the first, while the second, as a judgment promoted by the debtor, can continue[113]. The application confirms the accuracy of the interpretation presented.

Another criticality, that the delimitation of the scope of operation of the automatic stay to the proceedings instituted "against the debtor" involves, concerns the effects that the inhibitory produces on the appeals judgments. The reference, in particular, is to the question whether the proposition of an appeal by the debtor against a sentence pronounced before the application for admission to a bankruptcy procedure constitutes an activity in violation of the automatic stay. In this regard, some especially state courts, have found that an appeal judgment initiated by the debtor cannot be considered "against the debtor" procedure, so that such trial initiative would not be precluded by the automatic stay cause a potential benefit to the procedure, as it is suitable to remove a losing case against the debtor[114]. On federal level, a different reading has been

[113]See from the jurisprudence: Southern Bank & Trust Co. v. Harley, 295 S.C. 423 (1988).

[114] For the first affirmation of this principle, the case is read Association of St. Croix Condominium Owners v. St. Croix Hotel Corp., 682 F.2d 446 (1982), Farley v. Henson, 2 F.3d (1993); but we also read what was stated in Cathey v. Johns Manville Sales Corp., 711 F.2d 60.

affirmed, in the sense that the only criterion that can be used to resolve the issue is that based on the analysis of the trial position held by the debtor at the beginning of the procedure, i.e. during the first degree of judgment, if in this case the debtor held the position of defendant, the proposed appeal, albeit from this subject, against the sentence issued at the conclusion of that judgment, cannot be considered "against the debtor", as continuation of the first degree[115]. In the wake of this second orientation, the majority doctrine has also settled: If, in conclusion, with regard to the judgments to be established at first instance, the discretionary criterion to be used is founded on the subject who takes this initiative with the consequence that they will be precluded by the automatic stay the judgments established against the debtor, while those initiated by the debtor can proceed, the validity of this criterion is no longer valid when considering the appeals, where the absorbing value takes into account the position taken by the debtor in the previous grade, because if he held the status of a defendant in that office, the injunction in question is capable of indiscriminately affecting all appeals, regardless of whether they are proposed by or against the debtor himself[116]. Naturally, the possibility also remains for the debtor to request release from the automatic stay[117]. On the other hand, and as a logical consequence of the reconstruction proposed, the automatic stay will not have preclusive effects in relation to appeals, from anyone proposed, if the first instance judgment had been established by the debtor[118].

---

[115](1983), 62, in the sense "it would be anomalous for this Court to adjudge that the instant appeal is not "against the debtor" and therefore not subject to the automatic stay when it is undisputed that, should the merits of the appeal be reached and the action remanded for a new trial, the stay of proceeding would then attach since JM would have been returned to its initial status of defendant (...)".

[116]K.J. DERR, A.K. LAYDEN, The automatic stay: What are proceedings "against the debtor"?, in ABI Journal 13, 1994, pp. 27ss. P.A. AVRON, Does automatic stay apply to appeals being prosecuted by debtor of adverse order?, in ABI Journal, 31, 2012, pp. 22ss. A.N. RESNICK, H.J. SOMMER, Collier on bankruptcy, op. cit., § 362.03[3]. D.G. EPSTEIN, Bankruptcy and related law in a nutshell, op. cit., pp. 72ss. P. A. MURPHY, E.E. SAGERMAN, D. NEIER, Creditor's rights in bankruptcy op. cit., I. RAMSAY, Personal insolvency in the 21st century. A comparative analysis of the US and Europe, op. cit.

[117]P. A. AVRON, Does automatic stay apply to appeals being prosecuted by debtor of adverse order?, cit., 80. D. G. EPSTEIN, Bankruptcy and related law in a nutshell, op. cit., pp. 73ss.

[118]On the assumption, naturally, that, having the appeal the function of reviewing the

It is clear that the diverging of opinion illustrated is based and justified on the basis of two different qualifications of the appeal: An independent and overall procedure initiated at first instance. The approach is undoubtedly correct, since it is also necessary in the hypothesis in question to identify a case equivalent to the conduct of commencement or prosecution of a proceeding against the debtor[119]: In other words, if the appeal is considered a continuation of the procedure initiated at first instance, it will be necessary to refer back to that moment to check if it is a "against the debtor" procedure, and in this case its continuation mediates the proposition of the appeal, by anyone proposed, and regardless of which subject unsuccessful, will constitute an activity precluded by the automatic stay. On the other, if the appeal judgment is qualified as an independent procedure, a new assessment must be carried out, independent of the procedural positions taken at first instance, and thus precluding the only proceedings, in this case appeals, "against the debtor", and therefore proposed by the counterpart.

Among the proceedings concerned by the rule in question are finally included those of an enforceable nature established or continued against the debtor personally[120]: Please note that these proceedings are suitable to fall also in the inhibition set by the following number (2). An interesting question, in this regard, is represented by the fate of a forced sale, whose execution had already been arranged before the petition was filed: Strictly speaking, in fact, proceeding with the sale already arranged, but still to be carried out, can constitute the continuation of a pending proceeding, and therefore prohibited by the law in question. In this circumstance, the majority of US jurisprudence allows the creditor, even in the presence of the automatic stay, to request a postponement of the date of sale operations, in order to ensure the necessary time to advance, medium tempore, a request for release relief from the prohibition and, in

---

matters of law erroneously decided at first instance and resulting from the procedural documents, it will not be possible for the debtor's counterpart to widen the object of the judgment and to infer a new claim against the former. See, G.C. HAZARD, JR., J. LEUBSDORF, D. L. BASSETT, Civil procedure, op. cit., pp. 697ss.

[119]D.G. EPSTEIN, Bankruptcy and related law in a nutshell, op. cit. I. RAMSAY, Personal insolvency in the 21st century. A comparative analysis of the US and Europe, op. cit.

[120]In re Karis, 208 B.R. 913 (1997), 916.

the event of a concession, then proceed with the forced sale: This practice is completely consistent with the aforementioned purpose of the institution, namely the preservation of the status quo, which, evidently, the mere postponement of a previously arranged sale in no way can it conflict with this purpose[121]; another matter, of course, concerns its reconciliation with the principles of the par condicio creditorum, the opportunity whose derogation, however, is examined and absorbed by the relief provision in the given case.

10.Execution against the debtor. The case of a sentence obtained before the beginning of the procedure.

If the provision, referred to in Section 362 (a), number (1) is suitable to suspend the commencement or continuation of any proceedings against the debtor. The protection granted by the subsequent number (2)[122] is instead directed to the initiatives that, with respect to the pending judgment, are placed at a later time, since they are aimed at carrying out a sentence already obtained by the creditor, for the precision obtained before the start of the bankruptcy procedure[123]. In this limitation, the claim to decision object arose before the beginning of the procedure.

The provision, which appears to be a specification, in fact, a real

[121]A.N. RESNICK, H. J. SOMMER, Collier on bankruptcy, op. cit.; in jurisprudence see the case: In re Lynn Weaver, B.R. 7 (2008), 11, which is affirmed that: "A single continuance of a foreclosure sale following the filing of a petition is not a violation of the automatic stay if, before the continued sale date, the creditor filed an appropriate motion for relief from stay (...)".

[122]The section 362 (a) (2) of the Bankruptcy Code, in particular, provides that the filing of the application for admission to one of the procedures therein "operates as a stay, applicable to all entities, of (...) the enforcement, against the debtor (...) of a judgment obtained before the commencement of the case under this title (...)".

[123]A.N. RESNICK, H.J. SOMMER, Collier on bankruptcy, op. cit., § 362.03[4]. W.R. NORTON, JR., Norton bankruptcy law and practice, op. cit., § 36:6. B.A. BLUM, Bankruptcy and debtor/creditor, op. cit. L.B. BARTELL, Visualizing bankruptcy, op. cit., pp. 77ss. D.G. EPSTEIN, Bankruptcy and related law in a nutshell, op. cit., P.A. MURPHY, E.E. SAGERMAN, D. NEIER, Creditor's rights in bankruptcy, op. cit., pp. 185ss. A.N. RESNICK, Bankruptcy law manual, op. cit., pp. 72ss. F. R. KENNEDY, Automatic stays under the new bankruptcy law, op., pp. 14ss. R.A. JOHNSON, M.C. O'LEARY, Automatic stay provisions of the bankruptcy act of 1978, op. cit. S. PARSONS, Consumer bankruptcy law in focus.

repetition, probably dictated by legislator's concern to provide the debtor with the widest possible protection of the prohibition already set by the previous number (1), is likely to preclude enforcement of both sentences with pecuniary content and measures having a different content.

With regard to the first, the prohibition to carry out a sentence with a pecuniary content against the debtor personally also implies, and inevitably, the prohibition to proceed with (levy) attachment, including (garnishment) or (execution) sale towards the personal assets of the same, even if this entity is not expressly contemplated by the norm[124]. This appears to be completely consistent with the circumstance that the creditors here considered were to be satisfied with the bankruptcy proceedings and by the distribution of proceeds from the liquidation of summer property.

The injunction in question, as anticipated, also concerns judgments with different content, i.e. other measures that typically can be pronounced against a natural or legal person. This is the case, for example, of execution of an eviction provision pronounced against the debtor prior to the petition filing[125].

Within the scope of application of the law are also those proceedings that, in relation to the sentence, are placed in an ancillary position. Consider, for everyone, a civil contempt proceeding that is started in a coercive function in order to induce the debtor to fulfill the command enclosed in the sentence[126].

The specific ratio of provision is therefore twofold: In addition to the usual need to guarantee the debtor a shelter from the aggressive actions of others, the prohibition to carry out the judgments having pecuniary

---

[124]Of course, another hypothesis is the one represented by the judgments obtained after the petition was filed. This eventuality constitutes an infringement of the automatic stay, so that the sentence obtained will have no effect, or presupposes that the actor has previously obtained a provision of relief from the auto stay provided by the section 362 (a) (1), but, in this case, also the possibility of proceeding. For this obvious consideration see: S.V. KELLEY, Ginsberg & Martin on bankruptcy, op. cit., § 3.01[C][1], note 131. A.N. RESNICK, H.J. SOMMER, Collier on bankruptcy, op. cit. W.R. NORTON, JR., Norton bankruptcy law and practice, op. cit.

[125]W.R. NORTON, JR., Norton bankruptcy law and practice, op. cit., § 36:7, note 58; see also: In re Lewis, 15 B.R. 643 (1981).

[126]D.R. COWANS, Cowans bankruptcy law and practice, op. cit., pp. 495ss. A.N. RESNICK, H.J. SOMMER, Collier on bankruptcy, op. cit.

content is evidently connected to the opportunity to channel the moment of satisfaction of the creditorial claims before the bankruptcy court, in the competition of all creditors.

11. Acts aimed at recovering or collecting, towards the debtor, a credit arising before the beginning of the procedure.

Although the presence of the verb "to recover" may appear a repetition of the protection already granted by number (1), the provision enclosed in number (6) of Section 362 (a), where it requires the inhibition of any act that is in various ways to recover or collect, from the debtor, a credit arisen before the beginning of the procedure[127], it is of application scope far more extensive than the first, since suitable to include any initiative for this direct purpose, regardless of its connection with a proceeding, of a judicial nature or not. It is therefore on the out-of-court court that the law regains its autonomy and usefulness, also and above all with respect to the inhibition set by number (2), with regard to the execution of sentences with pecuniary content[128]. In other words, if the inhibitors referred to in numbers (1) and (2) are able to block, respectively, the proceedings aimed at recovering or collecting a right to claim against the debtor, and the forced executions of the sentences pronounced against the same subject, the large dictation of number (6) here examined lends itself (also, but above all) to precluding the equivalent activities that find

[127]A.N. RESNICK, H.J. SOMMER, Collier on bankruptcy, op. cit., § 362.03[8]. D.R. COWANS, Cowans bankruptcy law and practice, op. cit., pp. 504ss. L.B. BARTELL, Visualizing bankruptcy, op. cit., pp. 77ss. D.G. EPSTEIN, Bankruptcy and related law in a nutshell, op. cit., pp. 80ss. F.R. KENNEDY, Automatic stays under the new bankruptcy law, op. cit., pp. 22ss. R.A. JOHNSON, M.C. O'LEARY, Automatic stay provisions of the bankruptcy act of 1978, op. cit., pp. 607ss. S. PARSONS, Consumer bankruptcy law in focus, op. cit., I. RAMSAY, Personal insolvency in the 21st century. A comparative analysis of the US and Europe, op. cit.

[128]A.N. RESNICK, H.J. SOMMER, Collier on bankruptcy, op. cit., § 362.03[8][a]. S.V. KELLEY, Ginsberg & Martin on bankruptcy, op. cit., § 3.01[C]. W.R. NORTON, JR., Norton bankruptcy law and practice, op. cit., § 36:10. D.R. COWANS, Cowans bankruptcy law and practice, op. cit.; B.A. BLUM, Bankruptcy and debtor/creditor, op. cit. D.G. EPSTEIN, Bankruptcy and related law in a nutshell, op. cit. P.A. MURPHY, E.E. SAGERMAN, D. NEIER, Creditor's rights in bankruptcy, op. cit., pp. 186ss. A.N. RESNICK, Bankruptcy law manual, op. cit., pp. 77ss. I. RAMSAY, Personal insolvency in the 21st century. A comparative analysis of the US and Europe, op. cit.

fulfillment on the out-of-court plane[129].

It is therefore appropriate to fall within the prohibition in question, any conduct, whether judicial or informal, aimed at obtaining a payment from the debtor. This means that foreclosed from the automatic stay will also be, for example: A mere telephone contact between creditor and debtor concerning the request, addressed to the latter, to voluntarily proceed with the due fulfillment; sending a letter of intimation to fulfill; the threat of acting in court to obtain satisfaction of their claims; the decision, taken by a telephone company, to interrupt the provision of the service because of the refusal, by the debtor admitted to the bankruptcy procedure, to pay the bills. Subject to the prohibition are also pure conduct omissive including, for example, failure to interrupt by the creditor, activities prearranged for the collection of a credit: Think of the failure to stop the automatic deductions on salaries, authorized in pre-contamination period, which evidently become precluded as a consequence of the automatic operation of the automatic stay from the date of filing the petition[130].

It should be noted that, in most cases, the provision in question will have its effects especially with regard to unsecured creditors: Holders of pre-emptive rights, vice versa, will be more likely to take initiatives aimed at implementing the privilege held in numbers (4) and (5) of Section 362 (a)[131], perhaps in the provision in comment that it is possible to grasp the most genuine expression of the purpose of guaranteeing an effective fresh start to the debtor. If this subject is able to resume the ordinary course of business from the very day of petition's filing, is also and above all with regard to these extrajudicial activities, suitable to condition their daily life, that it is advisable to guarantee maximum protection.

---

[129] D.G. EPSTEIN, Bankruptcy and related law in a nutshell, op. cit.

[130] W.R. NORTON, JR., Norton bankruptcy law and practice, op. cit. P.A. MURPHY, E.E. SAGERMAN, D. NEIER, Creditor's rights in bankruptcy op. cit., pp. 185ss. F.R. KENNEDY, Automatic stays under the new bankruptcy law, op. cit. S. PARSONS, Consumer bankruptcy law in focus, op. cit.

[131] A.N. RESNICK, H.J. SOMMER, Collier on bankruptcy, op. cit., § 362.03[8][a]. D.R. COWANS, Cowans bankruptcy law and practice, op. cit. F.R. KENNEDY, Automatic stays under the new bankruptcy law, op. cit., pp. 22ss. S. PARSONS, Consumer bankruptcy law in focus, op. cit.

12.The compensation of a debt incurred before the beginning of the procedure with a claim against the debtor.

A disposition of absolute interest, also in a comparative perspective, is that contained in number (7) of Section 362 (a), which precludes the creditor from the possibility of offsetting the receivables due from the debtor with debts in the same subject[132].

Necessary, in order to fully understand the suspensive effect in question, is to refer to the subsequent section 553 that, in dictating the regulation of compensation within a bankruptcy procedure, specifies that special provisions contained in the bankruptcy law in no way affect the right of the creditor, recognized in general by ordinary law, to offset a debt to the debtor, established before the beginning of the procedure, with the credit claimed against the same subject, likewise raised before the petition was filed, except, in fact, as provided for in Section 362[133]. This means that, even if the creditor claims a right to set-off which, by virtue of the characteristics described above, is effective and enforceable in bankruptcy proceedings its ability to act only as the substantive content of the right and as typically happens as a consequence of the operation of the injunction, it is not in any way affected by the suspension precluded in the automatic stay of which the number (7) now in comment saves, naturally, the possibility of requesting a relief provision from the inibitoria[134].

---

[132] According to the section 362 (a) (7), in particular, the filing of the application for admission to one of the procedures envisaged by Bankruptcy Code "operates as a stay, applicable to all entities, of (...) the set off of any debt owing to the debtor that arose before the commencement of the case under this title against any claim against the debtor".

[133]The mentioned section 553, for the part that interests us, provides that "except as otherwise provided in this section and in sections 362 and 363 of this title, this title does not affect any right of a creditor to offset a mutual debt owing by such creditor to the debtor that arose before the commencement of the case under this title against a claim of such creditor against the debtor that arose before the commencement of the case".

[134]S.V. KELLEY, Ginsberg & Martin on bankruptcy, op. cit., § 3.01[E]. D.R. COWANS, Cowans bankruptcy law and practice, op. cit., pp. 506ss. A.N. RESNICK, Bankruptcy law manual, op. cit., pp. 80ss. D.G. EPSTEIN, Bankruptcy and related law in a nutshell, op. cit., pp. 107ss. B.A. BLUM, Bankruptcy and debtor/creditor, op. cit., pp. 249ss. F.R. KENNEDY, Automatic stays under the new bankruptcy law, op. cit., pp. 23ss. R.A. JOHNSON, M. C. O'LEARY, Automatic stay provisions of the bankruptcy act of 1978, op. cit. S. PARSONS, Consumer bankruptcy law in focus, op. cit., I. RAMSAY, Personal

The rationale of the provision lies in the opportunity to ensure that also the credit claimed by a person in turn forced towards the debtor, is subject to assessment in the proceedings instituted before the bankruptcy court, so that the right of compensation returns usable at the end of said verification[135].

The mutual claims of debt credit to be opposable to the procedure must have arisen both in the period prior to its opening: One, by express provision of the law, the other, for general condition of credit to tenders. This implies, of course, that this requirement of mutuality is not integrated where the opposing claims have arisen, one in an earlier period, and the other, in a period subsequent to that moment.

The compensating mechanisms prevented by Section 362, then, are only those that you would like to operate after the petition was filed: The compensations made before the opening of the procedure, on the contrary, are recognized by the same Section 553, which recognizes the general validity and opposition to bankruptcy[136].

The provision says nothing, on the contrary, with regard to the possibility of compensating mutual claims arising both after the petition was filed. It is clear that these are legal relations relating to the new course of debtor's business and made possible by the fresh start compensation will be freely practicable.

It is recalled that the rule in question refers to compensations made to the debtor: If the right of credit in question, in fact, passed through summer property, the compensating mechanisms will be impeded by

---

insolvency in the 21st century. A comparative analysis of the US and Europe, op. cit.

[135]Different, as is known, is the regulation of compensation pursuant to art. 56 of the American bankruptcy law, pursuant to which, for reasons of substantive justice, the creditors are entitled to compensate with their debts towards the bankrupt the claims they have against the same, where both claims arose on the date prior to failure. The norm, therefore, constitutes an exception to the principles of the formal and substantial competition, since it is not necessary to impose it in the passive state, and for the obvious exception to the principles of par condicio creditorum.

[136]A.N. RESNICK, H.J. SOMMER, Collier on bankruptcy, op. cit., § 362.03[9]. S.V. KELLEY, Ginsberg & Martin on bankruptcy, op. cit., W.R. NORTON, JR., Norton bankruptcy law and practice, op. cit., § 36:11. D.R. COWANS, Cowans bankruptcy law and practice, op. cit. L.B. BARTELL, Visualizing bankruptcy, op. cit. A.N. RESNICK, Bankruptcy law manual, op. cit., pp. 78ss. J.F. MURPHY, The automatic stay in bankruptcy, op. cit., pp. 577ss.

Section 362 (a) (3)[137].

Separated from the compensation is the case represented by the recovery of an overpayment made to the debtor in the period prior to the beginning of the procedure, implemented through a withholding (recoupment) of part of the payment due to the same debtor by virtue of a subsequent transaction. This type of recovery differs from compensation because, while in the latter the reciprocal debit credit relationships arise from distinct and separate legal relationships, the first involves the two parts of a single relationship; therefore, it is not considered in violation of the automatic stay in question, also because it would be unfair to allow the debtor to enjoy the benefits deriving from a contract without assuming the relative obligations[138].

13.The beginning or continuation of proceedings before the US Tax Court.

The last suspension concerning initiatives of the debtor is the one governed by the following number (8), which makes the beginning or continuation, at the US Tax Court, of a proceeding concerning debtor's tax[139]. See, in this regard, the classification made in In re Holyoke Nursing Home Inc. case, 273 B.R. 305 (2002), 311: "Set off is in the nature of a counterclaim, enabling a creditor on a mutual unrelated debt (...) recoupment is the from the same transaction, typically from the same transaction, to the reciprocal obligation arising from the same transaction (...)"[140].

---

[137]D.G. EPSTEIN, Bankruptcy and related law in a nutshell, op. cit. pp. 106ss.

[138]A.N. RESNICK, H.J. SOMMER, Collier on bankruptcy, op. cit., § 362.03[9][b]. S.V. KELLEY, Ginsberg & Martin on bankruptcy, op. cit., W.R. NORTON, JR., Norton bankruptcy law and practice, op. cit. D.R. COWANS, Cowans bankruptcy law and practice, op. cit. A.N. RESNICK, Bankruptcy law manual, op. cit., pp. 79ss, note 43.

[139]The section 362 (a) (8), in particular, prescribes that the filing of the application for admission to one of the procedures provided for by the Bankruptcy Code "operates as a stay, applicable to all entities, of (...) the commencement or continuation of a proceeding before the United States Tax Court concerning a tax liability of a debtor that is a corporation for a taxable period the bankruptcy court may determine or concerning the tax liability of a debtor who is an individual for a taxable period ending before the date of the order for relief under this title (...)". For further analysis see: F.R. KENNEDY, Automatic stays under the new bankruptcy law, op. cit., pp. 23ss. S. PARSONS, Consumer bankruptcy law in focus, op. cit.

[140]D.G. EPSTEIN, Bankruptcy and related law in a nutshell, op. cit. I. RAMSAY, Personal

Already mention has been made of the provision in question on the occasion of the analysis of the subjects that suffer the suspensive effects deriving from the automatic stay[141], the one in question constitutes the only hypothesis in which the debtor is exceptionally subject to the injunction envisaged in Section 362: Because, since the tax assessment is a proceeding that can be initiated only upon the request of tax payer, the recipient of the prohibition can only be that subject.

The rule concerns only the first level judgments, while the discipline concerning the appeals should be found in the prohibition set in the previous number (1)[142]. In this regard, therefore, it is necessary to refer to the criteria, elaborated above, useful to evaluate if and when the appeal judgment brought against a sentence issued by the U.S. Tax Court at the end of the proceedings initiated by the debtor and considered "against the debtor"[143]. Therefore, the position taken on the question of the nature of the appeal judgment will be decisive. In other words, whether it is an autonomous procedure or the continuation of the first degree. Applying these criteria to the case in question would therefore be that, following the first orientation, only appeals against the debtor should be suspended, while, following the second, no appeal could be prevented by the injunction, in any case of trial ab origin established by the debtor. From these conclusions it emerges, however, that the transfer of general criteria elaborated with regard to the automatic stay imposed by number (1) turns out, in reality, difficult to practice: Regardless of the preferred orientation about the nature of the appeal in fact, it follows that, while the judgments of first instance instituted by the debtor are always precluded by number (8) examined here, the establishment or continuation of the appeals by the same debtor would always be permitted[144]. It is therefore necessary to

insolvency in the 21st century. A comparative analysis of the US and Europe, op. cit.

141D.R. COWANS, Cowans bankruptcy law and practice, op. cit., pp. 508ss. A.N. RESNICK, H.J. SOMMER, Collier on bankruptcy, op. cit., § 03[10], where the recipient of the injunction is also found in the same Tax Court as the governmental unit affected by the automatic stay.

142A.N. RESNICK, H.J. SOMMER, Collier on bankruptcy, op. cit. D.R. COWANS, Cowans bankruptcy law and practice, op. cit.

143D.R. COWANS, Cowans bankruptcy law and practice, op. cit.

144The applicability of the mentioned criteria, with regard to the second orientation reported, would also be excluded from this, that if the law provides for the suspension of a

proceed with an adaptation, i.e. to conclude that all the appeals, regardless of the fact that they were initiated by the debtor or the financial administration, should be subject to the aforementioned injunction[145].

Furthermore, the suspension operates differently depending on whether the taxpaying debtor is a natural person or a company: In the first case, the suspended judgments are those relating to tax periods before the start of the procedure, while with regard to the companies, this limit of temporal ruling does not include the judgments relating to the tax periods following the petition filing, provided they are identified by the bankruptcy court[146].

This rule is completed with the provision contained in the following section 505, where the jurisdiction is attributed to the bankruptcy court in order to ascertain debtor's tax debts, as the realization of the ratio of convergence in the forum concursus of the related assessment judgments.

14.(Follows) Suspensions to protect bankrupt assets. The execution, against summer property of a sentence obtained before the beginning of the procedure.

The protections granted to summer property are, with the opening of the procedure, the following initiatives expressly precluded: (1) The execution, against the property merged into bankruptcy assets, of a sentence obtained before the start of the procedure; (2) acts aimed at obtaining possession or exercising control over the summer property; (3)

judgment that can be initiated only on the initiative of the debtor, which necessarily plays the role of actor, means that the determination of the appeals concerned by the prohibition in question can not depend on the procedural position of the defendant party taken by the debtor at first instance.

[145]Thus, the decision taken in the Freemen v case appears to be incorrect. Commissioner, 799 F.2d 1091 (1986), where it was affirmed that the appeal promoted by the debtor is not suspended by section 362 (a) (1) because it does not represent an action against the debtor, but this requirement is not required even to suspend the trial of first instance, so that an application of the provision cited to the case in question requires, for the purpose of compatibility, that this requirement is not required even with regard to appeals.

[146]A.N. RESNICK, H.J. SOMMER, Collier on bankruptcy, op. cit. S.V. KELLEY, Ginsberg & Martin on bankruptcy, op. cit., § 3.01[C]. W.R. NORTON, JR., Norton bankruptcy law and practice, op. cit., § 36:12. L.B. BARTELL, Visualizing bankruptcy, op. cit.

acts aimed at creating or implementing a pre-emption right of the same.

The suspension foreseen at number (2) of Section 362 (a), already analyzed, precludes the enforcement of a sentence obtained by the creditor in the period prior to the petition filing against the assets and rights transferred to bankruptcy assets[147].

So as the debtor also the summer property is protected from any attempt to obtain the enforced enforcement of the dictum enclosed in a judicial decision pronounced before the beginning of the procedure: Within the scope of the rule will therefore fall executive proceedings and again (levy) seizure, and (execution) sale[148]; since the automatic stay is not limited, as regards its operative field, from the criterion of custody legis, the suspensive effectiveness in speech can also benefit goods that are materially in possession of third parties, as happens with the writ of garnishment.

The overall consideration of the injunction ordered by number (2) allows us, however, to give it back its autonomy: If, with regard to the debtor, it appears a repetition, implemented through the specific identification of the procedures precluded, of the protection granted from the previous number (1), it fully regains its usefulness when it goes on to describe the suspensions operating for the benefit of bankruptcy assets, against which, as mentioned, the rule referred to in the aforementioned number does not intervene (1), reserved to the debtor.

The interests protected by the provision directly concern the insurance of bankruptcy assets integrity. This value, however, assumes different variations in the liquidation and conservative procedures: In the first, obviously, it is designed to prevent the risk of fragmentation of

---

[147]According to Section 362(a)(2) of Bankruptcy Code,in fact, the filing of the application for admission to one of the procedures provided for therein “operates as a stay, applicable to all entities, of (...) the enforcement (...) against summer property, of a judgment obtained before the commencement of the case under this title (...)”.

[148]A.N. RESNICK, H.J. SOMMER, Collier on bankruptcy, op. cit., § 362.03[4]. S.V. KELLEY, Ginsberg & Martin on bankruptcy, op. cit., § 3.01[C][2]. W.R. NORTON, JR., Norton bankruptcy law and practice, op. cit., § 36:6. D.R. COWANS, Cowans bankruptcy law and practice, op. cit., pp. 494ss. L.B. BARTELL, Visualizing bankruptcy, op. cit., pp. 77ss. B.A. BLUM, Bankruptcy and debtor/creditor, op. cit., pp. 248ss. D.G. EPSTEIN, Bankruptcy and related law in a nutshell, op. cit., P.A. MURPHY, E.E. SAGERMAN, D. NEIER, Creditor's rights in bankruptcy op. cit., pp. 182ss. I. RAMSAY, Personal insolvency in the 21st century. A comparative analysis of the US and Europe, op. cit.

summer property, in order to ensure orderly liquidation and subsequent distribution of assets among the creditors, respecting the legitimate causes of pre-emption; in the second, the object of protection is the possibility of devolving the assets that flowed into the summer property, the reorganization effort and, thus, to the success of the procedure initiated[149].

15.Acts aimed at obtaining possession of the property merged into bankruptcy assets or exercising control over the same.

With a very general formulation, the following number (3) makes the acts aimed at obtaining possession of the assets converged into the bankruptcy assets subject to an inhibitory action or at exercising control over them[150].

In this regard, it should be noted right now that the original formulation of the rule precluded the only initiatives aimed at obtaining possession of the aforementioned assets. Reference to other type of activities was added by an amendment of 1984[151], justified from the need to ensure that the protection extended even to the benefit of those initiatives that did not take place in the physical possession of the goods, and that therefore, in the absence of such a characteristic, would have escaped the prohibition in question[152]. Today, three types of conduct are expressly forbidden: The acts aimed at obtaining possession of assets on which summer property has a right; the acts aimed at obtaining possession of the assets converged in summer property, but on which the same is not the owner of a property right but of situations of mere possession or

[149]A.N. RESNICK, H.J. SOMMER, Collier on bankruptcy, op. cit. B.A. BLUM, Bankruptcy and debtor/creditor, op. cit.

[150]Section 362(a)(3) of Bankruptcy Code, to be precise, it provides for the filing of the admission application to one of the procedures provided for therein "operates as a stay, applicable to all entities, of (...) any act to obtain possession of property of the estate or of property from the estate or to exercise control over property of the estate (...)".

[151]Act of July 10, 1984, Pub. L. No. 98353, 98 Stat. 352 (1984).

[152]W.R. NORTON, JR., Norton bankruptcy law and practice, op. cit., § 36:7; on the difference between possession and controlling the sense of the greater comprehension of the second term, see also, D. G. EPSTEIN, Bankruptcy and related law in a nutshell, op. cit. pp. 93ss. I. RAMSAY, Personal insolvency in the 21st century. A comparative analysis of the US and Europe, op. cit.

detention[153]; finally, the acts aimed at exercising control over assets or rights of ownership of summer property.

The provision therefore lends itself to precluding a very wide range of initiatives, of a judicial or extrajudicial nature, aimed at carrying out the three described conduct[154]: And the common goal pursued is, of course, the same need to guarantee the integrity of bankruptcy assets, already illustrated at the end of the previous subparagraph[155].

Proceeding in the analysis of the foreclosed initiatives, to the first of the categories reported-acts aimed at obtaining possession of assets owned by the summer-, can be traced, for example, the conduct of the creditor holding a pre-emptive right that wants to enter the possession of the asset on which said pre-emption insists[156]; while it will fall into the second type of prohibited acts to obtain possession of assets from summer property, but not owned by the latter, the initiative of the subject who wants to recover from the mass a property which, however, has merged into summer property (think of the case of a car loaned to the debtor before the petition was filed): Obviously, he cannot be considered free to act but must request a relief measure from the automatic stay in order to prove his property right before the bankruptcy court[157].

Greater interest raises the third type of prohibited conduct, that is the one included the initiatives aimed at exercising control over assets or

---

[153]The automatic stay, it is remembered, concerns all the interests in property converged in the summer, and, therefore, also the situations of mere possession or detention of which the debtor was holder in the antecedent time Bankruptcy law manual, to the deposit of the petition: on point, P.A. MURPHY, E.E. SAGERMAN, D. NEIER, Creditor's rights in bankruptcy, op. cit., pp. 183ss. A.N. RESNICK, Bankruptcy law manual, op. cit., pp. 76ss. D.G. EPSTEIN, Bankruptcy and related law in a nutshell, op. cit., pp. 92ss. F.R. KENNEDY, Automatic stays under the new bankruptcy law, op. cit., pp. 15ss, note 55. R.A. JOHNSON, M.C. O'LEARY, Automatic stay provisions of the bankruptcy act of 1978, op. cit., pp. 606ss. J.F. MURPHY, The automatic stay in bankruptcy, cit., pp. 575ss. S. PARSONS, Consumer bankruptcy law in focus.

[154]A.N. RESNICK, H.J. SOMMER, Collier on bankruptcy, op. cit., § 362.03[5]. W.R. NORTON, JR., Norton bankruptcy law and practice, op. cit. L.B. BARTELL, Visualizing bankruptcy, op. cit. F.R. KENNEDY, Automatic stays under the new bankruptcy law, op. cit., pp. 15ss. S. PARSONS, Consumer bankruptcy law in focus, op. cit.

[155]A.N. RESNICK, H.J. SOMMER, Collier on bankruptcy, op. cit. W.R. NORTON, JR., Norton bankruptcy law and practice, op. cit., See also: In re Chateaugay Corp., 87 B.R. 779 (1988), 794.

[156]S.V. KELLEY, Ginsberg & Martin on bankruptcy, op. cit., § 3.01[D].

[157]A.N. RESNICK, H.J. SOMMER, Collier on bankruptcy, op. cit., § 362.03[5].

rights of ownership of summer property introduced, as was said, to free the prohibition referred to in number (3) obtaining the material possession of goods, and therefore suitable to include a wide and heterogeneous range of activities.

First of all, in the case under consideration, the initiatives aimed not to obtain, but to retain the possession, acquired prior to the petition, of assets owned by summer property: In this situation, as noted, the trustee can exercise his powers of turnover[158] to be included in the material availability of the asset; where the interested party refuses to return the goods to the procedure, he will incur the violation in question[159]. The same of course applies, more generally, for any hypothesis in which a subject retains the possession of an asset in the face of a restitution obligation towards the mass.

The reformulation of the law allows the protection to be extended to intangible assets, as such insurable possession. The subject connects us, first of all, with the question of the fate of contracts in progress: Pursuant to Section 365 of the Bankruptcy Code, in particular, the trustee can decide whether to take over or dissolve from the same; before this decision, however, since the legal relationships resulting from these contracts are considered legal positions belonging to the bankruptcy mass, they are protected against the other initiatives aimed at the dissolution of such shops or in any case against any interference that may jeopardize the subjective legal positions they derive. The reference is, to be precise, to the possibility of operating the bankruptcy termination clauses, or ipso facto clauses, or clauses that provide for the automatic termination of the contract in the event of admission to a bankruptcy procedure, or even the possibility of withdrawing from the contract by virtue of such event: Such initiatives are evidently precluded from the provision in question. The principle expressed, however, assumes particular importance in the matter

---

[158]A.N. RESNICK, H.J. SOMMER, Collier on bankruptcy, op. cit. L.B. BARTELL, Visualizing bankruptcy, op. cit. D.G. EPSTEIN, Bankruptcy and related law in a nutshell, op. cit., pp. 94ss. J.F. MURPHY, The automatic stay in bankruptcy, op. cit. I. RAMSAY, Personal insolvency in the 21st century. A comparative analysis of the US and Europe, op. cit.

[159]D.G. EPSTEIN, Bankruptcy and related law in a nutshell, op. cit. Section 365: "the trustee, subject to the court's approval, may assume or reject any executory contract or unexpired lease of the debtor (...)".

of leases, where the lessor incurs a violation of the prohibition in question whenever attempts to dissolve from the contract with the debtor or that it will also detect which conduct to obtain possession of assets on which the summer has an interest other than the right of ownership to deprive the latter of the possession of the premises. In the hypotheses examined up to now, it is worthwhile to note that the automatic stay is also used as an institution designed to assure the trustee the time necessary to decide whether to take over or to dissolve the pending contract.

Another interesting hypothesis is that relating to the fate of the rights of action which, by virtue of the petition, flow into the summer property: The protection in question implies, to be precise, that the sale of these rights is precluded, as well as, for example, the prohibition, in the hands of creditors, to promote liability actions against the directors of the debtor company, or to act in an ordinary way for the recovery of an asset that the debtor has transferred fraudulently (so-called fraudulent transfer); the prohibition is explained, of course, not with the suspension referred to in number (1) of Section 362 (a) which, it should be noted, operates only if the debtor takes the trial attorneys of the defendant, but with the belonging to the mass of these rights to act in court[160], so that an exercise by third parties involves an act aimed at exercise control over a right to ownership of summer property[161]. If the trustee abandons the right to action, however, it will cease to belong to the summer and, if it recovers

[160]The scenario is different if the lease comes naturally before or during the bankruptcy procedure. In this case, with regard to leases for nonresidential use, the sec. 362 (b) (10) expressly subtracts from the exclusive regime of the automatic stay the acts of the landlord aimed at obtaining possession of the premises: on the theme, for everyone, A.N. RESNICK, H.J. SOMMER, Collier on bankruptcy, op. cit., § 362.05 [10]. We keep in mind, however, that the sec. 541 (b) (2) excludes from the property of the summer the debtor's interests as a tenant in a nonresidential lease contract whose natural expiration occurred before or during the procedure (in this second case, the exclusion from the summer it intervenes at the time of the expiry of the contract), so that the termination of the automatic stay with regard to these assets follows already and only by virtue of this last forecast. See, D.G. EPSTEIN, Bankruptcy and related law in a nutshell, op. cit., pp. 100ss.

[161]D.G. EPSTEIN, Bankruptcy and related law in a nutshell, op. cit. pp. 96ss, however, there is a different justification with regard to fraudulent transfers. According to these authors, in fact, the summer would have an interest on the property subject of the fraudulent transfer evidently linked to the expectation to reinstate the bankruptcy assets with the asset being transferred, so the judicial action of the creditor would be prohibited precisely because it is directed towards an asset on which the summer has an interest.

in the ownership of the creditors, the latter, freed from the foreclosure in speech, will return free to act in court.

A further scenario is presented, then, in the case of competing automatic stays: When, that is, two subjects, both admitted to a bankruptcy procedure, are beneficiaries of the protective effects examined here and claim reciprocal claims. This situation arose in the conflict, well known to the American literature, between a company affiliated to Lehman Brothers Inc. ("Lehman")[162] and the SunCal group, including a consortium for the lending of Lehman[163]. Following the housing crisis in the United States in 2008, Lehman initiated enforcement proceedings against the SunCal group, which called for admission to a reorganization procedure under Chapter 11; in turn, Lehman also required admission to the same type of procedure, complicating the framework of claiming resolution between the two companies. In particular, in order to proceed with the forced execution initiated against the SunCal and obtain the repayment of the sums granted as a loan, Lehman requested the release from the automatic stay of which, from the time of application for admission to the reorganization procedure, it benefited the SunCal group; the latter, however, opposed the request for relief because some unfair conduct held by Lehman was quite suitable to justify the so-called equitable

---

[162]For further details and analysis see: G. XINYI, To recognise or not to recognise? Comparative study of Lehman brothers cases in Mainland China and Taiwan, in International Corporative Rescue, 10, 2013, pp. 240ss. J.L. WESTROOK, An empirical study of the implementation in the United States of the Model Law on cross border insolvency, in American Bankruptcy Law Journal, 87, 2013, pp. 247ss P.L. DAVIES, Resolution of cross-border groups, in M. HAENTJENS, B. WESSELS, Research handbook on crisis management in the sector, Edward Elgar Publishers, 2015, pp. 264ss, the author discussing how both the U.S. and the U.K. took unilateral action in the bailouts of non-national entities, including Lehman Brothers, in order to protect national interests. J.M. PECK, Cross-border observations derived from My Lehman Judicial Experience, in Butterworths Journal of International Banking & Finance Law, 30, 2015, pp. 132ss., the author explaining that cross-border conflicts and self-interested behaviours in the context of the Lehman insolvencies were unavoidable). S.L. BUFFORD, Coordination of insolvency cases for international enterprise groups: A proposal, in American Bankruptcy Law Journal, 86, 2012, pp. 685ss.K.P. WOJCIK, Bail-in in the Banking Union, in Common Markets Law Review, 53 (1), 2016, pp. 124ss. J. ALTMAN, A test case in international bankruptcy in international bankruptcy protocols: The Lehman Brothers insolvency, in San Diego International Law Journal, 12, 2011, pp. 477.

[163]See in argument the case: In re Palmdale Hills Property LLC, 654 F.3d 868 (2011).

subordination of the rights of credit claimed by the same[164], i.e. their degradation from privileged to unsecured, with consequent transfer in the bankruptcy assets of the pre-emptive rights of the SunCal that witnessed the same credit rights, in accordance with the provisions of Section 510 (c) (2) of the Bankruptcy Code[165]. In turn, Lehman replied, against this defense, that the equitable subordination of its right to claim together with the transfer of the right of first refusal was, in its turn, capable of violating the automatic stay placed in its protection, since an act aimed at exercising control over the rights flowing into its summer, in clear violation of the protection provided by number (3) under consideration. The bankruptcy court accepted the replies of Lehman, formulating, on that occasion, the principle of law whereby, in the presence of competing automatic stays, each debtor can act with purely defensive activities, but in the face of offensive initiatives the automatic stay arises as an insurmountable barrier.

The protective efficacy in question, as emerges from the text of the law, applies, however, regardless of the moment in which the claim arises which, through acts prohibited by the law, is intended to give satisfaction[166]. This is perfectly consistent and functional to the need to ensure that summer property constitutes a tool of satisfaction for the exclusive benefit of creditors whose title is prior to the petition filing: What, obviously, requires that the initiatives also of post-reconciliation creditors besides, of course, those aspiring to find satisfaction in the competition, against the summer property, are blocked; while, equally coherently, the creditors by title following the petition filing are free to

---

[164]By resorting to the equitative powers that traditionally belong to him, the bankruptcy court, pursuant to sect. 510 (c) of the Bankruptcy Code, may, in fact, derogate from the general rules on the order of distribution of the sums to subordinate the satisfaction of certain credits, where the relative owners have held a contrary conduct, in fact, to the principles of equity. This occurs, for example, where the behavior held was suitable to damage the other creditors or to cause an unjust advantage to the credit holder subject to subordination. For further details see: W.D. WARREN, D.J. BUSSEL, D.A. SKEEL, JR., Bankruptcy, op. cit., pp. 432ss.

[165]"(...) The court may (...) order that any lien securing such a subordinated claim be transferred to the estate". See the analysis of: V.C. DURRER II, K.D. JAIMEZ, Competing bankruptcies: What defenses survive the automatic stay?, op. cit., pp. 52ss.

[166]S.V. KELLEY, Ginsberg & Martin on bankruptcy, op. cit., § 3.01[C][2]. P.A. MURPHY, E.E. SAGERMAN, D. NEIER, Creditor's rights in bankruptcy, op. cit., pp. 185ss. See also the case: In re Garofalo's Finer Foods, Inc., 186 B.R. (1995), 436. For further details: A. BARRY CAPPELLO, Lender liability, Juris Publishing, New York, 2014, pp. 812ss.

take action, as already discussed in the number (1), by means of proceedings against the debtor even with direct initiatives towards the personal assets of the same, in line with the opportunity to guarantee the subject admitted to a bankruptcy proceedings.

16.An insistent right of pre-emption on the property merged into bankruptcy assets.

The last category of initiatives that Section 362 of the Bankruptcy Code precludes against summer property is the one defined in number (4), which subjects to acts that are aimed at creating, refining or exercising a pre-emption right (so-called lien) on bankruptcy assets[167].

The definition of the term "lien", moreover, is expressly set by the legislator in Section 101 (37), where it, with a very general definition, is identified in any "voluntary or legal or judicial nature of a charge against or an obligation or performance of an obligation"[168].

The prohibition in question concerns three different activities, united by having all, as object, a lien: Constitution, improvement, or the exercise of the rights connected to it. Remember, however, how, prior to the entry into force of today's bankruptcy law, the inhibitory effects that the Rules of Bankruptcy Procedures reconnected to the operativeness of the automatic stay were much more restrictive, concerning only the initiatives aimed at exercising the right of pre-emptive subsistence on bankruptcy assets. The reform has extended the scope of the suspension to include also the acts aimed at establishing and perfecting such a right, with the clear aim of avoiding that the order of pre-emptive causes is altered in the post-deposit petition period[169]. If, in fact, the pre-emptive rights

---

[167]See Section 362(a)(4) of Bankruptcy Code, where the provision that filing the application for admission to one of the procedures regulated therein "operates as a stay, applicable to all entities, of (...) any act to create, perfect, or enforce any lien against property of the estate". A.N. RESNICK, H.J. SOMMER, Collier on bankruptcy, op. cit., § 362.03[6]. S.V. KELLEY, Ginsberg & Martin on bankruptcy, op. cit., § 3.01[D]. L.B. BARTELL, Visualizing bankruptcy, op. cit., A.N. RESNICK, Bankruptcy law manual, op. cit., pp. 81ss. D.G. EPSTEIN, Bankruptcy and related law in a nutshell, op. cit., pp. 110ss. J.F. MURPHY, The automatic stay in bankruptcy, op. cit., pp. 576ss. I. RAMSAY, Personal insolvency in the 21st century. A comparative analysis of the US and Europe, op. cit.

[168]D.G. EPSTEIN, Bankruptcy and related law in a nutshell, op. cit. I. RAMSAY, Personal insolvency in the 21st century. A comparative analysis of the US and Europe, op. cit.

[169]W.R. NORTON, JR., Norton bankruptcy law and practice, op. cit., § 36:8. A.N.

acquired in the period prior to that moment are opposable within the procedure by the relative owners, it is necessary to ensure that the order of privileges thus constituted remains crystallized at that date, preventing the subsequent alteration through the establishment and completion of new pre-emption rights[170]. The provision, moreover, does not even limit its scope of operations to the only receivables that arose before the petition was filed: Conduits subject to inhibition, in other words, are always suspended, regardless of when the credit in question arises.

The very comprehensive tenor of the provision implies, on a concrete level, that, since the deeds constituting a lien are precluded, an unsecured creditor at the time the petition is presented will remain such for the purposes of the competition; secondly, for creditors who already hold a lien, judicial or extrajudicial initiatives[171] will be precluded, aimed at implementing this right of first refusal, including forced sale, and this, of course, even if the pre-emptive creditor is in possession of the asset on which the pre-emptive cause insists[172].

The impossibility, for the lender holder of a lien, to bring it to execution does not mean, however, that this subject loses its right of first refusal: The automatic stay, as known, is not suitable institution to affect

---

RESNICK, Bankruptcy law manual, op. cit., pp. 80ss. F.R. KENNEDY, Automatic stays under the new bankruptcy law, op. cit., pp. 17ss. D.R. COWANS, Cowans bankruptcy law and practice, op. cit., pp. 50ss. D.G. EPSTEIN, Bankruptcy and related law in a nutshell, op. cit., pp. 110ss, note 5. S. PARSONS, Consumer bankruptcy law in focus, op. cit., I. RAMSAY, Personal insolvency in the 21st century. A comparative analysis of the US and Europe, op. cit.

170 S.V. KELLEY, Ginsberg & Martin on bankruptcy, op. cit., § 3.01[C][2]. D.R. COWANS, Cowans bankruptcy law and practice, op. cit., pp. 502ss. B.A. BLUM, Bankruptcy and debtor/creditor, op. cit. D.G. EPSTEIN, Bankruptcy and related law in a nutshell, op. cit., pp. 110ss. I. RAMSAY, Personal insolvency in the 21st century. A comparative analysis of the US and Europe, op. cit. In jurisprudence see the case: In re Reserves Dev. Corp., 78 B.R. 951 (1986), 957.

171 A.N. RESNICK, H.J. SOMMER, Collier on bankruptcy, op. cit., § 362.03[6][b]. S.V. KELLEY, Ginsberg & Martin on bankruptcy, op. cit., § 3.01[D]. P.A. MURPHY, E.E. SAGERMAN, D. NEIER, Creditor's rights in bankruptcy op. cit., pp. 182ss. R.A. JOHNSON, M.C. O'LEARY, Automatic stay provisions of the bankruptcy act of 1978, op. cit., pp. 607ss.

172 A.N. RESNICK, H.J. SOMMER, Collier on bankruptcy, op. cit. L.B. BARTELL, Visualizing bankruptcy, op. cit. D.G. EPSTEIN, Bankruptcy and related law in a nutshell, op. cit. S.H. NICKELS, J.J. WHITE, Bankruptcy, West Group, Minnesota, 1993, where therefore the clarification about the indifference of the place where the good is physically located, for the purpose of the protection in question.

the substantial plan on legal situations pertaining to the subjects affected by it, as to simply preventing them from being exercised in an extra-competitive position or, in this case, that the creditor can bring to execution the right of pre-emption of which he is the owner outside the competition, therefore, of the proceedings managed by the bankruptcy court; on the other hand, this right will remain fully enforceable in the insolvency proceedings.

It should be noted that the protection in question extends only to assets over which the estate has a right of ownership: Where the interest claimed is a different right, for example, a purely possessory situation, the asset will not benefit from the protection offered bu number (4), but it may eventually fall under the general provision referred to in number (3), examined above, also stopping the residual possibility for the trustee or for the debtor in possession, if this is necessary, to request the granting an injunction pronounced on the basis of the equitable powers recognized by the bankruptcy court from Section 105[173].

17.(Follows) Suspensions intended to protect debtor's personal assets: Acts aimed at creating, refining or exercising a pre-emptive right to guarantee a credit arising prior to the start of the procedure.

The last entity to benefit from the protective effects offered by Section 362 is debtor's personal assets, consisting of, remember, all the assets and rights abandoned by the trustee, the exempt property claimed by the debtor, the assets, in the liquidation procedure, acquired after the petition was filed, and the others however they do not flow into bankruptcy assets.

In favor of the assets thus identified, the provision in question grants a single protective measure, prepared by number (5) of subsection (a) which, in assonance with the provisions of the previous number (4) with reference to summer property, inhibits all the acts aimed at creating, refining or exercising a right of pre-emption, with the further specification,

[173] A. N. RESNICK, H. J. SOMMER, Collier on bankruptcy, op. cit., § 362.03[6][c].

however, of the need for it to be used as security for a claim arising before the start of the procedure[174].

This temporal limitation, which follows that the protection applies only to bankruptcy creditors, while it falls short in relation to the receivables arising after the petition was filed, represents, as has already been pointed out several times, a figure consistent with the objective, precisely of any insolvency procedure, to guarantee from this moment the implementation of the fresh start, and therefore the establishment by the debtor of new legal relationships[175].

The consideration just carried out thus allows us to identify the peculiar rationale of the rule, which can therefore be found not only in the need to avoid preferential treatment for the benefit of some creditors, but also and above all in the opportunity to guarantee discharge to the debtor, and consequent effective fresh start, objectives that would be thwarted if it were possible to use debtor's personal assets, as a separate entity from summer property, only, as known, to satisfy creditors by way of pre-opening procedure, to guarantee satisfaction of bankruptcy creditors, evidently for the unpaid residue within the procedure. This prohibition, however, cannot leave perplexing where only one thinks of the possibility in which the discharge is denied: In this regard, the opinion of those who criticized the legislative choice to prevent bankruptcy creditors, holders of non dischargeable credits, to obtain a right of pre-emption on debtor's personal assets, and thus be able to compete with creditors by way of title following the petition filing[176]. In the reorganization procedures, vice

---

[174]Section 362 (a) (5) of the Bankruptcy Code, provides that the filing of the application for admission to one of the procedures therein "operates as a stay, applicable to all entities, of (...) any act to create, perfect, or enforce against property of the debtor any lien to the extent that such lien secures a claim that arose before the commencement of the case under this title (...)".

[175]A.N. RESNICK, H.J. SOMMER, Collier on bankruptcy, op. cit., § 362.03[7]. W.R. NORTON, JR., Norton bankruptcy law and practice, op. cit. L.B. BARTELL, Visualizing bankruptcy, op. cit. D.G. EPSTEIN, Bankruptcy and related law in a nutshell, op. cit. op., pp. 87ss. R.A. JOHNSON, M.C. O'LEARY, Automatic stay provisions of the bankruptcy act of 1978, op. cit., pp. 608ss. I. RAMSAY, Personal insolvency in the 21st century. A comparative analysis of the US and Europe, op. cit.

[176]F.R. KENNEDY, Automatic stays under the new bankruptcy law, op. cit., pp. 20ss. A.N. RESNICK, H.J. SOMMER, Collier on bankruptcy, op. cit., § 362.03[7][b]. S. PARSONS, Consumer bankruptcy law in focus, op. cit.

versa, the prohibition in question can be essential to guarantee the achievement of debtor reorganization purposes, to the extent that, for example, the exempt property is fundamental to ensure the successful outcome of the procedure[177].

The passage of assets and rights from bankruptcy assets to debtor's personal assets therefore changes the legal status, with regard to the effectiveness produced by the automatic stay: The assets that, abandoned by the trustee, or object of exemptions claimed by the debtor in fact, if at first they had protection against any initiative concerning receivables arising both before and after the petition was filed, with the aforementioned transfer to the property of the debtor they cease to benefit from the inhibitors specifically set up for the benefit of summer property. With this event, therefore, only the initiatives of bankruptcy creditors, intended to find satisfaction within the competition and, moreover, in case of supervening discharge, which, as we will see, happens temporally to the automatic stay, will see their claims to the payment of the residual definitively waived, will remain blocked, consistent with the need to ensure that the personal assets that the debtor begins to replenish is devolved to the new course of business[178].

18.Effects of automatic stay on the course of time.

An issue that usually accompanies any mechanism with an inhibitory effect, is that concerning the relationship between the same and the exercise of powers, rights or faculties that the law expressly subject to

[177]It should be noted, however, that it is very possible for the trustee to abandon an asset that has flowed into the summer not to the debtor but to a third party, and in particular to the holder of the right of preemption that insists on the same asset. In fact, the cessation of the automatic stay prepared for the benefit of the summer does not correspond to the sub-entry of any different protection since, with all evidence, the asset will not pass into the availability of an entity benefiting from the injunction, so that the creditor's executive initiatives preemptive will not be prevented. D.R. COWANS, Cowans bankruptcy law and practice, op. cit., pp. 504ss.

[178]A.N. RESNICK, H.J. SOMMER, Collier on bankruptcy, op. cit. S.V. KELLEY, Ginsberg & Martin on bankruptcy, op. cit., §§ 3.01[C][2] and [D]. W.R. NORTON, JR., Norton bankruptcy law and practice, op. cit. D.G. EPSTEIN, Bankruptcy and related law in a nutshell, op. cit., pp. 89ss.I. RAMSAY, Personal insolvency in the 21st century. A comparative analysis of the US and Europe, op. cit.

prescription or forfeiture: A problem that is generally solved by the provision for which, within the period in which the required initiatives are impeded by the injunction, the expiry of the related terms of exercise, envisaged under penalty of foreclosure, is also suspended.

Since in the US legal system there are laws (so-called statutes of limitations) which, safeguard the certainty of legal relationships, require that the exercise of a certain right must take place, under penalty of foreclosure, within a certain period of time. The silence observed by the bankruptcy law on the issue has turned the burden of the search for an appropriate solution to the jurisprudence.

First of all, since the null law provides for this, it is obviously not possible to state that the automatic suspension of the terms legally provided for the exercise of a right is reconnected to the automatic operation of the inhibitory effects connected to the stay: The automatic stay, in other words, does not interrupt or suspend the course of these terms[179].

Without prejudice to these premises, it is nevertheless possible to find in the bankruptcy law certain instruments useful for tempering a system that otherwise would appear to be absolutely unfair and prejudicial to the entity subject to the injunction, placed in front of the alternative between inertia, with consequent loss of their right, and acting in violation of the automatic stay (regardless, however, from the further question about the suitability of an act performed in violation of the injunction to operate as an impediment event of the expiration of the terms in question).

The reference is, in the first place, to Section 108 of the Bankruptcy Code, entitled "Extension of time", where under subsection (c) it is provided that in cases where the non-bankruptcy law (such as a statute of limitation, mentioned earlier), a court order or a contract set a deadline (so-called limitation period) for the commencement or prosecution of a legal action against the debtor, this term expires either on

---

[179]S.V. KELLEY, Ginsberg & Martin on bankruptcy, op. cit., § 3.01[C]. W.R. NORTON, JR., Norton bankruptcy law and practice, op. cit., § 36:4. P.A. MURPHY, E.E. SAGERMAN, D. NEIER, Creditor's rights in bankruptcy, op. cit., pp. 184ss. B.A. BLUM, Bankruptcy and debtor/creditor, op. cit., pp. 256ss. J.F. MURPHY, The automatic stay in bankruptcy, op. cit., pp. 586ss. In jurisprudence see: In re Margulis, 323 B.R. 130 (2005), 133ss.

its natural expiry or on the thirtieth day following the termination of the automatic stay, depending on which of the two events intervene subsequently[180]. In essence, the usefulness of the rule is taken in the event that the natural expiry of the term set to establish a judgment against the debtor intervenes during the bankruptcy proceedings and, therefore, in the vigor of the automatic stay, or even before the thirtieth day following its termination: In this case, the expiry of the term is automatically deferred to the extent indicated above[181].

The provision has limited, on an objective level, judgments already established or to be established against the debtor. In this regard, and with regard to all other types of acts, rescues again Section 105 (a) of the Bankruptcy Code, mentioned several times, to the extent that it is functional to the pronouncement of any necessary or appropriate provision to implement the provisions of the bankruptcy law or, as in the present case, to bring the system back to equity.

19.The initiatives removed from the protective effect: The exceptions expressed in Section 362 (b) of the Bankruptcy Code. Structure and possibility of using the equitative powers referred to in Section 105 (a) of the Bankruptcy Code.

The following subsection (b) contains a long series of initiatives to be exact, after the last changes made in 2005, this is twenty-seven different cases, which the law expressly excludes, that is, subtracts from the applicative scope of the automatic stay: In other words, it deals with actions that, by their nature, would have been fit to fall into any of the

---

[180]For a jurisprudential application see: Rogers v. Corrosion Products, Inc., 42 F.3d 292 (1995), 295ss. D.R. COWANS, Cowans bankruptcy law and practice, op. cit., pp. 474ss. B.A. BLUM, Bankruptcy and debtor/creditor, op. cit., pp. 257ss. J.L. SMAHA, Automatic stay under the 1978 bankruptcy code: an equitable roadblock to secured creditor relief, op. cit., pp. 1120ss.

[181]A.N. RESNICK, H.J. SOMMER, Collier on bankruptcy, op. cit., 3, § 362.05. W.R. NORTON, JR., Norton bankruptcy law and practice op. cit., § 36:14. D.R. COWANS, Cowans bankruptcy law and practice, op. cit., pp. 508ss. W.D. WARREN, D.J. BUSSEL, D.A. SKEEL, JR., Bankruptcy, op. cit., pp. 180ss. P. A. MURPHY, E.E. SAGERMAN, D. NEIER, Creditor's rights in bankruptcy, op. cit., pp. 192ss.

inhibitors prescribed by subsection (a), and that only by virtue of different legislative policy reasons, often, under pressure from certain lobbies, many exceptions have been made. As a reflection of precise and determined intentiones legislatoris, and set against a provision, such as the aforementioned subsection (a), to be interpreted extensively, the individual exceptions must be read strictly rigorously[182].

Between the two subsections, (a) and (b), here in comment, it is possible to appreciate a certain parallelism: If, in other words, the petition's deposit achieves the immediate and necessary operation of the automatic stay, at the same time it triggers, on an equally immediate and necessary basis, the operation of the exceptions to this injunction, and therefore the subtraction of the automatic imposition of the pre-exclusive effectiveness described for certain initiatives strictly required by law.

First of all, we need to move from what has already been stated in relation to the nature of the automatic stay: That is, to sum up that the subsection (a) contains a relative legal presumption, albeit sui generis, about the existence of a prejudice which, in lack of protection from the creditorial initiatives, derives from the interests of the procedure, as such suitable to trigger the immediate course of the injunction. Furthermore, it should be remembered that the introduction into the US bankruptcy system of the automatic stay did not entail the possibility of accessing protective measures otherwise not usable because in the previous era it was still possible for the debtor to obtain judicial orders with suspensive or inhibitory content, subordinately, however, to one of its initiatives in this sense, but has simplified, to the full advantage of the debtor, the process of obtaining these measures, now automatically reconnected to the petitions filing. Well, moving from these premises, it seems to us that the removal of a given initiative from the scope of the automatic stay as a consequence of the imposition of an exception means, more precisely, that this initiative is removed from the special regime that this institution is accompanied and, therefore, the aforementioned relative presumption. The

---

[182]A.N. RESNICK, H.J. SOMMER, Collier on bankruptcy, op. cit. S.V. KELLEY, Ginsberg & Martin on bankruptcy, op. cit., § 3.02[A]. D.G. EPSTEIN, Bankruptcy and related law in a nutshell, op. cit., pp. 61ss. In the same spirit see the case: In re Stringer, 847 F.2d 549 (1988), 552. A.N. RESNICK, H.J. SOMMER, Collier on bankruptcy, op. cit.

specific effect of the operation of an exception, in other words, is to re-establish, among the parties, the probative regime ordinarily in force with regard to the request for measures of an inhibitory nature. This means, in concrete terms, that the individual initiatives set aside for the exceptions to the automatic stay can be undertaken, or continued without the presence of a petition presenting any influence on them; while, on the contrary, it will be the party that intends to request a protective measure and, therefore, the debtor or the trustee, who must furnish proof of the prejudice suffered, in order to obtain the concession of the injunction, with a restoration, therefore, of the ordinary probation charges[183].

The effect resulting from the operation of an exception, in other words, is not that of subtracting tout court the initiative of a third party to any foreclosure: What happens, rather, is the cessation of the probative regime of favor for the debtor deriving from the vigor of the automatic stay, while remaining in any case the possibility, for this subject, to request a provision that also inhibits the completion of the shares subject to the exception, after the performance, as mentioned, of ordinary probationary charges, after demonstration of the injury otherwise suffered. The suspension provision, after verifying the existence of the conditions required for the ruling of an injunction, will be granted by the bankruptcy court on the basis of the equitable powers granted to it by Section 105 of the Bankruptcy Code.

The operation of an exception, in conclusion, shows the debtor at the time when, before the entry into force of the Rules of Bankruptcy Procedures, it was necessary to make a special request to the judicial authority to obtain the granting of a suspensive provision: An era in which the burden of the trial initiative was transferred to the debtor.

This datum reconfirms the essence and the peculiar trait of the modern automatic stay: It is not, therefore, the inhibitory content contained in it that constitutes the characteristic element of the institute that, as seen,

---

[183] A.N. RESNICK, H.J. SOMMER, Collier on bankruptcy, op. cit. S.V. KELLEY, Ginsberg & Martin on bankruptcy, op. cit., § 3.02[B]. W.R. NORTON, JR., Norton bankruptcy law and practice, op. cit. R.A. JOHNSON, M.C. O'LEARY, Automatic stay provisions of the bankruptcy act of 1978, op. cit., pp. 607ss. H.B. PICKARD, The new bankruptcy code, part II: the interests of secured creditors under the new bankruptcy code, op. cit., 233ss. See also in argument the case: Mirant Corp. v. Potomac Elec. Power, B.R. 152 (2003).

are other ways that can be used by the debtor to achieve the same result, but rather the automaticity and the necessity with which these effects are produced, at the moment and by virtue of petition deposit, as a reflection of the relative legal presumption that Section 362 has implemented, in its process of training and development. In conclusion, the exceptions provided for by subsection (b) are therefore not exceptions to the command of an inhibitory content, that is, one could say to the "stay" component of the institute, but rather exemptions from the automatic operation command connected to it, to the "automatic" component, it is still possible for the debtor to obtain the first (the "stay"), without however being able to benefit from the second (its "automatic" character)[184].

The initiatives that the subsection (b) subtracts from the automatic stay are twenty-seven: Given the cut, centered on the procedural profiles of the institute, which is intended to confer to the present discussion, we will not proceed to an analysis of each case contemplated by the norm, but we will shortly focus on those relevant to our purposes or for comparative purposes, or for reasons of systematic reconstruction of the matter that deals with it.

20.(Follows) The commencement or prosecution of criminal proceedings against the debtor. The proceedings on familiar lato sensu matter.

The first initiative subtracted from the automatic stay regime, and which therefore is not in any way affected by the automatic inhibition operating under the petition, is contemplated at number (1) of subsection (b), and concerns the beginning of the prosecution of a criminal proceeding against the debtor[185].

The rationale of the rule is quite clear: If the prohibition to initiate

---

[184]The section 362 (b) (1) of the Bankruptcy Code, provides that the filing of the application for admission to one of the procedures regulated therein "does not operate as a stay (...) under subsection (a) of this section, of the commencement or continuation of a criminal action or proceeding against the debtor (...)".

[185]A.N. RESNICK, H.J. SOMMER, Collier on bankruptcy, op. ult. Cit., § 362.05[1]. W.R. NORTON, JR., Norton bankruptcy law and practice op. cit., § 36:15. A.N. RESNICK, Bankruptcy law manual, op. cit., pp. 83ss. L.B. BARTELL, Visualizing bankruptcy, op. cit., pp. 79ss. B.A. BLUM, Bankruptcy and debtor/creditor, op. cit., pp. 250ss. M.A. FREY, S.K. SWINSON, Introduction to bankruptcy law, op. cit., pp. 249ss.

or continue proceedings against the debtor must also be functional in order to guarantee the latter an instrument to protect against the aggressive actions of others, it must not become a means to avoiding the consequences foreseen for the execution of criminal acts[186].

The provision takes particular interest to the extent that the result of the criminal proceedings can lead to payment by the debtor and in favor of a third party of a sum of money, which can lead to the risk of circumventing the prohibitions prescribed by the automatic stay: In this case, without prejudice to the criminal nature of the proceedings and, therefore, the applicability of the exception in question, the debtor can ask the bankruptcy court to pronounce an injunction pursuant to Section105 (a) where it proves that the main purpose of the proceeding is actually the obtainment of a payment from him[187]. Where criminal proceedings are accompanied by a civil action for compensation for damages deriving from the crime (such as, for example, a civil wrongful death action), this will naturally be blocked by the automatic stay.

Another extremely important provision is that contained in the following subsection (b) (2), in which the letters (A) and (B) subtract from the exclusive effect of the automatic stay a full-bodied initiative, all concerning internal relations to the family group. These include, among others: a) The commencement or continuation of a civil proceeding, i) for the declaration of paternity and maternity; ii) for the determination or judicial modification of the obligation to provide the food; iii) concerning the right of custody or visit of the minor; iv) for the dissolution of the marriage, excluding applications for division of assets that have merged during summer property; and b) of the acts aimed at obtaining payment of a maintenance obligation, provided they are not directed to summer property[188].

---

[186]W.R. NORTON, JR., Norton bankruptcy law and practice, op. cit. P.A. MURPHY, E.E. SAGERMAN, D. NEIER, Creditor's rights in bankruptcy op. cit. pp. 192ss. B.A. BLUM, Bankruptcy and debtor/creditor, op. cit. J.F. MURPHY, The automatic stay in bankruptcy, op. cit., pp. 578ss. R.M. HUTCHINSON, Automatic stay exceptions: Section 362(b), in Bankruptcy Developments Journal, 4, 1987, pp. 44ss, contra the direct applicability of automatic stay, A. N. RESNICK, Bankruptcy law manual, op. cit., pp. 83ss.

[187]D.G. EPSTEIN, Bankruptcy and related law in a nutshell, op. cit. I. RAMSAY, Personal insolvency in the 21st century. A comparative analysis of the US and Europe, op. cit.

[188]The section 362 (b) (2) of the Bankruptcy Code, provides that the filing of the application

The proceedings listed under a), introduced into the body of the standard by the Bankruptcy Reform Act of 1994[189] and the subsequent Bankruptcy Abuse Prevention and Consumer Protection Act (BAPCPA) of 2005[190] are clear expression of the principle by which the management of personal relationships of the debtor, which in no manner may have repercussions on the procedure, cannot be prevented or prejudiced by it.

As regards, then, the acts aimed at recovering a food obligation[191], it is easy to identify the rationale of the exception in the assistance reasons inherent in these obligations, aimed at meeting the essential needs of the beneficiaries who, moreover, are creditors who arise in a domestic context and not linked to the business activity carried out by the debtor[192]. Furthermore, these credits are declared non-deductible by Section 523 (a) (5) 156, so that the exception is functional to allow only the immediate payment, in the face of the primary needs of the person and, therefore, not delayed.

Please note that the law expressly limits the possibility of obtaining payment of a maintenance obligation to the fact that the resources to deal with it do not come from the summer but, obviously, from the property of the debtor; now, if we remember what has been said with regard to the regulation of the assets, and in particular of the salaries received by the debtor after the petition has been filed, it will also be recalled that in the procedures referred to in Chapters 11 and 13 such contingencies flow into the summer. In case of admission to one of them, the possibility for creditors to obtain food is, in fact, considerably restricted. In this regard, the changes made to the standard by the 2005

---

for admission to one of the procedures regulated therein "does not operate as a stay (...) under subsection (a)(A) of the commencement or continuation of a civil action or proceeding(i) for the establishment of paternity; (ii) for the establishment or modification of an order for domestic support obligations; (iii) concerning child custody or visitation; (iv) for the dissolution of a marriage, except to the extent that such proceeding seeks to determine the division of property that is property of the estate; […] (B) of the collection of a domestic support obligation from property that is not property of the estate (...)".

[189]Pub. L. No. 1098 (2005).

[190]Pub. L. No. 103394 (1994).

[191]A.N. RESNICK, H.J. SOMMER, Collier on bankruptcy, op. cit., § 362.05[2]. M.A. FREY, S.K. SWINSON, Introduction to bankruptcy law, op. cit.

[192]A.N. RESNICK, H.J. SOMMER, Collier on bankruptcy, op. cit. W.D. WARREN, D.J. BUSSEL, D.A. SKEEL, JR., Bankruptcy, op. cit., pp. 180ss.

BAPCPA have included a new exception in Section 362 (b) (2) (C) providing, in fact, the possibility of ordering the withholding of part of contingent assets that also flow into bankruptcy assets, in order to allocate them to the payment of a maintenance obligation, provided that it is established by a judicial or administrative provision[193].

On the contrary, the executive proceedings concerning a food credit do not fall within the scope of operation of the exception: They will therefore remain prevented by the injunction, without prejudice to the granting of a relief measure[194].

21.The beginning or prosecution of a proceeding by a governmental unit, for the protection of public interests.

The exception referred to in Section 362 (b) (4), considered among the most important as it subtracts from the exclusivity effects of the automatic stay the beginning or continuation of a procedure, including those of an executive nature, by a governmental unit, during the year of his police or regulatory powers[195].

The rationale of the provision is, apparently, very similar to the one formulated with regard to criminal proceedings: The automatic stay is an instrument aimed at guaranteeing the orderly management of the

---

[193]The section 362 (b) (4) of the Bankruptcy Code, provides that the filing of the application for admission to one of the procedures regulated therein “does not operate as a stay (...) under paragraph (1), (2), (3), or (6) of subsection (a) of this section, of the commencement or continuation of an action or proceeding by a governmental unit (...)to enforce such a governmental unit’s (...) police and regulatory power, including the enforcement of a judgment other than a money judgment, obtained in an action or proceeding by the governmental unit to enforce such governmental unit’s (...) police or regulatory power (...)”.

[194]A.N. RESNICK, H.J. SOMMER, Collier on bankruptcy, op. cit., § 362.05[5][a]. W.D. WARREN, D.J. BUSSEL, D.A. SKEEL, JR., Bankruptcy, op. cit., pp. 182ss. D.G. BAIRD, The elements of bankruptcy, op. cit., pp. 196ss. O. COUWENBERG, S. J. LUBBEN, Essential corporate bankruptcy law, op. cit.

[195]A.N. RESNICK, H.J. SOMMER, Collier on bankruptcy, op. cit., § 362.05[5][b]. S.V. KELLEY, Ginsberg & Martin on bankruptcy, op. cit., § 3.02[D]. W.R. NORTON, JR., Norton bankruptcy law and practice, op. cit., § 36:18. P. A. MURPHY, E.E. SAGERMAN, D. NEIER, Creditor's rights in bankruptcy op. cit., pp. 195ss. A.N. RESNICK, Bankruptcy law manual, op. cit., pp. 88ss. L.B. BARTELL, Visualizing bankruptcy, op. cit., pp. 80ss. R.M. HUTCHINSON, Automatic stay exceptions: Section 362(b), op. cit., pp. 49ss.

bankruptcy procedure, but cannot be transformed into a means of allowing transgressors to public rules or regulations to avoid the related responsibilities[196]. Among the most frequent applications of the exception in question, we can mention, for example, those concerning disciplinary proceedings, actions against discrimination at work, consumer and environmental protection[197].

The provision also allows the commencement of executive proceedings concerning the judgments obtained by the governmental unit: By express provision of the rule, exceptions are, however, the decisions concerning the payment of sums of money or the transfer of assets by the debtor, the execution of which, as it is directed towards the summer and suitable to interfere with the procedure, remains subject to the necessity of obtaining a provision of relief from the automatic stay.

22.The hypothesis of the petition filing by an ineligible debtor or in violation of a previous bankruptcy court order.

A very peculiar disposition is that enclosed in Section 362 (b) (21), also introduced by the aforementioned BAPCPA of 2005, where the acts aimed at bringing to execution an insistent right of pre-emption on an immovable property in the hypothesis in which the debtor are subtracted from the preclusive effects of the automatic stay instant present certain characteristics. It is, to be precise, the case in which he is "ineligible"

---

[196]A.N. RESNICK, H.J. SOMMER, Collier on bankruptcy,op. ult. cit., § 362.05[5][a]. S.V. KELLEY, Ginsberg & Martin on bankruptcy, op. cit., W.R. NORTON, JR., Norton bankruptcy law and practice, op. cit. W.D. WARREN, D.J. BUSSEL, D.A. SKEEL, JR., Bankruptcy, op. cit., P.A. MURPHY, E.E. SAGERMAN, D. NEIER, Creditor's rights in bankruptcy, op. cit., pp. 195ss. A.N. RESNICK, Bankruptcy law manual, op. cit., pp. 92ss. B.A. BLUM, Bankruptcy and debtor/creditor, op. cit., pp. 252ss. R. MARKER, When is a governmental unit's action to enforce its police or regulatory power exempt from the automatic stay provisions of section 362?, in Florida State University Law Review, 9, 1981, pp. 369ss.

[197]Section 362(b)(21) of the Bankruptcy Code, provides that filing of the application for admission to one of the procedures governed therein "does not operate as a stay (...) under subsection (a), of any act to enforce any lien against or security interest in real property (A) if the debtor is ineligible under section 109(g) to be a debtor in a case under this title; or (B) if the case under this title was filed in violation of a bankruptcy court order in a prior case under this title prohibiting the debtor from being a debtor in another case under this title (...)".

according to Section 109 (g) of the Bankruptcy Code, or, alternatively, deposited the petition in violation of a previous bankruptcy court order that forbade the presentation of a subsequent application for admission to a bankruptcy procedure[198].

The provision intervenes to fill a previous gap, and to soothe the related debate which, for the same reason, had for years had tired US doctrine and jurisprudence. In fact, before the introduction of the aforementioned provision, doubts existed around the question of whether the filing of a petition in violation of Section 109 (g) and, therefore, by a debtor considered by law ineligible would still be suitable to make the effects of automatic stay run: According to part of the jurisprudence, followed by certain doctrine[199], the application presented in violation of the command enclosed in Section 109 (g) was in fact affected by a radical nullity, with the consequent unsuitability, inter alia, to produce the operation of the injunction in comment; according to others[200], on the other hand, such an application should not be considered radically null, with the consequence that automatic stay would have entered into force, but there would have been room for its subsequent annulment ex tunc after judicial assessment of the debtor's actual ineligibility.

---

[198]A.N. RESNICK, H.J. SOMMER, Collier on bankruptcy, op. ult. § 362.05[19][b]. S.V. KELLEY, Ginsberg & Martin on bankruptcy, op. cit. § 3.02[J][11]. M.A. FREY, S.K. SWINSON, Introduction to bankruptcy law, op. cit. D.G. EPSTEIN, Bankruptcy and related law in a nutshell, op. cit., pp. 46ss. L.B. BARTELL, Visualizing bankruptcy, op. cit., pp. 81ss. S. LARSEN, Understanding the new semiautomatic stay, in ABI Journal, 25, 2006, pp. 75ss. I. RAMSAY, Personal insolvency in the 21st century. A comparative analysis of the US and Europe, op. cit.

[199]A natural person debtor, or a family farmer, are considered to be ineligible, pursuant to sect. 109 (g), if they had submitted a petition in the 180 days preceding the filing of the new application, and: a) The first procedure had been closed (dismissed) by the bankruptcy court as a result of the debtor's failure to comply with a provision o the nonappearance at the hearing to guarantee the continuation of the procedure; or b) when the same debtor has requested and obtained the closure of the procedure as a result of the presentation of a request for release (relief) from the automatic stay. Obviously, this is a provision of a sanctioning nature aimed at punishing abusive conduct and limiting the practice of the so-called serial filings that is, the serial deposit of applications for admission to a procedure for the exclusive purpose of benefiting from the automatic stay, through the foreclosure, for 180 days, of the possibility of presenting a new petition. In argument: A.N. RESNICK, H.J. SOMMER, Collier on bankruptcy, op. cit., 2, § 109.08. W.R. NORTON, JR., Norton bankruptcy law and practice, op. cit., § 18:14.

[200]See also the case: In re Casse, 198 F.3d 327 (1999), 342. For further details see: D.P. STEWART, International and transnational criminal law, Wolters Kluwer, New York, 2018.

23.The provision referred to in Section 362 (b) (21) intervenes on this context in a dual direction.

By regulating the hypothesis in the list of exceptions to the automatic stay, a choice is made that is partially favorable to the first cited guideline, to which the idea of inoperativity ex lege of inhibitory is accepted in the event that, inter alia, the debtor is ineligible, so any initiatives made by creditors after the petition will remain valid and effective[201]. In this regard, however, we must make a clarification: That the debtor in time falls within the categories contemplated by the rule here in question is obviously not a circumstance that appears simultaneously with the filing of the petition, as an impediment attached to the application to preclude the operation of automatic stay, but will emerge rather following a proper judicial assessment dedicated to the verification of the aforementioned circumstances; is to be considered, therefore, that the person interested in this matter can turn to the bankruptcy court to declare that the debtor falls into the category of persons to whom Section 362 (b) (21), with a provision that at the same time ascertains the inoperativity of the automatic stay, against the same, from the date of filing the petition, unless, naturally, a provision for dismissal of the procedure for ascertained ineligibility of the debtor pursuant to section 109 (g) not intervened[202].

Secondly, then, the initiatives excepted by the automatic stay are limited, on an objective level, only to acts aimed at bringing to execution an insistent right of pre-emption on an immovable property. In this regard, if you keep present on this point you will return extensively during the next section, which with regard to some qualified hypotheses of serial deposits of petitions. The same legislator of 2005 intervened to dispose the general inoperativity of the automatic stay (or the its early termination), without prejudice to the possibility, under certain circumstances, to benefit

[201]R. LEFKOWITZ, The filing of a bankruptcy petition in violation of 11 U.S.C. § 109(g): does it invoke the automatic stay? in Cardozo Law Review, 26, 2004, pp. 326ss. See also: In re Flores, 291 B.R. 44 (2003), 55ss.

[202]L.A. NAPOLI, The not-so-automatic stay: Legislative changes to the automatic stay in a case filed by or against an individual debtor, in American Bankruptcy Law Journal, 79, 2005, pp. 755ss.

from protection from a later date (or to obtain an extension of its duration). On this, however, we will have the opportunity to return treating the effectiveness time of the injunction, as a hypothesis of derogation from the general rules on production and termination of the automatic stay.

24.Additional exceptions to the automatic stay: Postponement

Lastly, two further cases are of particular interest that the subsection (b) subtracts from the inhibitory effects deriving from the automatic stay: This is in particular the forecasts contained in numbers (22) and (23), also introduced by the BAPCPA of 2005, which allow the procedure of specific initiatives concerning procedures and eviction actions, subject to the application of certain conditions. In other words, the legislator intended to codify exceptions operate not only as customary, by virtue of the petition filing, but also in the sense of neutralizing the rebuttable pre-assumption based on the automatic nature of the stay and at a later date, after assessing the occurrence of certain conditions as a case of early termination of the injunction. These very peculiar aspects of the legislation lead us, therefore, to a reflection if the subsection (b) is actually the most appropriate matter to bring such a discipline; or if it is not the case, rather, to treat such cases within the complex discipline concerning the temporal effectiveness of the automatic stay, to which the next Section will be dedicated. Several data, which we ca not anticipate now, lead us to prefer this second solution: In this context, naturally, having acquired the necessary notions, we will also try to offer a justification for the choice made here.

25.Disputes on the effectiveness of the protective effect: The identification of competent judge.

Things get complicated when you want to fall into the applicative reality, where the belonging of a given initiative to those affected by the injunction, rather than those made the subject of an exception, is often uncertain or object of dispute between the parties.

In cases where the applicability of the automatic stay is controversial, the parties obviously have an interest in obtaining a judicial decision suitable to bring certainty on the issue the entity that would suffer the suspensive effect, exposed to certain penalties in the case of prohibition violation. It is therefore inadvisable for the latter to act in the supposition that a certain exception applies, or that the automatic stay is otherwise not operational, being absolutely preferable to request the intervention of the judge on the matter.

The law, however, completely ignores the eventuality described, and in particular nothing provides for the identification of the competent judicial authority to know the question concerning the applicability of the automatic stay. This, also due to the complexity of the theme of jurisdiction division between bankruptcy and ordinary courts, results in a clear criticality in the case in which, in particular, the initiative in question is a judicial proceeding, a hypothesis in which there is therefore in the presence of two different courts where the judgment is incardinated, and the bankruptcy, both abstractly suitable to be invested in the matter.

Some decisions argue that competent to know the matter are both the courts before which the proceedings are pending, together with the determination of their jurisdiction, would also be competent to decide on the applicability of the automatic stay, not falling in the prohibition referred to in Section 362 (a) (1), both the bankruptcy court where the procedure was hinged[203]. Another decision, with reference to a decision taken by a state court, however, specified that the contribution, by Section 1334 (a) of Title 28 of the US Code, of exclusive jurisdiction in the district court. Therefore, the bankruptcy court for the district to which the jurisdiction has been delegated on cases regulated by the Bankruptcy Code, implies that the decision in question, however, belongs to that, or to the bankruptcy court, nor can this be opposed to the so-called collateral estoppel deriving from the sentence issued by the state judge[204]. This effect, more precisely defined issue preclusion, consists in the foreclosure,

---

[203]In this sense see: In re Baldwin United Corp. Litigation, 765 F.2d 343 (1985), 347. For further details: J.R. SULLIVAN, D.P. STEWART, International and transnational criminal law, Wolters Kluwer, New York, 2018. A.W. SHAIN, The effect of bankruptcy on State tax enforcement and proceedings, in Tax Analysts, 2012, pp. 948ss.

[204]The principles was expressed in the case: In re Gruntz, 202 F.3d 1074 (2000), 1083. For further details see: M. HOWARD, Bankruptcy federalism: a doctrine askew, in Pepperdine Law Review, 38, 2011, pp. 6ss.

for the parties, in a subsequent trial concerning a different cause of action, to re-examine the same question, in fact or law, controversial, decisive and explicitly decided by a sentence[205]. If, in this case, the effect of the issue of preclusion could have occurred, the definitive and indisputable nature of the decision on the applicability of the automatic stay issued by the State Court, with consequent foreclosure of the possibility of to know them again; the decision referred to, however, starting from the absence, in relation to the state court, of the necessary jurisdiction to rule on the matter, affirmed the nullity of the sentence pronounced by that body, and the consequent impossibility of verifying the described effect of issue preclusion[206]. In the wake of this orientation, the opinion opposed to the first mentioned is inserted, favoring to attribute exclusively to the bankruptcy court the competence to rule on the applicability of the automatic stay. The opinion is further supported by appealing to the need to avoid conflicts of decisions in the various extra-food holes and, in any case, in the opportunity to entrust the management of the procedure to the bankruptcy court[207].

26.Towards the search for a solution that requires us to delve into the complex discipline concerning the jurisdiction in bankruptcy matters in US law.

Precisely from the reference made by the sentence just mentioned in Section 1334 (a) of Title 28 of US Code[208], on the basis of which the exclusive jurisdiction of the district court was affirmed, thus, the bankruptcy court deciding on the question of the applicability of the automatic stay. Now, the argument does not seem decisive because it is not appropriate: As mentioned, in fact, the attribution of original and exclusive jurisdiction sanctioned in this rule is limited to "cases under title 11" and

[205]G.C. HAZARD, JR., J. LEUBSDORF, D.L. BASSETT, Civil procedure, op. cit., pp. 635ss. A.W. SCOTT, Collateral estoppel by judgment, in Harvard Law Review, 56, 1942.
[206]A. N. POLASKY, Collateral estoppel effects of prior litigation, in Iowa Law Review, 39, 1954, pp. 218ss.
[207]In this sense see: In re Hunt, 93 B.R. 484 (1988), 489.
[208]D.G. EPSTEIN, Bankruptcy and related law in a nutshell, op. cit. I. RAMSAY, Personal insolvency in the 21st century. A comparative analysis of the US and Europe, op. cit.

therefore, substantially, to procedure opening and to bankruptcy mass administration; on the other hand, as already known, for the express provision referred to in the following subsection (b), original but not exclusive jurisdiction is conferred with regard to civil proceedings concerning issues arising from or related to bankruptcy law or open competition procedure . Among the civil proceedings concerning issues arising at the opening of the insolvency procedure, it seems appropriate to be able to count the opinion that is established in order to determine the applicability of the automatic stay to a given initiative, in fact, situation that own exclusive source in the opening of the procedure.

Judgments of applicability determination of the automatic stay, constituting proceedings concerning a question arising at the beginning of the procedure and created by the Bankruptcy Code, are included among the judgments on which the district court and, generally, the bankruptcy court is equipped with original but not pure exclusive jurisdiction. It follows that the relative jurisdiction belongs, in principle, to the bankruptcy court, but the possibility of ruling also by other judicial authorities cannot be ruled out, since it is not an exclusive jurisdiction. In any case, it seems undoubtedly preferable, in practice, to reserve the questions about the applicability of the automatic stay to the knowledge of bankruptcy court, as well as to shared reasons already stated, also for the advantages connected to the specialization of the judge, certainly more experienced and competent in the evaluation of the matter in question. The same legislator has stated that, in regulating certain cases of early termination of the automatic stay, has attributed the power to issue a ruling ascertaining inability occurrence of the injunction to the bankruptcy court.

The conclusion would be different if the list referred to in Section 157 (b) (2) of Title 28 of US Code or the initiative considered in the context of "matters concerning the administration of summer property" referred to in letter (A) of the same law, and therefore the process under consideration was considered as core proceeding, whose jurisdiction is attributed, through referrals, to the bankruptcy court.

27.Temporal efficacy of automatic stay and procedure for granting relief

An analysis of this phenomenon has already been carried out, correctly intelligible only through a historical analysis of the evolution that the stays have known in US bankruptcy legislation, and in particular the progressive emergence of the need to provide for anticipation of the most possible the time of granting the injunction in favor of the debtor, in order to promptly remove the bankruptcy assets at any risk of disintegration: Evolution, as known, ultimately resulting in the current solution of presuming the existence of an injury to the procedural circumstance, this, previously subject to judicial assessment, so as to allow the production of protection only and exclusively by virtue, in fact, of the deposit of petition[209].

The textual data of the norm, in the body of Section 362 (a), expresses the discipline just illustrated about the initial term of effectiveness of the automatic stay providing that “a petition filed under sections 301, 302, or 303 of this title (...) operate as a stay”[210]. A brief analysis deserves the reference, performed there, in sections 301, 302 and 303. It should be remembered that the placement of the institute in Chapter 3 of the bankruptcy law, one of the so-called universal chapters, whose provisions are intended to be applied with regard to all operative chapter-indicative of its suitability to operate with regard to all the procedures governed by the Bankruptcy Code-the reference to these rules means that said operation also prescinds from the subject that takes the initiative for the deposit of the petition, both that is, the debtor himself (in the so-called voluntary cases, governed by Section 301)[211], a creditor or a third party

---

[209]A.N. RESNICK, H.J. SOMMER, Collier on bankruptcy, op. cit., § 362.02. S.V. KELLEY, Ginsberg & Martin on bankruptcy, op. cit., § 3.01[B]; W.R. NORTON, JR., Norton bankruptcy law and practice Norton bankruptcy law and practice, op. cit., § 36:4; B.A. BLUM, Bankruptcy and debtor/creditor, op. cit., pp. 244ss. F.R. KENNEDY, Automatic stays under the new bankruptcy law, op. cit., pp. 10ss. H.B. PICKARD, The new bankruptcy code, part II: the interests of secured creditors under the new bankruptcy code, op. cit., pp. 232ss. S. PARSONS, Consumer bankruptcy law in focus.

[210]D.G. EPSTEIN, Bankruptcy and related law in a nutshell, op. cit. I. RAMSAY, Personal insolvency in the 21st century. A comparative analysis of the US and Europe, op. cit.

[211]D.G. EPSTEIN, Bankruptcy and related law in a nutshell, op. cit. I. RAMSAY, Personal insolvency in the 21st century. A comparative analysis of the US and Europe, op. cit.

authorized to do so (according to Section 303, which regulates the so-called involuntary cases, which may be started with exclusive with regard to the liquidation procedures, as per Chapter 7, and reorganization, referred to in Chapter 11)[212], or again in the case of joint cases pursuant to Section 302, that is to say of an application submitted by the debtor (natural person) together with his spouse[213].

The petition is understood to mean the moment in which the application for admission to insolvency proceedings is lodged with the registry of the competent court, and the latter is taken over by the latter[214].

The operation of the stay as a necessary and automatic consequence of this fulfillment, however, not only excludes the need for a special provision for judicial grant, but also means that it is not necessary, either for its binding and enforceability to the entities subject to it, the making of any communication regarding its entry into force. These entities, in other words, will be subject to it from the moment the petition is filed and by virtue of that event only, even if they have not received notice of its operation or, upstream, of the opening of the competition procedure which, as is known, occurs with the notice referred to in Section 342 of the Bankruptcy Code[215], so that the activities that are equally accomplished in the guilty ignorance of the prohibition will still be affected by (broadly speaking) ineffectiveness.

Another issue, then, is that concerning the fate of the automatic stay in the case where the procedure initially initiated is converted into another, always governed by the Bankruptcy Code and, as far as we are concerned, if this conversion leads to the beginning of a new course of the

---

[212]D.G. EPSTEIN, Bankruptcy and related law in a nutshell, op. cit. I. RAMSAY, Personal insolvency in the 21st century. A comparative analysis of the US and Europe, op. cit.

[213]S.V. KELLEY, Ginsberg & Martin on bankruptcy, op. cit., D.G. EPSTEIN, Bankruptcy and related law in a nutshell, op. cit., pp. 64ss. I. RAMSAY, Personal insolvency in the 21st century. A comparative analysis of the US and Europe, op. cit.

[214]S.V. KELLEY, Ginsberg & Martin on bankruptcy, op. cit., § 3.01[B][4]. R.A. JOHNSON, M.C. O'LEARY, Automatic stay provisions of the bankruptcy act of 1978, op. cit., pp. 604ss.

[215]A.N. RESNICK, H. J. SOMMER, Collier on bankruptcy, op. cit., S.V. KELLEY, Ginsberg & Martin on bankruptcy, op. cit., § 3.01[B][1]. D.G. EPSTEIN, Bankruptcy and related law in a nutshell, op. cit. Bankruptcy and related law in a nutshell, op. cit., pp. 45. D.G. EPSTEIN, Bankruptcy and related law in a nutshell, op. cit. I. RAMSAY, Personal insolvency in the 21st century. A comparative analysis of the US and Europe, op. cit.

injunction. The question, is not purely speculative but has a considerable practical importance, insofar as, for example, the course of a new automatic stay would neutralize the relief measures from the inhibitor that the creditor can having obtained during the first procedure. The answer to this question is indeed provided by the same bankruptcy law, which in Section 348 (a), rubricated "effect of conversion" provides that "conversion of a case from one title to another is not a change in the date of the filing of the petition, the commencement of the case, or the order for relief"[216]. This means that the conversion does not involve the beginning of a new procedure and, as far as we are concerned, does not change the date of the first (and only) petition so that, since the latter is the only fulfillment suitable to produce the operation of the injunction in question, it follows that the stay in force still remains that originally produced, being to exclude, on the contrary, the trigger of a new and different stay.

The linear picture hitherto outlined has undergone radical changes following the entry into force of the aforementioned Bankruptcy Abuse Prevention and Consumer Protection Act, in 2005[217], which is perhaps the most significant reform intervention known from the current Bankruptcy Code not only, as will be seen shortly, for the incisive changes made to an institute, such as the one here commented, considered among the most important in the North American insolvency law, but also (and above all) for the underlying ideological change. If, in fact, before the use of one of the procedures governed by the Bankruptcy Code was considered an instrument in the full availability of the debtor, useful to fix his insolvency so as to guarantee him an agile and quick return to the business more than the number of voluntary cases , in US far exceeds that of the involuntary cases, the reformed intervent rules to limit the possibility of indiscriminate access to such an instrument with particular regard to the debtor person which, in particular, the consumer, placing some insurmountable limits against appeals that appear abusive, as clearly aimed at achieving purposes

[216]D.G. EPSTEIN, Bankruptcy and related law in a nutshell, op. cit. I. RAMSAY, Personal insolvency in the 21st century. A comparative analysis of the US and Europe, op. cit.

[217]J. CHIRCOP, The impact of bankruptcy abuse prevention and consumer protection act of 2005 repo "safe harbor" provisions in investors, in The European Journal of Finance, 24, 2018, pp. 18ss.

other than their own bankruptcy proceedings and, in particular, to profit exclusively from the benefits associated with the protection offered by the automatic stay without aiming at a serious and feasible arrangement of its failure[218].

This legislation therefore intervened to limit the operation of automatic stay in various ways, on the basis of some mandatory circumstances in which its course according to the ordinary discipline appears to be abusive or otherwise contrary to the principles of good faith[219]. The peculiarities that, in such eventualities, assume the temporal discipline of the automatic stay have moreover induced the American doctrine to describe such phenomenon, with expressions between them fungible, in terms of "not so automatic stay", or of "semi automatic stay"[220]. The examination of the overall system, as it came from BAPCPA, has suggested to us also the opportunity to subdivide the reformed regulation, with a certain systemic utility, into two distinct categories, effectively compendiable using just the two distinct phrases, coined by the North American doctrine. In particular, we will use the expression "not so automatic stay" to indicate those hypotheses in which, to the occurrence of certain circumstances, the automatic stay does not occur as a result of the petition, but the possibility remains for the debtor and the recurrence of the necessary prerequisites, to request the court to declare at a later time the deferred operation of the injunction which, therefore, is produced in a "not so automatic" way as happens in the normal hypothesis; while "semi automatic stay" will indicate the cases in which the suspensive effectiveness in comment comes into force with the deposit of the petition but, in the absence of the fulfillment by the debtor, of specific acts required

---

[218]J. BRAUCHER, A guide to interpretation of the 2005 bankruptcy law, in American Bankruptcy Institute Law Review, 16, 2008, pp. 376ss. B.A. BLUM, Bankruptcy and debtor/creditor, op. cit., 254ss. K. DAVIDSON, Bankruptcy-confusion and ambiguity. The post-BAPCPA uncertainty concerning the ride-though option in the eight circuit, in University of Arkansas at Little Rock Law Review, 36, 2014, pp. 492ss.

[219]P.A. MURPHY, E.E. SAGERMAN, D. NEIER, Creditors' rights in bankruptcy, op. cit., 180ss. L.A. NAPOLI, The not-so-automatic stay: Legislative changes to the automatic stay in a case filed by or against an individual debtor, op. cit., pp. 749ss. L.J. MARGULIES, Understanding the new semiautomatic stay, in ABI Journal, 25, 2006, pp. 26ss. S. LARSEN, Understanding the new semiautomatic stay, op. cit., pp. 22ss.

[220]P.A. MURPHY, E.E. SAGERMAN, D. NEIER, Creditors' rights in bankruptcy, op. cit.

by law, it comes to cease, in particular at a time before the one in which physiological cessation should intervene, so that it can be said that the activity of the inhibitory is only partly automatic. As a logical consequence of the characteristics outlined above, we also think it appropriate to discuss the not so automatic stay hypotheses in the immediate continuation of the treatment, constituting, as anticipated, hypothesis of derogation from the ordinary discipline regarding the initial course of protective efficacy, while the examination of the semiautomatic stay hypotheses will be carried out after analyzing the general discipline concerning the physiological cessation of the suspensive effect, implying, as said, an exceptional anticipation.

The described inversion of course, which characterizes the current evolution of US bankruptcy discipline in the sense of making recourse to the related procedures and benefits less free and in any case more closely monitored by the judicial authority, with a view to preventing abuse and greater protection of the interests of creditors, with partial sacrifice of the need for recovery at any cost of the debtor to the business world, for its part, is experiencing an evolution in the opposite direction, that is to a lesser affliction of insolvency against the debtor, to the full advantage of newly introduced institutions favoring this subject, especially in the context of the negotiation of business crises.

The order of the treatment chosen here to illustrate the temporal discipline of the automatic stay appears to be truly unpublished in the American literature, being the result of a systematic effort that, in that, customarily gives way to the most felt needs of pragmatism, and to a illustration of the matter that remains more faithful to the scans present in the text of Section 362. After completing the analysis of the discipline concerning the production of the suspensive effect with the provisions that derogate from the ordinary rule we will proceed to analyze the discipline concerning the cessation of the protective effect, further distinguishing two levels of investigation: The first, intended for the hypothesis of automatic termination of the injunction, including the ordinary discipline and the semiautomatic stay hypotheses; the second, widely devoted to the hypothesis of judicial cessation of the protective effect in comment, obtainable through the establishment of the special procedure for the release (relief) from the automatic stay.

28.The hypotheses of not so automatic stay: Previous presentation of two or more petitions.

The category in question consists of hypotheses in which the automatic stay does not occur as a necessary consequence of the petition filing, but can come into force at a later time, when certain conditions are met. The operability of the case of not so automatic stay, in other words, partially shares the mechanisms with regard to the actual exceptions to the automatic stay itself, which, in both cases, the legislator has identified some areas in which, for different reasons, the legal presumption placed on the basis of the operation of the injunction does not work, with consequent failure to automatically trigger the stay. In both cases, however, what is less is the automaticity of the stay and not the possibility tout court to obtain an injunction to protect the debtor or assets, having anticipated that even in the presence of a case of not so automatic stay is not excluded the possibility of benefiting from a protection subsequently triggered. It is therefore necessary to clarify in what, exactly, the two institutions differ and why, therefore, it was decided to treat them in different sessions. The answer is simple and probably already overshadowed in the concepts mentioned above, but the need for systematic clarity impose nevertheless to make it explicit. While in the exceptions, in fact, the disappearance of the automatic operation protection offered by Section 362 (a) is accompanied only by the possibility for the debtor to obtain a provision with an inhibitory content pursuant to Section 105 (a), subject to compliance with the probative burdens for these provisions envisaged, and with effectiveness limited to the single initiative contemplated therein, in the cases of not so automatic stay the special regime dictated by the aforementioned Section 362 (a) has not definitively lapsed, but rather suspended, since the conditions that the debtor is called to demonstrate are functional not to obtain a single and circumscribed protective measure according to Section 105 (a), but, as will be seen, precisely to the reactivation of the discipline enclosed in Section 362 (a), and therefore of the automatic stay, demonstrating the inexistence of the reasons of bad faith which, in legislator's project, had justified its temporary application. In conclusion, it is precisely the possibility of obtaining the subsequent reactivation of the automatic stay (and, with it, the related subjective and objective areas of effectiveness) that differentiates the cases in question from the exceptions, where on the contrary the vigor of the discipline posed by Section 362 (a) forever precluded; and the fact that the activation of automatic stay regulation may take place at a later date also justifies the choice of dealing with the cases in question during the analysis of the temporal scope of institution effectiveness as exemptions from the ordinary regime[221].

The first and most important exception to the automatic operation that usually characterizes the automatic stay as a consequence of the mere deposit of the petition, introduced with the BAPCPA of 2005, is governed by Section 362 (c) (4), where it is envisaged that the deposit of a petition by (or against) a debtor (natural person), in respect of which, in the year preceding such filing, were pending two or more insolvency procedures that have been closed with a dismissal provision, do not trigger an automatic stay[222].

The norm speaks, literally, of "individual", whose most correct translation appears, in fact, to be that of a natural person, regardless, however, from its qualification in terms of commercial entrepreneur, which allows us to bring you back the consumer figure[223].

It should be noted that the aforementioned provision is of a very general nature and, in particular, does not in any way limit its scope of application: This means that the automatic stay will not be operational against any entity that generally benefits from debt, bankruptcy and personal assets of the debtor, as well as with regard to the entire objective scope of its application[224].

---

[221]D.G. EPSTEIN, Bankruptcy and related law in a nutshell, op. cit. I. RAMSAY, Personal insolvency in the 21st century. A comparative analysis of the US and Europe, op. cit.

[222]The section 362 (c) (4), under subsections (A) (i), provides that: "if a single or joint case is filed by or against a debtor who is an individual under this title, and if two or more single or joint cases of the debtor were pending within the previous year but were dismissed (...) the stay under subsection (a) shall not go into effect upon the filing of the later case (...)".

[223]D. WARREN, D. J. BUSSEL, D. A. SKEEL, JR., Bankruptcy, op. cit., pp. 184ss.

[224]See in argument: S. V. KELLEY, Ginsberg & Martin on bankruptcy, op. cit., § 3.01[G][2]; contra, the decision adopted in the case: In re Johnson, 335 B.R. 805 (2006), 806, where it is stated that a systematic interpretation of the norm with the previous

The rule is obviously aimed at curbing the practice of serial filings, or rather the presentation, in a very short period of time, of multiple appeals for admission to one of the procedures governed by the Bankruptcy Code, which nonetheless reveal themselves, at a later date, not accompanied by a serious desire to settle the just dissapointed debt and leading to dismissal pronouncement, but moved only by the intent to gain the protective effects that the deposit of the petition, and the connected automatic stay, can assure the applicant[225].

The practice of serial filings constitutes, in fact, a problem felt by US jurisprudence since the 80s, which, before the repressive prediction introduced with the 2005 reform, had very often engaged in the search for suitable solutions to stem a phenomenon that it did not find direct regulation within the bankruptcy law. This had mainly occurred through the use of two different expedients[226]: The comminatory, at the time of the closing procedure by ruling the dismissal, of a prohibition to deposit another petition for a certain period of time (the so-called refiling bar); or, although this has been used in much rarer hypotheses, the pronunciation, based on Section 105 (a) of the Bankruptcy Code, a provision containing a prospective relief of the automatic stay[227], therefore suitable to ensure

---

subsection (c) (1) leads to limit the application of the sec. 362 (c) (4) exclusively towards the debtor and his personal assets; criticism of this pronunciation, L.J. MARGULIES, Understanding the new semiautomatic stay, op. cit., pp. 60ss.

[225]L.B. BARTELL, Visualizing bankruptcy, op. cit., pp. 85ss. M.A. FREY, S. K. SWINSON, Introduction to bankruptcy law, op. cit., pp. 254ss. L.A. NAPOLI, The not-so-automatic stay: Legislative changes to the automatic stay in a case filed by or against an individual debtor, op. cit., pp. 772ss.

[226]S.Z. BARETZ, Combating the Chapter 13 serial filer. An argument for orders containing prospective relief from the automatic stay provision, in Hofstra Law Review, 25, 1997, pp. 1316ss. J.D. KEY, The advent of the serial Chapter 11 filing and its implications, in Bankruptcy Developments Journal, 8, 1991, pp. 245ss. L.A. COLEMAN, Individual consumer "chapter 20" cases after Johnson: An introduction to non business serial filings under Chapter 7 and Chapter 13 of the Bankruptcy Code, in Bankruptcy Developments Journal, 9, 1992, pp. 357ss. K.L. NELSON, Abusive filings: Can courts stop the abuse within the confines of the Bankruptcy Code?, in Bankruptcy Developments Journal, 17, 2000, pp. 331, 336ss.

[227]A variant of this provision, for the procedures initiated pursuant to Chapter 13, consisted of the so-called "drop dead" orders, i.e. decisions where it was foreseen that, where in the course of the subsequent procedure the debtor did not show that he was able to complete it, or did not carry out the promised activities, the beneficiary would have enjoyed immediate release from the automatic stay, or the procedure would have been dismissed. In argument see: S.Z. BARETZ, Combating the Chapter 13 serial filer: An argument for

the release from the inhibitory to a particular creditor, evidently, whose aggressive initiatives the debtor aimed to foreclose through the serial claims, in case the deposit of a new petition had occurred; the latter was nevertheless free to request an injunction pursuant to Section 105 (a) so that, in fact, the described solution resulted in an inversion, to the detriment of serial debtor, of the proving burden of the protection needs[228].

The renewed legislative discipline is detached, however, from both solutions reported, while remaining closer, at least in the inspiring ratio, the second, operating as a preventive condition of the automatic operation of the stay.

Returning to the current standard, for application purposes of Section 362 (c) (4) it is therefore sufficient that in the year prior to the petition filing had been pending and subsequently closed with a dismissal measure, towards the instant debtor, two or more procedures pursuant to any of the operational chapters of the Bankruptcy Code (7, 11, 12 or 13)[229]. In this regard, it should be added that the rule is without prejudice to the case in which the last petition requires admission to a procedure other than the liquidation procedure (Chapter 7), after the previous procedure had been dismissed pursuant to Section 707 (b) 19, i.e. when the recourse to the liquidation procedure by the debtor, in consideration of the large monthly income of the same (means test), has appeared abusive[230]: Probably the underlying rationale behind this clause of salvation is contained in the intent to convey the debtor natural person on the most

---

orders containing prospective relief from the automatic stay provision, op. cit., 1323ss. K.L. NELSON, Abusive filings: Can courts stop the abuse within the confines of the Bankruptcy Code?, op. cit., pp. 345ss.

[228]See: In re Felberman, 196 B.R. 678 (1995). S.Z. BARETZ, Combating the Chapter 13 serial filer: an argument for orders containing prospective relief from the automatic stay provision, op. cit., pp. 1331ss. S.Z. BARETZ, Combating the Chapter 13 serial filer: An argument for orders containing prospective relief from the automatic stay provision, op. cit., pp. 1322ss.

[229]A.N. RESNICK, H.J. SOMMER, Collier on bankruptcy,op. cit., § 362.06[4]. D.G. EPSTEIN, Bankruptcy and related law in a nutshell, op. cit. pp. 49ss. I. RAMSAY, Personal insolvency in the 21st century. A comparative analysis of the US and Europe, op. cit. L. A. NAPOLI, The not-so-automatic stay: Legislative changes to the automatic stay in a case filed by or against an individual debtor, op. cit., pp. 769ss.

[230]A.N. RESNICK, H. J. SOMMER, Collier on bankruptcy, op. cit. L.A. NAPOLI, The not-so-automatic stay: Legislative changes to the automatic stay in a case filed by or against an individual debtor, op. cit., pp. 766ss.

suitable procedures to manage his/her failure (in this case, one of a recovery rather than liquidation), even if it is not possible to deny that also these cases, and the related dismissal rulings, are sometimes to sanction abusive conduct, so that their exemption from the discipline in question arouses, in reality, some perplexities; on the other hand, and consistently, the other hypothesis, contemplated by the same provision, in which, in the presence of the same preconditions, is proceeded, with the consent of the debtor, to the conversion of the liquidation procedure into a reorganization governed by Chapters 11 or 13, as noted, the conversion of the procedure does not imply the filing of a new petition, being considered a continuation of the previous one, so that we move outside the field of serial filings. If a party interested in this request and it will be, of course, anyone, confident in the application of the rule in comment, intends to act against the debtor, but wants to make sure not to run into a violation of the injunction, the bankruptcy court will have to issue an assessment that confirms that the automatic stay is not in force[231].

Automatic stay inoperativity towards the individual serial filer is not, however, definitive and irreversible, according to the peculiar characteristic that we have seen belong to the cases that can be counted among the hypotheses of the not so automatic stay, but surmountable through the special procedure contemplated by the same rule, which can be activated by anyone interested in it, aimed at obtaining an order from the bankruptcy court impositive, albeit deferred, of the stay. In particular, the interested party must take action within thirty days from the filing of the last petition, asking the court to pronounce an imposition of the injunction against all or some creditors, upon demonstration, to be provided in a specific hearing, which the filing of the last application was made in good faith, i.e. without the intention of prejudicing the creditors by means of the suspensive effects connected to it[232]; in this regard, the

---

[231]Read the following subsection (ii), where it is expected that "on request of a party in interest, the court shall promptly enter an order confirming that no stay is in effect (...)".

[232]So, in fact the norm continues "if within thirty days after the filing of the later case, a party in interest requests the court may order the stay to take effect in the case as to any or all creditors (subject to such conditions or limitations as the court may impose), after notice and a hearing, only if the party in interest demonstrates that the filing of the later case is in good faith as to the creditors to be stayed (...)".

law also introduces a rebuttable presumption, overcome by a "clear and convincing evidence to the contrary", predetermining a series of hypotheses in which the presentation of the application is to be considered as not in good faith[233].

Please note that when the law requires, for the purpose of ruling the impository measure of the stay, the demonstration, to be provided in any case, that the filing of the last petition occurred in good faith, the subsequent codification of the hypotheses, above mentioned, in which said deposit is presumed as having occurred in bad faith, it cannot assume any real significance on the basis of the allocation of the probative charges. Integrated the case in which the typical effects of the not so automatic are reconnected, the deferred operation in the inhibitory can be obtained by demonstrating that the filing of the last application was made in good faith, without, therefore, that the presence of hypotheses in which the existence of a state can assume a concrete significance of bad faith is presumed. It is therefore to be considered that these are merely exemplary cases, evidently accepted by the legislator by the previous jurisprudential practice, which do not add to the general rule, set out in the text, relating

[233]And its is precisely the following hypotheses: "(i) As to all creditors if (I) two or more previous cases under this title in which the individual was a debtor were pending within the 1year period; (II) a previous case under this title in which the individual was a debtor was dismissed within the time period stated in this paragraph after the debtor failed to file or amend the petition or other documents as required by this title or the court without substantial excuse (but mere inadvertence or negligence shall not be substantial excuse unless the dismissal was caused by the negligence of the debtor's attorney), failed to provide adequate protection as ordered by the court, or failed to perform the terms of a plan confirmed by the court; or (III) there has not been a substantial change in the financial or personal affairs of the debtor since the dismissal of the next most previous case under this title, or any other reason to conclude that the later case will not be concluded, if a case under chapter 7, with a discharge, and if a case under chapter 11 or 13, with a confirmed plan that will be fully performed; or (ii) as to any creditor that commenced an action under subsection (d) in a previous case in which the individual was a debtor if, as of the date of dismissal of such case, such action was still pending or had been resolved by terminating, conditioning, or limiting the stay as to such action of such creditor". See in argument: A.N. RESNICK, H.J. SOMMER, Collier on bankruptcy, op. cit. S.V. KELLEY, Ginsberg & Martin on bankruptcy, op. cit., op. cit., M.A. FREY, S.K. SWINSON, Introduction to bankruptcy law op. cit. W.D. WARREN, D.J. BUSSEL, D.A. SKEEL, Bankruptcy, op. cit., pp. 181ss. L.B. BARTELL, Visualizing bankruptcy, op. cit., pp. 86ss. L.A. NAPOLI, The not-so-automatic stay: Legislative changes to the automatic stay in a case filed by or against an individual debtor, op. cit., pp. 771ss. S. LARSEN, Understanding the new semiautomatic stay, op. cit., pp. 74ss.

to the probative charges in force on this matter, but which become indicative of a questionable regulatory technique.

Once ascertained, even through the administration of suitable evidence contrary to the aforementioned legal presumption, that the deposit of the last petition occurred in good faith, the bankruptcy court can pronounce a measure of imposition of the stay which, in accordance with the provisions of the same provision, it comes into force on the date of the issuance of said ruling[234].

The overall mechanism thus constructed appears to be a clear disincentive to the abuse because it intends to use an institution to achieve different purposes from those for which the law has coined the procedures referred to the Bankruptcy Code: The person who has already made multiple appeal, in time span of one year, to these instruments, for the sole purpose of benefiting from the protective effects connected to them as the outcome in a ruling by dismissal suggests, knows that at the presentation of a new and further application, that for such purposes both preordained, will not achieve the course of the automatic stay, evidently dealing with conduct affected by bad faith; however, and appropriately, the law saves the possibility in which the subsequent deposit aspires to the admission of a procedure to the genuine purpose of resolving a crisis situation by means of the tools offered by the law, assigning at the moment the possibility to demonstrate its own good faith and, with it, the faculty to request an imposition, even if deferred, from the stay. In any case, even in this second eventuality, the existence of a period of time, which can last up to at least thirty days, remains unavoidable, and in a certain sense irremediable (within which time the request in question must be presented[235]), in which the automatic stay does not work, and the debtor is left to the aggressive initiatives of its creditors: A certainly strange situation, where at the beginning of the procedure is not accompanied, at least in part, a full and

---

[234]A.N. RESNICK, H.J. SOMMER, Collier on bankruptcy, op. cit. S.V. KELLEY, Ginsberg & Martin on bankruptcy, op. cit., L.B. BARTELL, Visualizing bankruptcy, op. cit. B.A. BLUM, Bankruptcy and debtor/creditor, op. cit., pp. 256 L.A. NAPOLI, The not-so-automatic stay: Legislative changes to the automatic stay in a case filed by or against an individual debtor, op. cit., pp. 771ss.

[235]S.V. KELLEY, Ginsberg & Martin on bankruptcy, op. cit.,where it is stated that, if the application is submitted within thirty days from the filing of the last petition, the hearing, on the contrary, can not take place before the expiry of that period of time.

fair realization of competition in debtor's heritage.

A final clarification concerns the effects that the operation of the above-mentioned standard exercises on the codebtor stay, that is, you remember it, what, according to Section 1201 and 1301 of the Bankruptcy Code is produced in favor of the natural co-obliged or guarantor person for a consumer debt of the subject admitted to an adjustment of debts procedure referred to Chapters 12 or 13[236]: In such cases, it is expressly provided that the not so automatic stay referred to in Section 362 (c) (4), which affects the principal debtor, does not affect its negative effects on the aforementioned codebtor stay, which therefore continues to fully enjoy the protective effects with the filing of the last petition, also leaving it on the creditor the burden of requesting a relief measure. The choice appears to be consistent with the opportunity not to burden a subject of sanctions that the system poses for the repression of abusive behavior of others, all the more because it is characterized by qualified subjective states.

Finally, it should be noted that the majority jurisprudence considers that, even if there is no activation to obtain the deferred course of automatic stay, it remains possible for the party involved to request the pronouncement of an injunction pursuant to Section 105 (a) of the Bankruptcy Code, prior, obviously, demonstration of the legitimating conditions for the injunction ruling[237].

29.(Follows) Special discipline applicable to small business debtor.

A derogatory regulation of the ordinary time regime of production of the automatic stay is then dictated by Section 362 (n), also introduced by 2005 BAPCPA to stem and punish the phenomenon of serial claims.

If the first provision containing a hypothesis of not so automatic stay, was destined to individual debtor, that is, to the natural person debtor, among which, in particular, the consumer, the law of our attention is specifically dedicated to the small business debtor, to which the legislator

---

[236]A.N. RESNICK, H.J. SOMMER, Collier on bankruptcy, op. cit. S.V. KELLEY, Ginsberg & Martin on bankruptcy, op. cit.

[237]In re Williams, 346 B.R. 361 (2006). For further details see: A.N. RESNICK, H.J. SOMMER, Collier on bankruptcy, op. cit., § 362.06[7]; contra, In re Radson, 462 B.R. 911 (2011).

has therefore deemed it appropriate to devote an ad hoc discipline; this entity, moreover, is expressly defined by the law, which in Section 101 (51D) refers to the commercial individual or collective entrepreneur having an amount of liquid debts and payable not exceeding two million dollars, and who submits an application for admission to a reorganization procedure referred to in Chapter 11 in which no committee of creditors has been appointed (small business case)[238].

Section 362 (n) (1), in particular, provides that, where the small business debtor present a petition for admission to any of the operative chapters[239], the automatic stay does not come into force in a certain series of circumstances: a) If the instant, at the time of filing the new petition, is already subject to a small business case, still pending; b) if the instant has been subjected to a small business case that for any reason has been closed with a dismissal provision that has become definitive in the two years prior to the order for relief pronounced during the new petition; c) if the instant has been subjected to a small business houses whose restructuring plan has been confirmed in the two years prior to the last order for relief; d) if, finally, the instant is an entity that is the assignee of the business activity of a small business debtor in the cases referred to in lett. a), b), or c), unless it proves that the purchase took place in good faith, and not to circumvent the provisions of the section in comment[240].

Below is the text of Section 362 (n) (1): "Except as provided in paragraph (2), subsection (a) does not apply in a case in which the debtor (A) is a debtor in a small business case pending at the time the petition is filed; (B) was a debtor in a small business case that was dismissed for any

---

[238] T.E. CARLSON, J. FRASER HAYES, The small business provisions of the 2005 bankruptcy amendments, in American Bankruptcy Law Journal, 79, 2005, pp. 679ss. D.K. CASE, J.R. ALDERFER, BAPCPA and the new provisions relating to small businesses, in Widener Law Journal, 15, 2006, pp. 587ss. R. M. LAWLESS, Small business and the 2005 bankruptcy law: Should mom and apple pie be worried?, in Southern Illinois University Law Journal, 31, 2007, pp. 588ss.

[239] R.M. LAWLESS, Small business and the 2005 bankruptcy law: Should mom and apple pie be worried?, op. cit., pp. 595ss; contra, for the exclusion of the case in which the second procedure is initiated pursuant to Chapter 7, as it would not be possible to apply the subsequent subsection, T.E. CARLSON, J. FRASER HAYES, The small business provisions of the 2005 bankruptcy amendments, op. cit., pp. 689ss.

[240] D.G. EPSTEIN, Bankruptcy and related law in a nutshell, op. cit. I. RAMSAY, Personal insolvency in the 21st century. A comparative analysis of the US and Europe, op. cit.

reason by an order that became final in the two year period ending on the date of the order for relief entered with respect to the petition; (C) was a debtor in a small business case in which a plan was confirmed in the 2 year period ending on the date of the order for relief entered with respect to the petition; or (D) is an entity that has acquired substantially all of the assets or business of a small business debtor described in subparagraph (A), (B), or (C), unless such entity establishes by a preponderance of the evidence that such entity acquired substantially all of the assets or business of such small business debtor in good faith and not for the purpose of evading this paragraph"[241].

The order for relief is the equivalent of the actual declaration of bankruptcy, or of admission to a reorganization procedure. However, in voluntary and joint cases it coincides with the petition, as it is the same law that provides for the filing of a voluntary or joint petition to constitute an order for relief; in the involuntary cases, vice versa, between petition and order for relief there is a period of time necessary to allow the debtor to present an opposition, in which case the court is called to ascertain the existence of admission conditions to the procedure.

Also in this hypothesis, which can therefore be counted among the cases of not so automatic stay, the inoperativity of the inhibitory is not irreversible, as subsection (2) does not include certain circumstances in which the rule referred to in the aforementioned subsection (1) does not applies: a) In the involuntary cases provided that there is no evidence of collusion between the debtor and the instant creditors; b) where the debtor demonstrates, first, that the filing of the next petition is due to circumstances beyond his control and unforeseeable at the time the first procedure, currently pending, was applied for admission and, secondly, the the fact that the court approves a restructuring plan (with the exception of those with a liquidation content), within a reasonable period of time[242].

---

[241]D.G. EPSTEIN, Bankruptcy and related law in a nutshell, op. cit. I. RAMSAY, Personal insolvency in the 21st century. A comparative analysis of the US and Europe, op. cit.

[242]The subsequent subsection (2), in fact, provides that: "Paragraph (1) does not apply (A) to an involuntary case involving no collusion by the debtor with creditors; or (B)to the filing of a petition if (i) the debtor proves by a preponderance of the evidence that the filing of the petition resulted from circumstances beyond the control of the debtor not foreseeable at the time the case then pending was filed; and (ii) it is more likely than not that the court will confirm a feasible plan, but not a liquidating plan, within a reasonable period of time

Unlike what we saw dealing with Section 362 (c) (4), however, the legislator has not regulated a specific procedure aimed at demonstrating the circumstances connected to the inoperativity of the derogatory regime with the ordinary course of the automatic stay, or to clarify when, at the outcome of the positive demonstration of the same, the inhibitory enters into force. This led to bring the rule pursuant to art. 362 (n) in the list of authentic exceptions to the automatic stay, and to qualify the circumstances referred to in subsection (2) as impediments to the application of the exception itself. In this regard, and wanting to leave out the topographical argument that, as already mentioned, the choices of legislative technique made by the 2005 reform are, in our opinion, far from impeccable, we believe that the discipline contained in the aforementioned Section 362 (n) present aspects of complexity which prevent it from being combined with the linear regime of an exception, and which therefore advise to treat the subject among the hypotheses of derogation from the ordinary temporal regime of inhibition. This problem moreover, it does not have a speculative character, since the application of a different legal regime obviously derives from the classification of the case in one direction or the other.

In fact, with regard to the operative provision mechanism which, in the aforementioned circumstances, precludes the entry into force of the automatic stay with respect to small business debtor, the juxtaposition to the exceptions can also be correct. In this regard we think of the discipline referred to Section 362 (b) (21), which in part seems to work in a completely similar manner[243], passing to analyze the subsequent provision that, as seen, prevents the applicability of the last mentioned rule, allowing the automatic stay to produce its own effects. The imaginable scenarios in the silence of law on the point seem to be two: Small business debtor, when

---

(...)". A.N. RESNICK, H.J. SOMMER, Collier on bankruptcy, op. cit., § 362.05[28]; L. B. BARTELL, Visualizing bankruptcy, op. cit., pp. 88.

[243]R.M. LAWLESS, Small business and the 2005 bankruptcy law: Should mom and apple pie be worried?, op. cit., 596,deals specifically with the problem concerning the mechanism that allows deciding whether in the case in question it is versed in the hypothesis of small business serial debtor. Despite the law has the automatic inoperativity of the stay, in fact, he still considers preferable, for the creditor, to request bankruptcy court a ruling that ascertains the recurrence of the conditions set out in section 362 (n), and therefore the lack of vigor, by way of derogation from the ordinary regime, of the automatic stay.

the petition is filed, already provides, if necessary, to provide evidence of the above-mentioned circumstances that allow it to escape the inactive regime of the automatic stay, or that subject, at the said administration, will proceed in a next moment. But in any case, the administration of such proof implies and necessarily presupposes that it must be examined by the judge, who only upon careful evaluation will rule on the recurrence of the illustrated assumptions and, therefore, on the applicability or otherwise of the rule that prevents production of the automatic stay. It remains to be evaluated which procedural scheme should be followed by the judge, and what effect should be recognized to the provision that has excluded, in this case, the application of the last mentioned rule, pronouncing, in other words, for the applicability of the inhibitory. Also in this case the passable ways seem two. In fact, it is possible to hypothesise the faculty for the bankruptcy court to pronounce a provision declaring the operation ex tunc of the automatic stay, a choice that appears prima facie to be the fairest, as it is functional to remedy an error, in which it was decided to apply to the debtor a provision that is worse than the assumed existence of assumptions of which the non-existence of an interpretative hypothesis has been ascertained which, furthermore, would corroborate the classification in terms of exception of the standard under examination. But we know that this is not the road that, in the discipline of the phenomenon of serial filings, the US legislator has chosen to follow: The discipline contained in Section 362 (c) (4), in fact, allows the debtor, where it is subsequently proved that the initial assessment of his conduct as having been affected by bad faith had been incorrect, to obtain an imposition of the stay, whose start date, however, is deferred . And since the two standards now under examination seem to be supported by the same automatic inoperativity rationes of the stay towards serial debtors of small size, save the demonstration of circumstances all due to the presence of good faith or, if you prefer, the absence of evil faith does not seem risky to propose the application by analogy to the case of small business debtor of the procedure dictated by Section 362 (c) (4) (B), culminating with the issuance of an imposing provision of the stay with effect from ex nunc[244]:

[244]The ex nunc start of the stay seems to be overshadowed by T.E. CARLSON, J. FRASER HAYES, The small business provisions of the 2005 bankruptcy amendments, cit., pp.

This conclusion evidently, is coherent and supports the classification proposed here of the case under consideration in the category of not so automatic stay, connoted precisely by the possibility of knowing a deferred application of the real automatic stay.

30.Cessation of the protective effect. Automatic termination of protective efficacy against bankruptcy assets.

Starting from the ordinary discipline on automatic or legal termination of the automatic stay, the first data that emerges from the reading of Section 362 (c), numbers (1) and (2), is that, according to the same technique already followed in regulating the objective effectiveness referred to in previous subsections (a) and (b), the legislator has regulated the subject having distinguished with regard to the three beneficiaries of the injunction: Debtor, bankruptcy assets and debtor's personal assets[245]. It would seem to emerge a discrepancy in reality only apparent, between the discipline in the matter of production of the suspensive effect, which for all the mentioned subjects is found at the time of petition, and that, now in speech, concerning its legal cessation, that the subsection (c) reconnects at different times according to the beneficiary subject taken into consideration. In particular, briefly anticipating what will be more widely discussed further, if with regard to the debtor and his personal assets the termination of automatic stay is linked to the closure of the procedure, or to grant or denial discharge, the current injunction against bankruptcy assets continues as long as the asset taken into consideration remains a summer property, by failing, conversely, at the moment in which it ceases to belong. This, in reality, appears to be an obligatory choice entirely consistent with the system. On the one hand the automatic stay in favor of the debtor and his personal assets is functional, inter alia, to ensure that

688ss, where the operative mechanism of the provision is described in the sense of "denying the refiling debtor the protection of the automatic stay until the debtor establishes its entitlement to injunctive relief"; without comments in the argument see: D.K. CASE, J.R. ALDERFER, BAPCPA and the new provisions relating to small businesses, op. cit., pp. 597ss.

[245]D.G. EPSTEIN, Bankruptcy and related law in a nutshell, op. cit. I. RAMSAY, Personal insolvency in the 21st century. A comparative analysis of the US and Europe, op. cit.

immediate fresh start and the possibility of undertaking new legal relationships from the day of petition filing, and without the interference of bankruptcy creditors, so it is natural that such protection should continue until the procedure, aimed at the satisfaction of these, has exhausted its course (regardless, then, from the fact that these creditors have been satisfied completely or only partially, thematically). On the other the automatic stay with regards to bankruptcy assets is explained by the fact that this entity represents the object on which the satisfaction of bankruptcy creditors will have to take place, so that protective measures specifically aimed at ensuring the correct competition implementation on these assets is justified to the extent that these assets, in fact, actually form part of property summer[246], while where that membership should cease, simultaneously the automatic stay must also cease (regardless, then, from the possible subjection of these assets to different legal regimes and, in particular, to the possibility that they flow into debtor's personal assets, benefiting from the relative protective effects).

Also the regulation on legal termination of the automatic stay has undergone some modifications under 2005 BARPCPA, which introduced some exceptions to the rules just illustrated, which intervene to anticipate, with respect to the ordinary regime, the moment of injuction cessation. Moreover, even these semiautomatic stay cases can be classified according to the beneficiary entity of the protection that is taken into consideration: Their examination, therefore, will develop in parallel to the illustration of the ordinary discipline in the matter of legal cessation which, as already mentioned, it unfolds, in fact, following the same scans.

Returning, therefore, to general rule tenor, Section 362 (c) (1), as already mentioned, provides the automatic stay operating on deeds can be promoted in respect of property summer and will continue until the asset in question belongs to bankruptcy assets[247]; conversely, where, for any

---

[246]The Section 362(c)(1), in particular, provides that: "The stay of an act against property of the estate under subsection (a) of this section continues until such property is no longer property of the estate (...)".

[247]A.N. RESNICK, H. J. SOMMER, Collier on bankruptcy, op. cit., § 362.06[1]. S.V. KELLEY, Ginsberg & Martin on bankruptcy, op. cit., op. cit., § 3.07[A]. W.R. NORTON, JR., Norton bankruptcy law and practice, op. cit., § 36:13. W.D. WARREN, D.J. BUSSEL, D.A. SKEEL, JR., Bankruptcy, op. cit., pp. 183ss. L.B. BARTELL, Visualizing bankruptcy, op. cit., pp. 89ss. P.A. MURPHY, E.E. SAGERMAN, D. NEIER, Creditor's rights in

reason (consider, for example, sales assumptions being liquidated assets, abandonment or exemption) the asset ceases to belong to summer property, it obviously can no longer benefit of the protection afforded to that entity.

If, however, as a result of abandonment to the advantage of the debtor, or exemption claimed by the same, the asset goes to meet the personal assets of the debtor, it will benefit from the automatic stay that Section 362 (a) (5) puts it to the advantage of the latter, with the already known consequence that creditors by way of a later title will be free from the injunction at the beginning of the procedure; in the other hypotheses, vice versa, no protection will operate to the advantage of the same asset[248].

31.The hypotheses of semi automatic stay: Failure to perform legally due acts.

The cases of semi automatic stay introduced in 2005, unlike those of not so automatic stay, all attributable to prevention rations and the fight against the serial, and therefore abusive, applications to insolvency proceedings and to the injunction related to them, are characterized for their heterogeneity, of contents as reasons of justification, besides their scattered collocation in different subsections of Section 362, if not, even,

---

bankruptcy, op. cit., pp. 180ss. B.A. BLUM, Bankruptcy and debtor/creditor, op. cit., pp. 254ss. D.G. EPSTEIN, Bankruptcy and related law in a nutshell, op. cit., pp. 48ss. A.N. RESNICK, Bankruptcy law manual, op. cit., pp. 106ss. J.F. MURPHY, The automatic stay in bankruptcy, op. cit., pp. 613ss. F.R. KENNEDY, Automatic stays under the new bankruptcy law, op. cit., pp. 37ss. H.B. PICKARD, The new bankruptcy code, part II: The interests of secured creditors under the new bankruptcy code, op. cit., pp. 234ss. J.L. SMAHA, Automatic stay under the 1978 bankruptcy code: An equitable roadblock to secured creditor relief, op. cit., pp. 1120ss. S. PARSONS, Consumer bankruptcy law in focus, op. cit., I. RAMSAY, Personal insolvency in the 21st century. A comparative analysis of the US and Europe, op. cit.

[248] A.N. RESNICK, H.J. SOMMER, Collier on bankruptcy, op. cit. S.V. KELLEY, Ginsberg & Martin on bankruptcy, op. cit. § 3.07[F][1]; W. R. NORTON, JR., Norton bankruptcy law and practice op. cit. D.R. COWANS, Cowans bankruptcy law and practice, op. cit., 525ss. B.A. BLUM, Bankruptcy and debtor/creditor, op. cit. D.G. EPSTEIN, Bankruptcy and related law in a nutshell, op. cit, pp. 49ss. A.N. RESNICK, Bankruptcy law manual, op. cit., pp. 107ss. J.F. MURPHY, The automatic stay in bankruptcy, op. cit., pp. 614ss. R.A. JOHNSON, M.C. O'LEARY, Automatic stay provisions of the bankruptcy act of 1978, op. cit., pp. 611ss. F.R. KENNEDY, Automatic stays under the new bankruptcy law, op. cit., pp. 38ss. S. PARSONS, Consumer bankruptcy law in focus, op. cit., I. RAMSAY, Personal insolvency in the 21st century. A comparative analysis of the US and Europe, op. cit.

within rules different from the latter. A figure, this, to reconfirm the questionable legislative technique adopted by the legislator, who does not seem to have dedicated adequate reflection to the identification of the correct sedes materiae in which to intervene, to all disadvantage of the overall harmony of the system. The criterion adopted by us to bring to order the fragmented changes introduced by BAPCPA, in order to offer an illustration of material as coherent and organic as possible, is the one, already anticipated, identifying the provisions that make exceptions to the ordinary discipline in the issue of the automatic stay termination, and, thus, group these scattered and heterogeneous forecasts in the unitary category of semiautomatic stay, that is, cases characterized by the regular production of the inhibitor at the time of petition, but destined to see such effects cease automatically, at a time before the physiological one, governed by subsections (c) (1) or (2), in the event that the debtor (or the trustee) does not activate for the accomplishment of certain activities prescribed by law.

Derogation cases of ordinary discipline dictated in subsection (c) (1) with regard to automatic stay cessation of bankruptcy assets, to which our attention is now dedicated, can however be further grouped into two sub-categories: The first, to which the continuation of this paragraph will be dedicated, concerns the hypothesis in which the debtor or the trustee omits to perform certain acts due ex lege; the second one shares the substantial assumption but has specific regard to the eviction of residential buildings where the debtor has established his home.

Taking the moves, therefore, from the first sub-category mentioned, it includes two different hypotheses. The first is governed by Section 362 (h), where, with a very obscure formulation, it is provided that, in cases where the debtor is a natural person and begins a liquidation procedure pursuant to Chapter 7, the automatic stay placed to protect personal assets of the same, merged in summer property (think, for example, a car or home), and that are placed as collateral for a loan or subject to a pending lease terms, and these assets cease to belong to summer property if the debtor fails to fulfill the requirements prescribed in Section 521 (a) (2)[249], entitled "Debtor's duties"[250], that is: a) To file within thirty days from the petitions filing, or by the date of the creditors' meeting if earlier, a declaration of intent statement of intention containing the expression of desire to abandon or retain such assets and, in this second case, whether he wants to redeem them by paying the full amount of the secured credit, or if he intends to conclude an agreement of recognition by virtue of which he is obliged to pay for the whole of a debt otherwise subject to discharge, or again, if it is a pending lease, if he intends to take over from trustee's inertia; and b) to implement what was declared within the thirty days following the date of the creditors' meeting[251].

Provision's rationale lies in the need to encourage the debtor to

---

[249]When subject to a bankruptcy procedure is a debtor natural person who, in the list of assets and responsibilities that is required to prepare and deposit in the registry, indicates the existence of debts secured by a property converged in the summer, the sec. 521 (a) (2) requires him to declare what he intends to do in relation to such assets. If that is he intends to withhold them (by redemption or debt recognition even in spite of the possible discharge reaffirmation), or abandon them, renouncing thus to any claim of a petitorial or possessory nature over the same. In argument see: A. N. RESNICK, H.J. SOMMER, Collier on bankruptcy, op. cit., 4, § 521.14[1] e [2]. L.A. NAPOLI, Reaffirmation after the Bankruptcy Abuse Prevention and Consumer Protection Act of 2005: Many questions, some answers, in American Bankruptcy Law Journal, 81, 2007, pp. 284ss. L.A. NAPOLI, The not-so-automatic stay: Legislative changes to the automatic stay in a case filed by or against an individual debtor, cit., 756ss.

[250]The limitation of the scope of the rule to the liquidation procedure can be deduced from the combination of the section 362 (h) and section 521. See in argument: A.N. RESNICK, H.J. SOMMER, Collier on bankruptcy, op. cit., 3, § 362.11. S.V. KELLEY, Ginsberg & Martin on bankruptcy, op. cit., § 3.07[F]. W.D. WARREN, D.J. BUSSEL, D.A. SKEEL, JR., Bankruptcy, op. cit., pp. 181ss. L.B. BARTELL, Visualizing bankruptcy, op. cit., pp. 92ss. S. LARSEN, Understanding the new semiautomatic stay, op. cit., pp. 75ss.

[251]See the text of Section 362(h)(1): "In a case in which the debtor is an individual, the stay provided by subsection (a) is terminated with respect to personal property of the estate or of the debtor securing in whole or in part a claim, or subject to an unexpired lease, and such personal property shall no longer be property of the estate if the debtor fails within the applicable time set by section 521(a)(2): (A) To file timely any statement of intention required under section 521(a)(2) with respect to such personal property or to indicate in such statement that the debtor will either surrender such personal property or retain it and, if retaining such personal property, either redeem such personal property pursuant to section 722, enter into an agreement of the kind specified in section 524(c) applicable to the debt secured by such personal property, or assume such unexpired lease pursuant to section 365(p) if the trustee does not do so, as applicable; and (B) to take timely the action specified in such statement, as it may be amended before expiration of the period for taking action, unless such statement specifies the debtor's intention to reaffirm such debt on the original contract terms and the creditor refuses to agree to the reaffirmation on such terms (...)".

fulfill the duties that the law, through Section 521, prescribes against him for the eventuality in which there are debts secured by assets of a personal nature. And the sanction represented by the automatic stay termination in respect of the goods in question which, moreover, will cease to belong to summer property, produces, in other and more concise terms, as a consequence of one of these events: The failure to file the statement of intention and to indicate in the content of the latter, the position that the debtor intends to assume in relation to his personal assets, or the failure to implement the actions specified in intention statement[252].

In jurisprudence there is no peaceful agreement regarding the consequences deriving from the failure to carry out the activities described above. This arises, in particular, from the existence of a practice established prior to 2005 BAPCPA, known as "ride through", and which allowed the debtor to make payments due to the creditor holding a preemption, to retain possession of personal property subject to collateral, even in the absence of reaffirmation or redemption[253]. This possibility would still exist, also by virtue of the Section's 362 (h) (1) (B) final statement, which is without prejudice the possibility that the intention statement indicates the will of the debtor "to reaffirm such debt on the original contract terms and the creditor refuses to agree with the reaffirmation on such terms"[254]; according to others, on the contrary, where the debtor intends to retain his personal assets, he is bound to carry out the activities specifically set by the rule in question[255]. To this,

---

[252]J. BRAUCHER, Rash and ride through redux: The terms for holding on to cars, homes and other collateral under the 2005 act, in American Bankruptcy Institute Law Review, 13, 2005, pp. 478ss. L.A. NAPOLI, Reaffirmation after the Bankruptcy Abuse Prevention and Consumer Protection Act of 2005: many questions, some answers, op. cit., 287ss. K. DAVIDSON, Bankruptcy-confusion and ambiguity. The post-BAPCPA uncertainty concerning the ride-though option in the eight circuit, op. cit.

[253]In re Blakeley, 363 B.R. 225 (2007), 232. J. BRAUCHER, Rash and ride through redux: The terms for holding on to cars, homes and other collateral under the 2005 act, op. cit., K. DAVIDSON, Bankruptcy-confusion and ambiguity. The post-BAPCPA uncertainty concerning the ride-though option in the eight circuit, op. cit.

[254]In re Rowe, 342 B.R. 341 (2006), 351. L.A. NAPOLI, The not-so-automatic stay: Legislative changes to the automatic stay in a case filed by or against an individual debtor, op. cit., 758ss S.V. KELLEY, Ginsberg & Martin on bankruptcy, op. cit., § 3.02[J][4]. A.N. RESNICK, H.J. SOMMER, Collier on bankruptcy, op. cit.

[255]A.N. RESNICK, H. J. SOMMER, Collier on bankruptcy, op. cit.; L.B. BARTELL, Visualizing bankruptcy, op. cit. , op. cit; P. A. MURPHY, E.E. SAGERMAN, D. NEIER,

moreover, is connected the question concerning the taxability or otherwise the obligations prescribed by this section, in particular, the imperfect coincidence between the same and those referred to in Section 521 (a) (2), to which the law refers: According to some, in fact, the list in Section 362 (h) should not be considered mandatory, but should rather be integrated with that contained in the other mentioned standard, with the consequence that the automatic stay does not necessarily have to end where the debtor carries out one of the activities contemplated in the latter provision, but absent in section 362 (h)[256].

Since, however, the cessation of protective efficacy takes place automatically at the expiration of one of the aforementioned terms, without the court being obliged to issue an appropriate provision, the creditors wishing to act on the operability assumption of Section 362 (h) however, run the risk that, subsequently, is established that the debtor had performed the acts required by law and, so, that the stay was not, in fact, terminated: Preferable, therefore, it is for the same to apply to the court to pronounce a provision that ascertains, in fact, that the cessation of the automatic stay has occurred by virtue of the operation of Section 362 (h).

The following number (2) of Section 362 (h) provides, moreover, the possibility for trustee to present to the bankruptcy court, before the expiry of the deadlines set for the completion of the legally required acts to the debtor, a request aimed at preventing the application of the rule referred to in (1) and, thus, guarantee the permanence of the automatic stay; to this end, the trustee is required to demonstrate in a hearing that the personal assets in question represent a value or benefit for summer property, and once this assumption is established, the court will order that adequate protection be granted to creditor rights, as well as the transfer of assets possession as security for his claims to the trustee. If the court does not ascertain the aforementioned premise, vice versa, the stay will end at the time of the conclusion of the hearing culminating in the rejection of the petition proposed by the trustee[257].

Creditor's rights in bankruptcy op. cit., 185.

[256]D.G. EPSTEIN, Bankruptcy and related law in a nutshell, op. cit. I. RAMSAY, Personal insolvency in the 21st century. A comparative analysis of the US and Europe, op. cit.

[257]In particular, see number (2): "Paragraph (1) does not apply if the court determines, on the motion of the trustee filed before the expiration of the applicable time set by section

A second hypothesis of automatic stay's legal termination provided in advance with respect to the ordinary discipline, and dependent on the failure to carry out legally due acts, is to be found in Section 365 (p): Outside, therefore, the norm, referred to in the previous Section 362, governing the institute object of the present survey, although, albeit always, in the context of an innovation brought by 2005 BAPCPA.

Section 365 of the Bankruptcy Code, in particular, contains the discipline regarding pending contracts in which the debtor is part, including those of lease, dictating as a general rule the faculty for the trustee, subject to authorization by the bankruptcy court, to take over or withdraw from such relationships.

Subsection (p), introduced, as already mentioned, on the occasion of the 2005 reform, provides, at number (1), that where the trustee withdraws or does not promptly take over a pending lease contract concerning a property of a personal nature of the debtor (and think, therefore, to his dwelling house), such good ceases to belong to the summer, with consequent immediate cessation of the automatic stay[258].

The outflow of bankruptcy assets obviously implies that, as debtor's personal asset, conflicts with debtor's personal patrimony; however, the very general tenor of provision, which provides that the stay referred to in Section 362 (a) is automatically terminated, leads us to believe that the protective efficacy, in relation to that good, ceases tout court, and not only to the extent that it ceases to belong to summer property: What, in other words, means that the injunction which normally belongs to debtor's personal assets will not be applied to protect the same[259]. This reading, moreover, is supported by the discipline referred to

---

521(a)(2), after notice and a hearing, that such personal property is of consequential value or benefit to the estate, and orders appropriate adequate protection of the creditor's interest, and orders the debtor to deliver any collateral in the debtor's possession to the trustee. If the court does not so determine, the stay provided by subsection (a) shall terminate upon the conclusion of the hearing on the motion (...)".

[258]The norm affirms: "(...) If a lease of personal property is rejected or not timely assumed by the trustee under subsection (d), the leased property is no longer property of the estate and the stay under section 362(a) is automatically terminated (...)". In argument, see: L.A. NAPOLI, The not-so-automatic stay: Legislative changes to the automatic stay in a case filed by or against an individual debtor, op. cit., pp. 762ss. S.V. KELLEY, Ginsberg & Martin on bankruptcy, op. cit., op. cit., § 3.02[J][3].

[259]The standard in question, however, completes the provisions of Section 541 which, it

in the following numbers (2) and (3), which will shortly be returned.

The mechanism of activation useful to avoid inhibitory's legal cessation, and to preserve the protective effects in speech, typical of the case of semiautomatic stay, consists therefore in the timely manifestation of willingness on the part of the trustee to want to take over the pending lease.

The standard is applied in all operational chapters and with regard to all types of debtors (civil or commercial, individual or collective); however, it prepares two special provisions to regulate the proceedings initiated, on the one hand, pursuant to Chapter 7 and, secondly, pursuant to Chapters 11 and 13[260].

With regard to the former, number (2) of the regulation in question provides that the debtor is a natural person who, in view of the withdrawal intention expressed by the trustee, or at the end of the deadline for expressing his intention to take over, wants to continue the lease must communicate this will in writing to the landlord who, in turn, can communicate to the first his willingness to continue the relationship, without prejudice to the possibility, if any, to condition the continuation of remediation of previous breaches of obligations hired in the contract; if, in the thirty days following the notice of the landlord, the debtor sends him the written intention to continue the contact, the responsibility for the related obligations will naturally fall on the debtor personally, and not on the bankruptcy assets. The law continues by specifying that the automatic stay refers to, obviously, the one placed to protect the debtor, in particular with number (6) of Section 362 (a), is not violated by such communications and by the negotiations undertaken for the assumption of obligations to remedy previous defaults.

As part of the procedures established under Chapters 11 and 13, vice versa, it is the debtor (in possession) who has to decide whether to

---

should be remembered, regulates the composition of the summer; in subsection (b) (2), to be precise, bankruptcy assets are excluded: "Any interest of the debtor as a lessee under a lease of nonresidential real property that has terminated at the expiration of the stated term of such lease before the commencement of the case under this title, and ceases to include any interest of the debtor as a lessee under a lease of nonresidential real property that has terminated at the expiration of the stated term of such lease during the case (...)". A. N. RESNICK, H. J. SOMMER, Collier on bankruptcy, op. ult. cit., § 365.10[6].

[260] D.G. EPSTEIN, Bankruptcy and related law in a nutshell, op. cit. I. RAMSAY, Personal insolvency in the 21st century. A comparative analysis of the US and Europe, op. cit.

take over or dissolve the contract, before the reorganization plan is approved by the bankruptcy court; pursuant to number (3) of Section 365 (p), it is now expected that if the approved rehabilitation plan does not provide for the continuation of the lease contract, the contract must be declared dissolved at the end of the hearing for the approval of the plan itself. In this case, even the automatic stay operating to protect the personal property object of the loose rental contract ends immediately[261].

32. (Follows) Special regulations governing eviction actions on residential buildings constituting debtor's home.

With regard to the coordination between the law in question and the previous Section 362 (h), it seems that the latter must be applied when, within thirty days from petition's deposit, the trustee has already expressed a desire to withdraw from the lease or has remained inert.

Among the cases of early termination of automatic stay placed to protect bankruptcy assets, is then appropriate to include two particular hypotheses, which we have already mentioned in other parts of this discussion, which the legislator, with the 2005 reform, has actually introduced into the body of subsection (b) and, therefore, in the category of exceptions to protective efficacy: The latter, characterized by the inoperativity of the relative legal presumption placed on the basis of

---

[261]"(2) (A) If the debtor in a case under chapter 7 is an individual, the debtor may notify the creditor in writing that the debtor desires to assume the lease. Upon being so notified, the creditor may, at its option, notify the debtor that it is willing to have the lease assumed by the debtor and may condition such assumption on cure of any outstanding default on terms set by the contract. (B) If, not later than days after notice is provided under subparagraph (A), the debtor notifies the lessor in writing that the lease is assumed, the liability under the lease will be assumed by the debtor and not by the estate. (C) The stay under section 362 and the injunction under section 524(a)(2) shall not be violated by notification of the debtor and negotiation of cure under this subsection". "(3) In a case under chapter 11 in which the debtor is an individual and in a case under Chapter 13 if the debtor is the lessee with respect to personal property and the lease is not assumed in the plan confirmed by the court, the lease is deemed rejected as of the conclusion of the hearing on confirmation. If the lease is rejected, the stay under section 362 and any stay under section 1301 is automatically terminated with respect to the property subject to the lease (...)". For further details and analysis see: L.A. NAPOLI, The not-so-automatic stay: Legislative changes to the automatic stay in a case filed by or against an individual debtor, op. cit., pp. 763ss. S.V. KELLEY, Ginsberg & Martin on bankruptcy, op. cit.

automatic stay functioning and, therefore, of the preclusive effectiveness connected to it, in one with the deposit of the petition, with regard to the initiative addressed to the exception itself.

Although almost all the American doctrine addresses the analysis of the two cases in question respecting the sedes matter chosen by the legislator of 2005, operating mechanism study revealing all the complexity of the temporal discipline of automatic stay and, in particular, as an exception to the ordinary regime, among the hypotheses of semiautomatic stay[262].

The provisions that have so far been referred to are Sections 362 (b) (22) and (23), both concerning eviction proceedings concerning property for residential use; the peculiarities that characterize the temporal regime of injunction, in such cases, derive, moreover, from the combined disposition between these norms and, respectively, the successive subsections (l) and (m), to which the same norms express a reference.

Both these provisions, as will be immediately clear, were introduced in order to accommodate lessors concerns forced to suffer the effects of automatic stay triggered by the deposit of the petition by their tenants, in order to suspend the pending eviction proceedings and to be able to live "rent free"[263].

Starting from the first of the cases mentioned, Section 362 (b) (22) provides that "subject to subsection (l) the deposit of a petition does not produce the suspensive effects referred to in subsection (a) (3) that is, prohibition to perform acts directed to obtain possession of assets that have been transferred to bankruptcy assets, or exercise control over them, with regard to the prosecution of evictions, actions for the reinstatement of possession or other similar proceedings by the lessor in relation to the debtor, concerning property for residential use used to house the latter, in cases where the lessor has obtained before the date of filing of the petition

---

[262]The only authors, as far as we know, have noticed the discrepancy between substantial discipline and formal collocation of the two rules that will be immediately analyzed, are P.A. MURPHY, E.E. SAGERMAN, D. NEIER, Creditor's rights in bankruptcy, op. cit., pp. 194ss.

[263]A.M. AHART, The inefficacy of the new eviction exceptions to the automatic stay, in American Bankruptcy Law Journal, 80, 2006, pp. 126ss.

a sentence attributing the possession of the same assets[264]. As already mentioned, the provision is completed with the provision referred to in the following subsection (1): The latter, in its turn, disposes, at number (1), that the rule contained in Section 362 (b) (22) that is to say the non-production of the stay prepared by subsection (a) (3) in the cases described therein applies with effect from the thirtieth day following the petition[265], deposit, if the debtor, together with the latter, filing a sworn statement stating that the conditions exist to remedy the non-fulfillment of pecuniary obligations that led to the issuing of the sentence, and to have deposited, at the bankruptcy court's office, royalties to mature in the aforementioned period of thirty days following the petition[266] filing. This obviously implies that the discipline described above can only be applied to voluntary cases, because it is difficult for the debtor to provide the required deposits. Read the text of Section 362 (l): "(1) Except as otherwise provided in this subsection, subsection (b) (22) shall apply on the date that is 30 days after the date on which the bankruptcy petition is filed, if the debtor files with the petition to the courtesy of the lawyer in the jurisdiction of courtesy of the bankruptcy has been deposited with the clerk of the court, has been deposited with the clerk of the court, has been in the 30day period after the filing of the bankruptcy petition has been filed by a creditor, who, therefore, will not have to undergo even the suspension of thirty days just described[267].

Already from these few bars it is possible to draw the first considerations. First of all, with regard to the objective scope of

---

[264]See the text of section 362(b)(22): "Subject to subsection (l), under subsection (a)(3), of the continuation of any eviction, unlawful detainer action, or similar proceeding by a lessor against a debtor involving residential property in which the debtor resides as a tenant under a lease or rental agreement and with respect to which the lessor has obtained before the date of the filing of the bankruptcy petition, a judgment for possession of such property against the debtor (...)".

[265]W.D. WARREN, D.J. BUSSEL, D.A. SKEEL, JR., Bankruptcy, op. cit. op. cit. L.B. BARTELL, Visualizing bankruptcy, op. cit, pp. 81ss. S. LARSEN, Understanding the new semiautomatic stay, op. cit., pp. 76s. A.M. AHART, The inefficacy of the new eviction exceptions to the automatic stay, op. cit., pp. 128ss.

[266]A.M. AHART, The inefficacy of the new eviction exceptions to the automatic stay, op. cit.

[267]A.N. RESNICK, H. J. SOMMER, Collier on bankruptcy, op. cit., § 362.05[20]. See also: A.M. AHART, The inefficacy of the new eviction exceptions to the automatic stay, op. cit., 132 and 139ss.

application of the law, the limitation of the exception to the initiatives referred to in Section 362 (a) (3) implies, however, that the judicial proceedings aimed at executing the sentence and that, if this also presents a condemnatory head for the payment of the arrears, the lessor will remain precluded by the previous number (1) intends to act remains in any case held, for this part, to request a provision of relief from the automatic stay, resulting in the request for payment prevented by other provisions (think, for example, the general rule enclosed in subsection (a) (6))[268]. Secondly, then, and with regard to the strictly temporal profiles of the discipline, as emerges from the illustration completed the operativity of Section 362 (b) (22) as a genuine exception or as a hypothesis of automatic early termination of the automatic stay depends on the behavior observed by the debtor and, in particular, on its activation or otherwise with regard to the charges to file the sworn statement and fees for the location mentioned. This discipline, with all evidence, arises from the need to reconcile the conflicting interests of the landlord and the procedure: The former, in fact, has already obtained, in pre-bankruptcy, a favorable ruling that recognizes its right to the return of the leased property; on the other hand, the intervening deposit of the petition and the related operation of the automatic stay prevented it from acting for the recovery of the asset, as the subjective legal situation of advantage claimed on the same by the debtor was merged in the summer. Equitable requirements, therefore, have led to the development of a discipline suitable to protect the position of the lessor to a greater extent: Today, in fact, o the debtor undertakes concretely to remedy past failures, or the need to guarantee the position of the lessor involves the inoperativity of the protection offered by the automatic stay and the possibility, for this subject, to act immediately for the recovery of the asset.

At the first eventuality described, therefore, in the event that the debtor offers guarantees to protect the position of the lessor benefiting, in

---

[268]The following number (4), in fact, expressly specifies that if the debtor fails to meet the prescribed charges, the sect. 362 (b) (22) apply immediately, so that the lessor who wants to recover the possession of the property is not required to request a provision of relief from the automatic stay; moreover, to protect the requirements of legal certainty, the court registry is required to transmit to the lessor and to the debtor a communication about the non fulfillment of the charges and the application of the aforementioned exception.

fact, of a deferral in the production of the exception referred to in sect. 362 (b) (22) of thirty days, guaranteeing for this period the protection from the aforementioned proceedings[269], then the typical mechanism of each case of semiautomatic stay is reconnected and, therefore, the possibility of obtaining a restitution of the injunction ie, in the case of species, the definitive inoperativity of Section 362 (b) previum fulfillment of what is required by law. The reference is at number (2) of Section 362 (l), where it is prescribed that, where the debtor, within thirty days following the petition, deposits at the stationery a further sworn statement attesting to have remedied the defaults of the pecuniary obligations that had led to the ruling of restitution of the property in favor of the landlord, Section 362 (b) (22), in fact, does not apply[270]. Naturally, in the absence of the presentation of this declaration, at the expiration of the thirtieth day after the petition has been filed, the exception in comment will come into force, with the correlation ceasing the automatic stay operating on the initiatives specifically contemplated there. The situation, however, is complicated by the faculty, recognized to the landlord, to file an opposition to the declarations presented by the debtor: In this case, it is expected that, within the following ten days, a hearing is held specifically dedicated to ascertaining the veracity of such declarations; at the end of the same, if the court confirms the opposition of the lessor, the exception referred to in Sector 362 (b) (22) is applied immediately, so that the landlord can freely pursue the recovery of possession of the property, without the provision with specification, for true, superfluous-the need to request a provision of relief from the automatic stay.

The forecast referred to in the following section 362 (b) (23) is quite similar, where it is expected that "subject to subsection (m)" the filing of a petition does not produce the suspensive effects referred to in

---

[269]A.N. RESNICK, H.J. SOMMER, Collier on bankruptcy, op. cit.; A. M. AHART, The inefficacy of the new eviction exceptions to the automatic stay, op. cit., pp. 130.

[270]"(2) If, within the 30day period after the filing of the bankruptcy petition, the debtor (or an adult dependent of the debtor) complies with paragraph (1) and files with the court and serves upon the lessor a further certification under penalty of perjury that the debtor (or an adult dependent of the debtor) has cured, under non bankruptcy law applicable in the jurisdiction, the entire monetary default that gave rise to the judgment under which possession is sought by the lessor, subsection (b)(22) shall not apply, unless ordered to apply by the court under paragraph (3) (...)".

subsection (a) (3) with respect to eviction actions initiated by the lessor in against the debtor, concerning properties for residential use used as housing of the latter, in cases of endangerment or illegal use of substances in such property, where the lessor deposits with the bankruptcy court, and communicates to the debtor, a declaration sworn attesting that the eviction action has already been instituted or that the debtor has undertaken the described dangerous activities in the thirty days preceding the date of deposit of landford's declaration[271]. The reference made to the subsequent subsection (m), then, completes the discipline contained in the aforementioned exception by specifying the temporal regime of application: It is provided, in fact, that Section 362 (b) (23) is applied from the fifteenth day following the deposit, by the lessor, of the aforementioned sworn statement[272].

In other words, the regime of application of Section 362 (b) (23) is the following: It is applied by allowing, therefore, the continuation of the deportation action where the landlord provides to deposit the declarations provided for by the law, and in this case acquires force only once after fifteen days have elapsed from the time of this deposit[273]; it is not possible, therefore, and unlike what is seen with regard to the previous number (22), besides the other exceptions codified in subsection (b), that the rule applies already and only as a consequence of the petition[274].

---

[271]A.N. RESNICK, H.J. SOMMER, Collier on bankruptcy, op. cit. L.B. BARTELL, Visualizing bankruptcy, op. cit., pp. 82ss. S. LARSEN, Understanding the new semiautomatic stay, op. cit. A.M. AHART, The inefficacy of the new eviction exceptions to the automatic stay, op. cit., pp. 131ss.

[272]According to the text of the norm: "Subject to subsection (m), under subsection (a)(3), of an eviction action that seeks possession of the residential property in which the debtor resides as a tenant under a lease or rental agreement based on endangerment of such property or the illegal use of controlled substances on such property, but only if the lessor files with the court, and serves upon the debtor, a certification under penalty of perjury that such an eviction action has been filed, or that the debtor, during the thirty day period preceding the date of the filing of the certification, has endangered property or illegally used or allowed to be used a controlled substance on the property (...)".

[273]"(1) Except as otherwise provided in this subsection, subsection (b)(23) shall apply on the date that is 15 days after the date on which the lessor files and serves a certification described in subsection (b)(23) (...)". S.V. KELLEY, Ginsberg & Martin on bankruptcy, op. cit., L. B. BARTELL, Visualizing bankruptcy, op. cit.; A. M. AHART, The inefficacy of the new eviction exceptions to the automatic stay, op. cit., pp. 134ss.

[274]A.N. RESNICK, H.J. SOMMER, Collier on bankruptcy, op. cit. L.B. BARTELL, Visualizing bankruptcy, op. cit., S. LARSEN, Understanding the new semiautomatic stay, op. cit. A.M. AHART, The inefficacy of the new eviction exceptions to the automatic stay,

This period of automatic stay maintenance is provided, however, in order to allow the debtor to present an opposition in order to challenge the veracity of the affidavits filed by the lessor. With regard to this hypothesis, the law provides that Section 362 (b) (23) does not apply, unless otherwise ordered by the court: More correct, however, appears to conclude that the application, evidently deferred, of the exception remains suspended for the time necessary to hold an audience to hold within ten days from the presentation of the opposition, specifically appointed to verify the existence (or permanence) of the dangerous conditions reported by the landlord. Only in the event that, at the end of this hearing, the debtor is able to provide a positive demonstration of the non-existence conditions reported, the non-application of Section 362 (b) (23) will become definitive or, as stated in the standard, the stay prepared by subsection (a) (3) will remain effective until the physiological termination ordinarily provided for; in the opposite eventuality as well as in the case in which the debtor does not present any opposition, Section 362 (b) (23) will be immediately applied, so that it will be possible for the landlord to proceed with the eviction action without, of course, that it is necessary to request a relief measure from the automatic stay. Also with regard to the case in question, then, since the exception concerns only the actions described in subsection (a) (3), where the lessor intends to carry out different initiatives (such as, for example, the request for compensation for damages caused by the dangerous activity inside the leased property), must, on the contrary, request the release of the injunction, in particular that dictated by numbers (1) and (6).

33.(Follows) Debtor's personal assets. The temporal and functional relationship between automatic stay and discharge.

Taking now more in-depth analysis of legislation, Section 362 (c) (2), provides that the stay operating on "any other act under subsection (a)"[275] which, in conjunction with the provision referred to in the previous number (1), identifies the initiatives towards the debtor and of his personal

---

op. cit., pp. 136ss.

[275]L.B. BARTELL, Visualizing bankruptcy, op. cit.

patrimony, it lasts until one of the following three moments, according to which it intervenes first: a) That in which the procedure is closed for the attainment of its aims; or b) terminates due to the ruling of a dismissal order; or again c) the discharge[276] is granted or denied.

With regard to the first two hypotheses enunciated, it is evident that, where the procedure ends, due to its natural exhaustion or as a consequence of anomalous events, there is no longer any reason why the inhibitor should continue. By virtue of the supervening termination of the procedure, on the contrary, the bankruptcy court loses the jurisdiction it previously had on the administration of the case, so that this body is deprived of the powers to restore or order the continuation of injunction, also pursuant to Section 105 (a) of the Bankruptcy Code[277].

As far as the granting of the discharge is concerned, vice versa, automatic stay cessation is explained because the inhibitory effects connected to it are replaced by those deriving from the first[278]: The discharge provision, in other words, occurs temporally, and functionally replaces the automatic stay. If the latter, in fact, constitutes an impediment to the possibility, for creditors, to assert its claims against the debtor during the procedure, with the supervised ruling of the order of discharge, which results in the release of the debtor from all debts arising before the date of the order for relief and those equivalent to them, except those defined as

---

[276]According to the text: "The stay of any other act under subsection (a) of this section continues until the earliest of (A) the time the case is closed; (B) the time the case is dismissed; or (C) if the case is a case under Chapter 7 of this title concerning an individual or a case under chapter 9, 11, 12, or 13 of this title, the time a discharge is granted or denied (...)". A.N. RESNICK, H.J. SOMMER, Collier on bankruptcy, op. cit., § 362.06[2]; D.G. EPSTEIN, Bankruptcy and related law in a nutshell, op. cit., pp. 127ss. I. RAMSAY, Personal insolvency in the 21st century. A comparative analysis of the US and Europe, op. cit.

[277]See in argument: In re Income Property Builders, Inc., 699 F.2d 963 (1982), 964, regarding the possibility of restoring the stay and in case: In re Solar Equipment Corp., 19 B.R. 1010 (1982), 1011, with regard to the possibility of ordering the continuation. See in argument: D.R. COWANS, Cowans bankruptcy law and practice, op. cit., pp. 465ss. A.N. RESNICK, H.J. SOMMER, Collier on bankruptcy, op. cit.

[278]For the automatic stay see: S.V. KELLEY, Ginsberg & Martin on bankruptcy, op. cit., § 3.07[B]. B.A. BLUM, Bankruptcy and debtor/creditor, op. cit. S.V. KELLEY, Ginsberg & Martin on bankruptcy, op. cit., § 3.07[A]. J.F. MURPHY, The automatic stay in bankruptcy, op. cit., pp. 614ss.

non-dischargeable pursuant to Section 523[279], it is clear that the goals pursued by the automatic stay find a final settlement precisely in this definitive release from the responsibilities inherent in the procedure initiated; on the contrary, if the discharge is not granted, the creditors keep their remaining claims against the debtor intact and, simultaneously with the termination of the automatic stay, regain the free exercise of the shares against the same, but not also, obviously, in the with regard to bankruptcy assets, since the term of injuction cessation for this entity is different and independent from those examined above, so that the legal regime of the assets that have escaped from the same will be assessed on a case-by-case basis. A true cessation of the automatic stay, in other words, it is correct to speak only in the case of denied discharge, as mentioned, in case of granting the latter, the automatic stay will be rather absorbed by the same, assuming the appearance.

The consecration between automatic stay and discharge, however, is made possible by the fact that both differentiating themselves from the source from which they originate, being the first of legal origin and the second judicial, share the same legal nature: Even the discharge, in fact, constitutes an injunction to be precise, a permanent injunction, destined to absorb and replace the other, of a precautionary and temporary nature, represented by the automatic stay.

A final clarification seems absolutely appropriate: The circumstance that the law identifies, as distinct moments to which automatic stay cessation operating to protect the bankruptcy assets, the ruling on the discharge and the closure of the procedure obviously means that they moments do not coincide. Consider, in fact, that the declaration of bankruptcy, in the US bankruptcy system, also applies as a discharge request, since it is not necessary for the debtor to submit a specific request to that effect: The procedure for granting the discharge, in other words, it begins simultaneously with the opening of the procedure, and its duration, disconnected from the course of the procedure, depends exclusively on the fact that objections are presented by the legitimized subjects, and can

[279] D.G. EPSTEIN, Bankruptcy and related law in a nutshell, op. cit. I. RAMSAY, Personal insolvency in the 21st century. A comparative analysis of the US and Europe, op. cit.

therefore be concluded before or after the closure of bankruptcy case[280].

34.Previous presentation of another petition: A further hypothesis of semi automatic stay.

Also with regard to the timing of the cessation of the injunction against the debtor and his personal assets, the BAPCPA of 2005 intervened to make exceptions aimed at curbing and repressing the phenomenon of serial filings perpetrated by the natural person debtor, introducing hypotheses in which the automatic stay sees its effectiveness cease at an earlier time than the ordinary ones exposed in the previous paragraph[281].

Consider that the discipline enclosed in Section 362 (h), with regard to the obligations to which the debtor is obliged in relation to his personal assets placed as collateral for a loan or object of a pending lease, provides for the termination of the automatic stay not only towards summer property, but also debtor's property, so that even the aforementioned law must be numbered, mutatis mutandis, among the hypotheses of semi automatic stay now in comment.

The reference, in particular, is to Section 362 (c) (3), which provides that, in the event that a petition for access to a procedure governed by Chapters 7, 11 or 13 is filed by or against a debtor natural person, against whom, in the course of the last year, a termination procedure has been suspended with a ruling of dismissal, the automatic stay operating to protect the debtor, with regard to deeds concerning debts or assets placed as their guarantee, ends the thirtieth day following the date of deposit of the last petition[282].

The law, worthy of pointing out now, has raised several questions.

---

[280]D.G. EPSTEIN, Bankruptcy and related law in a nutshell, op. cit. I. RAMSAY, Personal insolvency in the 21st century. A comparative analysis of the US and Europe, op. cit.

[281]Section 362(c)(3), in particular was declared that: "If a single or joint case is filed by or against a debtor who is an individual in a case under chapter 7, 11, or 13, and if a single or joint case of the debtor was pending within the preceding 1year period but was dismissed, other than a case refiled under a chapter other than chapter 7 after dismissal under section 707(b) (A) the stay under subsection (a) with respect to any action taken with respect to a debt or property securing such debt or with respect to any lease shall terminate with respect to the debtor on the 30th day after the filing of the later case (...)".

[282]A.N. RESNICK, H.J. SOMMER, Collier on bankruptcy, op. cit., § 362.06[3][a]. S. LARSEN, Understanding the new semi automatic stay, op. cit., pp. 74ss. H. GERSHMAN, Automatic termination of the stay upon second filing under § 362(c)(3).

First of all, as regards its scope of application, it should be noted that, lacking any reference to the codebtor stay typical of the proceedings initiated under Chapter 13, the subsection now commented has no impact on the same, and therefore the co-obligor, in measure and in the manner seen at the time, will continue and benefit from the protection accorded to him[283].

Secondly, it is a duty to mention the complex question that the wording of the provision has raised in legal terms: It was noted, in particular, that the express limitation of automatic stay termination exclusively towards the debtor and his patrimony not, vice versa, also with regard to bankruptcy assets, it would not be binding, being indeed necessary to offer a reading of the provision capable of causing the protective efficacy cessation also with regard to summer protection, however in assonance to what happens under the subsection (c) (4) which, as seen, under this profile makes no distinctions whatsoever. Others, vice versa, have considered that the intention expressed by the legislator, to limit the applicative scope of the case of semiautomatic stay to the entities just identified, is unequivocal, even more so considering that the two provisions mentioned, referred to in numbers (3) and (4) of Section 362 (c), were introduced simultaneously by BAPCPA of 2005 and in very contiguous sedes matter[284].

The second reading, favorable to recognize the limitation of early automatic stay termination exclusively towards the debtor and his personal assets, seems to us preferable, and not only for the data, however not negligible, just exposed. In fact, it does not seem absurd that, with the discipline in question, the legislator intended to punish the debtor in first person, guilty of having abused the instruments offered by the Bankruptcy Code, without, at the same time, wanting to prejudice bankruptcy creditors, and therefore wanted at the same time to maintain the protection afforded to the property of the summer, which is exclusively reserved to the satisfaction of the same. On the other hand, the discrepancy does not appear to be incongruous, as is thus outlined in the following number (4):

---

[283]In re Curry, 362 B.R. 394 (2007), 397ss. H. GERSHMAN, Automatic termination of the stay upon second filing under § 362(c)(3).
[284]L.B. BARTELL, Visualizing bankruptcy, op. cit., pp. 224ss.

In the latter hypothesis, in fact, we are in the presence of a more serious case than the one now commented, in that the serial filings conduct described therein has a higher rate of recidivism and, correlatively, is punished with far more incisive penalties, i.e. with the provision of a mechanism of not so automatic stay, whose operation, however, differs a lot from the present hypothesis of semi automatic stay[285].

Finally, the subject of debate was the expression "with respect to any action taken", by which the legislator identifies initiatives aimed at returning to proceedings following the applicability of the provision in question. In fact, some courts have held, first, that the term "action" has a more circumscribed meaning of "act", often used in other provisions of Section 362, and indicates a specific and formal judicial or administrative initiative; secondly, it has been affirmed that the use of the verb "taken" would be to circumscribe on the temporal plane the list of precluded initiatives, limiting it in particular to those begun in the past and, more precisely, before the petition was filed[286].

The law then goes on to specify that at the request of a party who has an interest in continuing the automatic stay, the bankruptcy court may extend its term to some or all creditors, after having held a special hearing, better, complete the expiry of the aforementioned 30 day time limit, during which the requesting party is requested to demonstrate that the filing of the last petition took place in good faith in relation to creditors who are subject to the injunction pursuant thereto.

The dashed picture, with all the evidence, explains how the discipline introduced in Section 362 (c) (3) can be counted among the cases that have been defined as semiautomatic stay: Of inhibitory, that is, triggered by the petition filing, but fatally destined to see its effectiveness ceased at an earlier time than the ordinary one , in the absence of the

---

[285]A.N. RESNICK, H.J. SOMMER, Collier on bankruptcy, op. cit. W.D. WARREN, D.J. BUSSEL, D.A. SKEEL, JR., Bankruptcy, op. cit., L.A. NAPOLI, The not-so-automatic stay: Legislative changes to the automatic stay in a case filed by or against an individual debtor, op. cit., pp. 767ss. In jurisprudence see: In re Holcomb, 380 B.R. (2008), 815ss.

[286]In this sense see the case: In re Paschal, 337 B.R. 274 (2006), 279ss. For further details see: S.V. KELLEY, Ginsberg & Martin on bankruptcy, op. cit. § 3.01[G][1]. H. GERSHMAN, Automatic termination of the stay upon second filing under § 362(c)(3). cit., 58; contra, In re James, 358 B.R. 816 (2007), 820ss. Contro also: L.B. BARTELL, Visualizing bankruptcy, op. cit.

fulfillment of what is required by law in order, in fact, to remain in force. In this case, the law therefore requires that one party, presumably, will be the debtor, but the legitimacy is not explicitly circumscribed to that subject, it is activated to demonstrate that the repeated request for admission to a bankruptcy procedure, although abstractly hypothesis of serial filings, a good faith has been made, so that, since there is no abusive conduct to repress and punish, there is no reason to stop the automatic stay in advance[287].

Also with reference to the mechanism now commented, moreover, the law has codified a series of hypotheses integrating a legal presumption, surmountable through a "clear and convincing evidence to the contrary", based on the fact that the petition was not filed in good faith; these hypotheses, moreover, coincide with those already referred to above, with regard to the case of not so automatic stay enclosed in Section 362 (c) (4)[288].

The discipline just presented is completed, however, with the provisions of Section 362 (i), where it is provided that the legal presumption codified in subsection (c) does not apply, therefore, the subsequent filing can not be considered in bad faith, if the previous procedure had been dismissed as a result of the creation, by the debtor, of a debt repayment plan in favor of its creditors, although not yet fully fulfilled at the time of the next petition[289]: This circumstance, evidently, is

---

[287]"(B) on the motion of a party in interest for continuation of the automatic stay and upon notice and a hearing, the court may extend the stay in particular cases as to any or all creditors (subject to such conditions or limitations as the court may then impose) after notice and a hearing completed before the expiration of the thirty day period only if the party in interest demonstrates that the filing of the later case is in good faith as to the creditors to be stayed (...)". S.V. KELLEY, Ginsberg & Martin on bankruptcy, op. cit., M.A. FREY, S.K. SWINSON, Introduction to bankruptcy law, op. cit

[288]A.N. RESNICK, H.J. SOMMER, Collier on bankruptcy, op. cit., § 362.06[3][b]. L.B. BARTELL, Visualizing bankruptcy, op. cit., pp. 89ss. L.B. BARTELL, Visualizing bankruptcy, op. cit. B.A. BLUM, Bankruptcy and debtor/creditor, op. cit., pp. 256ss. S. LARSEN, Understanding the new semiautomatic stay, op. cit. L.A. NAPOLI, The not-so-automatic stay: Legislative changes to the automatic stay in a case filed by or against an individual debtor, op. cit.

[289]Section 362(c)(3)(C), provides that: "(...) For purposes of subparagraph (B), a case is presumptively filed not in good faith (but such presumption may be rebutted by clear and convincing evidence to the contrary) (i)as to all creditors, if (I) more than one previous case under any of Chapters 7, 11, and in which the individual was a debtor was pending

indicative of the fact that the debtor, far from having used the tools offered by the Bankruptcy Code for the sole purpose of making money of the benefits connected to them, he had rather sought in every way to compose his own insolvency situation with his creditors, in particular through the use of an out-of-court agreement that was accompanied by the dismissal of the prior insolvency procedure[290].

In the event that the automatic stay ends on the thirtieth day after the petition is filed, as a consequence of the non-activation of the interested party to its continuation, it has been argued, from a jurisprudence in a minority case, that it is also possible to apply to the case under examination. the provision enclosed in Section 362 (c) (4) (B), and thus obtain a judicial provision for deferred taxation of stay[291].

Also in this hypothesis, however, where a subject intends to act against the debtor or his personal assets trusting the operation of the legislation in question, prior activation is preferable in order to obtain from the bankruptcy court, pursuant to Section 362 (j), the ruling of a provision confirming that the stay is terminated in accordance with subsection (c) (3) herein[292].

Finally, even with regard to the case in point, as seen in relation to

---

within the preceding one year period; (II) a previous case under any of chapters 7, 11, and 13 in which the individual was a debtor was dismissed within such one year period, after the debtor failed to (aa) file or amend the petition or other documents as required by this title or the court without substantial excuse (but mere inadvertence or negligence shall not be a substantial excuse unless the dismissal was caused by the negligence of the debtor's attorney); (bb) provide adequate protection as ordered by the court; or (cc) perform the terms of a plan confirmed by the court; or (III) there has not been a substantial change in the financial or personal affairs of the debtor since the dismissal of the next most previous case under Chapter 7, 11, or 13 or any other reason to conclude that the later case will be concluded (aa) if a case under chapter 7, with a discharge; or (bb) if a case under Chapter 11 or 13, with a confirmed plan that will be fully performed; and (ii) as to any creditor that commenced an action under subsection (d) in a previous case in which the individual was a debtor if, as of the date of dismissal of such case, that action was still pending or had been resolved by terminating, conditioning, or limiting the stay as to actions of such creditor".

290 A.N. RESNICK, H.J. SOMMER, Collier on bankruptcy, op. cit.

291 In re Beasley, 339 B.R. 472 (2006), 473. L.J. MARGULIES, Understanding the new semiautomatic stay, op. cit., pp. 27ss. L.B. BARTELL, Visualizing bankruptcy, op. cit., contra, In re Williams, 410 B.R. 491 (2009), 494.

292 A.N. RESNICK, H.J. SOMMER, Collier on bankruptcy, op. cit., § 362.06[5]. S.V. KELLEY, Ginsberg & Martin on bankruptcy, op. cit. P.A. MURPHY, E.E. SAGERMAN, D. NEIER, Creditor's rights in bankruptcy op. cit., pp. 182ss.

the discipline referred to in subsection (c) (4), majority jurisprudence considers it possible, on the part of the party who is interested, to request an injunction pursuant to Section 105 (a) of the Bankruptcy Code, which provides for the termination of the automatic stay[293].

35.Judicial cessation of the protective effect: The procedure for automatic stay liberation (relief). Its function within the operating mechanism of inhibitory.

The presence of an institute such as the one in question, however, allows us to make an overall assessment of the phenomenon of the automatic stay, and we will see how this overview of the subject will allow us to achieve opposite results compared to those suggested from a more superficial or a narrower approach, it refers to the outcome of the examination at the institute that is the object of our discussion.

We refer, of course, to the possibility that the same Section 362 grants the entity subject to the injunction to request release (relief) from the automatic stay, and thus obtain a court order which, in the existence of the conditions required for this purpose, terminates the pre-exclusive effect with regard to subject, so that he can return free to act against the debtor or his assets or the property of the summer, despite the slope of the insolvency proceedings and the persistent subjection of other entities to the automatic stay, with a clear exception to the principles of par condicio creditorum. In other words, it is a further hypothesis of automatic stay termination: Only that, unlike those illustrated in the previous paragraphs, we are not in the presence of a specific case provided for by the law, but rather integrated by a judicial decision, and for the exclusive benefit of the subject by the latter concerned[294].

---

[293]The section 362(j) states that: "On request of a party in interest, the court shall issue an order under subsection (c) confirming that the automatic stay has been terminated (...)". For further details see: A.N. RESNICK, H.J. SOMMER, Collier on bankruptcy, op. cit., § 362.06[7].

[294]Whether it is a further hypothesis of cessation of the automatic stay, however, emerges from the same text of the section. 362 (c) dedicated, as is known, to the temporal discipline of the inhibitor just illustrated, whose incipit reads: "Except as provided in subsections (d), (e), (f) (...) of this section (...)". In argument see: A.N. RESNICK, H.J. SOMMER, Collier on bankruptcy, op. cit., § 362.06[6]. For further analysis see: Rules of Bankruptcy

We are obviously faced with an instrument that allows the subject hit by the injunction to overcome the bans imposed by law and obtain a judicial authorization to carry out activities that were otherwise prohibited: An instrument, in other words, capable of bringing elements of unquestionable flexibility to a normative connoted, otherwise, by a strong rigidity. The possibility of requesting the release from the automatic stay is instead to represent the rebalancing element of the entire system of protective effects related to the procedures governed by the Bankruptcy Code: If, in fact, upstream, the only presentation of the petition is suitable to trigger the automatic stay to foreclosure of the wide range of initiatives described, with a substantially all-encompassing formulation, from Section 362 (a) yes to immediately block any action against the debtor or assets, downstream it allows the individual entities affected by such effects to react to the inhibitor automatically taken against them to obtain their termination. It is a reflection, this, as we have already had the affirmation[295], of automatic stay's precautionary nature, which intervenes immediately, and without making any distinctions whatsoever, to protect the debtor and the procedure from the aggressive initiatives of others as a matter of urgency, however, the possibility for the individual subject to subsequently establish a special procedure where it submits to more careful assessment of the judge the actual existence of the reasons justifying the operation of the injunction, and with it the conditions that allow it to escape the related effects to this phenomenon.

A juxtaposition of the system just outlined thus makes it possible to disavow those statements, to which reference has just been made, which, arising from a prima facie knowledge of the subject, leads us to

---

Procedure, L. PEITZMAN, M.S. SMITH, The secured creditor's complaint: relief from the automatic stays in bankruptcy proceedings, in California Law Review, 1977, pp. 1216ss.

[295]Moreover, the different legal regime to which the acts carried out in violation of the inhibitory effects placed in protection of the debtor are subjected in the two legal systems: if, in fact, it is used to talk about the ineffectiveness of such acts, their exact qualification in The US system is, on the contrary, the subject of a very heated debate, and, in any case, the thesis that qualifies them as merely voidable appears particularly bad for the debtor and for safeguarding the interests of the procedure. For more analysis see: D.R. COWANS, Cowans bankruptcy law and practice, op. cit., pp. 527ss, is defined as: "A strong candidate for the most frequently used item of litigation in the bankruptcy court"; for more reflections see: B.A. BLUM, Bankruptcy and debtor/creditor, op. cit., pp. 268ss.

consider the automatic stay as an appropriate institution to offer the debtor a protection: It is indeed true, in fact, that from the objective point of view the scope of application of the automatic stay is much more comprehensive than the few and well identified activities that preclude the creditor against the debtor declared bankrupt or requesting admission to a procedure for the settlement of business crisis; but while the latter, are destined to remain irreversibly precluded in the slope of the procedure, in the US reality it is always possible for the creditor to request to be freed from the injunction, so that, ultimately, the debtor is condemned to a precarious situation, while the other creditors remain indefinitely in the uncertainty about the real consistency of the bankruptcy assets reserved for their satisfaction, also and above all in consideration of the frequency with which these proceedings are established.

Coming now to analyze the text of the norm, the subsections (d), (e), (f) and (g) of Section 362 are dedicated to the matter of liberation from the automatic stay. The first is dedicated to the substantial assumptions of the request for reliefs including, as will be seen, a peculiar hypothesis introduced by BAPCPA of 2005, and the other to procedural profiles of the related judgments to be integrated with the provisions placed between the Federal Rules of Bankruptcy Procedures, among which there are some deviations from the modules characterizing the ordinary procedure, of which it will be said, aimed at speeding up the process of granting the liberation provision[296].

Moving, therefore, from the rule contained in subsection (d), it is there that, upon request of a party interested in this, and after conducting a special hearing to ascertain the necessary substantive conditions, the court must grant release from inhibitory prepared by the previous subsection (a), ordering its termination, cancellation, modification or conditioning[297]. In the next paragraphs, we will therefore analyze this provision in detail, as well as the procedure for obtaining a judicial

---

[296]D.G. EPSTEIN, Bankruptcy and related law in a nutshell, op. cit. I. RAMSAY, Personal insolvency in the 21st century. A comparative analysis of the US and Europe, op. cit.

[297]Below, the text of the section 362 (d), in the part here considered: "On request of a party in interest and after notice and a hearing, the court shall grant relief from the stay provided under subsection (a) of this section, such as by terminating, annulling, modifying, or conditioning such stay (...)".

provision of relief from the automatic stay.

36.Active legitimization. The competent court.

Section 362 (d) specifies that the request for release from the automatic stay must come from a "party in interest", thus leaving to the interpreter the task of identifying the subjects that can be included in this phrase[298].

In this regard, the correct solution appears to be the most immediate, that is to recognize the legitimacy to request relief from all the entities subject to injunction, thus establishing a perfectly univocal relationship between subjection to its effects and legitimacy to avoid: If the automatic stay, as mentioned, is produced as a matter of urgency, indiscriminately and by virtue of the sole deposit of petition, with regard to a very wide range of subjects, the most equitable and reasonable solution appears to allow each of them, at a later stage, to initiate a procedure to further evaluate the actual opportunity of injunction itself, in order to obtain its release; on the other hand, no role can play, here, the existence of substantial requirements required by law for the ruling of this provision, which is a matter related to the merit of the trial for release, so, therefore, to be concluded, possibly, with a provision of denial, but which will not affect in any way the issue concerning the identification of legitimized subjects.

A solution different from the one proposed, denying the legitimacy to request the liberation from the automatic stay to all those

[298]A definition of "party in interest" is actually present in the Bankruptcy Code, and precisely in the section. 1109 (b), where this term refers to "the debtor, the trustee, a creditors' committee, an equity security holders' committee, a creditor, an equity security holder, or any indenture trustee", but its peculiar placement advises to refer the contents only to the procedure governed by Chapter 11. See in argument: A.N. RESNICK, H.J. SOMMER, o Collier on bankruptcy, op. cit., § 362.07[2]. D.R. COWANS, Cowans bankruptcy law and practice, op. cit., pp. 528ss. D.G. EPSTEIN, Bankruptcy and related law in a nutshell, op. cit., pp. 128ss. From the jurisprudence see: In re Vieland, 41 B.R. 134 (1984), gives legitimacy to the creditor or to the holder of the right to be operated prior to release from the automatic stay. S. V. KELLEY, Ginsberg & Martin on bankruptcy, op. cit., § 3.06[A]. In argument see also: D.G. EPSTEIN, Bankruptcy and related law in a nutshell, op. cit., pp. 50ss. F.R. KENNEDY, Automatic stays under the new bankruptcy law, op. cit. S. PARSONS, Consumer bankruptcy law in focus, op. cit., I. RAMSAY, Personal insolvency in the 21st century. A comparative analysis of the US and Europe, op. cit.

who, subject to the exclusionary effects deriving from it, are subjected, would mean, by all means, accept the absurd situation for which a part, necessarily subject to injunction in comment, cannot take any initiative in order to verify the appropriateness of such effects, thus renouncing that essential instrument for rebalancing positions between the parties that characterizes the US discipline on the protection of the debtor and interests of the procedure.

The proposed solution implies that, upon presentation of the request for relief from the automatic stay, the instant subject asserts his own qualification as an entity subject to the prohibition and, therefore, in the case in which it is a creditor, claims to boast a claim against the procedure, so as to qualify as a subject legitimized to advance the request in comment[299].

In the identification of judicial authority competent to pronounce the liberation provision from the automatic stay, the text of subsection (d) is limited to making a reference to "the court": A datum, this, that also by virtue of use of the definite article, immediately leads the mind to the bankruptcy court where the procedure is hinged. Since, however, as has already been pointed out several times, the matter inherent in the distribution, in the US legal system, of the bankruptcy jurisdiction is very complex, it seems appropriate to proceed with a more in-depth examination of the system of regulatory provisions of this matter, in order to seek confirmation of the conclusion that the literal interpretation has just suggested to us.

In this regard, the aforementioned Section 157 of Title 28 of the United States Code, in subsection (b), expressly includes among the core proceedings concerning the rights created by the bankruptcy law and which may arise exclusively in the context of a concurrent procedure "motions to terminate,cancel, or modify the automatic stay" or, in fact, the judgments for the release from the inhibitory[300].

Then, the core proceedings are represented by those judgments on

---

[299]S.V. KELLEY, Ginsberg & Martin on bankruptcy, op. cit., § 3.06[F]. J.F. MURPHY, The automatic stay in bankruptcy, op. cit., pp. 592ss.

[300]B.A. BLUM, Bankruptcy and debtor/creditor, op. cit., pp. 134ss. L.P. KING, Jurisdiction and procedure under the bankruptcy amendments of 1984, in Vanderbilt Law Review, 38, 1985, pp. 676ss.

which the bankruptcy court exercises its potestas iudicandi, as this has been referred to by the district court, since the latter has, in fact, the relative original jurisdiction.

This means, in conclusion, that with regard to proceedings for automatic stay liberation, the jurisdiction is, in principle, in the district court, with the possibility of referral to the bankruptcy court[301], which may decide on the matter with an appellable provision before the first. This solution, however, is certainly optimal both from the point of view of the needs of rationalization of the dispute, conveyed on a single forum and with a reduction in the risk of contradictory decisions, both to exploit the specialization of this judge[302].

37.Substantial conditions.

The discipline concerning the substantial presuppositions to which the existence subsists is linked to the power, for the court seised, to pronounce the liberation from the automatic stay in favor of the instant subject. In particular, these are four different hypotheses, naturally provided for in an alternative way, two of which, however, were introduced on the occasion of changes introduced by the 1994 and 2005 reforms.

The intervening assessment by the judge of their existence, integrating a contrary or incompatible with the presence of a prejudice to the procedure, constitutes the contrary evidence that allows the overcoming of the rebuttable presumption placed on the basis of the automatic stay operational mechanism, and with it the caducation of the connected protective effect, thus leaving free the instant that has obtained the positive provision to act against the debtor.

The first substantive assumption that the relief provision is

---

[301] Without, of course, that the procedure for obtaining the liberation of the automatic stay can be precluded by the Section 362(2). In this sense the case: In re Keaty, 350 B.R. 723 (2006), 726. In this sense see also: D. R. COWANS, Cowans bankruptcy law and practice, op. cit., pp. 556ss.

[302]The solution differs from what is stated above, Chap. III, Sec. II, § 11, regarding the competence to pronounce on the question about the applicability of the automatic stay. This inasmuch as the procedure for granting relief is expressly qualified by law as core proceeding, whose jurisdiction is attributed, through referrals, to the bankruptcy court, according to what emerges from the Section 157 (b) of Title 28 of the United States Code.

granted by the automatic stay is that described in number (1) of subsection (d), where it is expected that it may be required "for reasons, including the lack of adequate protection of an interest in property "claimed by the instant part[303].

The aforementioned law does not therefore indicate a precise justification for the granting of injunction but provides, with a very general formulation, that it may be granted whenever a justified reason is used, providing then, by way of example, to make reference to the most frequent hypothesis of granting the relief for a justified reason, namely the lack of adequate protection of a legal situation held by the individual subject[304].

The term "causes" is therefore suitable to include the heterogeneous range of situations in which it appears justified, in the specific case, to grant the individual person the release from the automatic stay[305]: It may be for example, the case where the court ascertains that the debtor had requested admission to the procedure in bad faith, and therefore only for the purpose of prejudicing his creditors by paralyzing their aggressive initiatives, or the possibility that the initiative subject to the request has no connection with the bankruptcy proceedings, the absence of prejudice is to be considered in re ipsa[306]; on the contrary, it is of course to be excluded that the request for relief may be based on the fact that the claim, whose satisfaction is blocked by the automatic stay, is destined to be extinguished in the event of granting the discharge[307].

---

[303]D.G. EPSTEIN, Bankruptcy and related law in a nutshell, op. cit. I. RAMSAY, Personal insolvency in the 21st century. A comparative analysis of the US and Europe, op. cit.

[304]D.G. EPSTEIN, Bankruptcy and related law in a nutshell, op. cit. pp. 58ss. I. RAMSAY, Personal insolvency in the 21st century. A comparative analysis of the US and Europe, op. cit. For the previous system see the analysis of: L. PEITZMAN, M. S. SMITH, The secured creditor's complaint: Relief from the automatic stays in bankruptcy proceedings, op. cit., pp. 1225ss.

[305]A.N. RESNICK, H.J. SOMMER, Collier on bankruptcy, op. cit., § 362.07[3]. S.V. KELLEY, Ginsberg & Martin on bankruptcy, op. cit., § 3.05[B]. D.R. COWANS, Cowans bankruptcy law and practice, op. cit., pp. 535ss. D.G. EPSTEIN, Bankruptcy and related law in a nutshell, op. cit., pp. 138ss. I. RAMSAY, Personal insolvency in the 21st century. A comparative analysis of the US and Europe, op. cit. R.M. MARTIN, Creditor alternatives to obtain relief from automatic stays in bankruptcy, in Banking Law Journal, 98, 1981, pp. 536ss. D.J. WARREN, Relief from the automatic stay: Section 362(d), in Bankruptcy Developments Journal, 3, 1986, pp. 199ss.

[306]In re Dixie Broadcasting, Inc., 871 F.2d 1023 (1989).

[307]A.N. RESNICK, H.J. SOMMER, Collier on bankruptcy, op. cit., § 362.07[3][a]. S.V.

Also with regard to judgments that, pending at an extra-food court, have been suspended due to the provision contained in Section 362 (a) (1), the established existence of a suitable "cause" may lead to the issuance of a relief measure that allows the continuation of the dispute with the aforementioned judicial authority. In this regard, it is interesting to note that the US jurisprudence has elaborated particular criteria on which to base an equitable balance test, i.e. a comparative assessment of interests at stake, at the end of which it will be possible to decide whether to allow the continuation of the judgment; in particular[308]: a) The fact that the prosecution of civil proceedings does not appear suitable to cause serious harm to the debtor or to the bankruptcy mass; b) the circumstance that the maintenance of the automatic stay is likely to cause greater damage to the performing party than those that would result in the debtor from his downfall; c) the probability of acceptance on the merits of reasons claimed by the performing party. On the basis of these assessments, of course, the relief measure may also be granted in order to allow the proposability of a counterclaim against the debtor who has initiated a judgment against an entity subject to the automatic stay[309]. A separate mention deserves, then, the hypothesis in which a judgment characterized by a joinder of defendants, in which the debtor takes the trial role of one of the defendants, is pending in an extra-bankruptcy court. In this case, especially where the

---

KELLEY, Ginsberg & Martin on bankruptcy, op. cit., § 3.05[B][4]. W.R. NORTON, JR., Norton bankruptcy law and practice op. cit., § 36:34. D.R. COWANS, Cowans bankruptcy law and practice, op. cit., pp. 535ss. D.G. BAIRD, The elements of bankruptcy, op. cit., pp. 199ss. P.A. MURPHY, E.E. SAGERMAN, D. NEIER, Creditor's rights in bankruptcy, op. cit., B.A. BLUM, Bankruptcy and debtor/creditor, op. cit., pp. 270. A.N. RESNICK, Bankruptcy law manual, op. cit., pp. 110ss. D.G. EPSTEIN, Bankruptcy and related law in a nutshell, op. cit., pp. 139ss. J.F. MURPHY, The automatic stay in bankruptcy, op. cit., pp. 604ss. R.A. JOHNSON, M. C. O'LEARY, Automatic stay provisions of the bankruptcy act of 1978, op. cit., pp. 615ss. F. R. KENNEDY, Automatic stays under the new bankruptcy law, op. cit., pp. 46ss. R.M. MARTIN, Creditor alternatives to obtain relief from automatic stays in bankruptcy, op. cit., pp. 536ss. S. PARSONS, Consumer bankruptcy law in focus, op. cit., O. COUWENBERG, S. J. LUBBEN, Essential corporate bankruptcy law, op. cit. I. RAMSAY, Personal insolvency in the 21st century. A comparative analysis of the US and Europe, op. cit.

308 In re Sawyer, 18 B.R. 661 (1982).

309 S.V. KELLEY, Ginsberg & Martin on bankruptcy, op. cit., D.R. COWANS, Cowans bankruptcy law and practice, op. cit., pp. 536ss. W.D. WARREN, D.J. BUSSEL, D.A. SKEEL, JR., Bankruptcy, op. cit., pp. 217ss. F. VAZQUEZ, Modification of automatic stay to permit litigation to proceed remains possible, op. cit., pp. 34ss.

debtor qualifies as an indispensable party, the granting of a provision of relief from the automatic stay is one of the solutions to cope with the criticalities related to the inhibitory operation in favor of only one of the necessary passive litigation, allowing the subjectively complex cause to continue despite the petition filing. Finally, an interesting question is that concerning arbitration proceedings: Since, as is clear from the Federal Arbitration Act, there is a strong federal policy in favor of this means of settling disputes out of court, in the presence of an arbitration agreement it will have to be preferably granted the release from the automatic stay to allow the establishment of the relative procedure, except of course the case in which this conflicts with the objectives pursued by the Bankruptcy Code and, in particular, the necessity that the assessment of credit claims takes place before the bankruptcy court[310].

As regards, then, the assumption, that the legislator expressly includes among the aforementioned causes, supplemented by "lack of adequate protection of an interest in property"[311] of ownership of the subject for the relief provision, is integrated by the circumstance therefore the interest in property claimed by the creditor does not find adequate protection during the automatic stay, for example because the value of the property has suffered a depreciation, a damage, or has been lost, so that, ultimately, the continuation of this inhibitor is likely to cause an injury to the subject[312]. This, of course, can only happen if, as mentioned, the subject in question is the owner of a right on an asset merged into summer property, or the debtor, protected by the automatic stay: It will be the case, first of all, holders of pre-emptive rights, but also, for example, landlords who have leased a property to the debtor, or co-owners of an asset that is

---

[310]Pub. L. No. 68401 (1925).

[311]D.G. EPSTEIN, Bankruptcy and related law in a nutshell, op. cit. I. RAMSAY, Personal insolvency in the 21st century. A comparative analysis of the US and Europe, op. cit.

[312]In this spirit the case: In re Gandy, 299 F.3d 489 (2002), 493. S.V. KELLEY, Ginsberg & Martin on bankruptcy, op. cit., § 3.05[B][1]. W.R. NORTON, JR., Norton bankruptcy law and practice op. cit., § 36:33. D.R. COWANS, Cowans bankruptcy law and practice, op. cit., pp. 545ss. B.A. BLUM, Bankruptcy and debtor/creditor, op. cit., pp. 276ss. D.G. EPSTEIN, Bankruptcy and related law in a nutshell, op. cit., pp. 143ss. R.A. JOHNSON, M.C. O'LEARY, Automatic stay provisions of the bankruptcy act of 1978, op. cit. R.M. MARTIN, Creditor alternatives to obtain relief from automatic stays in bankruptcy, op. cit., pp. 537ss. I. RAMSAY, Personal insolvency in the 21st century. A comparative analysis of the US and Europe, op. cit.

in the joint ownership of the debtor[313]. In order to identify the meaning of said adequate protection, however, reference should be made to the previous Section 361 which defines precisely when said form of protection exists, or not and verify if there is room for a measure of relief. The last-mentioned rule, in particular, with a merely illustrative list, provides that said adequate protection can be provided: a) Through periodic payments made by the trustee to the owner of the interest, to the extent necessary to compensate for any decrease in value caused by operativity of the automatic stay. This is the case, for example, of the creditor holding a pre-emptive right on an asset intended to see its value diminished over time, so that the delay in the realization of the claim caused by the operation of the injunction it translates into a lower value of the asset and a lower realizable value, which can be offset by such periodic payments[314]; b) by granting this entity an additional or replacement right of pre-emption, to the extent that the interest claimed has suffered a decrease in its value due the activity of bidding[315]; c) guaranteeing that entity another form of

---

[313]L.B. BARTELL, Visualizing bankruptcy, op. cit., P. A. MURPHY, E. E. SAGERMAN, D. NEIER, Creditor's rights in bankruptcy op. cit., pp. 209ss. B.A. BLUM, Bankruptcy and debtor/creditor, op. cit., pp. 275ss. D.G. EPSTEIN, Bankruptcy and related law in a nutshell, op. cit., pp. 52ss. I. RAMSAY, Personal insolvency in the 21st century. A comparative analysis of the US and Europe, op. cit.

[314]Section 361: "When adequate protection is required under Section 362, 363, or 364 of this title of an interest of an entity in property, such adequate protection may be provided by (1) requiring the trustee to make a cash payment or periodic cash payments to such entity, to the extent that the stay under Section 362 of this title, use, sale, or lease under Section 363 of this title, or any grant of a lien under Section 364 of this title results in a decrease in the value of such entity's interest in such property; (2) providing to such entity an additional or replacement lien to the extent that such stay, use, sale, lease, or grant results in a decrease in the value of such entity's interest in such property; or (3) granting such other relief, other than entitling such entity to compensation allowable under section 503(b)(1) of this title as an administrative expense, as will result in the realization by such entity of the indubitable equivalent of such entity's interest in such property". For further details see: J.R. SACK, Adequate protection, in Bankruptcy Developments Journal, 2, 1985, pp. 21ss. A.N. RESNICK, H.J. SOMMER, Collier on bankruptcy, op. cit., § 362.07[3][b][i]. S.V. KELLEY, Ginsberg & Martin on bankruptcy, op. cit., § 3.05[B][2]; D. G. BAIRD, The elements of bankruptcy, op. cit., pp. 201ss. L.B. BARTELL, Visualizing bankruptcy, op. cit., pp. 95ss. O. COUWENBERG, S. J. LUBBEN, Essential corporate bankruptcy law, op. cit.

[315]A.N. RESNICK, H.J. SOMMER, Collier on bankruptcy, op. cit., § 362.07[3][c]; S. V. KELLEY, Ginsberg & Martin on bankruptcy, op. cit., op. cit.; D. G. BAIRD, The elements of bankruptcy, op. cit. L.B. BARTELL, Visualizing bankruptcy, op. cit. O. COUWENBERG, S. J. LUBBEN, Essential corporate bankruptcy law, op. cit.

protection suitable to match the equivalent of that interest, so as to ensure that the position of the subject is not in any way prejudiced by the automatic stay.

The interested party in receiving an adequate protection must make a request at the moment in which they advance their application to obtain release from the automatic stay; where the protection so requested is not granted, through one of the behaviors described or other similarly suitable to ensure this result, the most recurrent reason for granting the relief provision "for causes" will therefore be integrated[316].

Since in the description of other conditions of relief provision the law provides the initiatives concerned or to identify the beneficiary of the injunction against which the same can be canceled, it is reasonable to conclude that the provision now under consideration assumes general and residual nature, being able to operate in all the circumstances not considered by these other norms, having a special character: This means that it can be applied with regard to any initiative considered by Section 362 (a), and regardless of the beneficiary entity of the injunction against which it intends to act[317]. The presence of such a rule of closure also seems indicative of legislator's desire not to excessively circumscribe the scope within which it is possible to obtain a provision of liberation from the automatic stay, once again to rebalance the equally vast and generic operation that this protection is recognized by subsection (a). the next number (2), Section 362 (d) identifies the substantial assumption to request the release of the automatic stay in favor of an "act against property", requiring the cumulative recurrence of two requisites[318]: That the debtor

---

[316] A.N. RESNICK, H.J. SOMMER, Collier on bankruptcy, op. cit., § 362.07[3][b]. D.G. BAIRD, The elements of bankruptcy, op. cit. J.F. MURPHY, The automatic stay in bankruptcy, op. cit., pp. 602ss. O. COUWENBERG, S. J. LUBBEN, Essential corporate bankruptcy law.

[317] B.A. BLUM, Bankruptcy and debtor/creditor, op. cit., pp. 270ss. D.G. EPSTEIN, Bankruptcy and related law in a nutshell, op. cit., pp. 50ss. I. RAMSAY, Personal insolvency in the 21st century. A comparative analysis of the US and Europe, op. cit. In particular for the analysis of "residual relief", see: D.G. EPSTEIN, Bankruptcy and related law in a nutshell, op. cit. J.F. MURPHY, The automatic stay in bankruptcy, op. cit., pp. 596ss. R.A. JOHNSON, M.C. O'LEARY, Automatic stay provisions of the bankruptcy act of 1978, op. cit., pp. 614ss. I. RAMSAY, Personal insolvency in the 21st century. A comparative analysis of the US and Europe, op. cit.

[318] A.N. RESNICK, H.J. SOMMER, Collier on bankruptcy, op. cit., § 362.07[4]. S.V.

does not have "equity in such property", and that this property it is not necessary to carry out an "effective reorganization"[319]. It is clear that the present case also essentially concerns the creditors who have a right of first refusal, the only ones who are evidently able to put in place an initiative directed against assets merged into the bankruptcy estate or belonging to debtor's personal assets. At the same time, it is equally evident that it is impossible to obtain, by means of this rule, the release from the automatic stay operating to protect debtor's person.

Focusing on the analysis of individual requirements described above, the term "equity" indicates the difference between the value (generally, the market value) of the asset in question and that of the charges on the same[320]. This means that the debtor has no equity in the property merged into the bankruptcy or personal mass when the amount of credits guaranteed by preemptive rights on that property and opposable to the mass exceeds the value of the property itself. In fact, in such cases, since the proceeds from the sale of the asset will be entirely devolved to the preferred creditors, while the mass will not receive any benefit from the liquidation, there is no reason why the procedure should maintain control of the asset and related operations. sale; in this case, in the procedures other than the liquidation procedure referred to in Chapter 7, unless a positive demonstration of the necessity of the asset in question is provided to ensure the effective restructuring of the debtor, the release from the automatic stay will be granted to the instant creditor, so

---

KELLEY, Ginsberg & Martin on bankruptcy, op. cit., § 3.05[C]. W.R. NORTON, JR., Norton bankruptcy law and practice, op. cit., § 36:35. D.R. COWANS, Cowans bankruptcy law and practice, op. cit., pp. 546ss. L.B. BARTELL, Visualizing bankruptcy, op. cit. B.A. BLUM, Bankruptcy and debtor/creditor, op. cit., pp. 271ss. D.G. EPSTEIN, Bankruptcy and related law in a nutshell, op. cit., pp. 56ss. I. RAMSAY, Personal insolvency in the 21st century. A comparative analysis of the US and Europe, op. cit.

[319] R.M. MARTIN, Creditor alternatives to obtain relief from automatic stays in bankruptcy, op. cit., pp. 540ss. D.J. WARREN, Relief from the automatic stay: Section 362(d), op. cit., pp. 210ss.

[320] S.V. KELLEY, Ginsberg & Martin on bankruptcy, op. cit., § 3.05[C][2]. W.R. NORTON, JR., Norton bankruptcy law and practice, op. cit. B.A. BLUM, Bankruptcy and debtor/creditor, op. cit. D.G. EPSTEIN, Bankruptcy and related law in a nutshell, op. cit, pp. 131ss. J.F. MURPHY, The automatic stay in bankruptcy, op. cit., pp. 600ss. D.J. WARREN, Relief from the automatic stay: Section 362(d), op. cit. I. RAMSAY, Personal insolvency in the 21st century. A comparative analysis of the US and Europe, op. cit.

that he can manage its sale[321].

Regarding the second requirement, by definition irrelevant in the liquidation procedure, the need for the asset in question in order to perform a reorganization that can qualify "effective" obviously requires something more than the mere instrumentality of the asset to the realization of the reorganization plan, also in consideration of the fact that, if that were the case, it would be very difficult to obtain a relief measure in the procedures initiated pursuant to Chapter 11 or other procedures with a recourse to recovery; the question has, moreover, been the subject of an important ruling by the Supreme Court of the United States, which in the United Savings Association of Texas v. Timbers of Inwood Forest Associates, Ltd., has specified that the adjective effective indicates the necessity of the recurrence of a feasible reorganization, that is of the reasonable possibility to reach a complete restructuring in reasonable time[322]: And only the good that is instrumental to the implementation of a reorganization having such characteristics will subtract the possibility of being subjected to a relief measure based on the assumptions under consideration[323]. It should be

[321]A.N. RESNICK, H.J. SOMMER, Collier on bankruptcy, op. cit., § 362.07[4][a]. S.V. KELLEY, Ginsberg & Martin on bankruptcy, op. cit., appropriately states that, in the assessment in question, all claims guaranteed by preemptive rights on the asset in question must be counted, and not only the credit of the individual: it is not, in fact, to establish whether there is equity for the creditor, but if there is for the debtor, and therefore for the procedure, which evidently can benefit from the liquidation of the asset where the proceeds are of a higher amount compared to the amount of the receivables guaranteed by it; in this sense see: P.A. MURPHY, E.E. SAGERMAN, D. NEIER, Creditor's rights in bankruptcy, op. cit., pp. 214ss. D.G. EPSTEIN, Bankruptcy and related law in a nutshell, op. cit. I. RAMSAY, Personal insolvency in the 21st century. A comparative analysis of the US and Europe, op. cit.

[322]S.V. KELLEY, Ginsberg & Martin on bankruptcy, op. cit., § 3.05[C]. W.R. NORTON, JR., Norton bankruptcy law and practice, op. cit. B.A. BLUM, Bankruptcy and debtor/creditor, op. cit., pp. 272ss. J.F. MURPHY, The automatic stay in bankruptcy, op. cit., pp. 608ss. R.M. MARTIN, Creditor alternatives to obtain relief from automatic stays in bankruptcy, op. cit., pp. 541ss.

[323]484 U.S. 365 (1988), which is affirmed that: "(...) There must be a reasonable possibility of a successful reorganization within a reasonable time". For further details see: A.N. RESNICK, H.J. SOMMER, Collier on bankruptcy, op. cit., § 362.07[4][b]. S.V. KELLEY, Ginsberg & Martin on bankruptcy, op. cit. § 05[C][1]. W.R. NORTON, JR., Norton bankruptcy law and practice, op. cit. D.R. COWANS, Cowans bankruptcy law and practice, op. cit., pp. 549ss. D.G. BAIRD, The elements of bankruptcy, op. cit., pp. 200ss. L.B. BARTELL, Visualizing bankruptcy, op. cit., pp. 96ss. P. A. MURPHY, E.E. SAGERMAN, D. NEIER, Creditor's rights in bankruptcy, op. cit., pp. 213ss. B.A. BLUM,

noted, however, that the rule is also considered applicable in the recovery procedures referred to in Chapters 12 and 13, with the only adaptation to understand the requirement referred to, rather than to reorganization, to debtor's rehabilitation[324]. In conclusion, where it appears that this subject has no possibility of feasible reorganization or rehabilitation, the release from the automatic stay may be granted (of course, where at the same time the subject has no equity in the asset in question); in the opposite case, instead, it will be necessary to go down to the next investigation plan, and to verify if the good object of the instance is functional to this reorganization, which therefore appears to be possible and reasonably practicable.

The third essential assumption for obtaining a release from the automatic stay was introduced by the reform of 1994[325] and subsequently amended by BAPCPA of 2005, and refers to the case called "single asset real estate case": This phrase, for the accuracy, is defined in Section 101 (51B), and indicates the procedure in which the active mass consists of a single immovable property (with the exclusion of the residential ones with less than four residential units), capable of generating substantially all debtor's income, which, moreover, do not exercise another business, except of the real estate asset[326]. Basically, we are dealing with a debtor whose sole economic activity is supplemented by the management of a

---

Bankruptcy and debtor/creditor, op. cit. D.G. EPSTEIN, Bankruptcy and related law in a nutshell, op. cit., pp. 57ss. D.G. EPSTEIN, Bankruptcy and related law in a nutshell, op. cit., pp. 134ss. J.F. MURPHY, The automatic stay in bankruptcy, op. cit. O. COUWENBERG, S. J. LUBBEN, Essential corporate bankruptcy law, op. cit. I. RAMSAY, Personal insolvency in the 21st century. A comparative analysis of the US and Europe, op. cit.

[324]A.N. RESNICK, H.J. SOMMER, Collier on bankruptcy, op. cit. S.V. KELLEY, Ginsberg & Martin on bankruptcy, op. cit., § 3.05[C]. B.A. BLUM, Bankruptcy and debtor/creditor, op. cit., pp. 273ss. D.G. EPSTEIN, Bankruptcy and related law in a nutshell, op. cit., pp. 130ss. J.F. MURPHY, The automatic stay in bankruptcy, op. cit., see also in argument the case: In re Scott, 121 B.R. 605 (1990), 607ss. I. RAMSAY, Personal insolvency in the 21st century. A comparative analysis of the US and Europe, op. cit.

[325]Pub. L. No. 103394 (1994).

[326]Section 101(51B): "The term "single asset real estate" means real property constituting a single property or project, other than residential real property with fewer than four residential units, which generates substantially all of the gross income of a debtor who is not a family farmer and on which no substantial business is being conducted by a debtor other than the business of operating the real property and activities incidental thereto (...)".

property he owns, and by the perception of the civil fruits deriving from it[327].

With regard to this case, Section 362 (d) (3) provides that the court must grant relief from the automatic stay operating on direct acts in respect of such immovable property, for the benefit of a creditor whose claim is guaranteed by an insistent right of pre-emption on the property itself, unless within a short time frame from the beginning of the procedure: a) The debtor deposits a recovery plan which presents a reasonable probability of being confirmed within a short period of time; or b) the debtor has started to make to all creditors, whose claim is guaranteed by such immovable property, monthly payments which, at the discretion of the former, may be made or by deductions from the rent received, or through other income generated from the asset itself before or after the start of the procedure, provided that such payments are also inclusive of the interest accrued by the creditors[328].

Law rationale, which evidently recognizes a considerable protection to privileged creditors, is that of repressing the abuses that, in the procedures considered therein, can be implemented to the detriment of the creditors themselves, prejudiced by the delays that forced sale transactions of the immovable property they inevitably suffer as a consequence of the operativity of the automatic stay, triggered by a pre-arranged deposit of the petition, implemented on the eve of the start of the executive procedure, and with the aim of delaying it. In such cases, where the possibility of reimbursement of the debtor is irrelevant, therefore, if a viable reorganization plan is not filed in good time, or the payments to creditors have not started, it is therefore stipulated that the relief provision, in the form of termination of the automatic stay, should be undoubtedly granted, to shorten the time necessary to

---

[327]B.A. BLUM, Bankruptcy and debtor/creditor, op. cit. J.B. BUTLER III, Section 362(d)(3): A singular provision of the Bankruptcy Code, in DePaul Business & Commercial Law Journal, 6, 2008, pp. 208ss.

[328]A.N. RESNICK, H.J. SOMMER, Collier on bankruptcy, op. cit., § 362.07[5]. S.V. KELLEY, Ginsberg & Martin on bankruptcy, op. cit., § 3.05[D]. W.R. NORTON, JR., Norton bankruptcy law and practice, op. cit., § 36:36. D.G. BAIRD, The elements of bankruptcy, op. cit., pp. 202ss. L.B. BARTELL, Visualizing bankruptcy, op. cit., O. COUWENBERG, S. J. LUBBEN, Essential corporate bankruptcy law, op. cit.

carry out the liquidation of the asset[329].

The fourth and last condition for granting the liberation provision from the automatic stay was introduced with the 2005 BAPCPA, and is known as "in rem relief", since it was founded, as will be seen, on a "in rem order", defined as directed against a specific asset. The particularity of this provision, as will be seen, is represented by its suitability to maintain its effectiveness even within the insolvency procedures that are initiated after the cessation of the one in which the provision was pronounced[330].

In detail, Section 362 (d) (4) provides that relief from the injunction to protect a property must be granted by the bankruptcy court for the benefit of a creditor holding an insistent right of pre-emption on it, where it is established that the deposit of the petition was part of a fraudulent design to the detriment of creditors, which provided for: a) The transfer of all or part of the property of that property without the consent of the privileged creditors or the approval of the court; or b) the serial filing of applications for admission to bankruptcy procedures all involving such immovable property[331].

---

[329]P.A. MURPHY, E.E. SAGERMAN, D. NEIER, Creditor's rights in bankruptcy, op. cit., pp. 217ss. D.G. EPSTEIN, Bankruptcy and related law in a nutshell, op. cit., A.N. RESNICK, Bankruptcy law manual, op. cit., pp. 113ss. J.B. BUTLER III, Section 362(d)(3): A singular provision of the Bankruptcy Code, op. cit., pp. 212ss. I. RAMSAY, Personal insolvency in the 21st century. A comparative analysis of the US and Europe, op. cit.

[330]To be precise, according to section 362 (d) (4) the bankruptcy court must pronounce release from the injunction, "(...) with respect to a stay of an act against real property under subsection (a), by a creditor whose claim is secured by an interest in such real property, if the court finds that the filing of the petition was part of a scheme to delay, hinder, or defraud creditors that involved either (A) transfer of all or part ownership of, or other interest in, such real property without the consent of the secured creditor or court approval; or (B) multiple bankruptcy filings affecting such real property". See, A.N. RESNICK, H.J. SOMMER, Collier on bankruptcy, op. cit., § 362.07[6]. S.V. KELLEY, Ginsberg & Martin on bankruptcy, op. cit., L.B. BARTELL, Visualizing bankruptcy, op. cit., P.A. MURPHY, E.E. SAGERMAN, D. NEIER, Creditor's rights in bankruptcy, op. cit., pp. 218ss. B.A. BLUM, Bankruptcy and debtor/creditor, op. cit., pp. 274ss. D.G. EPSTEIN, Bankruptcy and related law in a nutshell, op. cit., pp. 58ss. I. RAMSAY, Personal insolvency in the 21st century. A comparative analysis of the US and Europe, op. cit.

[331]Section 362 (b) (20) provides that filing of the application for admission to one of the procedures regulated therein: "(...) Does not operate as a stay […] under subsection (a), of any act to enforce any lien against or security interest in real property following entry of the order under subsection (d)(4) as to such real property in any prior case under this title,

Clearly, this is a provision similar to the one referred to in the previous number (3), since it also pertains an initiative concerning the immovable property of the debtor, but of more general application, and generically aimed at repressing fraudulent phenomena, integrated also through serial filings, suitable to jeopardize the possibility of satisfaction of a creditor who has a right of first refusal on said good. Moreover, unlike the previous rule, in this case, the court's assessment of the abusive conduct observed by the debtor will undoubtedly follow the granting of the provision of relief from the automatic stay, without the possibility for that subject to escape to this result by carrying out appropriate activities to ensure adequate protection of credit claims.

The provision, called "in rem order", pronounced under number (4), where it is noted in the appropriate registers, maintains binding effectiveness in bankruptcy proceedings that are launched in the two years following its ruling, with the effect, therefore, to prevent the application of automatic stay in respect of the goods considered in it, unless the debtor does not ask the court for its fall due to changed circumstances or due cause.

This discipline is completed with the exception codified in Section 362 (b) (20), where it is envisaged that in the procedures initiated in the two years following the ruling of the provision now in comment, the automatic stay does not operate with regard to the acts aimed at implementing a right of pre-emption existing on the real estate in this provision considered, except, again, that the debtor does not take action to obtain its removal: The registration of the relief provision and the exception connected to it allow, in other words, that the release from the preclusive effectiveness connected to the course of automatic stay can benefit all creditors in the next two years, and not just the one originally for liberation.

Finally, a special discipline is dictated with regard to the conditions for obtaining a relief measure from the codebtor stay[332]. In this

---

for a period of two year after the date of the entry of such an order, except that the debtor, in a subsequent case under this title, may move for relief from such order based upon changed circumstances or for other good cause shown, after notice and a hearing (...)".

[332]A.N. RESNICK, H.J. SOMMER, Collier on bankruptcy, op. cit., § 362.05[19][a]. S.V. KELLEY, Ginsberg & Martin on bankruptcy, op. cit., § 3.02[J][10]. L.B. BARTELL,

regard, Section 1301 (c) of the Bankruptcy Code provides, inter alia, that this provision may be granted, with the possibility for the creditor to act against the co-obligor, in cases where the recovery plan does not provide full payment of the secured credit from this subject, or in cases where the continuation of the codebtor stay, and the consequent delay in the possibility of carrying out its claim, derives irreparable damage to the interests of the creditor[333].

38.Nature and object of judgment.

As can be seen from rule 4001 of the Federal Rules of Bankruptcy Procedures, which in describing the introductory act (motion) of the judgment in question refers to the subsequent rule 9014[334], the procedure for the liberation from the automatic stay belongs to contested matters, i.e. a kind of deformed procedure, in which it is not necessary for the parties to make use of the patronage of a lawyer, nor, for the defendant, to present a defensive statement (answer)[335].

Visualizing bankruptcy, op. cit., pp. 81ss.

[333]A.N. RESNICK, H.J. SOMMER, Collier on bankruptcy, op. cit., 3, § 362.08[1]. S.V. KELLEY, Ginsberg & Martin on bankruptcy, op. cit., op. cit., § 3.06[A]. W.R. NORTON, JR., Norton bankruptcy law and practice, op. cit., § 36:32. D.R. COWANS, Cowans bankruptcy law and practice, op. cit., pp. 557ss. P.A. MURPHY, E.E. SAGERMAN, D. NEIER, Creditor's rights in bankruptcy, op. cit., pp. 200ss. B.A. BLUM, Bankruptcy and debtor/creditor, op. cit., pp. 268ss. J.F. MURPHY, The automatic stay in bankruptcy, op. cit., pp. 592ss. A.N. RESNICK, H. J. SOMMER, Collier on bankruptcy, op. cit., 8, § 1301.03[2][b] and [c]. L.B. BARTELL, Visualizing bankruptcy, op. cit., pp. 98ss. R.M. MARTIN, Creditor alternatives to obtain relief from automatic stays in bankruptcy, op. cit., pp. 544ss.

[334]The contested matters are opposed to the so-called adversary proceedings and, together with these, integrate the two forms of proceedings in which bankruptcy disputes are subdivided. The adversary proceedings, in particular, are characterized by a higher rate of formality and technical reason why generally the parties are represented by a lawyer, and start with the filing of a complaint to which the defendant must answer with a answer. It should also be noted that, as required by rule 9014 (c), the bankruptcy court may order that the disciplinary rules of the adversary proceedings must also be applied to a contested procedure. On this distinction, see: D.R. COWANS, Cowans bankruptcy law and practice, op. cit., pp. 417ss.

[335]In this, moreover, the discipline of the today's Federal Rules of Bankruptcy Procedures differs from the system of the previous rules, where the procedure for the liberation from the automatic stay was qualified as adversary proceeding. In the matter, W.R. NORTON, JR., Norton bankruptcy law and practice, op. cit., L. PEITZMAN, M.S. SMITH, The secured creditor's complaint: Relief from the automatic stays in bankruptcy proceedings, op. cit., pp. 1241ss.

The circumstance that in the procedure for the release of automatic stay, attributable to the contested matters, the debtor or the trustee is not required to proceed with the deposit of a answer is obviously reflected on the configuration of the thema decidendum of the related judgment: Being, in fact, the only procedural act unavoidably present on the scene constituted by the motion presented by the instant entity for the liberation, the minimum object of the judgment will be identified by the alleged motion contained in it. Secondly, the mere faculty of filing the answer is worth, then, to exclude the applicability, in the present judgment, of the discipline on compulsory counterclaims, namely that concerning the claims that the defendant must necessarily assert, under penalty of forfeiture, in the context of the already pending judgment[336]; but, even in the event that the debtor or the trustee decide to file a answer, the possibility of advancing a counterclaim seems to be excluded from the intentio legis expressed by House Reports, where it is clearly stated that the summary and deformed nature of the judgment, as well the requirements of rapidity that characterize it, make it unsuitable to become the seat for knowing and deciding different claims from its main object, that is the request for liberation from the automatic stay[337], with a foreclosure, in the end, of any possibility of widening the objective scope of the proceeding. Note, however, that what is said refers to the possibility that the counterclaims proposed in the context of a judgment of relief from the automatic stay are known and decided by the bankruptcy court with the efficacy of res judicata: Quite practicable, on the contrary, it remains the ability to know incidenter tantum, for the sole purpose, of course, to assess the actual existence of legitimacy and the substantial conditions for

[336]A.N. RESNICK, H.J. SOMMER, Collier on bankruptcy, op. cit., § 362.08[6]. W.R. NORTON, JR., Norton bankruptcy law and practice, op. cit. P.A. MURPHY, E.E. SAGERMAN, D. NEIER, Creditor's rights in bankruptcy, op. cit., pp. 203ss. For the previous system see: L. PEITZMAN, M.S. SMITH, The secured creditor's complaint: Relief from the automatic stays in bankruptcy proceedings, op. cit., pp. 1243ss. See also the case: In re Vitreous Steel Products Co., 911 F.2d 1223 (1990). For further details see: R.F. DUNCAN, W.H. LYONS, C.L. WILSON, The law and practice of secured transactions. Working with article 9, Law Journal Press, 2013, pp. 11ss.

[337]First Nat'l Bank of Denver v. Turley, 705 F.2d 1024 (1983), where a counterclaim claimed by the debtor was known for the sole purpose of denying the existence of a preemptive right for the instant creditor and thus denying him the legitimacy to promote the procedure for granting relief.

the granting of the provision and decide, thus, on the main claim, i.e. on the caducation of automatic stay[338].

In conclusion, judgment's object of liberation from the injunction must be reconstructed only on the basis of the motion presented by the instant subject: And it will be the right of that subject to obtain the relief provision, on the basis of the substantiated assumptions attached and tested[339].

39.(Follows) The procedure

It starts with a motion ("lift stay motion") presented by the entity that, subject to the injunction, has an interest in seeing it decayed. In this regard, the aforementioned rule 4001 continues by stating that such motion must be notified (served), as well as to debtor and his lawyer and trustee, to the creditors' committee, if appointed, or as an alternative to the creditors resulting from the list presented at the time of filing the petition, as well as any other person indicated by the court[340].

The parties to the proceedings will be, in addition to the instant subject, the trustee (debtor in possession), if the relief request relates to a property merged into the summer property or the debtor, if the initiative in question be directed against his person or his personal patrimony, even if the doctrine advises, for reasons of simplification, to quote both[341]. The other creditors, notified, as mentioned, of the presentation of the relief

---

[338]A.N. RESNICK, H.J. SOMMER, Collier on bankruptcy, op. cit., § 362.08[2]. S.V. KELLEY, Ginsberg & Martin on bankruptcy, op. cit. § 3.06[A]. J.F. MURPHY, The automatic stay in bankruptcy, op. cit., pp. 594ss. For the necessity of notifying the motion to the trustee, see the In re Doud case, 30 B.R. 731 (1983).

[339]D.R. COWANS, Cowans bankruptcy law and practice, op. cit., pp. 557ss. for the qualification of the trustee as an indispensable party, in the context of the previous rules, see the case In re DiBona, 7 B.R. 798 (1980). P.A. MURPHY, E.E. SAGERMAN, D. NEIER, Creditor's rights in bankruptcy op. cit., pp. 208ss.

[340]For some group reflections, and in particular for the qualification of the commented procedure and its accelerating characters as a re-balancing factor of a system in which the creditor necessarily sees and automatically blocked all his initiatives towards the debtor and the assets, W.R. NORTON, JR., Norton bankruptcy law and practice, op. cit., § 36:37. H.B. PICKARD, The new bankruptcy code, part II: The interests of secured creditors under the new bankruptcy code, op. cit., pp. 235ss. P.B. HAHN, Bankruptcy Code section 362(e): its application and effect, in Commercial Law Journal, 88, 1983, 195ss.

[341]S.V. KELLEY, Ginsberg & Martin on bankruptcy, op. cit. § 3.06[B]. P.A. MURPHY, E.E. SAGERMAN, D. NEIER, Creditor's rights in bankruptcy op. cit., 207ss. B.A. BLUM, Bankruptcy and debtor/creditor, op. cit.

request, may also intervene and oppose request, to the extent that, for example, they have an interest that the asset remains subject to the insolvency procedure and to distribution of proceeds in compliance with the principles of par condicio creditorum.

Although the judgment is counted among the contested matters, the legislation is not limited, in the position of the relative discipline, to make a deferment de plano to this system, but provides, with the subsection (e), to coin a special procedure, connoted, as will be seen, by accentuated characters[342]; this procedure, however, assumes different characteristics in the event that the debtor is a natural person subject to a procedure under Chapters 7, 11 or 13: We proceed, therefore, to examine, in the first instance, the ordinary regime, dictated by number (1) of the aforementioned subsection (e), and then turn the attention to the peculiar hypothesis just mentioned, governed by the following number (2).

However, it should be noted that the special procedure coined by subsection (e) meets application limits: The one governed by number (1), in fact, is intended to be applied with exclusive regard to relief requests from auto-stay to foreclosure "act against summer property", i.e. those based on the assumptions described in subsections (d) (2), (3) and (4), in which the markedly accelerating characters imprinted on the procedure find justification in the possible depreciation or risk of loss of the asset subject to the foreclosed initiative; on the other hand, the special procedure provided for in cases where the debtor is a natural person, governed by subsection (e) (2), does not encounter any limitations whatsoever. It remains therefore to ask what is the applicable procedure in the case in which a subject, different from the debtor natural person, demands the release from the inhibitory "for causes". In this regard, it seems reasonable to assume that the analogical application of the procedural modules dictated by Section (e), is justified in the case in which the instant subject shares the same risk of injury implied by the application of the accelerator modules of the same procedure[343].

---

[342]D.G. EPSTEIN, Bankruptcy and related law in a nutshell, op. cit. I. RAMSAY, Personal insolvency in the 21st century. A comparative analysis of the US and Europe, op. cit.

[343]The norm expected that: "(...) Thirty days after a request under subsection (d) of this section for relief from the stay of any act against property of the estate under subsection (a) of this section, such stay is terminated with respect to the party in interest making such

The reconstruction of the procedural procedure necessary to obtain a provision of relief from the automatic stay, is not, for real, an easy operation, and suffices, as confirmation of what has been stated, the reading of Section 362 (e) (1) that, instead of regulating the ordinary conduct of proceedings, provides to dictate the consequences related to a pathological outcome of the procedure. There is only provided, in fact, that within thirty days of the request of the aforementioned provision the bankruptcy court, at the end of a preliminary preliminary hearing, did not order the continuation of the injunction for the time necessary to reach the conclusion of the final hearing, the automatic stay terms with respect to the instant part for the provision[344]. The continuation, specifies the norm, will be ordered if a reasonable probability (reasonable likelihood) is found that the opposition proposed by the party opposing the request for relief is accepted in the final hearing[345]. Finally, it is expressly stipulated that it is not necessary to hold both hearings, but the preliminary can be "consolidated" to the final.

These fragmentary textual data allow us however to propose a reconstruction of the whole procedure and its possible developments. It is possible to state that within thirty days from the presentation of the motion a hearing must be held, where, presumably, the bankruptcy court will be called to carry out a prima facie assessment of the admissibility and the merits of application, also keeping in mind the opposition which, as incidentally tells us the norm, it can evidently be presented by the debtor or the trustee, as well as by other subjects (creditors above all) interested in it. Now, this evaluation appears preliminary to two possible developments: To the decision, that is, to consider such a hearing as final

---

request, unless the court, after notice and a hearing, orders such stay continued in effect pending the conclusion of, or as a result of, a final hearing and determination under subsection (d) of this section (...)".

[344]"The court shall order such stay continued in effect pending the conclusion of the final hearing under subsection (d) of this section if there is a reasonable likelihood that the party opposing relief from such stay will prevail at the conclusion of such final hearing (...)".

[345]The rule, in fact, requires that the final hearing be completed within thirty days of the conclusion of the preliminary hearing, unless the parties agree to extend the period of time or this is ordered by the court on the basis of force majeure. For more details see: A.N. RESNICK, H.J. SOMMER, Collier on bankruptcy, op. cit., § 362.08[5]. W.R. NORTON, JR., Norton bankruptcy law and practice op. cit., § 37, 37ss.

hearing and decide directly on the request for relief, or to qualify it as a preliminary, setting the final within a maximum of thirty days, in this second case, decide whether or not to order the continuation of the automatic stay until that date[346].

The first eventuality, that is, the assumption of an immediate decision on the request for relief without splitting between preliminary and final hearing, justified by the possibility of promptly providing on the relief requests of the easiest solution[347] appears to be the most reasonably practicable in the hypothesis of manifest inadmissibility, groundlessness o the validity of the question, what may happen, for example, when the subject appears to lack the necessary legitimacy to request release. In this case, it will be immediately notified of a provision rejecting the request for relief, with consequent survival of the automatic stay; and the same is true if, in the absence of opposition, the existence of presuppositions of the relief provision is manifest. All the other hypotheses, on the other hand, seem to merge into the other case mentioned, namely that in which it is necessary to proceed with a more in-depth examination of the material of the case and, thus, to follow a final hearing to the preliminary. When the court determines the final hearing is also required to issue a provision of continuation of the automatic stay for the hypothesis in which the opposition proposed by the debtor, the trustee or other legitimate subject has a reasonable probability of to be accepted. It is therefore necessary to distinguish according to whether the opposition is presented or not. In the first case, in particular, to the probable merits of the opposition will obtain the ruling of the conservative provision of the aforementioned prohibition. In the hypothesis of non-proposition of the opposition, or even of the absence of the requirement inherent to its probable acceptance accompanied, it is understood, by the necessity of subjecting to a more in-depth examination the existence of the substantial assumptions affirmed by the instant, the court, on the contrary, it must ascertain the termination of the automatic stay towards the applicant for release.

---

[346]A.N. RESNICK, H.J. SOMMER, Collier on bankruptcy, op. cit. P.A. MURPHY, E.E. SAGERMAN, D. NEIER, Creditor's rights in bankruptcy op. cit.

[347]In this sense see: A.N. RESNICK, H.J. SOMMER, Collier on bankruptcy, op. cit., § 362.08[4][b]. W.R. NORTON, JR., Norton bankruptcy law and practice, op. cit., § 36:38.

This, obviously, can only create complications for the true hypothesis, very rare given the composition of the judging organ, which remains the same in which in the subsequent final hearing it is ascertained that the summary evaluation performed in the preliminary hearing was erroneous, with consequent necessity to pronounce a provision modifying the provisionally pronounced one and affirming the persistent vigor of the automatic stay; note, however, that the effectiveness of this inhibition can only be retroactive to the date of the previous hearing. The found absence of the necessary conditions for the ruling of the relief provision, in fact, implies that the caduce provision of the automatic stay was ab origin unproductive effects, with the consequence that any acts carried out in the medium term should be considered in violation of the injunction[348].

The terms, of very short duration, dictated to mark the succession of procedural steps preliminary to the decision on the request for relief, are justified, as mentioned, in the need for the dispute in question to be resolved in quick times, especially in cases where the delayed realization of the claim of a privileged creditor risks of resolving into irreparable prejudice for this subject; for this reason, therefore, if these deadlines are not respected (the ruling, within thirty days following the presentation of the motion, of a provisional provision that orders the continuation of automatic stay or that decides on the application, to second that the preliminary and final hearing are consolidated or not, the conclusion of the final hearing within thirty days of the preliminary, in this second case), the automatic stay towards summer property will end, for the benefit of the instant subject, as sanction related to a development of the pathological process and contrary to the rationes legislatoris.

As mentioned, in the subsection (e) (2), inserted by 2005BAPCPA, the law provides to dictate a procedure for obtaining a relief measure in the cases in which the debtor is subject to a procedure governed by

---

[348]S.V. KELLEY, Ginsberg & Martin on bankruptcy, op. cit., W.R. NORTON, JR., Norton bankruptcy law and practice, op. cit., § 36:37. D.R. COWANS, Cowans bankruptcy law and practice, op. cit., pp. 559ss. L.B. BARTELL, Visualizing bankruptcy, op. cit., pp. 94ss. B.A. BLUM, Bankruptcy and debtor/creditor, op. cit. A.N. RESNICK, Bankruptcy law manual, op. cit., pp. 116ss. H.B. PICKARD, The new bankruptcy code, part II: The interests of secured creditors under the new bankruptcy code, op. cit. R.A. JOHNSON, M.C. O'LEARY, Automatic stay provisions of the bankruptcy act of 1978, op. cit., pp. 613ss.

Chapters 7, 11 or 13 and be a natural person; the disposition, differentiating itself in this from the prediction enclosed in the preceding number (1) which, as mentioned, is limited to the "stay of any act against the property of the summer", finds its application scope with undifferentiated regard to the "stay under subsection" (a)[349].

Also in this case the chosen normative technique was to regulate the sanction foreseen for the case of pathological development of the procedure, rather than to describe the joints of the same; however, the more straightforward conduct of the judgment does not pose the interpretative problems addressed earlier. In particular, it is provided that the automatic stay ends sixty days after the relief request has been submitted if by that date the court has not issued a final decision on the application, or has not provided for the extension of the mentioned period of sixty days at the request of all the interested parties or for the period deemed necessary by the recurrence of the right reasons[350].

Even here, obviously, the legislator intervenes to punish the developments of the procedure that do not respect the temporal scans impressed on it to give speed and speed to the judgment for obtaining release from the automatic stay and intervenes to the detriment of the procedure, right in function of the realization of the rebalancing of the positions of the parts involved in it, which has been said several times.

---

[349]Section 362(e)(2): "Not withstanding paragraph (1), in a case under chapter 7, 11, or 13 in which the debtor is an individual, the stay under subsection (a) shall terminate on the date that is sixty days after a request is made by a party in interest under subsection (d), unless (A) a final decision is rendered by the court during the 60day period beginning on the date of the request; or (B) such sixty day period is extended (i) by agreement of all parties in interest; or (ii) by the court for such specific period of time as the court finds is required for good cause, as described in findings made by the court (...)".

[350]W.R. NORTON, JR., Norton bankruptcy law and practice, op. cit., § 36:40. D.R. COWANS, Cowans bankruptcy law and practice, op. cit., pp. 564ss. L.B. BARTELL, Visualizing bankruptcy, op. cit. P.A. MURPHY, E.E. SAGERMAN, D. NEIER, Creditor's rights in bankruptcy, op. cit., pp. 204ss. B.A. BLUM, Bankruptcy and debtor/creditor, op. cit. A.N. RESNICK, Bankruptcy law manual, op. cit., pp. 119ss. H.B. PICKARD, The new bankruptcy code, part II: The interests of secured creditors under the new bankruptcy code, op. cit. R.A. JOHNSON, M.C. O'LEARY, Automatic stay provisions of the bankruptcy act of 1978, op. cit., pp. 614ss. F.R. KENNEDY, Automatic stays under the new bankruptcy law, op. cit., pp. 42ss. R.M. MARTIN, Creditor alternatives to obtain relief from automatic stays in bankruptcy, in Banking Law Journal, 98, 1981, pp. 552ss. S. PARSONS, Consumer bankruptcy law in focus, op. cit.

40.The unprecedented procedure alters part (ex parte relief).

In order to cope with the imminent and irreparable prejudices that even the special procedure illustrated in the previous paragraph does not seem to be able to avert, Section 362 (f) of the Bankruptcy Code, supplemented by rule 4001 (a) (2) of the Federal Rules of Bankruptcy Procedures, has introduced a procedure for the request for release from the automatic stay suitable to ensure that the subject is able to obtain the provision sought in even faster times[351].

The first provision mentioned above provides, in particular, that where the relief provision is indispensable in order to prevent irreparable damage to legal position of the entity subject to the injunction, which will occur before it is possible to arrange for the counterparty to meet a special hearing in order to guarantee the adversarial performance of the petition, the court, at the request of the instant party, can decide "with or without a hearing" but in any case without the fulfillment of prescribed formalities. The meaning of this rule is better clarified by the provisions of the aforementioned rule 4001 (a) (2) which, in delineating the procedural profiles of the judgment in question, immediately recognizes the possibility of obtaining the release from the injunction "without prior notice", i.e. without notification to the debtor, the trustee, or other interested parties of the presentation of the motion, and with the consequent possibility, therefore, that the court decides on the application without prior agreement of the adversarial towards such parties[352].

The practicability of this unprecedented process alters part, which

[351]Section 362(f) expects that: "(...) Upon request of a party in interest, the court, with or without a hearing, shall grant such relief from the stay provided under subsection (a) of this section as is necessary to prevent irreparable damage to the interest of an entity in property, if such interest will suffer such damage before there is an opportunity for notice and a hearing under subsection (d) or (e) of this section (...)".

[352]See: Rule 4001(a)(2) for the interesting part: "Ex Parte Relief. Relief from a stay under § 362(a) (...) may be granted without prior notice only if (A) it clearly appears from specific facts shown by affidavit or by a verified motion that immediate and irreparable injury, loss, or damage will result to the movant before the adverse party or the attorney for the adverse party can be heard in opposition, and (B) the movant's attorney certifies to the court in writing the efforts, if any, which have been made to give notice and the reasons why notice should not be required (...) ".

in the US bankruptcy system is known as "ex parte relief", is conditional on the existence of two cumulative circumstances: First, it must appear clearly, from specific facts provided evidence, that the instant would suffer an imminent and irreparable damage or loss in the time necessary to establish the adversarial towards the counterpart or his lawyer, in particular allowing them to present the objection to the request; secondly, the lawyer of the instant party must declare in writing any efforts made to perform the notification, and the reason why the execution of this cannot, in the end, be requested as necessary and indispensable. From this it emerges that the usability of the judgment inaudita altera presupposes not only the presence of a periculum in mora of such entity that it cannot be averted even through the use of the procedure referred to in subsection (e), in the sense of not tolerating the temporal extension imposed therein to allow the counterparts to propose an opposition, but also that the party, although prejudiced, has attempted to inform the other party of the presentation of the relief application, but this proved to be impossible, or rather it is appropriate it is not carried out at all, for example when the counterparty could, once the notice of such request has been received, perform acts that are suitable to whip the purpose of the provision. This last circumstance leads us to face a problem posed by the text of the norm. As said, these elements must be used, as expressly required by law, by using the conjunction "and", cumulatively: An aspect, this, which cannot leave perplexing, especially in the hypothesis in which case happens where periculum in arrears and the need to attach that the prior call of the counterparty could jeopardize the implementation of the provision with regard to requirements having their own autonomy, and which should therefore be placed as alternative conditions of access to the procedure in question. The system thus shaped, in the end, appears to be characterized by excessive rigidity, as well as by selectable choices even on a purely logical level.

The fact that the contradictory is initially omitted, so as to allow the instant subject to obtain as soon as possible a measure suitable to protect his interests, exposed to an imminent and irreparable prejudice, does not exclude that it may be established in the next epoch. We are in the presence, in other words, of a case of a possible and deferred contradiction. This is evidenced by the same rule 4001 (a) (2), which goes on to prescribe that the person who has obtained the relief provision in unprecedented forms alters part of communicating orally to the trustee (debtor in possession) and to the debtor the concession of provision, and to send by post or by other appropriate means a copy of the same; with two days notice (or even less, if the court decides so) to be guaranteed to the person who has obtained the relief provision, the other party can then request the restoration of the automatic stay: In this case, the court must proceed quickly to know and decide on this request[353].

41.The burden of proof.

In examining the substantial assumptions to which the possibility of obtaining a relief measure from the automatic stay is linked, we have limited ourselves to the description of the relevant cases, without even pushing into the procedural dimension to question the discipline concerning their proof, in particular for identify the onerous part of the demonstration of the individual facts integrating the cases illustrated, and the consequences of the failure to discharge this charge.

The reasons for the deferral of this analysis are soon explained: Section 362 of the Bankruptcy Code, in sub-section (g), expressly provides for the allocation of probative burdens on the existence of the substantial conditions of release from the automatic stay, so it was considered appropriate to devote a deepening party to this issue.

Starting from the textual data, the aforementioned standard places the release of the automatic stay "the burden of proof" on the requesting party regarding the lack of the equity debtor in property, and on the party who opposes such request "the burden of proof" on all other issues[354].

Before proceeding with a deepening of the law, it is however

---

[353]A.N. RESNICK, H.J. SOMMER, Collier on bankruptcy, op. cit., § 362.09. S.V. KELLEY, Ginsberg & Martin on bankruptcy, op. cit. § 3.06[D]. R. NORTON, JR., Norton bankruptcy law and practice, op. cit. P.A. MURPHY, E.E. SAGERMAN, D. NEIER, Creditor's rights in bankruptcy op. cit., pp. 205ss. A.N. RESNICK, Bankruptcy law manual, op. cit.

[354]Section 362(g), affirms that: "In any hearing under subsection (d) or (e) of this section concerning relief from the stay of any act under subsection (a) of this section (1) the party requesting such relief has the burden of proof on the issue of the debtor's equity in property; and (2) the party opposing such relief has the burden of proof on all other issues (...)".

appropriate to clarify the system of allocation of probative burdens in US system: If the expression "burden of proof", in fact, assumed in this context a meaning equivalent to our rule of the burden of proof is evident as the tenor of Section 362 (g) illustrated, would raise, not a few perplexities since, to say nothing of the fact that the rule often leads to the result of requesting the proof of a negative fact, with regard to the case governed by subsection (d) (1) the debtor would be required to prove the inexistence of the "cause" attached by the instant subject in order to avoid the granting of the provision of relief, therefore, with a distortion of the general rule according to which "who wants to assert a right in court must prove the facts which constitute the foundation"[355], while with regard to the following subsection (d) (2) the instant subject would be charged to prove only a fragment of the case constituting his right, namely the lack of equity in property for the debtor, while burden on the debtor the burden of proving that the property is necessary for the reorganization, delineating in conclusion a system that is struggling to appear to the criteria of absolute rationality, as well as to reconcile with the reconstruction, here proposed, which qualifies the judgment in comment as a tool aimed at giving the judge evidence contrary to the presumption legal relative based on the automatic stay.

However, it is known that the system of allocation of probative burdens diverges, in the United States, from the rules known to us, since there is a double level of such division, historically and conceptually justified by the presence, in this system, of the jury next to togato judge[356]: There is distinguished, in fact, between "burden of proof", understood as "duty of producing evidence to judge", i.e. a duty towards the judge, and "burden of persuasion", understood as "risk of non persuasion of the jury", and therefore descended from a relationship existing with the jury[357]. Since, in fact, the role of the judge, as administrator of justice, is also to

[355]M. REDMAYNE, Character evidence in the criminal trial, Oxford University Press, Oxford, 2015.

[356]J.H. WIGMORE, A treatise on the angloAmerican system of evidence, Little Brown, Boston, 1940, pp. 266, 278ss. J.B. THAYER, The burden of proof, in Harvard Law Review 4, 1890, pp. 48ss. M. REDMAYNE, Character evidence in the criminal trial, op. cit.

[357]J.H. WIGMORE, A treatise on the angloAmerican system of evidence, op. cit., pp. 266ss.M. REDMAYNE, Character evidence in the criminal trial, op. cit.

guide the action of the jury within the boundaries of reasonableness, the parties are charged, in the first instance, to demonstrate to that subject that they are in possession sufficient evidence to be considered by the jury and be reasonably placed on the basis of the verdict that the same is called to pronounce: This is obviously duty of producing evidence to judge, verified by a prima facie assessment[358]; only the fulfillment of this burden allows, therefore, the party to submit the material of the case, including the evidence produced, to the jury, and check if it is "persuaded". It is at this second level, in other words, that the burden of persuasion, which ultimately distributes the risk of non-persuasion of the jury between the parties, requiring the subject wishing to obtain a favorable verdict from the jury to persuade her about the truth of the facts that constitute the foundation of the requested decision. The identification of the facts on which the persuasion of the jury must take shape, is a determination that concerns the substantive law, while the procedural norms that, generally, distribute the burden of such persuasion between the parties, accepting the most disparate principles (including for example, the principle that the party attaching a positive fact, that is, the one that has the easiest means of knowing a certain kind of principle of closeness to the trial, is burdened by the relative burden of persuasion).

Now, the subject who wants to obtain a favorable provision on an affirmed situation (and therefore, in the last instance, the one who is burdened by the burden of persuasion about the existence of the attached facts), is generally also the subject who, in the first instance, must fulfill his duty of producing evidence to the judge, whose positive outcome will lead him, in fact, to the possibility of being submitted to the jury's judgment; at this point, two scenarios are possible: If the risk of non-persuasion is taken as the definitive criterion of judgment, the evaluation of the evidence produced by the parties will follow the rules of the preponderance of evidence and, if the subject incumbent fails to fulfill his burden of persuasion, he will suffer the consequences of the aforementioned rule, and cannot therefore obtain a favorable verdict, while

[358]J.H. WIGMORE, A treatise on the angloAmerican system of evidence, op. cit., pp. 278ss.; J. B. THAYER, The burden of proof, cit., pp. 57ss. E.M. MORGAN, How to approach burden of proof and presumptions, in Harvard Law Review 44, 1931, pp. 36ss.

the other party will win the case; but it is also possible that, for the operation of certain legal rules (for example, a presumption operating in favor of the instant subject), we cannot immediately decide based on the risk of non-persuasion of the jury but, to rebalance the position between the parties, the judge must ask the other party to produce sufficient evidence, suitable to fulfill his duty of producing evidence to the judge (which, in the proposed example, will overcome the legal presumption acting), so that, in the absence of such compliance, it will be the counterparty to be unsuccessful by judicial decision, while in the opposite case, its preliminary productions will pass to jury's examination, where it will come back to verify if the original subject was acquitted to his burden of persuasion according to the rules of evidence preponderance. The summary illustration of the system just carried out shows, in short, how the duty of producing evidence to judge is suitable for moving from one side of the judgment to another, depending on the stage in which it is located and the relative procedural developments; while the burden of persuasion, on the contrary, being established by law, remains unchanged, generally weighing on the part that affirms the fact whose existence is linked to the granting of the required protection.

Now, returning to evaluate the hypothesis of the allocation of probative burdens within the judgment for the liberation from the automatic stay, the phrase "burden of proof" present in the text of Section 362 (g) refers to the second of the aforementioned meanings, i.e. the distribution of the risk of non-persuasion between the parties to said judgment[359].

This means, firstly, that, according to the general rule mentioned above, the duty of producing evidence to the judge on the subject of immediate relief will be the burden of proving the prima facie existence of the conditions legitimizing the request: Therefore, evidently, the non-fulfillment of this charge implies that the request for relief must be immediately rejected by the court.

[359]A.N. RESNICK, H.J. SOMMER, Collier on bankruptcy, op. cit. S.V. KELLEY, Ginsberg & Martin on bankruptcy, op. cit. § 3.06[C]. W.R. NORTON, JR., Norton bankruptcy law and practice, op. cit., § 36:41; B.A. BLUM, Bankruptcy and debtor/creditor, op. cit., 270; In jurisprudence see: In re Eatman, 182 B.R. 386 (1995).

On the other hand, where the instant part provides to provide the evidence that, to this summary evaluation, appear suitable to found the request for relief, the next plan of the investigation, i.e. the distribution of the burden of persuasion, is dictated by the same Section 362 (g): Thus, it will be up to that party who opposes the relief request to demonstrate that adequate protection is guaranteed to the creditor and therefore, for example, that the asset on which the guarantee is insured is not being depreciated, while in view of the creditor's demonstration of the lack of equity in property held by the debtor, he must follow the demonstration by the latter or the trustee that such property is in any case necessary for the successful outcome of an effective reorganization or rehabilitation[360].

The discipline here exposed may appear excessively biased to the disadvantage of the subject/debtor or trustee who opposes the request for relief. This observation may also appear to be fundamental, however, to remember that the initial duty of producing evidence to the judge always weighs on the instant subject, yet such a discipline is perfectly compatible with the overall functioning system of the automatic stay, which has already been repeated several times. We have had the opportunity to describe: if this is automatically and unavoidably produced with the deposit of the petition, it must on the other hand be allowed the subjects who indiscriminately suffer such inhibitory effects an agile possibility of access to a procedure that allows them to overcome the rebuttable presumption placed against them, while those who had benefited at first from the discipline of favor should now have to prove the legitimacy of the suspensive effects gained[361]; on the other hand, the allocation of the burden of persuasion of the facts mentioned above to the debtor appears

---

[360]A.N. RESNICK, H.J. SOMMER, Collier on bankruptcy, op. cit., S.V. KELLEY, Ginsberg & Martin on bankruptcy, op. cit., L.B. BARTELL, Visualizing bankruptcy, op. cit., pp. 96ss. P. A. MURPHY, E.E. SAGERMAN, D. NEIER, Creditor's rights in bankruptcy, op. cit., pp. 221ss.

[361]For more analysis see: B.A. BLUM, Bankruptcy and debtor/creditor, op. cit., 270ss.: "The burden is allocated in this way because the stay is a form of injunction. As it is automatic, the trustee or the debtor do not have to apply for it and are initially relieved of the burden of establishing grounds for it. This places them in a better position than the normal applicant for an injunction, who must show grounds for relief. Therefore, once the continuation of the stay is challenged, the debtor or trustee must take up the burden of justifying its remaining in effect (...)".

to be an entirely reasonable solution, since it is entirely consistent with the principle of proximity to the means of proof which, as we have seen, also finds citizenship in the United States.

42.Possible contents of the final provision and its effectiveness.

Although reference has been made, in the preceding paragraphs, to a provision of "liberation" from the automatic stay, or, at most, to its generically caducatory effect, on this inhibitory, Section 362 (d) provides to articulate the possible contents of the relief provision that is granted to the instant party, specifying the possibility of operating "terminating, annulling, modifying, or conditioning" the automatic stay[362].

It emerges, therefore, how the effect linked to the provision of granting the liberation from the automatic stay is not unique and immutable, granting the law to the judge the possibility of modulating it according to four different contents, obviously in order to better adapt to the needs of the concrete case[363]. In particular, the possibilities of modifying or conditioning the automatic stay, as will be better seen, less radically affect the suspensive efficacy in question with regard to the cessation or cancellation measures: Since the system of protective effects is inspired, as mentioned, to a marked favor debitoris, the court will resort to the last two measures mentioned only if the appropriate part cannot be guaranteed adequate protection by resorting to the first, and least ablative, measures mentioned. The result is, in essence, a system of measures with progressively incisive content of the automatic stay, where the recourse to the one that most intervenes to impair its actual scope is justified only to the extent that a measure with a lighter impact is not suitable to guarantee to the subject in question the required protection[364]. We proceed, therefore, to analyze in detail the different contents that the provision of relief can

---

[362]D.G. EPSTEIN, Bankruptcy and related law in a nutshell, op. cit. I. RAMSAY, Personal insolvency in the 21st century. A comparative analysis of the US and Europe, op. cit.
[363]A.N. RESNICK, H.J. SOMMER, Collier on bankruptcy, op. cit., § 362.07[1]. P.A. MURPHY, E.E. SAGERMAN, D. NEIER, Creditor's rights in bankruptcy, op. cit., pp. 200ss. B.A. BLUM, Bankruptcy and debtor/creditor, op. cit., pp. 268ss.
[364]J.F. MURPHY, The automatic stay in bankruptcy, op. cit., pp. 612ss. D.R. COWANS, Cowans bankruptcy law and practice, op. cit., pp. 529ss. J.F. MURPHY, The automatic stay in bankruptcy, op. cit., pp. 597ss.

take, in order of increasing intensity.

First of all, the automatic stay can be conditioned, that is, maintained in the condition that the debtor or the trustee perform some specific obligations, indicated in the same provision, obviously functional to ensure that creditor's situation is adequately protected: If, for example, the request for relief is based on the fact that the interest in property claimed by the subject is suffering, the court can pronounce the continuation of the automatic stay on the condition that the trustee takes steps to ensure that this prejudice ceases, or is adequately compensated. It is therefore immediately apparent that this represents the mildest form of judicial intervention on the automatic stay.

The provision to modify the automatic stay, then, has the peculiarity of affecting the injunction allowing the party subjected to the free exercise of some, but not the whole, of its rights, or the fulfillment of only some "procedural steps": An example is represented by the provision that allows a subject to initiate forced expropriation (foreclosure action), but prohibits it from proceeding with the sale of the asset, ie the one that allows to start or continue a judgment in the extra-bankruptcy (possibly also through the possibility of invoking an arbitration agreement), but not to continue with the execution of the sentence obtained there[365]. The amendment provision is the most frequently granted against a request for release.

The possibility for the court to adjudicate by ordering the cessation of the automatic stay, then, allows the instant party to free himself from the prohibitions connected to the injunction and to start or continue the action previously precluded; the termination of the automatic stay operates, of course, from the ruling of the judicial provision, and therefore ex nunc[366].

Finally, the possibility of pronouncing the cancellation of the

---

[365]A.N. RESNICK, H.J. SOMMER, Collier on bankruptcy, op. cit. D.R. COWANS, Cowans bankruptcy law and practice, op. cit. J.F. MURPHY, The automatic stay in bankruptcy, op. cit., 596ss.

[366]B.A. BLUM, Bankruptcy and debtor/creditor, op. cit.; on the possibility of modifying the automatic stay to allow the continuation of a civil judgment, see also the contribution of F. VAZQUEZ, Modification of automatic stay to permit litigation to proceed remains possible, op. cit.

automatic stay, in addition to being a central aspect of the discipline in the matter of relief, assumes a more general systematic value, especially as it can be inferred with regard to the discussed regime of acts performed in violation of the injunction. The possibility of canceling the automatic stay, in fact, implies that the related provision is effective retroactively or ex tunc differentiating, in this, from the mere cessation measure just illustrated, as well as from the other measures, all operating ex nunc, with the possibility, i.e. to validate the acts performed by the instant subject even in the presence of inhibition: Since, in fact, even US law excludes the possibility of validating a null act (void), subsisting this power only with regard to a voidable act (voidable), part of the doctrine and jurisprudence has deduced that the act performed in violation of the automatic stay is merely voidable, and not void[367]. The provision in question, for the particular effects that connote it, is regarded as an exceptional provision, and therefore only accessible in particular circumstances, such as when the debtor has abused the procedure and the creditor, in good faith, did not know of the entry in force of the injunction[368].

Finally, a mention deserves the provision that rejects the request for relief from the automatic stay: In this case, obviously, the inhibitory will remain in force, subject to the legal regime of termination prepared by Section 362 (c), with possible fulfillment of the discharge order, where this is granted. With regard to the effectiveness of the provision of relief from the automatic stay, it has already been possible, in the course of the discussion, to anticipate some aspects.

First of all, the reference is to what we have just observed in relation to the relative course, connected to the peculiar content that it assumes: Ex tunc, in the event of a cancellation of the injunction, ex nunc, from the date of its ruling , in all other cases. It should be added that rule 4001 (a) (3), registered as "stay of order" provides that the provision that

---

[367]A.N. RESNICK, H.J. SOMMER, Collier on bankruptcy, op. cit. S.V. KELLEY, Ginsberg & Martin on bankruptcy, op. cit., § 3.01[B][2]. D.R. COWANS, Cowans bankruptcy law and practice, op. cit. P.A. MURPHY, E.E. SAGERMAN, D. NEIER, Creditor's rights in bankruptcy, op. cit., pp. 201ss. B.A. BLUM, Bankruptcy and debtor/creditor, op. cit. J.F. MURPHY, The automatic stay in bankruptcy, op. cit., pp. 597ss.

[368]S.V. KELLEY, Ginsberg & Martin on bankruptcy, op. cit., B.A. BLUM, Bankruptcy and debtor/creditor, op. cit., pp. 269ss. In jurisprudence see case Franklin Sav. Ass'n v. Office of Thrift Supervision, 31 F.3d 1020 (1994).

accepts the request for relief remains suspended for fourteen days from its ruling, unless the court decides otherwise: Because, however, the ability to shorten or eliminate this suspension is generally recognized in the cases in which this would entail for the creditor the risk of irreparable damage, the aforementioned provision does not, by definition, operate with regard to the measures obtained at the outcome of the unprecedented procedure[369]. Once this period of suspension has elapsed, the provision in question becomes provisionally enforceable, in accordance with the rooms of urgency and speed that characterize the procedure for granting relief; the proposition of the appeal (appeal) against the provision is not, however, capable of automatically suspending its effectiveness, so that in the case where, for example, the debtor fails to obtain from the court of second instance a ruling that suspends provisionally the contested relief measure, the creditor may proceed in its action even while the judgment of encumbrance is pending.

But already it has been possible to mention also the regime of conservation of the effects produced by the measure in comment, especially in the case of conversion of procedures: Since, in fact, this case does not involve the change of the date of filing of the first (and only) petition, the automatic operating stay during the second procedure is that originally produced, so that even the relief measures that had been obtained during the first one also preserve their effects even after the conversion.

It is also necessary to ask whether, in the course of the same procedure, the same subject, in the course of the same procedure, can re-submit a new application to obtain the release from the automatic stay: This possibility is obviously conditioned applicability, in this case, of the principles of res judicata, and in particular of the rule of bar, under which the rejection of the application prevents its re-proposal in the context of a new process. The application of the principles of res judicata, in particular, requires the participation of three requirements. The provision must be valid, must contain a decision on the merits, and must be final[370]. The latter

---

[369]A.N. RESNICK, H.J. SOMMER, Collier on bankruptcy, op. cit., § 362.13. W.R. NORTON, JR., Norton bankruptcy law and practice, op. cit., § 36:42.

[370]J.H. FRIEDENTHAL, M.K. KANE, A.R. MILLER, Civil procedure, op. cit., pp. 646ss.

connotation, in particular, is closely linked to the quality of the assessment contained therein[371], so that it seems to have to exclude its recurrence in a judgment, such as the one in question, characterized, as mentioned, by the summary of cognition, besides, by a decision taken rebus sic stantibus, and therefore subjected to the constant mutability of the facts made on the basis of the decision taken (consider, for example, the case in which only later the asset weighed by a right of pre-emption undergoes a real depreciation)[372].

For the same reason, it seems to us that a relief measure obtained in the course of a procedure is destined to lose its effectiveness when it reaches its epilogue, so that in no way can this provision be invoked in the context of a procedure subsequently initiated: in other words, it would have a merely endoconcessional effect, and not, as we said, res judicata[373]. On this point, however, the jurisprudence does not seem unanimously oriented: On the one hand, in fact, there are those who affirm the effectiveness of res judicata of the relief provision, while more detailed solutions propose to put the same on the basis of a rebuttable presumption operating at in favor of the creditor who, during the second procedure, again asks for release from the automatic stay[374].

43.The voluntary derogation of the protective effect: prepetition waiver agreements

The hypothesis of termination, legal and judicial, of the automatic stay, the examination of which has been dedicated to this Section, do not exhaust, however, the list of suitable cases to lead to the fall of the injunction ordered by Section 362 of the Bankruptcy Code.

In fact, it is necessary to mention a practice, established in the wake of the wide freedom that, in the American legal system, is

---

L.L. TEPLY, R.U. WHITTEN, Civil procedure, op. cit., 985ss. G.C. HAZARD, JR., J. LEUBSDORF, D. L. BASSETT, Civil procedure, op. cit., pp. 610ss.

[371]J.F. MURPHY, The automatic stay in bankruptcy, op. cit., pp. 626ss. Has excluded the effects of res judicata in case: In re Sun Valley Ranches, Inc., 43 B.R. 641 (1984).

[372]D.R. COWANS, Cowans bankruptcy law and practice, op. cit., pp. 467ss. See also the case: In re Taylor, 77 B.R. 237 (1987). M.E. TRACHT, Contractual bankruptcy waivers: Reconciling theory practice and law, in Cornell Law Review, 82, 1997, pp. 306ss.

[373]In re Norris, 39 B.R. 85 (1984).

[374]In re Bystrek, (1982).

traditionally recognized for the autonomy of the parties, consisting in the stipulation of prepetition waiver agreements, i.e. agreements concluded by the debtor with one or more creditors, containing the agreement that, in case of subsequent presentation by the former, of an application for admission to one of the procedures provided by the Bankruptcy Code, such subject will renounce automatic stay, often by taking on the commitment not to challenge the request for relief submitted by the creditor[375].

The contractual instrument in question has historically arisen spontaneously in situations in which the creditor was willing to make some concessions to his debtor in difficulty (including, for example, the refusal to make use of the proper routes of forced execution), but at the same time he wished to take precautions against the possibility that the latter, by filing a petition, precluded in any case the feasibility of any aggressive initiative[376].

While, moreover, in the force of the previous Rules of Bankruptcy Procedures, the rule 401, in subsection (b), expressly provided that the stay would persist, among other things, until the bankruptcy renounced this right[377], thereby implicitly recognizing citizenship to the prepetitions waiver agreements, no provision of such a tenor can be found in today's Section 362[378]. From here today's debate about the legitimacy of such a practice and, secondly, the value that such agreements can assume in a bankruptcy procedure.

44.(Follows) Lines of interpretation of the solutions proposed by jurisprudence and doctrine...

On the two extremes, of course, the opposite positions: According

---

[375]A.N. RESNICK, H.J. SOMMER, Collier on bankruptcy, op. cit., § 362.07[7][b]. S.V. KELLEY, Ginsberg & Martin on bankruptcy, op. cit., § 3.05[F]. M. E. TRACHT, Contractual bankruptcy waivers: Reconciling theory, practice, and law, in Cornell Law Review, 82, 1997, pp. 312ss.

[376]W.D. WARREN, D. J. BUSSEL, D. A. SKEEL, JR., Bankruptcy, op. cit., pp. 221ss.

[377]Rule 401(b) affirms that: "(...) The stay shall continue until (...) the bankrupt (...) waives (...) his right thereto". For further details see: J. W. MOORE, L. P. KING, Collier on bankruptcy, 14th ed., 1A, op. cit., § 11.012.

[378]E.S. ADAMS, J.L. BAILLIE, A privatization solution to the legitimacy of prepetition waivers of the automatic stay, in Arizona Law Review 38, 1996, pp. 9ss.

to some, that is, the prepetition waiver agreements must be considered self executing within the competition procedure, in the name of the superior values of the contractual autonomy of the parties and the opportunity to favor out-of-court compositions of the crisis, so that, where the creditor acts for the request of relief from the automatic stay, the court cannot do anything else but grant it, by defining this agreement as a "cause" in accordance with Section 362 (d) (1)[379]; on the completely opposite side, vice versa, we find the opinion of those who deny any efficacy to such agreements, considered contrary to the public interests protected by the Bankruptcy Code. Finally, an intermediate opinion is visible, which, although denying automatic execution to agreements in question, however, does not come to deny, to the same, any value within the procedure, rather leading to their conclusion to the group of circumstances that the court is called to assess, together with the others, when deciding whether there is a "cause" to grant the relief measure[380].

First of all, it seems easy to agree on the point that the agreements in question can not be considered self executing. Remember, in fact, that during the investigation carried out on the interests to which protection the automatic stay is preordained, it has emerged that this institute does not is exclusively functional to the protection of the debtor, but also of the entire creditor class, as essential to ensure that the distribution of bankruptcy assets takes place in compliance with the principles of equal conditions, as well as the public interests to an efficient management of bankruptcy proceedings. Recognizing the self-executive effectiveness of the prepetition waiver agreements would obviously mean allowing the debtor to unilaterally arrange for an effect of which he is by no means the sole owner: A power which, in no way, can be recognized[381].

---

[379]As we can see in case: In re Club Tower L.P., 138 B.R. 307 (1991). For further details see: J. FERRIELL, E.J. JANGER, Understanding bankrutptcy, LexisNexis, New York, 2013. D.A. AUSTIN, S.P. PARSONS, Business bankruptcy law in focus, Wolters Kluwer, New York, 2016.

[380]P.A. MURPHY, E.E. SAGERMAN, D. NEIER, Creditor's rights in bankruptcy, op. cit. W. BASSIN, Why courts should refuse to enforce prepetition agreements that waive bankruptcy's automatic stay provision, in Indiana Law Review, 70, 1994, pp. 9ss. In jurisprudence see the case: Matter of Pease, 195 B.R. 431 (1996), 435.

[381]E.S. ADAMS, J.L. BAILLIE, A privatization solution to the legitimacy of prepetition waivers of the automatic stay, op. cit., pp. 25, 31ss. See also the case: In re Desai, 282 B.R.

But even the favorable solution to consider the conclusion of such an agreement between the circumstances that the court is called to assess in ascertaining the existence of a just "cause" for relief provision granting, does not convince. Notwithstanding the risk of fueling a practice which, in fact, can result in the constraint of a party in a situation of weakness to conclude an agreement by which it renounces a fundamental protection, it must not be forgotten, then, that this the last is granted by an imperative discipline. The normative system of the automatic stay is in fact fixed by the law to protect situations which, with the deposit of the petition, escape the privatistic sphere of the relationship between the debtor and his creditor, and vice versa, in a universal dimension, involving the entire creditor class within a procedure managed by public bodies, i.e. the jurisdictional ones; this system, in other words, happens in its entirety to the privatistic management of debtor relations with its own creditors, so that only on the basis of the rules operating there can the fundamental protections offered be eliminated, while no relief can be recognized to an agreement individually assumed when the debtor was still in bonis.

However, the eventuality in which it is precisely the law, and therefore the special rules operating in the insolvency system, to recognize some importance to an agreement concluded by the debtor with its own creditors is different: This is the case governed by rule 4001 (d) of the Federal Rules of Bankruptcy Procedures, where a special procedure is established aimed at obtaining the recognition of agreements concluded, during the procedure and, in particular, before or after the deposit of a motion, between the debtor and a creditor, concerning the modification or termination of the automatic stay. In particular, it is provided that the recognition procedure should be initiated with a motion, to be notified to all interested parties and therefore, in particular, to other creditors, who within the next fourteen days may present their opposition to such agreement; only in case of presentation of an opposition the court is obliged to set a specific hearing, and in any case this body remains free to grant recognition, and therefore in the ruling of the relief measure, evaluated all the circumstances[382].

---

527 (2002). D.A. AUSTIN, S.P. PARSONS, Business bankruptcy law in focus, op. cit.

[382]A.N. RESNICK, H.J. SOMMER, Collier on bankruptcy, op. cit., § 362.08[8]. D.R.

The peculiarities that characterize this case with respect to the practice of prepetition waiver agreements are notable. First of all, as mentioned, these are agreements concluded in the course of the insolvency procedure, at a time when, therefore, the debtor enjoys the full benefits associated with the automatic stay, and with the annulment, therefore, of the risk of constriction of the part in a situation of weakness that is accompanied by agreements concluded during the pre-competitive period; secondly, it is the law itself that recognizes its legitimacy, evidently for the purpose of externalizing the resolution of controversial issues which, if faced during the relief judgment, would entail an aggravation and a delay in the procedure[383] also surrounding the procedure of special precautions, including, above all, the need to involve other subjects holding the interests to whose protection the automatic stay is aimed, to allow them to exercise their right to the adversarial. These expedients, together with the freedom of judgment of which, in any case, they remain the owner the court, therefore, allow to avoid that the conclusion of the agreement remains relegated to the purely private dimension of the bilateral relationship between debtor and individual creditor, but they lead the same agreement to the supervision of all the subjects holding the interests protected by the automatic stay.

45.Consequences of protective effect cessation.

With regard to the consequences deriving from the cessation of the automatic stay, it is appropriate to distinguish between legal and judicial cessation of the injunction.

As for the cases of legal cessation, in fact, while, as we have seen, those taken in respect of bankruptcy assets are linked to the fact that the asset in question comes out of summer property in consequence, for example, of bankruptcy liquidation, abandonment or exceptioner ultimately subject to a different legal regime, the injunction against the debtor and his personal assets ends with the exhaustion of the procedure: So, from the fact that the discharge is granted or denied, depends on the

---

COWANS, Cowans bankruptcy law and practice, op. cit., pp. 563ss. P.A. MURPHY, E.E. SAGERMAN, D. NEIER, Creditor's rights in bankruptcy, op. cit., pp. 208ss. W.D. WARREN, D.J. BUSSEL, D.A. SKEEL, JR., Bankruptcy, op. cit.

[383]S.V. KELLEY, Ginsberg & Martin on bankruptcy, op. cit., § 3.07[D].

possibility for the bankruptcy creditors subsequently act, once the automatic stay has ceased, with respect to these entities in order to seek the satisfaction of their residual claims[384]. Consider also that with the closure of the procedure the jurisdiction of the bankruptcy court is no longer valid. This means, therefore, that once the automatic stay is terminated due to the causes provided for by the law, the court will not be able to restore it. Evidently, he will be able to pronounce an ad hoc injunction pursuant to Section 105 (a) of the Bankruptcy Code[385].

With regard to the grant of a relief measure, on the other hand, reference has already been made to the fact that the release operates exclusively towards the subject and within the limits exactly described in the provision, while the legal situation of the beneficiary entity of the injunction does not change with regard to the generality of other subjects who undergo the automatic stay. The effects deriving from the judicial cessation of the automatic stay differ greatly, therefore, from those resulting from the case of legal cessation, since the provision in question does not involve the escape of the asset that constitutes its object from bankruptcy assets, so that, the other entities remain subject to the prohibitions descending from Section 362 (a). Once the relief provision has been granted, however, the court will not be able to order the restoration of the automatic stay referred to in Section 362 (a); however, if the presumptions occur, it will obviously be a case of very exceptional cases, it may grant the debtor an injunction pursuant to Section 105 (a) of the Bankruptcy Code, and thus impose on the party that at first had obtained the liberation from the automatic stay the prohibition to proceed further with its own aggressive initiatives[386].

---

[384]D.R. COWANS, Cowans bankruptcy law and practice, op. cit., pp. 465ss; In jurisprudence see. In re Nagel case, 245 B.R. 657 (1999).

[385]J. F. MURPHY, The automatic stay in bankruptcy, op. cit., pp. 618ss.

[386]In re Terramar Mining Corp., 70 B.R. 875 (1987), 877, where it is precisely an affirmation that the bankruptcy court can: "(...) On properly filed complaint for injunctive relief pursuant to § 105 of the Bankruptcy Code, grant injunctive relief in an extraordinary situation, and prohibit the party who originally obtained relief under the motion for relief from stay to proceed any further with the action to enforce a lien against property of the estate (...)".

46.Automatic stay violation. Conditions for violating automatic stay.

Concluded the analysis of the institute governed by Section 362 of the Bankruptcy Code, in all its characteristic moments, all that remains is to pass to the illustration of the pathological aspects that can invest such a system of protection of the debtor, and therefore of the consequences that the law reconnects to the accomplishment of activities precluded by the vigor of automatic stay.

An action carried out in violation of automatic stay is, obviously, any initiative suitable to fall under the circumstances described in Section 362 (a) without at the same time integrating an exception to the prohibition set forth in the following subsection, put in place by the entities that the law subjects to the prohibitions prescribed therein, and against the subjects that, of the same prohibitions, are beneficiaries. It can then consist of both active behavior and omission: An example of the second case is represented, as seen, by the hypothesis in which debtor's counterpart in an extra-food judgment fails to take the necessary steps to ensure that this procedure is actually suspended.

Above all, it is important to carry out an important clarification, which, together with the elements collected so far, will further explain the essence of automatic stay, especially where it concerns its first moment, i.e. as a protection necessarily operating in favor of the debtor from the time of petition filing. Since, in fact, the automatic stay consists in a prohibition imposed on certain subjects identified ex lege, lawful is wondering if its operation as well as, in particular, the possibility of applying the consequences expected in the event of its violation, including the ineffective side sensu[387] of the completed activity, require that these subjects have been effectively informed of injunction's validity, or if, in the absence of any warning or communication, and therefore to the verification of their good faith, the need to protect their entrustment, with salvation, therefore, of the effects of accomplished activity. The Bankruptcy Code, in fact, prescribes with the Section 342, that the creditors and other

[387]S.V. KELLEY, Ginsberg & Martin on bankruptcy, op. cit., § 3.01[B][4]. A.N. RESNICK, Bankruptcy law manual, op. cit., pp. 120ss.

interested parties are informed of the opening of the bankruptcy proceedings, and in addition the Official Form 9 includes, among the specific contents of this notice, also the warning of the entry into force of the automatic stay, but generally this notice is received by the same several days after the petition is filed. In the course of the discussion, moreover, we have already had the opportunity to anticipate the answer to this question, namely in the sense that the automatic stay acquires efficacy with the sole deposit of the petition, without being necessary, in order to subject a part to the its preclusive efficacy, the actual knowledge of the event itself, so that, consequently, the actions that it performs while ignoring the force of the injunction will nevertheless be considered contra legem, with the relative consequences [388].

This rigorous discipline is evidently explained by the prevalence that the law recognizes to the interests[389], of a public nature, to which the automatic stay is pre-arranged. The need to ensure that bankruptcy assets are preserved in their entirety and devolved to satisfaction of bankruptcy creditors, and that the procedure can be managed efficiently, clearly require that the protective effects are produced with absolute certainty starting from a single and predetermined moment for all the subjects affected by them, while avoiding the aggravations which, otherwise, it would involve the need to ascertain whether the entity in question, in the specific case, had received news of the operation of the automatic stay or not.

The fact that the person affected by the injunction was not aware of the operation of the latter when he took a prohibited action, is not completely irrelevant, however, for the purposes of applying the regulation in question. In fact, it is seen that the innocuous ignorance of the operativeness of the automatic stay can lead, at the outcome of the judgment for the liberation from the injunction, and together with the existence of substantial assumptions required for this purpose, to the ruling of a provision of cancellation, with an amnesty ex tunc of the completed activity; and it will be seen later, as more severe penalties are foreseen for

[388]S.V. KELLEY, Ginsberg & Martin on bankruptcy, op. cit., § 3.01[B][1]. D.R. COWANS, Cowans bankruptcy law and practice, op. cit., pp. 476. B.A. BLUM, Bankruptcy and debtor/creditor, op. cit., pp. 257ss. See also the case: In re Calder, 907 F.2d (1990), 956.
[389]A. N. RESNICK, H. J. SOMMER, Collier on bankruptcy, op. cit., §§ 362.02 e 362.12.

the hypothesis of violations perpetrated in the awareness of automatic stay vigor (willful violation).

Subject to any such additional sanctions, depending on the subjective attitude that may be found by the entity that has violated the automatic stay, the unavoidably foreseeable consequence of any act carried out in contravention of the prohibitions posed by Section 362 (a) is represented, as anticipated, by the inability, of such act, to produce or consolidate its legal effects; the exact legal regime of such activities, in the absolute silence of the law on this point, is nevertheless one of the most debated issues concerning automatic stay, in the matter of debt restructuring agreements[390].

US jurisprudence, on this point, appears to be divided between two opposing theses: The majority, which supports the nullity of acts carried out in violation of inhibition (void approach), and the one that, vice versa, supports its mere voidability (voidable approach).

47.The thesis according to which the initiatives carried out in violation of the automatic stay are voidable (voidable approach).

The opposing interpretations, in order of the legal regime proper of the acts performed in violation of the inhibition, are the result of two different interpretative approaches. While the nullity of such initiatives is argued by moving from the presumable intention of the legislator, and therefore through a teleological interpretation of the overall discipline of the automatic stay, attentive to the nature and the purpose that the same intends to pursue, their annullability, as will be seen immediately, is argued by the proper meaning of the words (plain meaning approach), and therefore by a literal interpretation of Section 362 of the Bankruptcy Code.

---

[390]A. Sikes v. Global Marine, Inc., 881 F.2d 176 (1989), 178, where it is the statement for which: "(...) By strict definition that which is void is nugatory and of no effect and cannot be cured; that which is voidable may be either voided or cured (...) we are persuaded that the better reasoned rule characterizes acts taken in violation of the automatic stay as voidable rather than void (...) in section 362(d) Congress empowered the court to grant relief from the automatic stay "by terminating, annulling, modifying, or conditioning" the stay. The power to annul authorizes retroactive relief even unto the date of the filing of the petition giving rise to the automatic stay. The power to annul authorizes the court to validate actions taken subsequent to the impressing of the section 362(a) stay (...)".

The argument that, unequivocally, seems to lead to the conclusion just mentioned, would be represented by the subsection (d), regulating, as is known, the procedure for granting relief, and in particular by the power attributed to the court to retroactively cancel the automatic stay, with ex tunc of the activities carried out in its vigor: Since, in fact, this faculty implies the possibility of validating such acts, and the validation is to be excluded in the hypothesis of radical nullity, they would unequivocally derive their qualification in the sense of mere annulment; once the judgment of relief has been established for the cancellation of the automatic stay, in other words, the court would be called to choose between the validation of the initiative or its cancellation.

To further support the thesis now in comment, we add the presence of provisions of contents of Sections 542 (c) and 549 (c) of the Bankruptcy Code: The first, in particular, excludes the need for turnover of summer property the deeds of disposition that are made in good faith by a person in possession of assets that have been transferred to the bankruptcy assets, who were not aware of the beginning of the procedure or of automatic stay vigor; the second, then, has as its object the postpetition transactions, excluding the possibility for the trustee to exercise his avoiding powers with regard to the sale of real estate belonging to the bankruptcy assets perfected in favor of a bona fide purchaser who had no knowledge of the beginning of the procedure. In other words, these rules, by providing for the salvation of certain legal acts carried out during the bankruptcy proceedings, would ultimately rule out the possibility of considering them radically ineffective.

In this sense, the fifth[391] and sixth circuits in particular appear to be oriented, as well as a minority part of the doctrine[392]. The same conclusion, however, was reached through a different argumentative path, typical of the instruments proper to the economic analysis of law, and peculiar to US legal system, i.e. the use of information forcing paradigm: The latter, in particular, would consist of a rule aimed at stimulating the disclosure of certain information between contractual counterparties,

---

[391]Easley v. Pettibone Michigan Corp., 990 F.2d 905 (1993).

[392]T.A. BARNES, The plain meaning of automatic stay in bankruptcy: The void/voidable distinction revisited, in Ohio State Law Journal, 57, 1996, pp. 315ss.

especially if they concern the risk for one of them to suffer a certain damage, and incentivized by allocating the risk of same damage to the part that, being aware of this information, was able to avoid it by communicating it to the other party, so as to induce it, in fact, to greater transparency, and to achieve an overall greater efficiency of the system[393]. The application of this rule to the matter that deals with us leads to questioning what the part is aware of the relevant information, that is the force of the automatic stay, and therefore, with a lower overall cost, is able to communicate it to counterpart. This is evidently the debtor who, better than anyone else, is aware of the filing of a petition against him, and on which, therefore, the burden of disclosing this event to the creditors, as well as the consequent risk of its violation. From this, it follows that the legal regime that best enables the realization of this arrangement of relations between debtor and creditors is that of the mere annulment of the initiative, which, on the one hand, entails the initial validity and effectiveness of the deed performed in violation of the automatic stay against the debtor the risk of the violation itself and, secondly, it will charge the subsequent procedural initiative aimed, in fact, to make the act invalid[394].

The adherence to this interpretative thesis is ultimately reflected in a greater attention paid to the protection of entrusting the third party and the effects of the activities performed by them: Which, as we know, could well have not been, at the time of completion of the action, aware of the force of the injunction, finding itself consequently in a subjective state of good faith, as such deserving of some form of recognition.

---

[393]R. R. NICCOLINIA, The voidability of actions taken in violation of the automatic stay: Application of the information forcing paradigm, in Vanderbilt Law Review, 45, 1992, pp. 1679ss.

[394]With reference to the possibility of canceling the automatic stay retroactively, with validation of the deed performed in its force, provided for in section 362 (d), we spoke among the proponents of the void approach of "void unless annulled" standard. In argument see: D.R. TOBAR, The need for a uniform void ab initio standard for violations of the automatic stay, in Whittier Law Review, 24, 2002, pp. 24ss. D.G. EPSTEIN, Bankruptcy and related law in a nutshell, op. cit., pp. 156ss. I. RAMSAY, Personal insolvency in the 21st century. A comparative analysis of the US and Europe, op. cit.

48.The thesis according to which the initiatives carried out in violation of automatic stay are void (void approach).

The opposing argument aimed at bringing the acts committed in violation of the automatic stay into the legal category of nullity is based on legislator's intention (purposive approach), and therefore on a teleological interpretation of the discipline, enhancing the goals that, through it, the Congress intended to reach.

It is noted that the automatic stay constitutes a fundamental instrument of protection aimed at the protection of both debtor and reditors, freeing the former from the aggressive initiatives of the latter which, in turn, can rely on the integrity of bankruptcy assets, and on its suitability to be distributed in compliance with the principles of a level playing field; finally, this institute is also directed to protect public interest, guaranteeing an efficient management of the bankruptcy procedure[395]. Now, since these interests are to be considered unavailable, it follows that the acts carried out in violation of a rule, obviously unavoidable, aimed at the protection of the interests themselves, should be considered affected by radical nullity, also in consideration of the fact that a less rigorous discipline, as that descending from a qualification in terms of mere annullability, would end up betraying the objectives pursued by the overall legislation, encouraging those affected by the injunction to act anyway, being able to trust in the consolidation of their own initiative. In this reconstruction, moreover, the cases in question, which we have said, which seem to imply the possibility of validating the deed carried out in violation of the injunction and which would seem to undoubtedly exclude, in this way, their classification as radically void. The provisions in Sections 362 (d), 542 (c) and 549 (c) of the Bankruptcy Code, to be exact, would constitute "equitable exceptions" to the voidness rule, and therefore capable, when recourse to of an equitable nature, to subtract a specific initiative to the rigorous regime of radical nullity, otherwise in force, foreseen for acts carried out in violation of the automatic stay[396]. This is the opinion pursued

[395]In re Soares, 107 F.3d 969 (1997), 976.
[396]Rexnord Holdings Inc. v. Bidermann, 21 F.3d 522 (1994), 527.

by the prevailing jurisprudence, and in particular by the first[397], second[398], third[399], ninth[400], tenth[401] and the eleventh circuit, as well as the absolutely majority doctrine[402].

In the sense of radical nullity of the acts committed in violation of the automatic stay, it was also expressed the only sentence of the Supreme Court of the United States found on the issue, pronounced in Kalb v. Feuerstein case of 1940[403]. A precedent that for the supporters of the void approach would represent an inescapable voice in support of its reasons. However, it should be noted that this ruling concerns the special procedure set out in Section 75 (s) of the Bankruptcy Act of 1898, introduced with the Frazier Lemke Act of 1934[404] in which, however, the relief provision could only order the modification and termination of the stay, and not even

---

[397]In re Siciliano, 13 F.3d 748 (1994), 751, which is affirmed that: "The inclusion of the word "annulling" in the statute, indicates a legislative intent to apply certain types of relief retroactively and validate proceedings that would otherwise be void ab initio (...)".

[398]In re Schwartz, 954 F.2d 570 (1992), 571, which is affirmed that: "Given the important and fundamental purpose of the automatic stay and the broad debtor protections of the Bankruptcy Code, we find that Congress intended violations of the automatic stay to be void rather than voidable (...)".

[399]Ellis v. Consolidated Diesel Elec. Corp., 894 F.2d 371 (1990), 372.

[400]In re Albany Partners Ltd., 749 F.2d 670 (1984). For further details see: G.W. NEWTON, R. LIGUERMAN, Bankruptcy and insolvency taxation, op. cit.

[401]A.N. RESNICK, H.J. SOMMER, Collier on bankruptcy, op. cit., § 362.12[1]. P. A. MURPHY, E.E. SAGERMAN, D. NEIER, Creditors' rights in bankruptcy, op. cit., pp. 232ss. D.G. EPSTEIN, Bankruptcy and related law in a nutshell, op. cit., pp. 155ss. R.A. JOHNSON, M.C. O'LEARY, Automatic stay provisions of the bankruptcy act of 1978, op. cit., pp. 618ss. J.F. MURPHY, The automatic stay in bankruptcy, op. cit., pp. 591ss. M.J. LICHTENSTEIN, Violations of the automatic stay: Void or voidable?, in ABI Journal, 23, 2004, pp. 54ss. D.R. TOBAR, The need for a uniform void ab initio standard for violations of the automatic stay, op. cit., pp. 35ss. B.A. BLUM, Bankruptcy and debtor/creditor, op. cit., I. RAMSAY, Personal insolvency in the 21st century. A comparative analysis of the US and Europe, op. cit.

[402]D.G. EPSTEIN, Bankruptcy and related law in a nutshell, op. cit. B.A. BLUM, Bankruptcy and debtor/creditor, op. cit., I. RAMSAY, Personal insolvency in the 21st century. A comparative analysis of the US and Europe, op. cit.

[403].308 U.S. 433 (1940).

[404]In this sense case: A. Sikes v. Global Marine, Inc., 179, note 2, which is affirmed that: "(...) Our decision today does not conflict with the Supreme Court's holding in Kalb v. Feuerstein (...) When the Supreme Court decided Kalb in 1940, bankruptcy referees had the express statutory power only to modify or terminate the automatic stay. The power to annul the stay had not been authorized. Accordingly, where the violation of the stay was statutorily proscribed and an applicable exception did not exist, the violative action was void. That scenario no longer applies (...)".

its cancellation, a circumstance that, for supporters of the opposing opinion, would make a non-binding ruling within the current system.

49.Distinction's practical consequences: Burden distribution of trial initiative.

The question concerning the legal regime to which the acts carried out in violation of the automatic stay are subjected does not evidently have an exclusive speculative value, since the different qualification of such activities is likely to produce practical consequences of absolute importance, capable, however, of repercussing on the intimate nature of the debtor protection system set up by the United States bankruptcy law.

Consider, in fact, that while a null act is an unproductive origin of effects, so that the debtor must not in any way act to react to creditor's behavior, being able, in fact, to rely on the radical unsuitability of the activity to produce any kind of effect in the juridical order, a merely annulable act is, vice versa, initially endowed with validity and efficacy, attributes, however, which are liable to be canceled at a later time, where the subject to which the aforementioned annullability is codified, therefore, the debtor acts in order to request a judicial ruling instrumental to this result[405].

In other words, from the preference for one or the other, of the two interpretative thesis follows, more generally, the recognition of a different regime of favor towards the subjects variously participating in the procedure, as well as, ultimately, a different overall structure of the protection regulation of the debtor dictated by the Bankruptcy Code. In particular, as already emerges from the above, the debtor and the procedure

---

[405]As we can see from the case: In re Soares, op. cit., par. 976, "(...) this semantic difference has practical consequences because the characterization of an infringing action as "void" or "voidable" influences the burden of going forward. Treating an action taken in contravention of the automatic stay as void places the burden of validating the action after the fact squarely on the shoulders of the offending creditor. In contrast, treating an action taken in contravention of the automatic stay as voidable places the burden of challenging the action on the offended debtor (...) the former paradigm, rather than the latter, best harmonizes with the nature of the automatic stay and the important purposes that it serves". See in argument: B.A. BLUM, Bankruptcy and debtor/creditor, op. cit. M.J. LICHTENSTEIN, Violations of the automatic stay: Void or voidable?, op. cit. D.R. TOBAR, The need for a uniform void ab initio standard for violations of the automatic stay, op. cit.

appear to be more protected by the system resulting from the void approach, as the initiative taken against them will be unproductive effects regardless of an activation by the debtor himself or the trustee, while the creditor, who wants to see his action validated, has to institute a procedure for granting relief pursuant to Section 362 (d); while the voidable approach leads to recognizing a debtor treatment as a debtor and trustee, obliging them, in order to obtain the termination of the activity committed in violation of the prohibition prescribed by the automatic stay, to appeal to the judge in order to obtain a sentence that cancel this initiative. It is clear, therefore, that the two theses allocate the so-called in a differentiated way. burden of going forward, i.e. the burden of the resulting judicial initiative[406].

This different structure, moreover, constituted one more argument in support of the void approach, since leaving the burden of activation on the part of the person who has violated the automatic stay is certainly better suited to the protective aims that the institute intends to pursue, and, where appropriate, allows the debtor to better concentrate on the effort reorganization, without having to worry about acting in court to contest the initiatives of others. Especially since, as noted above, among the supporters of the voidable approach we tried to find a justification of the allocation of the activation charge to the debtor, implied by this interpretative hypothesis, according to a different criterion, that is based on the allegedly more efficient placement of the costs of an overall legal operation, typical principles of the economic analysis of law[407].

[406]Thus, in the aforementioned case In re Schwartz, 572, where it effectively opines that: "(...) The Bankruptcy Code does not burden the debtor with a duty to take additional steps to secure the benefit of the automatic stay". A.N. RESNICK, H. J. SOMMER, Collier on bankruptcy, op. cit. D.R. TOBAR, The need for a uniform void ab initio standard for violations of the automatic stay, op. cit., pp. 25ss.
[407]R.R. NICCOLINIA, The voidability of actions taken in violation of the automatic stay: Application of the information forcing paradigm, op. cit., pp. 1677ss.

50.Need to verify further interpretative hypotheses: Absolute invalidity or relative ineffectiveness of the initiatives carried out in violation of automatic stay.

The dry alternative between nullity and voidability of the acts carried out in violation of the automatic stay does not exhaust, indeed, the catalog of the possible legal regimes to which such violations can be subjected.

An interesting development of interpretation can derive, first of all, moving from the first of the two theses previously illustrated, namely that in favor of the mere annullability of the acts performed in violation of the injunction, a thesis that, in fact, might appear more persuasive, at least in the a measure in which it is more compatible with the possibility of validation of the same acts, deriving from the power of retroactive cancellation of the automatic stay referred to in Section 362 (d) of the Bankruptcy Code. What, on the contrary, of this thesis is not convincing, is the fact that leaving the possibility of reacting to invalidate the unlawfully carried out initiative exclusively by the debtor, or the trustee, ends, in definitive, to entrust the protection of interests by automatic stay to their exclusive availability, so that their inertia ultimately translates into the inevitable sacrifice of interests belonging to a multiplicity of other subjects (that is, of course, creditors and procedure). Ultimately, this structure would lead to encouraging the performance of acts in violation of automatic stay, the agent being able to trust in lack of activation, for whatever reason may derive, in particular, from the contemporary and absorbing efforts related to debtor's or trustee's procedure, and therefore on the salvation of his own initiative, with considerable diseconomies, and in clear contrast with the objectives, of protection as well as efficient management of the procedure and implementation of the par condicio, subtended to the institute in comment.

A solution to this misunderstanding, however, could be usefully sought through the extension of the legitimacy to take action to request the invalidation of the act performed in violation of the automatic stay to all subjects, to whose protection this institution is aimed: In particular, therefore, to other creditors and interested parties. A qualification, in other words, in the sense of absolute nullification of the initiatives carried out in injunction violation, which on the one hand allows to restore a correspondence between the group of subjects protected by it, and those entitled to take action to make it worth eliminating the misunderstanding the unilateral availability of interests belonging to different groups, and, on the other, allows a reduction in the position of the debtor and the trustee, who can also count on the collaboration of other subjects, equally interested, in the repression of conduct of automatic stay violation.

Secondly, it is natural to wonder about the opportunity to extend, in this case, the category of acts ineffectiveness committed in violation of the injunction against the procedure[408], in the sense that such acts would be valid and effective inter partes, but they would remain unproductive to the mass as long as the automatic stay continues. In light of this reconstruction, therefore, in the cases of annulment ex tunc of automatic stay, or in the cases contemplated in Sections 542 (c) and 549 (c), there would be no validation of the deed performed in injunction violation, on the contrary, the condicio iuris would be necessary, so that it could produce its own juridical effects in relation to the procedure.

Even if the juxtaposition with the solution is undoubtedly seductive, it is necessary to keep in mind that one moves in the context of an order quite different from the domestic one, and, moreover, that the institute of which it is speaking arises from a branch of the whole peculiar to the common law system, and unknown to us: It is, of course, the equity system from which the inhibitory powers of the bankruptcy courts have emerged, then progressively evolved into the modern institution of automatic stay.

In particular, the automatic stay constitutes an injunction, although operating, today, as a matter of fact, so that it is a more correct methodological solution to derive the consequences of the violation of the institute starting from the general discipline of injunctions. In this regard, the acts committed in violation of an injunction are peacefully qualified as void, and therefore void, as illegal.

The solution of the nullity of the initiatives carried out in violation

---

[408]J.E. MARTIN, Hanbury & Martin modern equity, Sweet & Maxwell, London, 2001, pp. 799ss.

of the automatic stay undoubtedly constitutes, and as has already been observed in the previous paragraphs, the one that is best reconciled with the unavailability of the interests protected by a rule, obviously mandatory, as Section 362 of the Bankruptcy Code. But, in our opinion, there is a further argument to support this conclusion. In the chapter dedicated to the temporal discipline of automatic stay, in fact, it has been observed that, in the case in which the discharge is granted, the latter happens both from a temporal and from a functional point of view to the inhibition imposed by Section362 (a), a consecution that is made possible by the common legal nature-precisely of injunction-proper of the two institutions: More precisely, the discharge constitutes a permanent injunction, intended to absorb and replace the other, of a precautionary nature and provisional, represented by the automatic stay. Now, with regard to discharge, the bankruptcy law, unlike what has been seen with regard to institution that deals with it, explicitly qualifies the legal regime of the acts affected by it: Section 524 of the Bankruptcy Code, entitled "effect of discharge", provides, inter alia, that "a discharge in a case under this title (...) voids any judgment at any time obtained, to the extent that such judgment is a determination of the personal liability of the debtor with respect to any debt discharged"[409], declaring the nullity of the activities set out therein. In short, if the consecration between automatic stay and discharge is explained by the homogeneity of the legal effects deriving from these institutions, both representing injunctions, and if with regard to discharge the legislator qualifies in terms of void the activities of the same concerned, the same consequence must be extended with reference to the acts carried out in violation of the automatic stay.

The option now made in favor of the void approach recalls, however, the problem of reconciling the regime of radical nullity of the acts carried out in violation of the automatic stay with the rules, mentioned several times, referred to in sections 362 (d), 542 (c) and 549 (c) of the Bankruptcy Code.

Regarding the procedure for the granting of relief from the automatic stay, it is necessary to remember the role it assumes in the

---

[409]D.G. EPSTEIN, Bankruptcy and related law in a nutshell, op. cit. I. RAMSAY, Personal insolvency in the 21st century. A comparative analysis of the US and Europe, op. cit.

overall structure of the institute. It has been said, in fact, that by means of this judgment the party subject to the injunction proposes to give the judge evidence contrary to the rebuttable presumption underlying the operation of automatic stay demonstrating, in other words, the non-existence of prejudice that justifies a protective measure in favor of the beneficiaries identified by law. The non-existence of the injury, or the presence of another just cause, determines, in other words, automatic stay application. This allows, as has already been intended, to reconcile the regime of nullity of the acts carried out in violation of the bans in question, with the power of the court to order automatic stay cancellation. It consists, in reality, in a non-application ex tunc of injunction, and more precisely in the assessment made by the judge that, given the substantial assumptions proven by the instant party, the automatic stay towards the latter was, in fact, never produced, so that ultimately, we are faced with the verification of institution's inoperativity, and not of a ruling that, having detected the validity of the automatic stay and, with it, the invalidity of the completed activity, provides to dispose of an amnesty.

The same conclusion can be extended to the aforementioned cases, which exclude certain deeds of assets that flowed into the summer from the possibility of exercising turnover or avoiding powers of the trustee: Moreover, it is necessary to reflect on the fact that they are based on the faultless ignorance of the automatic stay operation, exactly as it happens in the cases of cancellation pursuant to Section 362 (d).

In conclusion, it should be noted that, for the reasons set out above, the sole ignorance of injunction lawfulness is not, in itself, sufficient grounds for granting the relief measure, a kind of cancellation, but requires the appeal of other substantial presuppositions required for this purpose. If, in fact, such ignorance does not preclude the triggering of automatic stay by virtue of the sole deposit of the petition, it cannot be consistently stated, then, that its allegation is sufficient to obtain a subsequent ruling that ascertains the inoperativity from that moment.

51.The sentence for court contempt

Other consequences derive from the qualification of the automatic stay in terms of injunction, in terms of its violation. Generally, the non-compliance with an order contained in an injunction, prohibitory or mandatory, temporary or definitive, constitutes in fact a conduct in the context of court or, literally, in court contempt.

The court contempt, as is known, constitutes a sanction, operating in personam, which can be imposed by the court if the person who receives a command enclosed in a measure pronounced by him/her refuses to comply with it: More precisely, the judge can declare that the party acted in contempt, with the consequent application of a custodial or pecuniary sanction[410]. The contempt of court, in particular, may be civil or criminal: In the first case, the sentence to detention and/or pecuniary sentence, to be paid to the offended party, continues until the party agrees to obey court's command, and the purpose of forcing it to execute the provision; in the second, the sentence to the imprisonment or pecuniary sanction accesses the crime consisting in the refusal to execute the order of the court, and is aimed at both the manager's punishment, and the deterrence of any non-compliance of others[411].

While, therefore, the criminal contempt only aims to punish a past conduct, the civil contempt also has a coercive function, aimed at the future, and tense, in fact, to obtain the fulfillment on the part of the one who, currently, does not comply with court's provision[412].

Automatic stay violation, as injunction, therefore implies, in addition to consequences just seen in relation to the legal regime of deed, the possibility for the court[413] to pronounce, against the entity in question,

---

[410]More precisely, one speaks of coercive contempt when the sanction continues until the person who complies with the judicial provision; of compensatory contempt, when it is aimed at compensating the damaged party of the damage suffered; of punitive contempt, when the penalty is aimed at punishing the violator on such concepts, see: G.C. HAZARD, JR., J. LEUBSDORF, D.L. BASSETT, Civil procedure, op. cit., pp. 399ss. G.C. HAZARD JR., M. TARUFFO, Civil procedure, pp. 240ss.

[411]L.L. TEPLY, R. U. WHITTEN, Civil procedure, op. cit., pp. 633ss. J.H. FRIEDENTHAL, M.K. KANE, A.R. MILLER, Civil procedure, op. cit., 752ss. J.H. BEALE, JR., Contempt of court, criminal and civil, in Harvard Law Review, 21, 1908, pp. 162ss. W.S. PARKINSON, The contempt power of the bankruptcy court fact or fiction: The debate continues, in American Bankruptcy Law Journal, 65, 1991, pp. 592ss.

[412]R. WEISS, Contempt power of the bankruptcy court, in Bankruptcy Developments Journal, 6, 1989, pp. 212ss. J.A.E. POTTOW, Rethinking criminal contempt in the bankruptcy court, in Law & Economics working papers n. 126, 2017, pp. 12ss.

[413]We take in consideration that historically the existence of the powers of court contempt has always been debated, a problem deriving from the uncertain location and qualification

the conviction for court contempt[414], a possibility, this, which finds its source, once again, in Section 105 (a) of the Bankruptcy Code, in the part in which it recognizes the power, of an equitable form, to pronounce "any order, process, or judgment that is necessary or appropriate to carry out the provisions" of the Bankruptcy Code[415].

It should however be noted a very peculiar aspect, and which denotes subject matter speciality of the present survey. It has been said, in fact, that court contempt is a sanction that arises from non-compliance, by a subject, to a provision pronounced by the court. In the case that concerns us, however, the automatic stay is not enclosed in a judicial order, but constitutes a phenomenon that, as known, is produced ex lege in virtue of provisions of Section 362 (a) of the Bankruptcy Code[416]. The persistent punishment by way of contempt of the conduct in violation of this rule is evidently a historical residual of this institute, which from judicial injunction has progressively evolved into an injunction of a legal source, which, however, has retained the nature and remedies typically associated with it, further confirmation of the correctness of the overall reconstruction proposed by us.

---

of this organ in the American judicial system, and often resulted in the solution of recognizing these powers exclusively in the district court; on this point, we refer to the analysis of R. WEISS, Contempt power of the bankruptcy court, op. cit., pp. 206ss. W.S. PARKINSON, The contempt power of the bankruptcy court fact or fiction: The debate continues, op. cit., pp. 593ss. W.R. NORTON, JR., Norton bankruptcy law and practice, § 36:44 and 45. B.A. BLUM, Bankruptcy and debtor/creditor, op. cit., pp. 144ss. and 260ss. J.A.E. POTTOW, Rethinking criminal contempt in the bankruptcy court, op. cit.

[414]A.N. RESNICK, H.J. SOMMER, Norton bankruptcy law and practice, op. cit., § 362.12[2]. S.V. KELLEY, Ginsberg & Martin on bankruptcy, op. cit., § 3.01[B][3]. W.R. NORTON, JR., Norton bankruptcy law and practice, op. cit., § 36:43. D.R. COWANS, Cowans bankruptcy law and practice, op. cit., pp. 477ss. B.A. BLUM, Bankruptcy and debtor/creditor, op. cit. A.N. RESNICK, Bankruptcy law manual, op. cit. D.G. EPSTEIN, Bankruptcy and related law in a nutshell, op. cit., pp. 170ss. J.F. MURPHY, The automatic stay in bankruptcy, op. cit., pp. 589ss. R.A. JOHNSON, M. C. O'LEARY, Automatic stay provisions of the bankruptcy act of 1978, op. cit. I. RAMSAY, Personal insolvency in the 21st century. A comparative analysis of the US and Europe, op. cit.

[415]B.A. BLUM, Bankruptcy and debtor/creditor, op. cit., pp. 144ss. L.B. BARTELL, Visualizing bankruptcy, op. cit., pp. 99ss. P. A. MURPHY, E.E. SAGERMAN, D. NEIER, Creditor's rights in bankruptcy, op. cit., pp. 232ss. For a jurisprudential application see the case: In re Skinner, F.2d 444 (1990), 447.

[416]D.R. COWANS, Cowans bankruptcy law and practice, op. cit., pp. 480ss, however, the meaning of the statement made by B.A. BLUM, Bankruptcy and debtor/creditor, op. cit., pp. 260ss, according to which: "Although the automatic stay, it is nevertheless a court order (...)".

It should be added, then, that the general requirements to be able to pronounce the contempt include provision, content specificity and, of course, a conduct in violation of the command enclosed. Consequently, in the case where the subject who act in violation of an injunction either in good faith, or otherwise ignore without such a measure it cannot be convicted for court contempt[417].

These general principles, of course, also apply with regard to the special injunction now under consideration, so that it is necessary to conclude that the act carried out in the guilty ignorance of automatic stay operation, even if it gives place to the nullity of the same act the possibility of obtaining a declaration of inoperativity ex tunc of the injunction, will never lead, also, to the ruling of contempt against the entity in question. This solution, if it has always found consistent confirmation in US doctrine[418] and jurisprudence[419] has also received a definitive consecration with 2005BAPCPA, which intervened on Section 342 of the Bankruptcy Code, dedicated to interest parties' communication, adding a subsection (g) (2), where the possibility of imposing a pecuniary sanction for automatic stay infringement is excluded, unless , the subject in question had not already received the communication in speech[420]. Moreover, if it proves that the entity has in any case had actual knowledge of automatic stay, this compensates the lack of communication in speech, with applicability, therefore, of the sanctions provided for the contempt[421].

---

[417]D.R. COWANS, Cowans bankruptcy law and practice, op. cit., pp. 477ss.

[418]A.N. RESNICK, H.J. SOMMER, Collier on bankruptcy, op. cit. S.V. KELLEY, Ginsberg & Martin on bankruptcy, op. cit., M.A. FREY, S.K. SWINSON, Introduction to bankruptcy law, op. cit., pp. 251ss. P.A. MURPHY, E.E. SAGERMAN, D. NEIER, Creditor's rights in bankruptcy, op. cit., pp. 232ss. J.F. MURPHY, The automatic stay in bankruptcy, op. cit., pp. 590ss.

[419]In re Crysen/Montenay Energy Co., 902 F.2d 1098 (1990); See also case: In re Zartun, 30 B.R. (1983), where it is specified that the knowledge of the deposit of the petition, unaccompanied by the knowledge of the operativity of the automatic stay, is a sufficient condition for the conviction for contempt.

[420]It should also be remembered that the Official Form 9 completes the content of the notice specifying that it must indicate the validity of the automatic stay. This data together with the provision referred to in sect. 342 (g) (2), would seem to disprove those jurisprudential opinions, mentioned in the previous note, according to which the only knowledge of the deposit of the petition, unaccompanied by the knowledge of the operativity of the automatic stay, would be sufficient for the purpose of contempt.

[421]R.A. JOHNSON, M.C. O'LEARY, Automatic stay provisions of the bankruptcy act of 1978, op. cit.

With regard to the procedure for obtaining a ruling by court contempt, the possibility for the court to issue "its own accord", that is, of its own office, rule 9020 of the Federal Rules of Bankruptcy Procedures provides that it may be requested by the party affected by a motion according to the previous rule 9014, i.e. the one that, as seen, regulates contested matters[422].

52.Automatic stay guilty (willful) violation

Automatic stay speciality compared to the general category of injunctions, which we have already seen consists, inter alia, in its operation ex lege, is also reflected in remedies specifically provided by the same law, preparing the Bankruptcy Code some penalties peculiar to the hypothesis of automatic stay violation.

The reference, in particular, is to Section 362 (k) of the Bankruptcy Code, where is envisaged that the individual who suffers an injury due to a willful violation of the automatic stay, of a violation made aware of the operation of the prohibition, has the right to compensation of the actual damages, including the expenses and professional compensation of the judgment, as well as, under certain circumstances, of the punitive damages[423].

To be precise, if the entity subjected to the injunction makes a prohibited initiative, after having acquired knowledge of the deposit of the petition and, with it, of automatic stay operativity[424], it intervened through the communication referred to in Section 342, or brought to the attention

---

[422]In this regard, see, in fact, the text of the section 342 (g) (1), where it is envisaged that a communication made to the creditor to an address different from that which the creditor himself has for this purpose indicated: "(...) Shall not be effective notice until such notice is brought to the attention of such creditor (...)". For further details see: A.N. RESNICK, H.J. SOMMER, Collier on bankruptcy, op. cit., § 362.12[2][a].

[423]Section 362(k): "(...) An individual injured by any willful violation of a stay provided by this section shall recover actual damages, including costs and attorneys' fees, and, in appropriate circumstances, may recover punitive damages (...)".

[424]A.N. RESNICK, H.J. SOMMER, Collier on bankruptcy, op. cit., § 362.12[3]. S.V. KELLEY, Ginsberg & Martin on bankruptcy, op. cit., D.R. COWANS, Cowans bankruptcy law and practice, op. cit., pp. 480ss. M.A. FREY, S.K. SWINSON, Introduction to bankruptcy law, op. cit. D.G. EPSTEIN, Bankruptcy and related law in a nutshell, op. cit., pp. 163ss. I. RAMSAY, Personal insolvency in the 21st century. A comparative analysis of the US and Europe, op. cit. In jurisprudence: In re Chestnut, 422 F.3d 298 (2005).

of the addressee in another appropriate and proven way; also with regard to the case now commented, in fact, the rule applies, as per Section 342 (g) (2), which excludes the application of a pecuniary sanction in the event of failure to receive the information in speech[425]. The proof of knowledge of automatic stay operativeness looms, naturally, on the subject that acts for the compensation of the damage[426]. However, an innocent violation can turn into a willful violation if, after having received the communication of the beginning of the procedure, the party fails to remedy the action performed (through, for example, the restoration of the status quo ante, or the interruption of the action in progress, or the return of the asset subtracted from the summer property)[427].

On the contrary, it is not required to ascertain the intention, in the case of non-compliant subject, to violate the automatic stay, and therefore of a subjective attitude of intent[428].

As for the subjective requirement inherent in the willful violation of automatic stay, it should be added that it is common to the possibility of condemning part of court contempt, so that it will be possible, in certain cases, to cumulate said generic sanction prepared for injunctions violations with the special ones, referred to in Section 362 (k) now under consideration, specifically designed to protect automatic stay.

53.The textual data of the norm...poses some problems.

First of all, it refers exclusively to “individual”, that is, first of all,

---

[425]A.N. RESNICK, H.J. SOMMER, Collier on bankruptcy, op. cit. S.V. KELLEY, Ginsberg & Martin on bankruptcy, op. cit., D. WARREN, D.J. BUSSEL, D.A. SKEEL, JR., Bankruptcy, op. cit., pp. 184ss. L.B. BARTELL, Visualizing bankruptcy, op. cit.

[426]D. WARREN, D.J. BUSSEL, D.A. SKEEL, JR., Bankruptcy, op. cit., B.A. BLUM, Bankruptcy and debtor/creditor, op. cit., pp. 259ss.

[427]S.V. KELLEY, Ginsberg & Martin on bankruptcy, op. cit., W.R. NORTON, JR., Norton bankruptcy law and practice, op. cit. D.R. COWANS, Cowans bankruptcy law and practice, op. cit., pp. 482 and 485.

[428]A.N. RESNICK, H.J. SOMMER, Collier on bankruptcy, op. cit. S.V. KELLEY, Ginsberg & Martin on bankruptcy, op. cit., D.R. COWANS, Cowans bankruptcy law and practice, op. cit., pp. 481ss. B.A. BLUM, Bankruptcy and debtor/creditor, op. cit. D.G. EPSTEIN, Bankruptcy and related law in a nutshell, op. cit. op. cit. In jurisprudence see the case: In re Repine, 536 F.3d 512 (2008). For further details see: B.A. BLUM, Bankruptcy and debtor/creditor, op. cit.

to the natural person debtor, while legal entities and, in particular, companies would be excluded from the scope of the law[429]. The literal interpretation of this rule did not fail to meet with the resistance of part of the jurisprudence which it considered appropriate to extend the applicability of the provision also to companies, to avoid unjustified discrimination[430]; others, vice versa, have considered that they can guarantee access to the possibility of obtaining compensation for the damages suffered also by the entities other than the debtor natural person, through, again, the rule contained in Section 105 (a) of the Bankruptcy Code[431]. But the use of the term "individual", instead of that, more specific, of "debtor" suggests something more, namely the possibility of access to compensation for damages provided by the standard under consideration also for other subjects protected by the automatic stay, including, on all, the creditors. Since this institution also protects the interests of the latter, in fact, it is right and consistent to grant the same remedy compensatory descendant from the violation of the bans placed by the institution in question[432].

As regards the compensable damage, the law as anticipated, distinguishes between actual (or compensatory) damages, to which the individual would always have rights[433], aimed at compensating the subject of damage, patrimonial and not, immediately, and the possibility, purely eventual, to impose punitive (or non compensatory) damages, having rather a sanctioning and deterrent purpose in relation to other similar initiatives.

---

[429] A.N. RESNICK, H.J. SOMMER, Collier on bankruptcy, op. cit. S.V. KELLEY, Ginsberg & Martin on bankruptcy, op. cit., D. WARREN, D.J. BUSSEL, D.A. SKEEL, JR., Bankruptcy, op. cit. P.A. MURPHY, E.E. SAGERMAN, D. NEIER, Creditor's rights in bankruptcy, op. cit., pp. 233ss.

[430] See Budget Service Co. v. Better Homes of Virginia, 804 F.2d 289 (1986), 292. D.R. COWANS, Cowans bankruptcy law and practice, op. cit., pp. 479ss. J.F. MURPHY, The automatic stay in bankruptcy, op. cit., pp. 591ss.

[431] See In re Spookyworld, Inc., 346 F.3d 1 (2003). For more analysis see: B.A. BLUM, Bankruptcy and debtor/creditor, op. cit., pp. 258ss. J. FERRIELL, E.J. JANGER, Understanding bankruptcy, op. cit.

[432] D.G. EPSTEIN, Bankruptcy and related law in a nutshell, op. cit. op. cit., pp. 162ss. In jurisprudence, see In re Dawson, 390 F.3d 1139 (2004), 1146. I. RAMSAY, Personal insolvency in the 21st century. A comparative analysis of the US and Europe, op. cit.

[433] S.V. KELLEY, Ginsberg & Martin on bankruptcy, op. cit., D.G. EPSTEIN, Bankruptcy and related law in a nutshell, op. cit. op., pp. 163ss. I. RAMSAY, Personal insolvency in the 21st century. A comparative analysis of the US and Europe, op. cit.

It must be said that the prediction, for which the individual would always be entitled to compensation for compensatory damages, and therefore, in fact, the prediction for which this type of damage would be in re ipsa, is entirely consistent with the structure of automatic stay, and therefore to the fact that its operation is connected to the presumption of the existence of a prejudice otherwise suffered by the debtor and procedure. Are not therefore those jurisprudential opinions that want to exclude the right to compensation in cases where there is no evidence of a prejudice[434], because, in fact, where there is an automatic stay, the risk of a prejudice is always there.

The compensatory damages include, first of all, the pecuniary loss suffered for economic prejudices incurred by the individual[435]. But it has already been mentioned that this item also includes a non-pecuniary damage component. An interest current in jurisprudential, emerging but increasingly shared, has in fact expressed itself in favor of the redress of the existential (emotional distress damage) damage, presumably configurable only for the debtor as a result of the conduct of his creditor who has violated to protect the former as evidently capable of provoking worries, anxieties and pangs of mind[436]. From the textual data of law, vice versa, it is inferred that the expenses and professional fees of the lawyer must also be included in this category; on the consistency of this item, however, there is no unanimous interpretation in jurisprudence, since a minority share would limit it only to the fees due for the professional activity carried out to stop the violation of automatic stay[437]; absolutely part of the majority, vice versa, in the wake of a ruling by the Supreme Court, seems oriented to include all the fees due to the lawyer, and therefore also those related to the subsequent stages aimed at obtaining full

[434]In re Brock Util. & Grading, Inc., 185 B.R. 719 (1997). B.A. BLUM, Bankruptcy and debtor/creditor, op. cit., pp. 259ss.

[435]A. N. RESNICK, H. J. SOMMER, Collier on bankruptcy, op. cit. S.V. KELLEY, Ginsberg & Martin on bankruptcy, op. cit., B.A. BLUM, Bankruptcy and debtor/creditor, op. cit.

[436]In jurisprudence, however, there is no consensus that it is necessary, in order to obtain compensation for this type of damage, proof that it has also suffered damage of a financial nature: In the affirmative the Aiello v. Providian Financial Corp. case, 239 F.3d 876 (2001); in a negative sense, the aforementioned In re Dawson case.

[437]As we can see in the case: Sternberg v. Johnston, 595 F.3d 937 (2010).

recovery of the breach occurred[438].

The law also recognizes the possibility of condemning the person who acted in automatic stay violation to compensate punitive damages. Obviously, this faculty requires a greater degree of guilt than the one present in simple willful violation, which is characterized by malice and bad faith, a situation that is often defined as "egregious", i.e. striking, violation[439]. An example can be represented by the creditor's conduct who, although aware of the start of the procedure and automatic stay operation, makes numerous and repeated calls to his debtor, for the sole purpose of embarrassing and humiliating him[440]. In such hypotheses, with all the evidence, the conditions for a conviction for the compensation often also occur emotional distress damages.

Further possibility of condemning the entity violating the automatic stay to payment for punitive damages is moreover an express limitation in the same Section 362 (k), which in the following number (2) states that in the event that said violation consists in an action carried out by a person who, in good faith, was convinced that, in relation to the debtor, the rule referred to in the previous subsection (h) or, in other words, the semiautomatic stay case that prescribes the early termination of injunction in the event that the debtor natural person or the trustee fails to perform certain obligations pursuant to law with regard to some personal assets placed as collateral for a loan or the subject of a pending lease, and therefore that the automatic stay had ceased, the compensation for

---

[438]See tha case: Pennsylvania v. Delaware Valley Citizens' Council for Clean Air, 478 U.S. (1986).

[439]S.V. KELLEY, Ginsberg & Martin on bankruptcy, op. cit. B.A. BLUM, Bankruptcy and debtor/creditor, op. cit., pp. 260ss. D.G. EPSTEIN, Bankruptcy and related law in a nutshell, op. cit., pp. 164ss. I. RAMSAY, Personal insolvency in the 21st century. A comparative analysis of the US and Europe, op. cit.

[440]In re White, 410 B.R. 322 (2009), 328, which is affirmed: "Platinum Protection's actions in this case were also egregious. The Debtor contacted Platinum Protection on numerous occasions to notify it as to the pendency of the bankruptcy case, and yet calls to the Debtor continued. Moreover, Platinum Protection engaged in practices intended to expose the Debtor to embarrassment and humiliation by calling the Debtor's workplace and emergency contacts to inform them of the Debtor's delinquent status. These circumstances constitute the "appropriate circumstances" under which punitive damages should be awarded, under any standard. Based on the egregious nature of the conduct of Platinum Protection, the Court finds that an award of $ 10,000 in punitive damages is an appropriate punishment and deterrent (...)".

damages is limited, in fact, to actual damages[441]. Since, moreover, the payment of expenses and professional fees due to the lawyer are items included in this category, the limitation imposed by the aforementioned provision does not affect the compensation of such items of damage[442].

---

[441]Section 362(k), affirmed that: "(...) If such violation is based on an action taken by an entity in the good faith belief that subsection (h) applies to the debtor, the recovery under paragraph (1) of this subsection against such entity shall be limited to actual damages (...)".

[442]A.N. RESNICK, H.J. SOMMER, Collier on bankruptcy, op. cit. D.G. EPSTEIN, Bankruptcy and related law in a nutshell, op. cit., I. RAMSAY, Personal insolvency in the 21st century. A comparative analysis of the US and Europe, op. cit. S.V. KELLEY, Ginsberg & Martin on bankruptcy, op. cit., L.B. BARTELL, Visualizing bankruptcy, op. cit., A.N. RESNICK, H.J. SOMMER, Collier on bankruptcy, op. cit.

PART 2

Legal analysis, reflections and observations of bankruptcy crimes in the insolvency system of North America

1.Introduction.

The federal bankruptcy system of the state is a historically deriving burden, in parallel with the application of punitive criminal offenses, from the same civil discipline of insolvency and bankruptcy, which considered, presumptively, the insolvent as a subject "in odor of fraud", according to the brocardo decoctor, ergo fraudator.

From a methodological point of view this study will be carried out through the analysis of sources from different extraction. Alongside the proper reading of materials of academic and doctrinal origin, particular attention will be paid to the exposition of professional resources made available to the operators of bankruptcy system (mainly trustees and prosecutors) by the US federal office administration.

Last, only in this preliminary presentation, but obviously fundamental as to specific weight, will be the analysis of the case law of the federal superior jurisdictions (mainly, if not exclusively, of the jurisprudence elaborated by the various circuits of the federal court of appeals, since, in subject matter of this work, essentially the courts of last resort)[443].

---

[443]The 94 US judicial districts are organized into 12 regional circuits (Circuits), each of which houses a Court of Appeal. The jurisdiction of the Court of Appeals, therefore, encompasses appealing appeals from each of the district courts located within the membership circuit. These are the districts of the US Court of Appeals: -Federal Circuit: Washington headquarters; A.D. Circuit (Washington headquarters): District of Columbia; - 1st Circuit (Boston headquarters): Maine, Massachusetts; New Hampshire; Puerto Rico; Rhode Island; - 2nd Circuit (home of New York): Connecticut; New York; Vermont; - 3rd Circuit (Philadelphia office): Delaware; New Jersey; Pennsylvania; U.S. Virgin Islands; - 4th Circuit (Richmond headquarters): Maryland; North Carolina; South Carolina; Virginia; West Virginia; - 5th Circuit (home of New Orleans): Louisiana; Mississippi; Texas; - 6th Circuit (home of Cincinnati): Kentucky; Michigan; Ohio; Tennessee; - 7th Circuit (Chicago

If, on the one hand, the interpretation of courts plays a fundamental role in the approach (though necessarily limited and, inevitably, incomplete) to the bankruptcy criminal provisions in force in the legal system taken for comparison purposes; on the other, it is necessary to stress from now on that, from an absolute and relative point of view (having, in other words, the scarcity of the statistical resources that accompany, or should accompany, the local judicial activity), the federal jurisprudential production (and only to this can be referred to, given the federal nature and not the state of crimes related to insolvency) is in bankruptcy extremely rarefied.

Even with all the limitations due to the lack of (cultural) tools necessary for a comparative study that is, and cannot be, always in progress, the approach to the American bankruptcy criminal system requires the abandonment of certainties related to theoretical, practical and national experiences and requires to reevaluate and, often, to leave out certain categories vice versa fundamental in the criminal sub-system of origin of the writer.

One of the most significant examples is that related to the characteristics of the active elements subject to incrimination under the rules that will be exposed. The rules contained in title 18 of the US Code (the US Federal Code, hereinafter 18 USC) from § 152 to § 157 contemplate, for the most part, figures of common crime and are applicable, indifferently, to the commercial entrepreneur, to the figures companies (directors, auditors, etc.), but also, and this is certainly the original element, to natural persons.

This does not reflect but the marked difference between the US system of insolvency procedures (governed by the various paragraphs of title 11 of the U.S.C.). A figure similar to bankruptcy, (which, despite the name that refers to our criminal equivalent, has no criminal connotation) depending on different forms summarized in the various paragraphs of title

---

headquarters): Illinois; Indiana; Wisconsin; 8th Circuit (home of St. Louis): Arkansas; Iowa; Minnesota; Missouri; Nebraska; North Dakota; South Dakota; 9th Circuit (home of San Francisco): Alaska; Arizona; California; Guam; Hawaii; Idaho; Montana; Nevada; Northern Mariana Islands; Oregon; Washington; -10th Circuit (home of Denver): Colorado; Kansas; New Mexico; Oklahoma; Utah; Wyoming; -11th Circuit (Atlanta headquarters): Alabama; Florida; Georgia.

11 USC, a purely liquidation procedure or debt restructuring, intended, in the physiology (excluding that of conducts attributable to frauds, in the sense both criminal and civil law of the term, by the debtor) to the debit (discharge) of the bankrupt, is, in fact, applicable indifferently to the commercial entrepreneur (individual or corporate) and to the natural person (consumer)[444]. At the same time, the US system has a criminal armament that applies to both categories and indeed, in practice, given the very clear prevalence of bankruptcy claims presented by o towards consumers compared to those affecting commercial entrepreneurs, the application of bankruptcy criminal cases is mainly aimed at the former rather than the latter.

If a first important difference concerns the active subjects of bankruptcy crimes, no less important is the one concerning the role of bankruptcy in the offense structure. Problematic not negligible moment in the bankruptcy criminal system: That on the nature of the bankruptcy sentence in the structure of bankruptcy crimes, so much so that it is intended as a constitutive element, a condition of punishment (extrinsic or intrinsic)[445], of procedure[446], of existence o presupposed (in the post-bankruptcy hypotheses)[447], it acquires an unavoidable resolution, given the indispensability of the same for the prosecution of criminal cases. The declaration of bankruptcy also marks, in the national legal system, a watershed that is particularly important also in a descriptive key, making it possible to distinguish between cases of pre and post bankruptcy offenses.

---

[444]It could be said that the US bankruptcy system, although still in a disorganized manner, is born with a humanitarian vocation, precisely to cope with situations of over-indebtedness of natural persons. Indeed, of a physical person. In 1800, prior to the adoption of the first organic codification dated 1898, an exemption discipline was adopted unanimously by the Congress to allow the release from prison for debts (due to a failed construction speculation) by Robert Morris, one of the signatories of the Declaration of Independence and the American Constitution, as well as one of the first two senators of the state of Pennsylvania. See in argument: G.F. MUNITZ, Keynote address: Stories in the development of bankruptcy law, in Golden Gate University Law Review, 42, 2012, pp. 4ss.

[445]D. SKEEL JR., Debt's dominion. A history of bankruptcy law in America, Princeton University Press, Princeton and Oxford, 2014, Introduction, pp. 6ss. S.J. LUBBEN, A new understanding of the bankruptcy clause, in Case Western Reserve Law Review, 64, 2013, pp. 326ss. K. AYOTTE, D.A. SKEEL, Bankruptcy law as a liquidity provider, in University of Chicago Law Review, 80, 2013, pp. 1560ss.

[446]D. SKEEL JR., Debt's dominion. A history of bankruptcy law in America, op. cit.

[447]D. SKEEL JR., Debt's dominion. A history of bankruptcy law in America, op. cit.

Limiting ourselves to mentioning what will be shown with reference to individual incriminating cases, in US bankruptcy criminal system, on the contrary, the focus is on a different (and earlier) element (and moment), that of signing the application pursuant to of one of paragraphs of Title 11 USC (petition), whether promoted by the active subject (debtor/reo) or by the creditors (involuntary petition), who can (not necessarily) be victims of crime, but not offended people (ample space will be dedicated, infra, to the good legal framework protected by bankruptcy crimes).

Moreover, it is certainly an aspect of greater breakage with respect to the domestic system certain conduct carried out prior to the signing of the bankruptcy petition (in-house or by creditors) and in anticipation of it can be criminalized even if no bankruptcy is ever declared, nor is any instance brought to that effect.

Always considering the subjective element, the fact that no US bankruptcy criminal offense is punishable under the guilt and that the distinction between fraudulent and simple bankruptcy cannot be reproduced in that system will not be overlooked.

These cases, do not ever contemplate bankruptcy as a necessary event, due at a particular moment in the life of company/individual, and, consequently, do not incriminate, contrary to what happens in the national system, the omission or delay in the presentation of the related request, nor the aggravation of the disruption caused by the continuation of the business activity, in the absence of further relevant conduct pursuant to title 18 USC § 152 and 157[448].

The exposition of incriminating offenses just mentioned could hardly be effective if the statutory context of reference is totally excluded, that governed, that is, by the already mentioned aforementioned title 11 U.S.C.; for this reason the following paragraph will be dedicated, albeit in a manner that is not exhaustive and necessarily rapid, to some notes on the insolvency procedures in force in the US federal system.

[448]B. RIDER, Research handbook on international financial crime, Edward Elgar Publishers, Cheltenham, 2015, pp. 210ss.

2.The system of insolvency proceedings in federal US law.

Even in our days the major commentators of US federal bankruptcy system could not fail to notice the absolute uniqueness of the same in the world panorama[449]. Correctly, the element of greatest surprise for the foreign interpreter is identified in the fact that, in that system, the recourse to bankruptcy procedures (henceforth also bankruptcy) is not considered, either by natural persons, or by entrepreneur of last resort. Certainly no one would like to declare their bankruptcy, but most US debtors consider this eventuality as a normal resource to achieve a healthy composition of their debts and certainly not as the "end" of any activity.

Also from a numerical point of view, in the last 15 years the recourse to bankruptcy procedures has reached top numbers. For the first time in 1996, petitions submitted by natural persons exceeded one million per year, as well as those signed by commercial entrepreneurs (more precision will be observed in the last paragraph of this chapter, there where we will also try to give an account of the multiple and contrasting opinions on the reasons why the recourse to the North American bankruptcy system is, from the mid-nineties until today, literally exploded).

What he wants to emphasize, again with the words of authoritative doctrine, is that "US bankruptcy law is certainly more favorable (sympathetic) towards the debtor than that of most other nations (...)"[450].

Unless we return to the individual paragraphs of title 11 U.S.C. (and, therefore, on the different insolvency procedures available to debtors), adopting a perspective key "from above", we can see that one of the elements of greatest interest, and favor towards the moment, of the North American system is linked to the "control" that the debtor exercises on the procedure. First of all in the choice phase, where the debtor is, in fact, who can opt for purely liquidatorial plans (which provide for the delivery of the most relevant assets to the procedure, but guarantee immediate debts, at least for natural persons) rather than reorganization in continuity. In this second case, having in mind the procedures initiated by

[449]"Bankruptcy law in the United States is unique in the world" for D. SKEEL JR., Debt's dominion. A history of bankruptcy law in America, op. cit.

[450]D. SKEEL JR., Debt's dominion. A history of bankruptcy law in America, op. cit., pp. 8

the commercial entrepreneur, it is the latter that maintains control of the business activity and is not automatically replaced by a curator.

Another distinctive element is that linked to the strong jurisdictionalization of procedures and the pre-eminence of the role played by specialized legal assistance[451]. The origins of US bankruptcy system are to be found in the last decades of the eighteenth century and reflect the particular cultural ideology, far outdated at the time, according to which the North American future would have been assured by the development of trade. In this sense, bankruptcy laws should have played a fundamental role to protect non-fraudulent debtors, as well as creditors, and to encourage the development of a credit on speculative grounds that would fuel the growth of trades[452].

The current bankruptcy code, issued in 1978, is addressed, as already mentioned, to different categories of subjects: Natural persons (insolvent civilians), commercial entrepreneurs (distressed corporations), as well as other economic entities, however, similar to discipline, to the latter (limited partnerships, general partnerships).

The main purpose of the bankruptcy code is to regulate a procedure (or a series of procedures) through which some insolvent debtors (the honest but injured debtor)[453] can reorganize their business,

---

[451]D. SKEEL JR., Debt's dominion. A history of bankruptcy law in America, op. cit., pp. 2ss notes that in spite of the strong similarities between the US and British business system and the common origins of bankruptcy regulations in the nineteenth century, there is now a large gap between the two countries. For example, the British system is more oriented towards the liquidation of the insolvent firm and the procedures, even if there is a judicial declaration of bankruptcy, have a more markedly administrative footprint. This is evidenced by the absence of specialized legal assistance throughout the first phase of contact between the debtor and the curator, as well as the expulsion of the debtor from the control of the insolvent enterprise, entrusted to a representative of the credit mass, the trustee. For more references, also in historical terms, to the British system. See in argument: V. MARKAM LESTER, Victorian insolvency: Bankruptcy, imprisonment for debt, and company winding-up, in Nineteenth Century England, Oxford University Press, Oxford, 1995.

[452]D. R. MCCOY, The elusive Republic: Political economy in Jeffersonian America, University of North Carolina Press, 1980, pp. 179ss. For an interesting overview of the historical evolution of the US bankruptcy through its various arrests (1898, 1938, 1978, pp. 169ss. D. SKEEL JR., Debt's dominion. A history of bankruptcy law in America, op. cit., G.F. MUNITZ, Keynote address: Stories in the development of bankruptcy law, cit., pp. 2ss.

[453]K. GEBBIA, Debt and crime: Inevitable Bedfellows, in Golden Gate University Law

make peace with their creditors and enjoy a new opportunities in life, a clean path that can be pursued without the pressure and the sword of damocles of pre-existing debts[454].

The cardinal figure of the personal bankruptcy system (the one addressed to natural persons) is the concept of discharge, the cancellation of debt or debit. The element of the discharge, the idea, that is, that once the goods have been delivered, if present, to the procedure, a subject is no longer obliged to face any debt surplus with his future assets, if we consider the history century of bankruptcy, it has relatively recent origins[455]. When, at the end of the procedure, the individual obtains the discharge the contracted (asset) bonds are canceled and the creditors will no longer be able to obtain the fulfillment.

Pursuant to current legislation (without any pretense of exhaustive or technical analysis, which goes beyond the scope of this work), the debtor natural person can essentially follow two paths to obtain discharge. The first is that of straight liquidation pursuant to 11 U.S.C. § 7 (commonly called Chapter 7). In these cases, the debtor, after having lodged an application for bankruptcy, is called upon a series of declaratory obligations (on his own assets and income, as well as on recent economic and financial movements) and on the delivery of his property[456] to the Bankrupty Court (a Federal Court).

After the appointment of a trustee (trustee), the latter provides to

---

Review, 42, 2012, pp. 532ss.

[454]Grogan vs. Garner, 498 U.S. 279, 1991; Janus v. American Federation of State of 27 June 2018, Supreme Court of US n. 16-1477, Castro-contreras v. U.S. of 11 June 2018, n. 17-8861, the new route is normally defined as "fresh start" with regard to natural persons and "financial rehabilitation" with regard to corporations. K. GEBBIA, Debt and Crime, cit., pag. 530.

[455]This institue was introduced for first time in England in 1705. See in argument: C.J. TABB, The historical evolution of the bankruptcy discharge, in American Bankruptcy Law Journal, n. 65/1991, pag. 325. E. KADENS, The Pitkin affair: A study of fraud in early english bankruptcy, in American Bankruptcy Law Journal, n. 84, 2010, pag. 483ss. J. REIS, S. BATTILOSSI, State and financial systems in Europe and the USA. Historical perspectives on regulation and supervision in the nineteenth and twenthieth century, ed. Routledge, London & New York, 2026.

[456]Albeit with exceptions. For example, the debtor is authorized to retain ownership of certain assets, such as work tools, or portions of real estate value. See, 11 U.S.C. section 522. These exceptions are aimed at allowing the debtor, even in the face of a bankruptcy procedure, to be guaranteed, but we will return, a so called fresh start.

liquidate the assets and distribute the proceeds to the creditors, in an equal manner according to the respective classes of privilege. This procedure, however, actually takes place in a narrow minority of cases. On average, 75% of the instances under Chapter 7 concern debtors who do not own (or declare not to own) any good to repay their creditors (so-called "no asset" cases). In these cases, the debtor can benefit from immediate discharge within one or two weeks of petition presentation[457].

The second alternative offered to the debtor consists in the presentation of a rehabilitation plan pursuant to title 11 U.S.C. § 13[458]. According to this regulation, the applicant maintains possession and control over its assets and undertakes to meet a rate of its debt exposure over a period ranging from three to five years.

Since the entry into force of the new bankruptcy code (1978), most instances of bankruptcy concerning natural persons are submitted in person by the debtor (voluntary petition). There is the theoretical possibility that the petition is presented also by the creditors (involuntary petition), but, in practice, this happens rarely, given the impossibility, once the procedure has started, to achieve, for the creditor, the complete and individual satisfaction of one's credit (each individual judicial action is suspended, so-called automatic stay) and the relative ease, for the debtor, of obtaining the discharge[459].

However, this institute knows some exceptions: Some, so to speak, physiological, linked to the particular nature of debt[460]; others, however, linked to a distorted use of the bankruptcy system, following,

---

[457]D. SKEEL JR., Debt's dominion. A history of bankruptcy law in America, op. cit., pp. 7ss.

[458]B. RIDER, Research handbook on international financial crime, op. cit.

[459]It is no coincidence that the latest reform of the bankruptcy code launched by the Bush administration in 2005, the Bankruptcy Abuse Prevention and Consumer Protection Act (BAPCP), which we will briefly discuss in the last paragraph of this chapter, is an attempt to dramatic increase in consumer bankruptcy through a tightening of controls assigned to the US Trustee Program in the process of signing the applications. An inspired reform, in the words of an authoritative commentator from a "very anti-consumer debtor" logic. G.F. MUNITZ, Keynote address: Stories in the development of bankruptcy law, op. cit., pp. 546ss. J. CHIRCOP, The impact of the bankruptcy protection act of 2005 repo "safe harbor" provisions on investors, op. cit., pp. 1724ss.

[460]As far as natural persons are concerned, they are examples of exception to the discharge, for example, the debts relating to student loans. See, 11 U.S.C.

again in general terms, fraud.

Similarly to what happens to natural persons, commercial entrepreneurs (generally in company form) can also opt for the signing of an application for liquidation, as for reorganization. The liquidation takes place in accordance with the same Chapter 7 of the Bankruptcy Code, but the regulations envisaged present only weak analogies with respect to that applicable to consumers. Once the common section has been chosen for liquidation, it is represented by the appointment of a trustee[461] who proceeds with the sale of corporate assets and the distribution of the proceeds among the creditors, equally, according to the respective classes of privilege. Unlike what happens to natural persons, however, the company that signs an instance under Chapter 7 has no right to consider any good and, above all, is not destined to benefit from discharge[462].

3.The alternative to the straight liquidation procedure is, once again, that of reorganization pursuant to Title 11 U.S.C. § 11 (Chapter 11).

Once submitted for reorganization the managers[463] of the distress corporation are authorized to benefit from a variable period (at least four months, except for the possibility of extensions granted by the Bankruptcy Court) called exclusivity period during which these without interference from the organs of the procedure (if the appointed judge opts for the appointment of a judicial commissioner), they have the task of preparing and proposing the reorganization plan.

The signing of the petition (and for the whole course of the procedure) makes the operative the automatic stay, according to which the social creditors are inhibited from proposing individual actions (even

---

461Normally the trustee is appointed by the Bankruptcy Court among the members of a federal agency, U.S. Trustee; however, it may happen that the trustee is chosen by the social creditors, when an instance representing at least 20% of the unsecured debt is applied for.

462D. SKEEL JR., Debt's dominion. A history of bankruptcy law in America, op. cit., pp. 9ss

463For D. SKEEL JR., Debt's dominion. A history of bankruptcy law in America, op. cit., pp. 214ss the central role of the managers of the company in the reorganization procedure - to the detriment of the figure of the curator-designated by the 1978 bankruptcy code reform was strongly influenced by the political will to guarantee greater contendibility of the ownership structure and favor the corporate takeover operations based on leverage.

extrajudicial) to recovery of their credit[464].

Another recurring figure is that of "(...) White Knight" Bleedouts (...) a business consultant is hired by a troubled business to assist it in acquiring new financing and streamlining operations. On occasion, the "white knight" is given an ownership interest in the business. The consultant takes control of the financial operations of the business. He/she uses the position to convert company assets, including failure to pay withholding taxes, failure to make pension fund contributions, diverting receivables, paying personal expenses with company funds, taking an excessive salary and bonuses and, in some situations, paying false invoices to entities or individuals related to him/her (...)[465].

---

[464]A bankruptcy regulation favorable to the debtor, in fact, encourages buyers to resort to a strong indebtedness in order to carry out acquisitions with the awareness of having significant possibilities to maintain control of the newly acquired company, possibly signing a reorganization request, even if the revenues achieved post takeover were not sufficient to repay the debt incurred to carry out the transaction. At the same time, the contestability is guaranteed even if the point of view of the target company is adopted: a common defense strategy, in the face of a hostile acquisition attempt, is to contract a considerable amount of debts, in order to discourage the potential buyer from carrying out the operation. Obviously, this strategy involves risks related to a possible future insolvency. A system that ensures managerial continuity also in the latent sense of bankruptcy, however, does not lead the management of the target company to "lock" the ownership structure by favoring the entry into the share capital of institutional investors such as banks or investment funds. See in argument: M.J. ROE, Strong managers, weak owners. The political roots of American Corporate Finance, Princeton University Press, Princeton, 1966, Chapter 10. It should be noted that these entrepreneurial phenomena often represent the occasion for the realization of criminal operations punishable under the bankruptcy criminal law subject to forthcoming exposure. A rundown of the most relevant criminal penalties in this area, which go under the name of bleed out, is found in the United States Trustee Manual, Bankruptcy Fraud & Abuse Enforcement Program, August 1997, pp. 60ss. The description offered by the Corporate Raider Bleedouts: "(...) A stable company with very liquid assets, such as a large pension and/or profit sharing fund, is acquired in a leveraged buyout. The company is operated for the sole purpose of allowing the insiders to loot the company. A chapter 11 is filed to allow the insiders to complete their scheme. Business transactions are complex and purposefully confusing, which makes fraudulent conveyance actions expensive and difficult to prove. Scheme is used in all types of industries (...).

[465]Bankruptcy proceedings, also by virtue of the aforementioned automatic residence rule, have been, over the years, used by the American business system as a real lifeline to protect the continuity and profitability of the company even against future and economic risks. The bankruptcy has been, since the 80s of the 1900s, used as a real preventative solution to the potential liabilities deriving from legal actions for widespread damage (mass tort liability). See, K.J. DELANEY, Strategic bankruptcy: University of California Press, Berkeley and Los Angeles, 1992, pp. 60ss. Which cites, for example, the paradigmatic case of Johns

The reorganization plan is then subject to negotiation between the management of social debtor and the creditors (but only the most important among them), meeting in committees[466].

The plan, therefore, is submitted to the approval (by a two-thirds majority) by the various committees. Should the debtor not be able to obtain the approval of a category of social creditors, the bankruptcy court may, however, approve the reorganization plan pursuant to the so called cramdown provision. To be confirmed, however, a cramdown plan must satisfy the absolute priority rule with respect to the dissenting credit class. At the latest, this rule provides that the debtor is authorized to satisfy creditors belonging to a lower class than the dissenting class, as well as the shareholders, only after having repaid in full the creditors belonging to the committee that has not approved the plan[467].

The role of the curator (trustee) re-emerges with reference, essentially, to his power of control and cancellation on preferential[468] and fraudulent payments[469]. The revocation regulation, however, seems to be rather limited, since the trustee has the power to revoke, by virtue of a presumption of preferentiality, the payments made by the company (but the discipline is also common for natural persons) in the ninety days prior

---

Manville (but it is only one of many-see, for example, the example of Dow Corning undertaking a reorganization procedure to protect itself from legal proceedings for damage caused by defective silicone implants for cosmetic surgery). Johns Manville was (and still survives as Manville Inc.) one of the leading companies in the United States for the production of asbestos, essentially for home insulation and large vessels. Beginning in 1939, but particularly after 1964, Johns Manville became the target of an ever-increasing number of actions

[466]In each reorganization case there is necessarily a committee representing the seven largest unsecured creditors, but the bankruptcy court can order the creation of other committees representing the other categories of creditors and shareholders. The figure often absent, in the Chapter 11 cases, under the current law (which revolutionized the previous Bankruptcy code of Roosveltiana of 1938 which provided for a penetrating control on the reorganization procedures by the Security and Exchange Commission) is that of the trustee (curator) who intervenes in the reorganization plan only in a minority of certain cases. "The assumption is that the corporation's current managers will continue to run the show (...)". D. SKEEL JR., Debt's dominion. A history of bankruptcy law in America, op. cit., pp. 10ss

[467]D. SKEEL JR., Debt's dominion. A history of bankruptcy law in America, cit., pag. 10.

[468]11 U.S.C. § 547. For further details see: M.A. FRY, P. HURLEY, S.K. SWINSON, Introduction to bankruptcy law, Thomson & Reuters, New York, 2012, pp. 262ss.

[469]11 U.S.C. § 548. M.A. FRY, P. HURLEY, S.K. SWINSON, Introduction to bankruptcy law, op. cit.

to the signing of the petition. This time margin extends to one year if the payments are made in favor of corporate insiders (shareholders, managers) on the presumption that these, having greater chances of knowing the state of bankruptcy of the corporation, may have arranged the payments in order to take advantage of the generality of creditors. Consequently, the trustee who sees the existence of preferential payments, or of other anti-doubt conduct by the management of the distressed corporation (such as the frauds that we will deal with in the next paragraphs), has the right to advance to the Bankruptcy Court an instance of transformation of the procedure from Chapter 11 to Chapter 7, i.e. from reorganization to liquidation[470].

4.Overview of incriminating cases.

Coming, therefore, in medias res, at the heart of indictments, you can easily notice how the same go to cover conduits, in large part, overlapping those considered criminally relevant even in the local system. On the other hand, however, they see each analogy weaken and present themselves as markedly original. As we will see, it is the opinion of the writer that this depends, essentially, on the legal good protected by the US criminal offenses, which is, unequivocally, the administration of justice[471].

The Congress drew a normative (the explicit reference is to title 18 USC § 152) which, in the interpretation of the major commentators, taken from the settled jurisprudence, "tries to cover every possible method by which the bankrupt, or any other person, may try to circumvent the bankruptcy law, striving to prevent a fair distribution of assets among creditors"[472].

The objective of criminal protection, except to return, later, on a jurisprudential analysis that, in interpreting the elements of crime of the

[470]M.A. FRY, P. HURLEY, S.K. SWINSON, Introduction to bankruptcy law, op. cit.
[471]S. DUBERSTEIN, Are bankruptcy Criminals?, in St. John's Law Review, 25 (2), 1951, pp. 234ss.; in fact, the criminal protection of bankruptcy proceedings has accompanied the US system since the first, and already mentioned, bankruptcy statute of 1800: L.P. KING, (eds.) Collier on Bankruptcy, Matthew Bender, New York, 1997, §7-201.
[472]L.P. KING (eds.), Collier on Bankruptcy, op. cit., § 1151. From the jurisprudence see: Stageman vs. U.S., 425, F.2d, 984, 9th Circuit, 1970. in Re Westmoreland coal Company of 29 December 2018, S.D. Texas Houston of U.S. bankruptcy courts, case n. 18-35672 adversary 18-3300.

single cases[473] will confirm what has been supported so far, is even better summarized by the words of the then attorney general Janet Reno, who in 1996, emphatically defined the "total disclosure"[474] operation as a sign of the "constant effort of the department of justice to repress and deter fraud, protect the integrity of the bankruptcy system and reinvigorate public confidence in this system"[475].

Turning to the list of criminal cases will be considered in detail only those that have more elements of analogy with national bankruptcies as these are contained in paragraphs 152 to 157 of Title 18 of the U.S.C.[476]; paragraph 152 is, without fear of denial, the cardinal rule of the whole system and, for this reason, will be analyzed separately.

§153[477] punishes the undue appropriations perpetrated by certain

---

473See in particular the par. of the Title 18 U.S.C. § 152 and Title 18 U.S.C. § 157.

474Memorandum of Attorney General Janet Reno of 10 October 1995, which is affirmed that: "(...) It is imperative that the integrity of the bankruptcy system, an integral component of our national economy, be preserved and enhanced (...). Bankruptcy is a public process, and we must aggressively pursue those who would use the system to avoid their valid legal obligations, delay or evade their Federal and State tax obligations, and otherwise distort the process witch offers deserving debtors the opportunity to seek a fresh start. We must not allow under-serving participants to use the process improperly (...)".

475P. GAUMER, Operation total disclosure, in American Bankruptcy Institute Journal, 15 (10), 1996, pp. 10ss. Legal damages for the causation of related asbestos diseases: Asbestosis, in the first period, pleural mesotheliomas and pulmonary carcinomas once the etiology has been scientifically ascertained. In 1982 the number of legal actions taken exceeded 16,500 and increased at the rate of three per hour. Given the latency time of the carcinogenic events produced, the management of J-M realized that, even if it had immediately stopped the production of asbestos, it would have been exposed to a possible/probable risk of compensation for the next thirty years. On 26 August 1982, therefore, despite being, at the time, a perfectly solvent company, Johns Manville signed a reorganization request pursuant to Chapter 11. The reorganization ended with the final approval (after a first rejection of the plan) of Bankruptcy Court in 1988. The company created a two billion dollar trust to meet the compensation of current and future victims, but the newly established Manville Inc. could continue its business activity free of any compensation risk. K.J. DELANEY, Strategic bankruptcy, op. cit., preface, assigns a value judgment (negative) on this use of the bankruptcy system, considered-in some cases-more than a refuge for the fragile entrepreneur, an instrument of offense of the powerful entrepreneur.

476For the elements of crimes see: United States Trustee Manual, pp. 19ss.

47718 USC § 153-Embezzlement against estate: a)Offense. A person described in subsection (b) who knowingly and fraudulently appropriates to the person's own use, embezzles, spends, or transfers any property or secretes or destroys any document belonging to the estate of a debtor shall be fined under this title, imprisoned not more than 5 years, or both; b)Person to Whom Section Applies. A person described in this subsection is one who has access to property or documents belonging to an estate by virtue of the person's

active subjects against the bankruptcy asset (summer)[478]. This rule does not apply to bankruptcy and is instead directed to those subjects who have access, for professional reasons, to assets or documents referable to the bankruptcy assets such as trustees, custodians, lawyers, public officials appointed by the bankruptcy court or persons named by them coadjutors. The object of the conduct is represented by the assets and documents forming part of the bankruptcy axis. The conduct, briefly, consists in the distraction of such assets to their advantage or in the destruction of documents. The subjective element is described by the know and fraudulently adverbs referring to an intentional intent figure[479]. § 154[480] governs situations of conflict of interest of procedure officers. Once again, the norm is addressed to curators, custodians or other public officials appointed by the Bank of insolvency.

The criminally relevant conduct is manifold and gives back an all-public connotation (good performance of the procedure) of the protected legal asset. The offensive structure of the case would seem to refer to the pattern of abstract danger crimes, since the judge is not required to make any assessment of the conflict of interest effectiveness in which the agent would pay, nor the screening of any damage, or danger of it; from the conduct to the purpose of the procedure, or the equitable distribution of the bankruptcy axis towards the credit mass. The incriminating conduct

---

participation in the administration of the estate as a trustee, custodian, marshal, attorney, or other officer of the court or as an agent, employee, or other person engaged by such an officer to perform a service with respect to the estate.

[478]According to the Title 11 U.S.C. § 541, are included in the concept of ownership of the summer "all the interests of the debtor in the property from the date of commencement of the procedure" and also "the fruits, products, income or profits deriving from ownership received after the beginning of the procedure".

[479]For a detailed analysis of the concepts of knowingly and fraudulently, which describe the intent required by all the bankruptcy criminal offenses, see the next paragraph on 18 U.S.C. § 152.

[480]USC § 154-Adverse interest and conduct of officers: A person who, being a custodian, trustee, marshal, or other officer of the court-knowingly purchases, directly or indirectly, any property of the estate of which the person is such an officer in a case under title 11; -knowingly refuses to permit a reasonable opportunity for the inspection by parties in interest of the documents and accounts relating to the affairs of estates in the person's charge by parties when directed by the court to do so; or -knowingly refuses to permit a reasonable opportunity for the inspection by the United States Trustee of the documents and accounts relating to the affairs of an estate in the person's charge, shall be fined under this title and shall forfeit the person's office, which shall thereupon become vacant.

ranges from the purchase (direct or indirect) by the contractor of assets owned by the summer (note that there is no reference to the purchase price and therefore no reference to a concrete danger for the correct distribution bankruptcy assets) to the denial of a reasonable request for access to the accounting records of the summer made by the interested parties or by the US trustee.

The subjective element required (generic fraud) is, in relation to this last case, less pregnant than the one seen previously, being described only by the adverterly knowingly (it is no longer required that the party acted fraudulently). A last notation about the sentence: If, contrary to the other cases, there is no custodial sanction, but only pecuniary, the provision contemplates a significant penalty (which in our system we would define) accessory such as removal from office.

§155[481] punishes agreements, explicitly or implicitly, contracts knowingly and fraudulently, to set the rates of services rendered by the various parties involved in the procedure (debtors, creditors, curator, legal representatives). § 156[482] punishes the conscious (awarely) violation of bankruptcy rules governing the procedure by a particular active subject, a professional figure, as far as the writer is aware, unknown to the national experience, but, on the contrary, extremely widespread in the US panorama, especially considering the context of consumer bankruptcy.

---

[481] 18 USC § 155-Fee agreements in cases under title 11 and receiver ships: Whoever, being a party in interest, whether as a debtor, creditor, receiver, trustee or representative of any of them, or attorney for any such party in interest, in any receivership or case under title 11 in any United States court or under its supervision, knowingly and fraudulently enters into any agreement, express or implied, with another such party in interest or attorney for another such party in interest, for the purpose of fixing the fees or other compensation to be paid to any party in interest or to any attorney for any party in interest for services rendered in connection therewith, from the assets of the estate, shall be fined under this title or imprisoned not more than one year, or both.

[482] 18 USC § 156-Knowing disregard of bankruptcy law or rule: (a) Definitions. In this section-(1) the term “bankruptcy petition preparer” means a person, other than the debtor’s attorney or an employee of such an attorney, who prepares for compensation a document for filing; and (2) the term “document for filing” means a petition or any other document prepared for filing by a debtor in a United States bankruptcy court or a United States district court in connection with a case under title 11. (b) Offense. If a bankruptcy case or related proceeding is dismissed because of a knowing attempt by a bankruptcy petition preparer in any manner to disregard the requirements of title 11, United States Code, or the Federal Rules of Bankruptcy Procedure, the bankruptcy petition preparer shall be fined under this title, imprisoned not more than 1 year, or both.

The case is, in fact, addressed to the bankruptcy petition preparer or that person, other than a lawyer (or his employee) who, by way of compensation from the debtor, prepares, in favor of it, the necessary documents, or related, to the presentation of a petition. The rule applies if an instance of bankruptcy is declared inadmissible (dismissed) by the Bankruptcy Court because of the aware (but not necessarily fraudulent) attempt by a bankruptcy petition preparer to violate the rules governing the procedure. It should be noted that this case does not postulate a participation of the debtor to the conduct of the preparer and seems, rather, aimed, as well as to protect the smooth performance of the bankruptcy proceedings, also to ensure that it is able to exert its favorable effects precisely in against the subscriber (generally a weak person who relies on the preparer for the presentation of the application).

5.Single indictment cases: 18 U.S.C. § 152.

The cardinal rule of the whole system of bankruptcy frauds (bankruptcy crimes) is represented by paragraph 152[483] of title 18 of the

[483] 18 USC § 152-Concealment of assets; false oaths and claims; bribery: A person who-(1) knowingly and fraudulently conceals from a custodian, trustee, marshal, or other officer of the court charged with the control or custody of property, or, in connection with a case under title 11, from creditors or the United States Trustee, any property belonging to the estate of a debtor; (2) knowingly and fraudulently makes a false oath or account in or in relation to any case under title 11; (3) knowingly and fraudulently makes a false declaration, certificate, verification, or statement under penalty of perjury as permitted under section 1746 of title 28, in or in relation to any case under title 11;(4) knowingly and fraudulently presents any false claim for proof against the estate of a debtor, or uses any such claim in any case under title 11, in a personal capacity or as or through an agent, proxy, or attorney; (5) knowingly and fraudulently receives any material amount of property from a debtor after the filing of a case under title 11, with intent to defeat the provisions of title 11; (6) knowingly and fraudulently gives, offers, receives, or attempts to obtain any money or property, remuneration, compensation, reward, advantage, or promise thereof for acting or forbearing to act in any case under title 11; (7) in a personal capacity or as an agent or officer of any person or corporation, in contemplation of a case under title 11 by or against the person or any other person or corporation, or with intent to defeat the provisions of title 11, knowingly and fraudulently transfers or conceals any of his property or the property of such other person or corporation; (8) after the filing of a case under title 11 or in contemplation thereof, knowingly and fraudulently conceals, destroys, mutilates, falsifies, or makes a false entry in any recorded information (including books, documents, records, and papers) relating to the property or financial affairs of a debtor; or (9) after the filing of a case under title 11, knowingly and fraudulently withholds from a custodian, trustee, marshal, or other officer of the court or a United States Trustee entitled to its possession, any recorded information (including books, documents, records, and papers)

Federal Code. This is a rule that describes a plurality of cases (offenses), specifically, nine[484], intended to operate separately and, depending on the case, in a concurrent manner (in the sense of the material competition of crimes)[485]. It does not exist, under the name of unitariness of the bankruptcy[486], this also explains the relative, only apparent, meekness of the sanctioning component envisaged by the rule in question, which contemplates a maximum sentence of five years of imprisonment.

Still in general terms, for purely descriptive purposes, the offenses described can be divided into four categories: Case of concealment/distraction

---

relating to the property or financial affairs of a debtor, shall be fined under this title, imprisoned not more than 5 years, or both.

[484]See in argument: W.L. NORTON JR., (eds.), Bankruptcy law and practice, Thomson Reuters, New York, 1997, § 49.2, 49ss. T. OGIER, J.D. WILLIAMS, Bankruptcy crimes and bankruptcy practice, in American Bankruptcy Institute Law Review, 6 (2), 1998; contra N.M. GEWERTZ, Act or assets: Multiplicitous indictments under the bankruptcy fraud statute: 18 U.S.C. 152, in The University of Chicago Law Review, 76 (2), 2009, pp. 927ss. G.P. SPENCER, A simple solution for stub rent? How proposed changes to the treatment of stub rent could lead to unforeseen consequences, in Review of Banking & Financial Law, 26, 2017, pp. 926ss.

[485]"(...) May be separately charged and separately punished" for R.C. MCCULLOUGH II, Bankruptcy fraud: Crime without punishment II, in Commercial Law Journal, 102, 1997, pp. 15, with ample jurisprudential quotations in support, among which, by way of example, U.S. vs. Schireson, 116 F.2d 155, 3rd Circuit, 1940; with regard to the specific figure of the concealment envisaged by § 152 (1), however, according to a non-granitic case law, all the hypotheses of concealment of assets attributable to the bankruptcy assets created before the petition are considered a single offense , while those carried out post petition are contested and punished separately, see, U.S. vs. Haymes, 610 F.2d 309, 5th Circuit, 1980.

[486]This, however, does not mean that, when the sentence is commuted, the condemned will automatically be destined to suffer a material accumulation of the penalties, but only that this is abstractly possible. Without wanting to go into the rules (extremely detailed, especially if compared to Article 133 of the Criminal Code, see 28 USC §944 and following) governing the activity of sentencing in the federal courts, we report how, after the guilty verdict rendered by the jury (all the processes for bankruptcy frauds are jury trials) the Court, in hypothesis, can order that the penalties imposed for each of the disputed cases are concurrently executed (more recurrent hypothesis) or separately. In the first case, imagining a sentence of three years imprisonment for each of the different charges challenged (eg concealments and false oaths), these will run simultaneously, making sure that the total period to be discounted is still three years. In the second case, on the contrary, the penalty for the second case begins to expire only once expired for the first case, bringing the total period to be deducted from six years of imprisonment. For an overview on sentencing in bankruptcy crimes v. United States Trustee Manual, cit., § 5.14.1 et seq .; report the latest changes, in the sense of greater severity, on the subject of sentencing guidelines. M.A. TIGHE, R.R. CALO, Congress, the courts, and the feds agree-bankruptcy crime does not pay, in Annual Survey of Bankruptcy Law, sess. 1, 11/12/2004, pp. 355ss.

(concealment); case of false declarations within the procedure (false oaths, false declarations); documentary cases; cases aimed at criminalizing the conduct of creditors[487].

This cataloging is only partially super impossable to that of our own, which makes a summa of divisions between patrimonial and documentary bankruptcy conduct. In particular, the differences become more profound with reference to the legal good protected by the cases that incriminate the various forms of concealment, certainly the closest to the hypotheses of bankruptcy assets operating in various national systems.

Without going further into the description of the individual sections of § 152, in order to correctly identify the legal asset to which these forecasts are safeguarded, it is appropriate to quote what is sustained by authoritative doctrine[488], and constantly taken up by the jurisprudence of the courts of appeals[489]: "Orientation of title 11 (USC) towards the rehabilitation of the debtor and the equitable distribution (of bankruptcy assets) among the creditors rests almost exclusively (heavily) on the honesty of the protagonists of the procedure. When the honesty is absent, pursuing the purpose of the civil system component of the bankruptcy system becomes more expensive and more illusory. To protect the civil system, bankruptcy crimes do not focus on[490] the losses of individuals (creditors, also understood as mass and not individually) nor are they

---

[487]This classification is the result of the union made by the writer of the (partially) different catalogs offered by T. OGIER, J.F. WILLIAMS, Bankruptcy crimes and bankruptcy practice, op. cit., pp. 2ss. M.A. TIGHE, A guide to making a criminal bankruptcy fraud referral, in American Bankruptcy Institute Law Review, 6, 1998, § 409.

[488]L.P. KING (eds.) Collier on bankruptcy, op. cit., §7-01 A.N. RESNICK, H.J. SOMMER, Collier guide to chapter 11: Key topics selected industries, Lexis Nexis, New York, 2016.

[489]U.S. vs. Gellene, 182 F.3d 578, 7th Circuit, 1999, § II.1. For further details see: K.F. BRICKE, J. TAUB, Corporate and white collar crime: Cases and materials, Wolters Kluwer, The Hague, 2017.

[490]In the original text "material". On the concept of material we will deal with the case governed by the 18 U.S.C. 152 (2) false oaths, that the jurisprudence, even if some alternations, considers punishable only if the false declarations made under oath by the debtor possess this attribute. For the configuration of the other cases, on the contrary, no verification of the actual offensiveness is required (also in terms of danger). In any case, but it will be object of specific treatment, the requirement of materiality, even where required, does not contemplate the realization of a pecuniary damage to the creditors, nor that the conduct causes a danger for the correct distribution of goods. See: U.S. vs. Gellene, 182 F.3d 578, 7th Circuit, 1999, § II.2 "we conclude that the materiality does not require proof of the potential impact on the disposition of assets".

sensitive to certain acts (criminal conduct) cause a particular damage to someone, on the contrary, the disciplinary norms in federal bankruptcies try to prevent and remedy the abuses of the bankruptcy system.

Therefore, most of the cases do not require that the offending conduct be concretely offensive[491] with regard to the effects generated on the procedure for the distribution of assets, or that the active subject (defendant) has benefited (not only) from them, or that some of the creditors are actually damaged[492].

Still remaining on a descriptive plan of the elements common to each different case, it should be emphasized that bankruptcy crimes are distinguished from abusive conduct with only civil status, as well as many other federal crimes, by virtue of the specific subjective element (intent) that must cover the pipelines[493].

Each of the specific offenses governed by § 152 requires that the prosecutor demonstrate that the accused acted knowingly and fraudulently[494]. The requirement of awareness/voluntariness is that which has offered minor hermeneutical problems; the most significant jurisprudential arrests have been attested to a literal interpretation of the term knowingly and require that the criminal relevance of the conduct be affirmed if the proof is reached that the active subject acted voluntarily, intentionally and not affected by error[495].

---

[491]The writer has decided to freely translate this part ("with regard to the effects generated on the procedure of distribution of goods") to emphasize the meaning of the passage reported. In the original text (...) most of the crimes do not require that the acts are to be found in the grand scheme of things (...).

[492]R.C. MCCULLOUGH II, Bankruptcy fraud, op. cit., pp. 19, according to: "(...) illegal activity can result in prosecution and conviction for criminal bankruptcy fraud even when no monetary harm ultimately results when, for example, a perjurer recants his testimony (...)".

[493]M.A. TIGHE, A guide to making a criminal bankruptcy fraud referral, cit., § 411.

[494]"(...) The object of Congress in passing this criminal statue was to punish those debtors who, although wanting relief from their debts, did not want to surrender what property there was to the creditors (...) for U.S. vs. Shapiro, 101, F.2d 375, 379, 7th Circuit, 1939. in the same spirit see: in Re Tinsley of 26 December 2018, U.S. Bankruptcy Court, D.n. Jersry, case n. 17-28611-ADA, adv. n. 17-1622-ABA.

[495]For W.L. NORTON JR., (eds.) Bankruptcy law and practice, op. cit., § 49.2, 49-4 "(...) word knowingly in used by the courts in ordinary sense and requires that the defendant's acts or conduct be voluntary, intentional, and not by result of mistake, accident, or other innocent reason (...); in jurisprudence see ex multis, U.S. vs. Zehrbach, 47 F.3d, 1258, 3rd Circuit, 1994; U.S. vs. Defazio, 899 F.2d, 626, 635, 7th Circuit, 1990 according to: "(...)

However, more problems are linked to the definition of the concept of fraudulently[496]. In fact, an intent to defraud is normally accompanied by the desire or the purpose, by the active subject, to obtain a profit or an advantage from his own conduct, rather than for the purpose of causing damage to the taxable person[497].

The application of bankruptcy criminal offenses to conduct supported by a purpose (profit or damage) patrimonial would be inconsistent with the object of protection, all public (good performance of the insolvency proceedings), just the crimes in comment (and the option hermeneutics followed by majority jurisprudence constitutes a further element of confirmation about the nature of crimes against the administration of justice of bankruptcy crimes). For this reason, the courts attested to a rather extensive interpretation of the term fraudulently considering it sufficient, in order to affirm the criminal relevance of the conduct, that the subject acted with the intent to deceive (cheat) or mislead (deceive) creditors or the procedure (trustee or bankruptcy judge), without requiring, however, any specific patrimonial purpose[498]. At the same time, it is not required that the active subject be aware of the civil anti-prudence of his/her conduct[499].

An example of the majority opinion reported here can be found in the aforementioned US vs. Gellene[500]. In the present case, the defense able

---

Knowingly (...) means that the defendant realized what he was doing and was aware of the nature of his conduct and did not act through ignorance, mistake or accident (...)". For further analysis see: D. BROWNING WEBB, RICO conspiracy law and the Pinkerton doctrine, Xlibris Corporation, US, 2013. C.B. MUELLER, L.C. KIRKPATRICK, L. RICHTER, Aspen treatise for evidence, Wolters & Kluwer Law & Business, New York, 2018.

[496]"Defining "fraudulent" is somewhat more artificial" for T. OGIER, J.F. WILLIAMS, Bankruptcy crimes and bankruptcy practice, cit. § I.

[497]M.A. TIGHE, A guide to making a criminal bankruptcy fraud referral, op. cit., § 411. In this sense see a minority trend in jurisprudence: U.S. vs. Zehrbach, 47 F.3d, 1258-59, 3rd Circuit, 1994, "(...) proving fraudulent element of bankruptcy fraud requires finding that defendant acted knowingly with purposeful, specific intent to deceive for purpose of causing financial loss to creditor or bringing about financial gain for oneself (...)".

[498]U.S. vs. Lerch, 996 F.2d, 158, 161, 7th Circuit, 1993.

[499]U.S. vs. Zehrbach, 47 F.3d, 1258-59, 3rd Circuit, 19 §94, which is stated that: "(...) that: The act be voluntary and intentional, and not that a person knows he is breaking the law" and the knowledge of conduct's illegality is not element of § 152 violation.

[500]U.S. vs. Gellene, 182 F.3d 578, 7th Circuit, 1999, § II.1.

to appeal the defendant Gellene, blamed two false hypothesis hypotheses under 18 U.S.C. 152 (3) contains precisely in the critique of the jury's instructions (jury instruction)[501] made by the court of first instance concerning the concept of fraudulence.

According to the defensive interpretation, to anchor the punishment of the conduct to the test of a mere intent to deceive (to make false or to deceive)[502] would not have satisfied the statutory provision, according to which, the subjective element requested could not understand an intent to fraud, or to defraud the taxable person of a particular right, interest, or property through fraudulent conduct[503].

This argument stemmed from a consideration of the legal good protected by the case in point which, in the opinion of defense, could not be considered in the mere preservation of integrity of the bankruptcy system (in terms of regular procedure), but necessarily had to be anchored to a content assets, linked to the correct distribution among creditors of bankruptcy assets[504].

The court of appeal, however, disregards this restrictive argument precisely on the assumption that the rules in question do not have, at least exclusively, an object of purely patrimonial protection, but are oriented towards protecting the integrity of the system of bankruptcy proceedings, that may well be endangered by conduct perpetrated without any immediate purpose of altering the correct distribution of bankruptcy assets to the mass[505].

---

[501]The Court of First Instance had instructed the jury (Jury Instruction No. 18) in the sense of having to assume the requirement of fraudulence if the prosecutor had succeeded in proving that the defendant had acted "with intent to deceive", U.S. vs. Gellene, cit. § II.1.

[502]"To deceive is to cause to believe the false or to mislead", U.S. vs. Gellene, op., cit. § II.1.

[503]"To defraud is to deprive of some right, interest or property by deceit", U.S. vs. Gellene, op. cit. § II.1.

[504]"(...) Under § 152 of the Bankruptcy Code (...) the defendant must have specific intent to alter or to impact the distribution of a debtor's assets and not merely to impact the integrity of the legal system, as the government argued", U.S. vs. Gellene, op. cit. § II.1.

[505]"(...) we cannot accept Mr. Gellene's narrowly circumscribed definition of "intent to defraud" or "fraudulently". Mr. Gellene would limit exclusively the statute's scope to false statements that deprive the debtor of his property or the bankruptcy estate of its assets. In our view, such a parsimonious interpretation was not intended by the Congress. First the plain wording of the statute suggests no such limited scope. Rather, the plain wording of the statute punishes making a false statement "knowingly and fraudulently". The common

From a probative standpoint, jurisprudential interpretation aims to satisfy the burden of prosecution of the intent sought in the presence of mere indirect and circumstantial evidence[506].

6.§ 152 (1) Concealment of assets.

This case punishes anyone (not only the debtor), knowingly and fraudulently, conceals any property belonging to the bankruptcy unit against custodians, curators, or officers appointed by the bankruptcy court, or, in connection with an open procedure under title 11 USC, operate said conduct against creditors or the US office trustee.

The meaning of concealment has been interpreted from the earliest jurisprudential applications in an extremely broad way and is suitable to broadly cover many of the behaviors that are contemplated in paragraph 1 of art. 216.

This concept refers to all operations of secrecy, concealment, forgery or destruction concerning assets destined to fall within the bankruptcy or information relating to such assets[507]. Conduct can have content that is as active as it is omissive: preventing the discovery of goods or not communicating their existence falls peacefully in the provision of

---

understanding of the term "fraudulently" includes the intent to deceive (...) whether the deception at issue is aimed at thwarting the bankruptcy court or the parties of the bankruptcy, § 152 is designed to protect the integrity of the administration of a bankruptcy case": U.S. vs. Gellene, op. cit. § II.1.

[506]In this sense: M.A. TIGHE, A guide to making a criminal bankruptcy fraud referral, op. cit., § 412. R.C. MCCULLOUGH II, Bankruptcy fraud, op. cit., pp. 20ss. In jurisprudence see: U.S. vs. McCormick, 72 F.3d, 1404, 9th Circuit, 1995, "(...) circumstantial evidence is sufficient to find fraudulent intent (...)"; interesting instructions to the jury rendered during the first degree hearing then led to the appeal in case U.S. vs. Ciampaglia, 628 F.2d 632, 642, 1st Circuit, 1980 "one cannot look inside a person's mind (...) the intent should be judged by what a person does or says or fails to do or to say (...) including willful blindness to the existence of a fact that should have been obvious (...)" (the one on voluntary blindness is commonly referred to as ostrich instruction). See also: U.S. vs. Howard, 619 F.3d 723, 727, 7th Circuit, 2010, "(...) because direct evidence of a defendant's fraudulent intent is typically not available, specific intent to defraud may be established by circumstantial evidence and by inference drawn from examining the scheme itself (...)".

[507]U.S. vs. Phillips, 196, F.574, S.D.N.Y. 1912, "secretion, falsifying and mutilating property or information (...)".It should be noted that judicial interpretation considers criminally relevant not only total omissions, but also partial information and "half-truths". The obligation on the debtor is to offer "complete and truthful information to the trustee, an officer of the court" for U.S. vs. Webster, 125 F.3d 1024, 7th Circuit, 1997.

the incriminating norm[508].

However, the interpreter is unaware of the absence, in this list, of one of the most significant behaviors in the system of origin, the distraction[509]. Certainly, within the concept of concealment are those forms of expulsion of personal or corporate assets in favor of third parties (or nominees)[510], however, it would appear to be foreign to the order being compared, any judicial activity aimed at syndicating the correctness/economy of personal and (above all) entrepreneurial choices prior to signing the petition (excessive expenses, sponsorship contracts, underselling sales, increase in debt exposure, if not when intrinsically fraudulent and accompanied by a particular intent, according to § 157)[511].

The discourse is understandably different with regard to the conduct subsequent to the signing of an instance, eg, according to Chapter 11. In such cases, the debtor, pending the reorganization procedure, is commonly authorized to retain possession of assets (debtor in possession) and to continue business, but only for what concerns the extraordinary course of business and execution of the plan. In this case, therefore, judicial screening can go to union under the lens of § 152 (1) the correctness of entrepreneurial choices and their traceability/extraneousness (and therefore punishability) to the concept of ordinary course of business as circumscribed by the bankruptcy court in the authorization of the

---

[508]Burchnal vs. U.S., 342, F.2d, 982, 10th Circuit, 1965, "preventing discovery or withholding knowledge of the assets is sufficient to find concealment"; U.S. vs. Turner, 725 F.2d 1154, 8th Circuit, 1984. "Concealment means, not only secreting, falsifying, mutilating as specified in section 1 of the Bankruptcy Act but also includes preventing discovery, fraudulently transferring or withholding knowledge or information required by law to be made known". R.C. MCCULLOUGH II, Bankruptcy fraud, op., cit., pp. 19ss.

[509]U.S. vs. Camp, 140 F.Supp., 98, D. Hawaii, 1956, "(...) the crime of concealment is concealment. It is not an improper use of funds, it is not the use of corporate funds for personal expenses, it is not even the use of funds in fraud of creditors (...)".

[510]U.S. vs. Moody, 923 F.2d 341, 89-6271, 5th Circuit, 1991, concerning the concealment to the trustee of a trust within which the debtor's assets had been conveyed. The fiduciary headings (transfer of ownership to a third party with maintenance of an interest in the asset) were considered as concealment in In re Vecchione, 407 F Supp 609, E.D.N.Y., 1976.

[511]M.A. TIGHE, A guide to making a criminal bankruptcy fraud referral, op. cit., § 412. In jurisprudence see: U.S. vs. Gigli, 573 F. Supp. 1408, 1414, W.D.Pa., 1983; the concept of ordinary course of business has, however, been more investigated by civil jurisprudence, see: Medical Malpractice Ins. Ass'n vs. Hirsch (In re Lavigne), 114 F.3d 379, 385, 2nd Circuit, 1997; Erickson vs. Citizens First National Bank (In re Erickson), 216 B.R. 938m 941, Bankr. C.D.Ill, 1998. U.S. v. Fuller, U.S. Court of Appeal. Eight circuit n. 18-1706.

reorganization application.

The relevant element in the analysis of this case is not so much the declaration of bankruptcy (which takes the form of the discharge or the refusal of it) as the start of the bankruptcy procedure by signing the petition (by the debtor or of creditors). This is the moment from which arise the declaratory and delivery obligations to be borne by the debtor in relation to the assets to be allocated to the bankruptcy assets and the creditors' insolvency. The rule, therefore, applies to the conduct that accompanies the signing of the petition (pending the procedure) or that follows it[512].

Constitutive elements of the case are, therefore, in addition to the already described intent and the conduct of concealment, the existence of a bankruptcy procedure and the traceability of the material object to the concept of property of the summer.

This last requirement is certainly the most complicated interpretation[513]. This is because it requires the analysis of civil law rules concerning the traceability of the hidden asset to the bankruptcy axis[514], both abstractly and in the concrete procedure initiated (or concluded). Note, however, how the belonging of the property to the concept of property of the summer, as considered a matter of fact and not of law, is totally devolved, within the criminal process, to the decision of the jury[515], and is susceptible to be called into question even if the bankruptcy court has already made a determination to do so[516].

---

[512]M.A. TIGHE, A guide to making a criminal bankruptcy fraud referral, op. cit., § 412.This does not mean that the conduct prior to the start of the bankruptcy procedure is not indicted in the US system. In fact, these behaviors are relevant according to the 18 U.S.C. 152 (7) which we will analyze below.

[513]M.A. TIGHE, A guide to making a criminal bankruptcy fraud referral, op. cit., § 412.

[514]In relation to this requirement, the US jurisprudence rejects formal interpretations related to the nominal heading of the goods but is, on the contrary, informed to a principle of effectiveness, see, ex multis, U.S. vs. Cherek, 734 F.2d 1248, 1254, 7th Circuit, 1984. It is not possible to delve into the subject specifically, but it should be borne in mind that the curator in the US system has ample powers to recover assets that are formally registered to legal entities under the cd "Alter ego" theory; for an example in jurisprudence, see: Steyr-Daimler-Puchof America Corp. vs. Pappas, 852 F.2d 132, 4th Circuit, 1988.

[515]U.S. vs. Weinstein, 834 F.2d 1454, 1461, 9th Circuit, 1987, "(...) questions of which assets are inclusive in bankruptcy estate is question for jury (...)".

[516]U.S. vs. Robbins, 997 F.2d 390, 393, 8th Circuit, 1993 which affirms this principle on the basis of the lower probative standard required in the bankruptcy process compared to that imposed in the criminal trial "quantum of proof necessary to sustain bankruptcy court";

In order to overcome the complexities linked to the ascertainment of this requirement, the majority jurisprudence, through an extensive interpretation of the case that raises more than one reserve in the writer[517], has decided to apply the obligation of disclosure to all assets, even those which, at the time of signing the petition, appear to be due to the bankruptcy.

Following this (consolidated and, it would seem, undisputed) jurisprudential address[518], § 152 (1) is, therefore, suitable to incriminate behaviors that deprive the bank of bankruptcy of the possibility of expressing itself about the traceability of the asset to the summer, even if, following the discovery of the asset itself, this, on the basis of the regulation contained in title 11 of USC, is, lastly, excluded from the bankruptcy axis[519].

On the other hand, this interpretation, however debatable, is consistent with the offensive structure of the case (abstract danger) and with the protected legal asset (administration of justice). This is perceived even more clearly, having regard to the jurisprudence that has developed about the value of the assets subject to concealment as well as about their destination.

The absolute lack of interest in the patrimonial moment of the offense can be found in those rulings that confirm the responsibility,

---

but the principle is valid in both senses, so it will be possible to initiate a prosecution for fraudulent concealment even if, for example, in the bankruptcy proceedings, the trustee, after the discovery, renounces a particular asset, see: U.S. vs. Grant, 971 F.2d 799, 805-06, 1st Circuit, 1992, (...) abandonment of asset by trustee in civil administration of estate does not assure later prosecution for concealment of asset (...)".

[517]Reservations not shared by the US doctrine consulted, which does not raise any problem of constitutionality. For an expressed position, but in the sense of reasonableness of this interpretation, see also in argument: M.A. TIGHE, A guide to making a criminal bankruptcy fraud referral, op. cit., § 412.

[518]Ex multis, U.S. vs. Jackson, 836 F.2d 324, 330, 7th Circuit, 1987, "the debtor must disclose even those assets whose bankruptcy status is uncertain (...)"; even more clear U.S. vs. Beard, 913 F.2d 193, 197, 5th Circuit, 1990, "(...) the debtor must disclose all assets even if likely to later be excluded from estate (...)". For more analysis see: T. TARVIN, The privilege against self-incrimination in bankruptcy and the plight of the debtor, in Seton Hall Law Review, 44, 2014, pp. 78ss.

[519]See also: U.S. vs. Cherek, 734 F.2d 1248, 1254, 7th Circuit, 1984, "(...) even if the asset is not ultimately determined to be property of the estate under the technical rules of the Federal Bankruptcy Code, Section 152 properly imposes sanctions on those who preempt a court's determination by failing to report the asset (...)".

regardless of the perception of the acting subject, about the value of the assets removed from the procedure. "(…) The debtors have an absolute duty to report whatever interest they hold in property, even if they believe the assets are worthless or are unavailable to the bankruptcy estate (...)[520].

Notwithstanding this argument, however, has breached the appealed court of appeal, which also considered the failure to communicate a mere potential expectation of future gain in the investment to be criminally significant.

Nor does it reveal, once proven the non-delivery of goods to the procedure with the signing of the petition, that they were actually used for the satisfaction of creditors[521].

An example in this sense comes from an already quoted jurisprudential decision[522] which, despite the apparent lack of consistency of the matter of contending in terms of the patrimonial values involved[523], offers particularly interesting ideas for reconstructing the structure of the offense in question. In the present case, the accused Turner was charged with the crime referred to § 152 (1) in relation to the failure to note the proceeds of a commercial sale transaction in the accounting records of the company being reorganized. The trial, however, was able to show how the

---

[520]See ex multis U.S. vs. Allen, 524 F.3d 814, 822, 7th Circuit, 2008; U.S. vs. Grant, 971 F.2d 799, 809, 1st Circuit, 1992, "(...) value of asset concealed from trustee is not relevant to determine whether a violation of 18 U.S.C. § 152 occurred"; Kanner vs. U.S., 21 F.2d 285, 287, 2nd Circuit, 1927, "value of concealed assets is not essential element of § 152 (...)". An interesting argument, in a defensive key, was raised in U.S. vs. Standard, 1996 WL 207157, 9th Circuit, 1996. The defendant on that occasion claimed that the failure to exhibit an investment made by the corporation subject to insolvency proceedings in an oil company (Transwestern) could not be criminally relevant under the § 152 (1) since it is valueless in terms of corporate reorganization. The criminal irrelevance of the omission would fall from the point of view of defense, not from the lack of an objective element of the case (hidden asset), but from the impossibility of attributing to the conduct the required subjective attribute of fraudulence.

[521]In general, as already underlined, damage to creditors is irrelevant for the purposes of the punishment of concealments, see: U.S. vs. O'Donnell, 539 F.2d 1233, 1237, 9th Circuit 1976 "false statement by debtor about assets need no harm to creditors in order to be proof of concealment (...)".

[522]U.S. vs. Turner, 725 F.2d 1154, 8th Circuit, 1984.

[523]The sentence, in fact, as part of the reorganization procedure pursuant to Chapter 11 of a car dealership, whose majority shareholding was held by the accused Turner, deals with the concealment of the proceeds from the sale of a single car, a Ford Thunderbird, for the small sum of $ 6,500.

defendant, although not having noted in the company books the amount of the sale in question, had used this sum to satisfy some social creditors. The defense, therefore, affirmed the criminal irrelevance of the conduct, given the subjection of the sum to the purposes proper to the procedure.

However, the court of appeal, according to which, once the non-exposition of an active member to the organs of the procedure was proved, the actual use of the sums was shown, even if destined for the final aim of the procedure itself (satisfaction of creditors), it loses all relevance[524].

Some further considerations are due as regards the moment of consumption and the statute of limitations[525] applicable to the case governed by § 152 (1). The crime in question is perfected at the time of the conduct[526]. This makes the behavior of the active person subsequent to it irrelevant, even if earlier than the term of the insolvency procedure, and even if coinciding with the return of the assets subject to conciliation to the procedure (further proof of the non-pecuniary nature of the offense)[527].

If the moment of conduct is that of the perfection of the offense, its consummation, for procedural purposes linked to the applicability of the statute of limitations[528] (but not only, see below) is, however, postponed in time[529].

---

[524]"(...) Turner's crime was not in selling the car, possessing the proceeds, or using the proceeds to pay debts, but rather in preventing the discovery, by the trustee or the corporate debtor, of what he had done with the car and the money (...)".What makes this case interesting, besides its contribution to the correct determination of the protected legal asset, is the use of § 152 (1) could have detected as a preferential bankruptcy. The correct instrument for the repression of preferential payments, however, is constituted by § 152 (7) which will be the subject of forthcoming exposure.

[525]18 U.S.C. § 3283ss.

[526]See from the jurisprudence the case: U.S. vs. Chambron, 43 F.3d 1468, 4th Circuit 1994which affirms the punishment of self-laundering (18 U.S.C. 1957) compared to a predicate offense of concealment, even if both conducts (that of the predicate offense and that of money laundering) occurred before the bankruptcy. See also: J.M. SCHEB II, Criminal Law, Cengage learning, U.S., 2014, pp. 255ss.

[527]See in aegument: Kalin vs. U.S., 2 F.2d 58, 59, 5th Circuit, 1924, "return of concealed property to benefit creditor does not purge concealment of its criminality (...)". See also: U.S. vs. Klupt, 475 F.2d 1015, 1019, 2nd Circuit, 1973, "although assets eventually benefited creditors, deliberate diversion of assets equaled concealment (...)".

[528]For the statute of limitations see the analysis of: R. BOLES, Easing the tension between Statutes of limitations and the continuing offense doctrine, in Nothwestern Journal of Law & Social Politics, 7, 2012, pp. 219ss. C. KAVENY, Ethics at the edges of law: Christian moralists and American legal thought, Oxford University Press, Oxford, 2017.

[529]R.C. MCCULLOUGH II, Bankruptcy fraud, op. cit., pp. 35ss, "(...) the offense dates

The statute of limitations establish "a time limit to pursue a crime, based on the date on which it is consumed"[530]. These rules, of purely legislative creation (unknown to common law), have the function of inhibiting government power to prosecute a crime (albeit with exceptions) if the prosecutor has not been able to formalize an accusation within a given (variable, with regard to bankruptcy crimes equal to five years) period of time (it is then irrelevant the moment of final conviction). While sharing certain characteristics of our prescription (especially with reference to the objectives pursued[531]), the statute of limitations provide for a purely procedural discipline (the course of time determines the expiry of the power to exercise the action and is, therefore, a condition of non-procedeability) and do not extinguish the offense to which they apply.

With regard to § 152 (1), this is subject to an autonomous statute of limitations[532] that deserves to be described: "(…) The concealment of assets of a bankrupt or other debtor must be interpreted as a continuing offense until such debtor the discharge is granted or denied (i.e., at the end of the bankruptcy procedure[533]), and the period of limitation (forfeiture of the power to exercise the action) does not begin to run until that moment (of grant or denial of the discharge).

The concept of continuing offense (as opposed to that of instant crime) is, in some way, comparable to the local figure of the permanent

---

from the time of bankruptcy, not from the initial time of concealment (...)". BLACK'S LAW DICTIONARY, 1546, 9 ed. 2009 "A criminal statute of limitations establishes a time limit for prosecuting a crime, based on the date when the offense occurred".

[530]R. BOLES, Easing the tension between Statutes of limitations and the continuing offense doctrine, op. cit. pp. 223ss.

[531]This is the purpose of the statutes of limitations in the interpretation of the Supreme Court, Toussie vs. U. S., 397 U.S. 112, 114–15, 1970, its purpose of a statute of limitations is to limit exposure to criminal prosecution to a certain fixed period of time following the occurrence of those acts the legislature has decided to punish by criminal sanctions. Such a limitation is designed to protect individuals from having to defend themselves against charges when the basic facts may have become obscured by the passage of time and to minimize the danger of official punishment because of acts in the far-distant past. Such a time limit may also have the salutary effect of encouraging law enforcement officials promptly to investigate suspected criminal activity (...)".

[532]18 U.S.C. § 3284.

[533]If the application is judged inadmissible (dismissal of bankruptcy) by the bankruptcy court, such decision, for the purposes of the statute of limitation, is equivalent to the negation of the discharge. See: U.S. vs. Dolan, 120 F.3d 856, 867, 8th Circuit, 1997.

crime. As defined in jurisprudence[534], with an expression made its own by the doctrine[535], it constitutes continuing offense a continuous flow of conduct that causes an offense that lasts for a time equivalent to that of the conduct itself.

It is not possible to concentrate here on the dogmatic problems raised by this particular figure[536], but we can fail to notice how to interpret § 152 (1) which a continuing offense does not reflect solely on the procedural discipline of the statute of limitations (guaranteeing of course, the prosecutor has a longer time to formalize the accusation on a par with what happens when the limitation begins to run from the court declaration of bankruptcy[537]), but produces significant material effects.

In jurisprudence[538], in fact, the doctrine of continuing offense is used to suppress chronologically previous behaviors with respect to the signing of the petition by the active subject. This is because, a concealment carried out even at a considerable distance[539] compared to the start of the procedure, but maintained during this, is destined to become a bankruptcy offense once the petition has been signed, consummated at the time of discharge (or of the denial of it).

The main road, however, to repress the pre-petition conduct is represented by § 152 (7) which will be the subject of the next exhibition.

---

[534]U.S. vs. Morales, 11 F.3d 915, 922, 9th Circuit, 1993, "an ongoing course of conduct that causes a harm that lasts as long as that course of conduct persists (...)".

[535]R. BOLES, Easing the tension between Statutes of limitations and the continuing offense doctrine, op. cit. pp. 228ss.

[536]R. BOLES, Easing the tension between Statutes of limitations and the continuing offense doctrine, op. cit.

[537]M.A. TIGHE, A guide to making a criminal bankruptcy fraud referral, op. cit., §§ 152(7),Transfer and Concealment of assets in contemplation of a bankruptcy.

[538]See, In re May, 12 B.R. 618, N.D. Fla. 1980; U.S. vs. Chambron, 43 F.3d 1468, 4th Circuit 1994.

[539]On the notion of considerable distance, however, it is fair to understand, as far as the writer is aware, judicial actions aimed at repressing behaviors that have come to life, when not decades, before the start of the procedure are almost completely unknown in the United States. The forms of concealment pre petition referred to in the text, in the absolute majority of cases, precede by days or, at most, months the signing of the application. Rarely, and in this sense are paradigmatic and cited as examples of limitations of criminal behavior, the interest of prosecutors goes to investigate conducted years before the subscription. The sentence that deals with the pre-dating concealment that dates back to the instance that it was able to find punishes a previous four-year conduct, see U.S. vs. Willey, 57 F.3d 1374, 1380-81, 5th Circuit, 1995.

This case punishes anyone, either on their own or as a representative (as an agent) of a natural person or a corporation, knowingly and fraudulently transfer (transfers) or covert (conceals) their personal assets, or assets owned by the third party or corporation , in anticipation (in contemplation) of the commencement of a bankruptcy procedure governed by title 11 on its behalf, or towards the third party or the corporation, or for the purpose of circumventing the discipline contemplated by the same title.

The notion of concealment, of course, follows the one elaborated in doctrine and jurisprudence with reference to § 152 (1). § 152 (7)[540], however, incriminates, alternatively[541] (and possibly concurrently with respect to concealment) a new conduct, that of transfer of assets.

The notion of transfer, which is also applicable for criminal purposes, is the subject of a specific legal definition within the bankruptcy code[542].

It can be noted that this standard adopts a particularly extensive meaning of the term transfer to include (in a residual way) any direct or indirect, absolute or conditional, voluntary or involuntary way of disposing or subdividing a property or an interest in a property. It should also be noted that, according to this discipline, the mere transfer of possession of an asset (regardless of the passage of property) constitutes a

---

[540]S. PATERSON, Bargaining in financial restructuring-market norms, legal rights and regulatory standards, in Journal of Corporate Law Studies, 14 (2), 2014, pp. 336ss. B. ADLER, V. CAPKUN, L. WEISS, Value destruction in the new era of Chapter 11, in The Journal of Law, Economics, and Organization, 29 (2), 2013, pp. 462ss. C.J. TABB, Credit bidding, security and the obsolescence of Chapter 11, in University of Illinois Law Review, 103, 2013, pp. 104ss. M.B. JACOBY, E.J. JANGER, Ice cube bonds: Allocating the price of process in Chapter 11 bankruptcy, in The Yale Law Journal, 123 (4), 2014, pp. 870ss. C.J. TABB, The bankruptcy clause, the fifth amendment and the limited rights of secured creditors in bankruptcy, in University of Illinois Law Review, 2015, pp. 766ss.

[541]See, U.S. vs. Shapiro, 101, F.2d 375, 379, 7th Circuit, 1939. in this sense see. M. PONTANI, Pre-bankruptcy crimes and entrepreneural behaviour. Some insights from American and italian bankruptcy laws, in German Working Papers in Law and Economics, Berkeley Electronic Press, 2004, paper 14.

[542]11 U.S.C. § 101 (54) a)the creation of a lien; b)the retention of title as a security interest; c) the foreclosure of a debtor's equity of redemption; or d) each mode, direct or indirect, absolute or conditional, voluntary or involuntary, of disposing of or parting with-i)property; or (ii) an interest in property.

transfer to both bankruptcy and criminal effects[543].

According to the most prestigious doctrine[544] and followed in jurisprudence, within the notion of transfer dictated by § 152 (7) figures must also be included that are not directly governed by title 11 U.S.C. § 101 (54), but provided for in relation to a similar purpose of protection, the correct distribution of social assets, compared to that pursued by the criminal case in question. Thus, preferential transfers (preferences)[545] and fraudulent transfers (fraudulent transfers) must be considered criminally relevant (if accompanied by the other requisites).

Another element of differentiation from the discipline dictated by § 152 (1) can be found in the description of the object of the conduct. In fact, the law punishes the operations carried out, with reference to the assets of the active subject (his property), and with reference to the assets of the person, physical or legal, in favor of which the conduct is carried out (or the property of such other person or corporation).

Therefore, for the purposes of punishment with respect to the case referred to in § 152 (1), the necessary linkability of the assets subject to the conduct to the bankruptcy (summer) is no longer applicable.

The expression "his property" is suitable to cover both the assets that can be entered in the summer concept as well as those of the debtor's exclusive property, formed or acquired, both subsequently and prior to the opening of the procedure (and therefore to the creation of the bankruptcy)[546].

The issue is of particular interest with reference to the (legal) fruits deriving from the assets covered by the pipeline since, with reference to them, it is possible to perceive an evident difference between the case referred to in § 152 (1) and that referred to in § 152 (7).

In US vs. Mitchell[547], the appealed court was confronted with the conviction at first instance of the accused Mitchell pursuant to § 152 (1). The accusation against the defendant concerned the concealment of the

---

[543]M. PONTANI, Pre-bankruptcy crimes and entrepreneural behaviour., op. cit., pag. 13. 263 Collier on bankruptcy, 15 ed., revised 1998, vol. 1, 7-73.
[544]11 U.S.C. § 547.
[545]11 U.S.C. § 548.
[546]Collier on bankruptcy, 15 ed., revised 1998, vol. 1, 7-75.
[547]U.S. vs. Mitchell, 06-2844/2419, 8th Circuit, 2007.

income received, before the signing of a petition of personal bankruptcy, from the shareholding in a company, Wood Floors Import Inc.; shareholding transferred, two years before signing the application, from the defendant to his wife.

The prosecutor, supporting the sham nature of the transaction (on the paper only), formalized a concealment accusation pursuant to § 152 (1) concerning the income related to the Wood Floors Import Inc. received by the defendant in the years since 1998 (date of the fictitious equity sale) to 2000 (date of the signing of a petition in which Mitchell did not report said income among its balance sheet)[548]. A first instance sentence for concealment followed, pursuant to par. 152 (1), of "pre petition income".

The court of appeal, however, correctly annulled the conviction, not considering a constitutive element of the case, or the traceability of the hidden asset, on the basis of the following argument. An essential element "of the case referred to in § 152 (1) (...) is that the concealment concerns an asset belonging to the bankruptcy asset"[549]. Overall, the bankruptcy axis (summer) includes the assets and interest attributable to the debtor, starting from the beginning of the insolvency procedure, as well as all proceeds which, from that moment on, derive from the former.

Following this chronologically definition of property of the summer, the income derived from an asset before signing the petition, will never be able to become part of this legal entity (summer), as it was earlier than its coming to existence[550].

In the opinion of the writer, a result of opposite sign (with respect

---

[548]In the opinion of the prosecution: Mitchell was the owner of Wood Floors Import; this company should have entered the bankruptcy axis; even the pre-petition income deriving from Wood Floors Import, therefore, should have been traced back to the ownership of the same axis "(...) the Government's case was that Mitchell owned WFI, which became part of the estate, and that therefore pre-petition income derived from WFI was property of the estate as well (...)".

[549]U.S. vs. Mitchell, op. cit., pag. 6.

[550]U.S. vs. Mitchell, op. cit., pag. 7, "The filing of the bankruptcy petition creates a new legal entity: the bankruptcy estate". In jurisprudence see also: In re Marlmueller, 51 F.3d 775, 776, 8th Circuit, 1995. The Court also relies on the doctrinal position found in Collier on Bankruptcy, P. 541.17, 15 ed., Revision of 2006 according to which (...) included as property of the summer under section 541 (a) (6) are all proceeds, products, offspring, rents, or profits of property of the summer, acquired after [underlined in the Court's citation] the case is commenced (...)".

to the annulment on appeal) could have been achieved if the prosecutor had challenged the accused Mitchell, rather than the case referred to in § 152 (1), the one governed by § 152(7). The burden of proof would have been certainly more burdensome with reference to the intent (in contemplation), but the pre-petition income would have been attributable to the material object of the conduct indicted by this last case, his property (personal property of the debtor) and a conduct of concealment on them could have been declared criminally significant[551].

The case in question is participated by a subjective element of particular significance. The active subject must have acted: i) In anticipation of his bankruptcy (or that of the natural or legal person for which he operates) or ii) for the purpose of circumventing the discipline dictated by title 11 U.S.C.

The first mental state required (in contemplation) requires proof of a psychological connection between the conduct of the active subject and the signing of the bankruptcy petition[552].

Clearly the case is designated as a priority (and the burden of proof is simpler to satisfy) to cover the cases of voluntary bankruptcy, i.e. those hypotheses in which the same agent is an agent who makes a bankruptcy on his own (or in favor of the corporation for which it acts)[553].

As seen with regard to the mens rea reation in the hypothesis of concealment pursuant to § 152 (1) of also the cases governed by § 152 (7) require that the agent acted knowingly and fraudulently, the proof of the particular intent in commentary is taken from the jurisprudence through an inferential procedure based on a series of elements: First of all the awareness about the condition of failure or pre-insolvency of the debtor[554].

551As we can see in the case: U.S. vs. Moody, 923 F.2d 341, 5th Circuit, 1991. In that case the defendant was accused, according to the § 152(7) which has in contemplation of his bankruptcy, concealed the profits deriving from a trust in his favor, received before signing the petition. "(...) Under this statute it is not necessary for the property to be an asset of the bankruptcy estate. It is sufficient if in concealing or transferring his own property the defendant has the intent of the concealment or transfer to defeat the bankruptcy law (...)".

552M. PONTANI, Pre-bankruptcy crimes and entrepreneural behaviour, op. cit., pp. 14ss.

553U.S. vs. Haymes, 610 F.2d 309, 312, 5th Circuit, 1990, "this proof may be easier in case of voluntary petition, because of the defendant's control over the action (...)".

554U.S. vs. Martin, 408 F.2d 949, 954, 7th Circuit, 1969, "defendants' conviction of concealment in contemplation of bankruptcy is based on circumstantial evidence of defendant's actions and knowledge before the petition was filed"; in U.S. vs. Haymes, 610

The case is finalized only if the requested intent is held by the agent at the time of the conduct and not when it arises subsequently to it[555].

The hypotheses governed by § 152 (7) apply, however, to established case law, also to involuntary bankruptcy cases, i.e. those cases in which the bankruptcy petition is filed by creditors (personal or social). A paradigmatic example in this sense is the pronunciation US v. Ayotte[556].

The personal history and the blatantly criminal conduct of the active subjects[557], in the case in question, has certainly influenced the decision of the court of appeal, which, however, will have to affirm a principle of law that will be constantly cited by the subsequent jurisprudence.

The conduct of the defendants was due to a situation of bust out[558].

F.2d 309, 312, 5th Circuit, 1990, starting from the awareness of the defendant about the weak economic and financial conditions of the corporation he administered, the Court of Appeal held that the jury was justified "in putting two and two together in finding that debtor's transfer of funds revealed contemplation of bankruptcy"; requires, however, a particularly severe burden of proof and that the intent is proven on the basis of specific factual circumstances and non-assumptions, Burke Vs. Dowling, 944 F. Supp. 1036, E.D.N.Y., 1995. Other circumstantial elements are: a close relationship between the parties to the transaction; personal retention of the proceeds of the transaction; the extemporaneous nature of the transaction and the absence of an earlier economic assessment, etc. For further details and analysis, see: T. OGIER, J.F. WILLIAMS, Bankruptcy crimes and bankruptcy practice, op. cit., § 2.c.

[555]U.S. vs. Tashjian, 660 F 2.d 829, 1st Circuit, 1981.

[556]U.S. vs. Ayotte, 385 F.2d 988, 6th Circuit, 1967.

[557]"Appellants' venture was short-lived and transparently criminal". This is the begging of the sentence in comment.

[558]Another example of bases we could find in the case: Harris vs. Roberto, 966 F.2d 1442, 4th Circuit, 1992, "The plan for the particular type of fraud involved in this case, known as a "bust-out," generally begins when a person or group of people establish a business concerned with the sale of consumer goods. Front men are used to run the day to day operations of the business. Using start-up funds, modest orders are placed with manufacturers and suppliers, and prompt payment is made for the purposes of establishing credit and obtaining credit references. Additional orders are then placed with the same suppliers using credit. Actual retail trade is minimal and most of the goods ordered are immediately shipped after receipt to warehouses and consumer good outlets controlled by the parties that provide the start-up funds and inventory. After an agreed-upon cut-off date, payments to suppliers are stopped. Shipments of goods by the front men to their backers continue until valuable inventory has been exhausted. As the creditors' demands for payments increase, the "bust-out" occurs with the business declaring Federal bankruptcy or, in this case, the state equivalent: assignment for the benefit of creditors. The creditors are left with a less valuable inventory to satisfy their claims (...)". The case of the tax bust out is particularly significant and generally punished pursuant to art. 223 co. 2 n. 2 L.F., as a malicious cause of bankruptcy. This is the description offered by United States Trustee

The bust out operations are perpetrated by companies, usually created ad hoc in order to acquire goods on credit (often on the basis of a false documentation proving the financial soundness of the same), sell them under cost in cash and fail at the time of having to honor your debts with suppliers[559].

In the present case, the defendants, after setting up a bust out scheme linked to the Palm Forniture company, had disappeared, leaving a considerable unpaid debt to the suppliers and making any remaining goods disappear from company's warehouses. The latter (the creditors), therefore, presented to Bankruptcy Court an instance of bankruptcy against Palm Supplies. The trial was unable to return the evidence on the contrary, it established the contrary of defendants knowledge of the application for bankruptcy (approved by the Bankruptcy Court in absentia) against the company they administered.

The lack of knowledge of the bankruptcy procedure represented, therefore, the defense able to appeal of Ayotte and Correi, in whose opinion, the case referred to in § 152 (7) could not be integrated due to lack of the subjective element required (having acted in contemplation of own bankruptcy).

On the contrary, the court of appeal upheld the first instance condemnation based on the following argument: People must be understood as capable of understanding the natural and reasonable consequences of their acts. If, in a situation of insolvency, over-indebtedness and evident crisis in the conduct of its business, some deliberately concealing its assets, or a considerable part thereof, it must be considered that this person acted in anticipation (in contemplation) of the normal consequences of one's own conduct, or the application of bankruptcy legislation on the instance of social creditors[560].

The second mental state required, alternatively, from § 152 (7) is

Manual, cit., pag. 60: "An individual operates a series of businesses in the same industry and fails to pay taxes. He/she then usually files chapter 11 bankruptcy for the company just prior to or at the time the Internal Revenue Service files a lien on the debtor's assets. The company operates for a brief period of time in chapter 11 before the case is converted or dismissed. A new business is then started with the debtor's assets (...)".

[559]For a roundup on the most common cases of bust out schemes see: United States Trustee Manual, cit., pp. 59ss.

[560]U.S. vs. Ayotte, cit., § 18.

to have acted in order to circumvent the provisions of title 11 U.S.C.; according to the doctrinal opinion, this requirement is satisfied if the active subject has acted in order to carry out an intentional deviation from the liquidation procedure, distribution of bankruptcy assets governed by title 11[561]. We have chosen to deal with the paragraph dedicated to the exposure of § 152 (7) the issue concerning a further constituent element of some of the crimes in question, namely the existence of a bankruptcy. In fact, the establishment of a bankruptcy procedure is a fundamental requirement pursuant to § 152 (1), which incriminates the conduct of concealments carried out on assets belonging to the bankruptcy (summer, as we have already seen, which arises juridically only with signing a petition)[562].

The existence of a bankruptcy procedure (which culminates in the grant or denial of the discharge) is by no means required for the realization of the case referred to in § 152 (7). Theoretically, (the case in point) can be improved in anticipation of a, only apparently inevitable, bankruptcy, that the debtor will succeed, subsequently with respect to the conduct, to avert[563].

The doctrinal opinion reported was confirmed by jurisprudence in Burke vs. Dowling case[564]. This sentence arises from a civil action arising

---

[561]Includes the existence of bankruptcy among the elements of crime del § 152(1) R.C. MCCULLOUGH II, Bankruptcy Fraud, cit., pag. 17.

[562]R.C. MCCULLOUGH II, Bankruptcy fraud, op. cit., pag. 23ss.

[563]See: Burke vs. Dowling, 944 F. Supp. 1036, E.D.N.Y., 1995. For further details see: M. SCHUSTER, Die Regulierung von Invetsment Crowdfunding in den USA: Der USA amerikanische Crowdfund Act im Spannungsfeld von Anlegenschutz und Kapitalzugang, Nomos Verlag, Baden-Baden, 2018.

[564]18 U.S.C. 1961-64. For more analysis see: G.E. LYNCH, RICO: The crime of being a criminal parts I&II, in Columbia University Law Review, 87, 1987, pp. 661ss, "(...) one of the most controvertial statute in federal criminal code (...)". J.K. STRADER, Understanding white collar crime, LexisNexis, New York, 2006, pp. 306ss. For the purpose of this presentation it is sufficient to bear in mind that this case was introduced in order to repress repeated criminal conduct, carried out by means of company vehicles. Elements constituting the case are: i) The existence of a company; ii) the commission by the active subject of two or more determined criminal conduct (predicate offenses, predicate acts); iii) that the commission of predicate offenses can qualify as a criminal path (pattern of racketeering activity); iv) that the active subject: a) Has used the company as a vehicle of the criminal path; b) participate in the ownership or control of said company; c) conduct business affairs through the criminal path; v) that criminal activity has effects on inter-state trade. § 152 (7), as a federal offense, is one of the predicate offenses for the application of RICO. The statute can be invoked by both the prosecutor and the damaged individuals.

from a crime committed by an individual for the application of the Racketeer Influenced and Corrupt Organizations Statute (RICO) which saw, among the predicate offenses of the criminal activity of the corporation treated in court, among others, a hypothesis of bankruptcy fraud pursuant to § 152 (7).

The court, therefore, in order to respond to the petitum of the plaintiff, had to concentrate on the constituent elements of the allegedly disputed crime, § 152 (7). The defendant's defense, to support the non-configurability of the offense in question, had focused its defense, rather than on the nonexistence of the disputed conduits of concealment (dates, however, for granted, also in this case it was a bust out scheme), on the fact that, in respect of the company administered by the latter, no bankruptcy proceedings had been opened (neither voluntarily nor by the creditors) pursuant to title 11 of USC.

These arguments, however, have been rejected by the court, in the opinion of which the existence of a bankruptcy procedure is a constituent element only of § 152 (1), but not also of § 152 (7). Based on the literal tenor of the case, the court seised stated that "all that is required (from § 152 (7)) is that the defendant has transferred his assets, with the ultimate aim to circumvent the bankruptcy court, remaining instead , completely indifferent whether the bankruptcy procedure has actually started or not"[565].

Although aware of the certainly exceptional nature of the case taken into consideration by the aforementioned sentence, the interpretation in comment offers considerable insights to analyze the offensive structure of the case referred to in § 152 (7): We are in the presence of a crime of mere disobedience, certainly of abstract danger to the protected legal asset, the good performance of the insolvency procedure.

7. "Declarative" cases in accordance with § 152 (2) (3)

The second macro category envisaged by § 152 is that relating to the crimes of nature, so to speak, declarative, consistent, in broad terms,

---

[565]Burke vs. Dowling, cit., II. § 12(2)(C). The court, however, rejects the alleged claiming that it has not proved the intent required by the law.

in lying to the organs of the procedure[566].

§ 152 (2) (again a common crime) punishes false declarations made, knowingly and fraudulently, under oath during any type of hearing related to bankruptcy proceedings, as well as during debtor's hearings (or possible witnesses) carried out before the editor. § 152 (3) instead, incriminates the false statements made, once again knowingly and fraudulently, in the signing of written documents related to the bankruptcy procedure (first of all the petition and attached forms, in which the debtor is called to indicate their equity and the commercial and financial operations carried out in a specific period of time)[567].

The false term used, in relation to the statements, from the case in point, in the jurisprudential interpretation, covers both the ideological falsehoods and any type of conscious and voluntary omission, made in order to mislead the organs of the procedure or to hide goods from submit to the distribution among creditors[568]. Sometimes, but the address is not consolidated[569], in jurisprudence the notion of falsity has been extended to the point of including also formally true statements, but, with regard to the

---

[566]M.A. TIGHE, A guide to making a criminal bankruptcy fraud referral, op. cit., § 425.

[567]It is interesting to note that the prevailing jurisprudence considers that the case of false declarations pursuant to § 152 (3) can be compared with that of concealment pursuant to § 152 (1) even if the conduct concerns the same asset. See, U.S. vs. Cluck, 143 F.3d 174, 179, 5th Circuit, 1998; U.S. vs. Christner, 66 F.3d 922, 929-30, 8th Circuit, 1995. This interpretation raises many doubts of constitutionality in relation to the fifth amendment which expresses the US equivalent of the ne bis in idem principle, under the name of Double Jeopardy Clause: "Nor shall be any person for the same offense to be twice put in jeopardy of life or limb". The fifth amendment protects the defendant both from the establishment of a second criminal trial for the same fact already subject to conviction or acquittal, as from the risk of multiple convictions for the same fact within a single process. For a broad summary of the problem and an interpretative proposal that puts the assets at the center of the analysis and not conducted (in order to protect the accused from multiple charges for the same fact). See in argument: N.M. GEWERTZ, Act or assets: Multiplicitous indictments under the bankruptcy fraud Statutes: 18 U.S.C. 152, op. cit., pp. 912ss. However convincing we believe that the proposal put forward by the author is bound to encounter little success in jurisprudence, given the asset declination of the legal asset assumed as the object of protection of the case in question, as well as the refusal-far from unmotivated-of the consolidated opinion that considers the different paragraphs of § 152 independent offenses.

[568]U.S. vs. Sobin, 56 F.3d 1423, 1428, D.C. Circuit, 1995, "false statements includes knowing omissions of facts made with intent to deceive or conceal (...)".

[569]M.A. TIGHE, A guide to making a criminal bankruptcy fraud referral, cit., § 425.

general context, misleading[570].

The requirement, which is entirely jurisprudential, that differentiates the case in question from those of concealment already analyzed is given by the materiality.

To be punishable, that is, declarative conduct must have as its object a material matter[571]. The requirement of materiality is one of the few institutions from which it is possible to deduce the need to recover indices of offensiveness in practice in the entire US bankruptcy criminal system.

A concrete offensiveness, however, that the declarative conduct must possess in relation to the legal good protected by the case in question which remains, in any case, the administration of justice. The materiality requirement, therefore, has no patrimonial content and a conduct can be considered material even if it does not cause any damage (patrimonial note) to social creditors[572].

A wide attention to the notion of offense incorporated by the US jurisprudence with reference to the cases referred to in § 152 (2) (3) is dedicated in US vs. Gellene[573], which we have already mentioned with reference to the interpretation of the subjective element (fraudulently) in the hypothesis of concealment.

The defendant's defense consistently with the patrimonial interpretation of the legal asset protected by the norms governed by § 152 sustained that the statements made in object from § 152 (2) were to be considered material only if related to the assets of bankruptcy axis and, therefore, to aspects related to the concursive distribution of the debtor's assets. According to this reading, the conduct would be considered

[570]U.S. vs. Robbins, 997 F.2d 390, 395, 8th Circuit, 1993 confirmed a conviction for a false oath accusation based on formally true but misleading claims. Particular attention was paid to the element of the context also in U.S. vs. Bonacorsa, 528 F.2d 1218, 1221, 2nd Circuit, 1976, (...) perjury charge may not be defended by isolating statements from context and changing its meaning (...)".

[571]See ex multis, U.S. vs. Key, 859 F.2d 1257, 1261, 7th Circuit, 1988; U.S. vs. O'Donnell, 539 F.2d 1233, 1237-38, 9th Circuit, 1972; Metheany vs. U.S., 365 F.2d 90, 93, 9th Circuit, 1966. For further details see: S.L. MICHAEL, White collar crime: Law, procedure, theory and practice, Kluwer Wolters, New York, 2014.

[572]See also: U.S. vs. O'Donnell, op. cit. S.L. MICHAEL, White collar crime: Law, procedure, theory and practice, op. cit.

[573]U.S. vs. Gellene, 182 F.3d 578, 7th Circuit, 1999, § II.2.

offensive (material) only when it affects (negatively) the liquidation procedure of the assets of the bankrupt towards the mass.

The court of appeal agrees with the above opinion, but only in the sense of believing that false information of the kind described above actually satisfies the requirement of materiality, but does not exhaust it.

Certainly, states the court, false representations concerning "debtor's commercial transactions, estate assets, the discovery of such assets and the history of financial transactions"[574] are eligible to be defined as material. However, it cannot be said that only this kind of information is relevant.

On the negative side, it is incorrect to state, in the opinion of the cited jurisprudence, that only declarations that damage creditors, or that confer an advantage on the debtor must be considered criminally relevant. On the positive side, however, the definition of material becomes rather elusive and dominated by a logic of case by case[575].

It seems to be affected by tautology, or at least by poor explanatory value, the statement that the requirement of materiality requires that the false statements are related to significant aspects of the bankruptcy procedure within which they are rendered.

Equally ineffective and a sign of a certain logical perversion that according to which the statement that the active subject deems to be sufficiently important and therefore material in order to achieve the intended purpose should be considered material.

Following this line of thought, proper to the cited jurisprudence, the requirement of materiality loses any selective function of the criminal relevance of the conduct.

8.Other cases governed by § 152

It has been decided to jointly deal with the remaining cases

---

[574]U.S. vs. Gellene, cit. § II.2. S.L. MICHAEL, White collar crime: Law, procedure, theory and practice, op. cit.

[575]Here is the same Court that seems to betray a certain embarassment: "(...) just what is significant is difficult to say for the general case: failing to disclose ownership of a ream of paper in a multi-million dollar bankruptcy is probably not material, but in many cases a false social security number or a false prior address may be (...)". U.S. vs. Gellene, cit. § II.2.

governed by § 152 because, either they are not very practical, or in any case share the same legal issues already analyzed in the previous paragraphs below (the common subjective element of all the cases in question) it is given, also in this case, by having acted knowingly and fraudulently)[576].

§ 152 (4) punishes anyone (the figure is addressed to creditors) present instances of insinuation to bankruptcy passive based on false evidence of credit. § 152 (5) punishes anyone, after the signing of the petition by the debtor, receives from it assets (belonging to the summer) in order to frustrate the procedure of the insolvency distribution. § 152 (6) punishes anyone who gives, offers, receives or seeks to obtain money or other assets, remunerations, compensations, rewards, advantages or promises to act, or to avoid acting within a procedure governed by title 11 (agreements between debtor and creditors). § 152 (8) governs the documentary hypotheses. The law contains both pre and post-petition conduct and incriminates anyone, after the initiation of a insolvency procedure, or in anticipation of it, hidden, destroy in whole or in part, falsify (in both material and ideological sense, make false annotations) any recorded information (books, documents, balance sheets, registers) relating to the balance sheet or reconstruction of a debtor's financial movements. § 152 (9) punishes anyone who, after initiating a insolvency procedure, retains and does not make available to the organs of the procedure any recorded information (books, documents, balance sheets, registers) relating to the financial situation or reconstruction of financial movements of a debtor.

It should be noted that, for these last two figures, the case law does not require any materiality requirement.

9.Single indictment cases: 18 U.S.C. § 157.

The reform of bankruptcy proceedings of 1994 in one with a reorganization of the cases covered by the previous analysis, all however, already contained in the previous legislation of 1898 introduced a new type of crime, the only legislative term called bankruptcy fraud.

---

[576]Foe a panoramic of these figures of crime see: v. United States Trustee Manual, cit., pag. 27-34.

§ 157[577] of title 18 U.S.C. incriminates anyone, having devised (devise), or in an attempt to devise, a fraudulent scheme, in order to perpetrate or conceal this scheme, or in an attempt to do so. This case, which constitutes a sort of reserve clause[578], has been foreseen in order to attribute criminal importance to conduct that, pursuant to the previous statute, could not be prosecuted[579].

An example in this sense is represented by the presentation of ideologically false documentation, if it is not expressly foreseen that the annotations contained in it are made by the declarant under oath. Furthermore, the representation, not necessarily in the context of a procedure, of the existence of a proceeding under title 11 (in order to be able to benefit from the automatic stay) becomes punishable when in fact, this has never been established[580].

Criminal policy reasons linked to the introduction of the new case are based on experience, starting by the late 80s and during the 1990s, linked to the emergence of previously unknown fraudulent phenomena.

If, until then, most of criminal conduct was essentially aimed at the concealment of assets against the procedure (and therefore found an adequate legislative response in § 152)[581], the emergence of the phenomenon of distorted use of the bankruptcy system by individuals who, using automatic stay as a true artificial instrument, carried out extensive fraudulent transactions, only incidentally linked to the insolvency

---

[577] 18 U.S.C. § 157-Bankruptcy Fraud: Subscribes a petition pursuant to Title 11, including an involuntary petition ex par. 303; False or fraudulent representations, requests or promises concerning, or in relation to, an existing bankruptcy procedure or whose existence is falsely declared, at any time, before or after signing the petition.

[578] A person who, having devised or intending to devise a scheme or artifice to defraud and for the purpose of executing or concealing such a scheme or artifice or attempting to do so-files a petition under title 11, including a fraudulent involuntary petition under section 303 of such title; -files a document in a proceeding under title 11; or -makes a false or fraudulent representation, claim, or promise concerning or in relation to a proceeding under title 11, at any time before or after the filing of the petition, or in relation to a proceeding falsely asserted to be pending under such title, shall be fined under this title, imprisoned not more than five years, or both.

[579] The expression is of the: M. PONTANI, Pre-bankruptcy crimes and entrepreneural behaviour, op. cit., pp. 15ss.

[580] M.A. TIGHE, A guide to making a criminal bankruptcy fraud referral, op. cit.

[581] J.A. CASTLE and others, Bankruptcy crime Statutes governing debtors, in Bankruptcy Strategist, 15, 1998, pp. 6ss.

procedure[582].

Synthetically, elements constituting the offense are: The existence of a fraudulent scheme, in consummate or attempted form[583]; the behaviors described, linked to the operability of the active subject in relation to the insolvency procedure; instrumentalization of the bankruptcy system to the success or the concealment of fraud[584]. This last requirement is of particular importance in the legislative genesis of the institute itself. Specifically, during parliamentary work, the applicability of this case to cases where the conduct contained in numbers 1 and 2 of the standard are not perpetrated as an essential component in the pursuit of the fraudulent scheme, has been excluded[585].

The most widespread examples in application practice concern the creation of fraudulent schemes within the expropriation or eviction procedures, also due to the rapid surge of such phenomena following the repeated real estate crises of the last decades (and, in a disruptive way, since 2005 on).

Active subjects of such fraudulent operations are professional scammers, who approach, in various ways, real estate owners in difficult financial situations, planning a way out of the imminent expropriation of the home by creditors (usually credit institutions).

The real estate owner is persuaded to sell his house in favor of the

---

[582]M.A. TIGHE, A guide to making a criminal bankruptcy fraud referral, op. cit.

[583]It should be noted that the jurisprudence does not require that, in the presence of an artifice, the punishability is subordinated to the verification of its actual success (ex post), nor of its concrete aptitude (ex ante) to deceive the passive subject. See U.S. vs. Wagner, n. 03-4313, 6th Circuit, 2004.

[584]This case could well apply also to the bust out operations already described, as well as to Ponzi schemes. They deal with the issue concerning the satisfaction of damaged investors in the light of the antinomies between bankruptcy and criminal confiscation. K.B. PHELPS, Handling claims in Ponzi scheme bankruptcy and receivership cases, in Golden Gate University Law Review, 42, 2012, pp. 567ss. M.A. SULLIVAN, When the bezzle bursts: Restitutionary distribution of assets after Ponzi schemes enter bankruptcy, in Washington & Lee Law Review, 68, 2011, pp. 1589ss.

[585]Declaration of defendant Brooks, 140 Congr. Rec. H 10771, 4 October 1994, "It would also not be a crime under this section for a person to make a false statement or promise concerning a proceeding under title 11, as long as the false statement or promise was not made as part of a scheme to defraud involving the bankruptcy proceeding. Similarly, a person who conveys incorrect information about the pendency of a bankruptcy or the planned filing of a bankruptcy case would not be within the scope of this section unless that information was conveyed fraudulently and to further a fraudulent scheme (...)".

active subject or, more frequently, of a nominee (or a company) who, on the eve of the forced sale procedure of the property, submits an application pursuant to Chapter 7. In this way, by virtue of the principle of automatic stay, the individual actions of forced execution on the debtor's assets are inhibited throughout the course of the bankruptcy procedure (regardless of whether this ends with a ruling of inadmissibility, or with the concession or the denial of the discharge); the action is intended, for each individual property, to be repeated indefinitely (with the transfer of the same to different subjects/companies) to the aim, in case of success, to avoid the forced execution for an indefinite time[586].

An example in this sense is constituted by the US vs. Daniels case. Even more important than the specific case of the judgment, however, is the fact that on this occasion the court found itself having to face a question of constitutional legitimacy of § 157, advanced by the accused, under the "void for vagueness" doctrine[587] (principle of taxation, sufficient determinability of the case).

In the opinion of the appellant Daniels, the rule in question would be to be censured as it would not describe nor did the blame, in the concrete case with sufficient clarity the passive subject of fraudulent activity (perpetrated through the instrumental use of bankruptcy regulation)[588].

Specifically, it would not be possible to understand whether the case aims to protect against frauds: Any physical person, one or more identified creditors or, indeed, the bankruptcy system considered in itself[589].

The court certainly not spreading in a particularly detailed analysis considers the argument raised by the fatuous defendant[590]. Law

---

[586]L.F. CHAVES, In rem bankruptcy refiling bars: Will they stop abuse of the automatic stay against mortages?, in California Bankruptcy Journal, 24, 1998, pp. 3ss.

[587]L.F. CHAVES, In rem bankruptcy refiling bars: Will they stop abuse of the automatic stay against mortages?,

[588]See the case from the Supreme Court: Kolender vs. Lawson, 461 U.S. 352, 357, 1983, "(...) the void for vagueness doctrine requires that a penal statute define the criminal offense with sufficient definiteness that ordinary people can understand what conduct is prohibited and in a manner that does not encourage arbitrary and discriminatory enforcement (...)".

[589]U.S. vs. Daniels, op.cit. "Daniels claims that the vagueness in the bankruptcy fraud statute is that it is unclear who is supposed to be protected from the fraudulent conduct-the bankruptcy system itself, a member of the general public, or some creditor (...)".

[590]U.S. vs. Daniels, op. cit., "(...) the argument proclaiming Daniels' confusion as to who

constitutionality is supported by referring to a previous ruling of another circuit[591] that had solved a similar question (sufficient determination) with reference to the case of email fraud[592].

In the opinion of the sentence in question, § 152 is also followed, in the choice of legislative language, on § 134, which represents a general anti-fraud prediction, against which it is not possible to postulate any reproach of intrinsic vagueness[593].

In the present case, then, the defensive argument is judged to be worthless, and the question of irrelevant constitutional legitimacy (to use domestic terminology), since, according to the court, the defendant could not have run into confusion about the passive subject protected by the case, having the first place in being a fraudulent conduct, both in respect of the debtors, that of the creditors, that of the bankruptcy system considered in itself[594].

Criminal phenomena in some way similar to those just treated see the distorted use of the bankruptcy system, through the abuse of the automatic stay, in order to delay the eviction procedure. In these cases, the active subject, representing himself as a qualified person, often a lawyer, assisting the tenants in disputes with the landlords and paying a fee, subscribes, in favor and, basically, without the knowledge of the former, of the petitions of personal bankruptcy finalized precisely to hinder the execution of the eviction.

A case of this kind was taken into consideration by an important

he might be prohibited from defrauding is fatuous (...)".

591 U.S. vs. Feinberg, 535 F.2d 1004, 1010, 7th Circuit, 1976.

592 18 U.S.C. § 1341. The § 157 is modeled on the case of mail fraud is also apparent from the parliamentary work that accompanied the approval of the rule, see statement of the deputy Brooks, 140 Congress Record H10752-01, October 4, 1994.

593 U.S. vs. Daniels, op. cit., "The mail fraud statute contains identical language-criminalizing conduct that "devise[s] or intend[s] to devise a scheme or artifice to defraud"-leading us to the conclusion that there is nothing inherently vague in the notion of a general anti-fraud provision (...)".

594 U.S. vs. Daniels, op. cit., "(...) as is clear from the facts of this case, Daniels defrauded not only the homeowners, but also the bankruptcy system and the mortgage companies. The bankruptcy fraud statute, as applied to Daniels, is constitutional (...)".

how controversial[595] ruling of the ninth circuit, US vs. Millwitt[596], which will be taken as a starting point for an analysis of the case in question.

First of all some system considerations. The pronunciation in question gives the sign of the very poor application of § 157: Firstly, the court[597] expressly recognizes that, although twelve years after the entry into force of the law, the one under examination constitutes the first opportunity to interpret the constituent elements of the case; secondly, as already established by another circuit in the aforementioned US vs. Daniels case, who § 157 shares the structure of some federal statutes, primarily those incriminating other types of fraud, mail and wire frauds[598] (of very frequent application)[599]. The interpretative elaboration developed by the courts with reference to these different figures of crime will, therefore, be the same as in US vs. Daniels, also used for the benefit of bankruptcy fraud[600].

10.US vs. Millwitt case would seem to be moving away from US vs. Daniels.

In short, these are the facts that were the subject of the imputation, pursuant to § 157, of the accused Millwitt: Having enticed a plurality of tenants in economic difficulty; to have made them believe in defending them in disputes with the owners; on the contrary, having signed a series of personal bankruptcy requests on their behalf; finally, having convinced them to remunerate it, with rents no longer paid to landlords (pending a bankruptcy procedure unknown to tenants) for services rendered in delaying eviction.

The annulment of the sentence of first instance in appeal, even if

---

[595]Controversial both when compared to other pronunciations, primarily U.S. vs. Daniels, cit., Both in his own collegiate genesis. The decision was taken, in fact, by a majority of two judges in three and the dissenting opinion of Judge Wallace is rather harsh in criticizing the conclusions of the majority.

[596]U.S. vs. Millwitt, 475 F.3d 1150, 9th Circuit, 2006.

[597]It is, moreover, a very wide circuit which includes, among others, the California district

[598]18 U.S.C. § 1343.

[599]U.S. vs. Millwitt, cit., § II "(...) while we have not interpreted 18 U.S.C. 157, we have discussed the elements of U.S.C. § 1341 and 18 U.S.C. § 1343, the mail and wire fraud statutes upon which § 157 was modelled (...)".

[600]See the § 157 ed il § 1341, v. Collier on bankruptcy, 15 ed., revised 1998, vol. 1, 7-07 "Section 157 was consciously patterned on the federal mail fraud statute".

due, essentially, to prosecutor's adoption of a questionable strategy and, probably, a basic error in the formulation of the imputation, son, however, of a date interpretation of the norm disavowed by the court, allows to appreciate the most important differences between the two sentences. Indeed, the indictment explicitly qualified, as passive subjects of the fraudulent conduct of Millwitt, the owners of the apartments rented out[601]. Thus, in the indictment, there was no reference to fraudulent conduct perpetrated against the conductors[602].

Contradictually, however, compared to the object of the act of blaming, the prosecution of the prosecution focused exclusively on demonstrating to the jury the fraudulent conduct held by the accused against the tenants[603]: Having deceived about the fact of being a lawyer[604], having signed bankruptcy claims on behalf of them without their knowledge[605], having defrauded them of rent fees[606].

The same instrumentalization of the bankruptcy system was presented, in the investigation of the prosecution, as functional to conceal the (non) judicial activity of Millwitt in the eviction procedure: The conductors, noting a setback in the eviction process (due to the operation , without their knowledge, of the principle of automatic stay), they were

[601]U.S. vs. Millwitt, cit., § III, "(...) as we have noted, the government charged Millwitt with "fraudulently obstruct[ing] the creditors' legal right to collect back rents, and repossess the properties". In sum, the fraudulent scheme was one to prevent the landlords from exercising legal rights, and the alleged victims were the landlords. The required bankruptcy nexus alleged was the filing of sham Chapter 13 bankruptcy petitions (...)".

[602]U.S. vs. Millwitt, cit., § III "(...) there were no allegations in the indictment concerning a scheme to defraud the tenants, nor were the tenants identified as victims of the fraudulent scheme (...)".

[603]U.S. vs. Millwitt, cit., § III, "(...) throughout the trial, the government referred to the tenants, rather than the landlords, as the victims of Millwitt's fraudulent scheme (...)".

[604]U.S. vs. Millwitt, cit., § III, citing the opening declaration of the Prosecutor: "(...) The evidence will show that the defendant intended to deraud the [tenants named in the bankruptcy petitions]. He did it by passing himself off as an attorney and by telling them he would be representing them and performing various legal services (...)".

[605]U.S. vs. Millwitt, cit., § III, citing ex novo the opening declaration of the Prosecutor: "(...) [n]One of the victims authorized [Millwitt] to file bankruptcy on their behalf (...)", but, the court continues, to demonstrate the reference made by the prosecutor to the tenants as passive subjects of fraud (victims) "(...) Millwitt never filed bankruptcy on behalf of anybody but the tenants (...)".

[606]U.S. vs. Millwitt, cit., § III, "(...) the evidence showed that (...) the fraudulent scheme was one by Millwitt to deprive the tenants of money by fraudulently representing them that he was representing their interests (...)".

convinced of the goodness of the defendant's defense and continued to remunerate it[607].

On the contrary, the prosecutor did not concentrate any probative effort in proving the existence of a fraudulent scheme against the owners, nor the fact that the signing of the petitions was instrumentalized to execute or to conceal this scheme[608].

The confirmation of the conviction in the appeal albeit in terms of the appeal, that is the sufficiency of the evidence of the specific intent required by the law would necessarily have to go through a hermeneutical operation about the constituent elements (elements of crime) of the crime in question.

Specifically, if § 157 requires that the prosecutor, in demonstrating the required intent, must prove the existence of a fraudulent scheme designed to mislead a particular taxable person (natural or legal).

In fact, if the thesis supported in US v. Daniels, § 157 applies, without distinction, to fraud against the debtor, the creditor, another physical person, but also, generally, the bankruptcy system in itself considered the investigatory inefficiencies of the prosecutor in US v. Milwitt could have been exempt from censorship.

However, this is not the interpretation of the ninth circuit in the judgment under examination. Recalling the previous jurisprudence concerning e-mail fraud[609], the court, on the one hand, emphasizes the

---

[607]U.S. vs. Millwitt, cit., § III, "The government argued that the effect of the bankruptcy filing was that it allowed Millwitt to continue to represent to the tenants that he was taking care of their legal issues with their landlords. As the government stated, the defendant's supposed clients were aware that they were not being evicted despite having received this notice to be evicted, and the defendant led them to believe that was because he was working diligently on their behalf, he was defending them against [sic] these eviction proceedings. The tenants had not idea that a bankruptcy stay had anything to do with the delay-with the halt in the eviction proceedings (...)".

[608]U.S. vs. Millwitt, cit., § III, "In sum, when the government rested the case, it had presented no proof that there was a scheme to defraud the landlords, much less that the bankruptcy petitions had been filed as a means of executing or concealing the scheme". When, on the basis of the formulation of the conclusions in the trial of the first instance, of the error committed, the prosecutor tried to present the lessors as passive subjects, indirectly, damaged by the conduct of the accused "Millwitt directly deceiv[ed] the clients and indirectly deceiv[ed] the landlords (...)".

[609]McNally vs. U.S., 483 U.S. 350, 107 S.Ct. 2875, 97 L.Ed.2d 292, 1987; U.S. vs. Mitchell, 867 F.2d 1232, 9th Circuit, 1989. For further details see: D.K. WEBB, R.W.

patrimonial nature of the protected legal property (by § 1341, and, by analogy by) § 157[610], on the other, affirms how this case requires, among its constituent elements (object, therefore, of trial demonstration), that, through a given fraudulent scheme, the active subject has the specific intent to defraud a victim, or a class of victims, identifiable[611]. The probative deficiencies about the trial of the specific intent against the victims identified in the indictment (lessors), in this specific case, have therefore led to an annulment of the sentence.

Cancellation decided only by majority. Judge Wallace, in his articulate dissenting opinion, calls into question the fundamental postulates made by the majority and denounces a surreptitious over-rulling of the precedents of the same circuit, however, by a court (in terms of composition) incapacitated to such an act[612].

Beyond the factual data, relating to the specific case, presented by the dissenting judge, he refuses to include among the elements of crime of § 157 the need to identify a specific victim of the fraudulent activity. This refusal goes through the citation of a precedent of the same ninth circuit, linked to the case of wire fraud, US vs. Crawford[613].

On that occasion, with regard to the similar figure of wire fraud, the court had denied that the prosecutor should give evidence of a specific intent to defraud a particular taxable person, taking a position and rejecting all the precedents cited by the majority in his support in US v. Millwitt.

Majority that, in the opinion of the dissenting judge, would have, in fact, adopted the interpretation that, in US vs. Crawford, was supported in the dissenting opinion of judge Tashima, thereby achieving an undue

---

TARUN, S.F. MORO, Corporate international investigations, Law Journal Press, New York, 2018.

[610]McNally vs. U.S., op. cit., (in this point over rulled from introduction of § 1346) "the mail fraud statute only reached the loss of money and property and not to "the intangible right of the citizenry to good government".

[611]U.S. vs. Millwitt, cit., § II, "Given all of these considerations, we conclude that the crime of bankruptcy fraud under 18 U.S.C. § 157 requires a specific intent to defraud an identifiable victim or class of victims if the identified fraudulent scheme".

[612]U.S. vs. Millwitt, cit., Wallace, Senior Circuit Judge, dissenting, § I and II. The criticism, however, becomes sharp when it accuses the majority of having deviated from the same principles of the court system of accusation having raised, ex officio, a question of law (identified victim) not remitted to the decision by the parties.

[613]U.S. vs. Crawford, 239 F.3d 1086, 9th Circuit, 2001.

overruling of his own precedent. In addition to the internal jurisprudence of the circuit, Judge Wallace also rests his dissent on the precedents of other courts that, likewise, do not consider that the type of mail fraud requires the existence of an identified victim[614].

The question is still open. The small number of precedents in this field does not allow to draw certain conclusions. However, it is the writer's opinion, based on the generally unanimous interpretation of the public legal good protected by US criminal offenses, that the position advocated in the dissenting opinion of Judge Wallace will find greater support in future jurisprudence.

11.Single indictment cases: 18 U.S.C. 1519 (Sarbanes-Oxley Act)

In response to the scandals of the early 2000s, which involved primary corporations such as Enron and WorldCom, whose managers were the protagonists of massive criminal activities (and equally sensational, as to the penalties imposed, criminal proceedings), the Congress inaugurated a new legislative-corporate and criminal law-that also affects the area of bankruptcy crimes, the so-called Serbanes-Oxley Act[615].

At least for what concerns the bankruptcy criminal field, the new discipline is nothing but the inevitable, economic and, sadly, predictable muscular and irrational response of the legislator to the scandals that have shaken public opinion[616].

---

[614]U.S. vs. Munoz, 430 F.3d 1357, 1369, 11th Circuit, 2005, "the crime of mail fraud does not include an element requiring a contemplated harm to a specific identifiable victim"; U.S. vs. Henningsen, 387 F.3d 585, 590, 7th Circuit, 2004; U.S. vs. Loayza, F.3d 257, 260, 4th Circuit, 1997 "indictment which do not identify specific mail fraud victims by name are sufficient".

[615]Serbanes-Oxley Act, Public Company Accounting Reform and Investor Protection Act, Pub.L. 107-204, 30 July 2002, 116 Stat. 745.

[616]M.A. PERINO, Enron's legislative aftermath: Some reflections on the deterrence aspects off the Serbanes-Oxley Act of 2002, in Columbia Law School, working paper n. 212, 2002. "Some things are inevitable (...) when scandals erupt or horrific crimes capture public attention, Congressmen want to show that they are doing something about it. There is a long, and sometimes ignominious, history in Congress of (...) addressing public outcry over some recent event through new criminal laws, even in areas in witch there appeared to be little need for new federal legislation (...); an opposite opinion would seem to be supported by the practical (governmental bankers, prosecutors and trustees), probably-but it is a personal assessment- wishing to vent the system inefficiencies in a critique of the previous

The new § 1519[617] is aimed, in the same intentions of the legislator, to widen the margins of applicability of cases of documentary infidelity not only in the bankruptcy sphere mostly already existing in US criminal system[618].

Certainly, a large area of overlap between the new law and the already existing case is in the field of bankruptcy. Conduct of alteration, destruction (total or partial), concealment, falsification (material or ideological) of documents or registers-previously perpetrated (in anticipation) or subsequent to the signing of a petition-were, even earlier, peacefully punishable under the historical case governed by § 152 (8).

With respect to the legislation already (and still) in force, § 1519 requires a less meaningful subjective element: If § 152 (8) applies to behaviors done knowingly and fraudulently, the the new case abandons the intent to deceive (to deceive, mislead, reverse) described by the adverbulently fraudulently, to apply to the actions put in place in order to prevent, obstruct or influence a procedure pursuant to title 11, allowing, in this sense, a weakening of the burden of proof of the subjective requirement for the prosecutor[619].

---

legislation and applaud the new. So for A. TIGHE, R. CALO, Congress, the courts, and the feds agree-Bankruptcy crime does not pay, in Annual Survey of Bankruptcy Law, 2004, pag. 351, "(...) while the number of bankruptcy crime prosecutions may not be as high as many desire, these developments demonstrate that engaging in criminal activity in bankruptcy court is a higher risk activity than ever before because, if caught, prosecution may be easier and sentences higher (...)".

[617] 18 USC § 1519-Destruction, alteration, or falsification of records in Federal investigations and bankruptcy "(...) whoever knowingly alters, destroys, mutilates, conceals, covers up, falsifies, or makes a false entry in any record, document, or tangible object with the intent to impede, obstruct, or influence the investigation or proper administration of any matter within the jurisdiction of any department or agency of the United States or any case filed under title 11, or in relation to or contemplation of any such matter or case, shall be fined under this title, imprisoned not more than 20 years, or both (...)".

[618] 148 Congr. Rec. S7419, 26 July 2002 which defines the § 1519, "(...) a new general anti-shredding provision (...). Currently, provisions governing the destruction or fabrication of evidence are a patchwork that have been interpreted often very narrowly by federal courts (...) Section 1519 is meant to apply broadly to any acts to destroy or fabricate physical evidence (...)".

[619] A. TIGHE, R. CALO, Congress, the courts, and the feds agree, op. cit., pag. 352. For a first jurisprudential application, to one case, moreover, blatantly punishable also under the previous legislation, see also: U.S. vs. Thrower, No. 03-CR00341, Docket n. 18, Northern District of Ohio. U.S. vs. Johns, n. 11–3299, 7th Circuit, 2012.

Again, with reference to the material object of the crime, this has been extended making applicable the case also to the conduct perpetrated on any tangible object (creating, in the opinion of the writer, many problems of certainty), not necessarily related to assets or business financial statements of the debtor (as required by § 152 (8))[620].

The result, however, is paradoxical. The crime of more recent coinage, in fact, although regulating conduct supported by a subjective element of less intensity, and less connoted in terms of fraudulence easier to prove, but also an index of less offensive and also applying to material objects, in hypothesis, from the lower probative/demonstrative value (any tangible object) with respect to books and accounting records, it foresees a quadrupling of the sanction, which reaches the draconian measure of twenty years of imprisonment[621].

12.A reflection and observations on the effectiveness of the criminal protection system of bankruptcy.

The analysis of the American bankruptcy criminal system, in the opinion of the writer, could not be considered exhaustive if not accompanied by a brief reflection on the effectiveness of the system itself, or rather its practical application at the jurisdictional level. On the other hand, the one linked to the concreteness of the penal system in the prevention and repression of the abuses of bankruptcy proceedings is an issue that is anything but neglected in the same American doctrine[622].

If we wanted to offer a comparison, even if we repeat it, without any pretense of statistical scientificity[623], we would note that, in 2005

---

[620]In this sense, the extension of punishability is not measured by the elimination of the link between the subject of the conduct and the patrimonial and financial situation of the debtor, a requirement already interpreted in jurisprudence in a rather extensive manner. Rather, the new law reaches a greater scope of applicability with reference to documents not attributable to the debtor tout court, but to creditors or, even, to subjects unrelated to the bankruptcy procedure. See for further details: A. TIGHE, R. CALO, Congress, the courts, and the feds agree, op. cit., pag. 353.

[621]M. PONTANI, Pre-bankruptcy crimes and entrepreneural behaviour., op. cit., pp. 19ss.

[622]R.C. MCCULLOUGH II, Bankruptcy fraud: Crime without punishment II, op. cit.

[623]R.C. MCCULLOUGH II, Bankruptcy fraud: Crime without punishment II, op. cit., pp. 2ss. It expresses itself in terms of paradoxical recalcitrance to the application of bankruptcy criminal cases "(...) Section 152 of the Federal Criminal Code in Congress's answer to

alone, 5,595 criminal proceedings were instituted for bankruptcy cases.

In short, if one compares the number of insolvency proceedings initiated in US with that of the reported offenses unless one considers that the rate of loyalty to the system of North American citizens is close to 100%, one can only conclude of the absolute virtuality and non ineffectiveness of the bankruptcy criminal system.

An example is worth more than the numbers: The trials of the executives of Enron and WorldCom (respectively the second and the first greatest failure in world history) did not see, among the charges, no case of bankruptcy fraud[624]. The problem has not recently emerged, but accompanies the enforcement of the discipline examined since its origins[625].

The total disclosure operation, of which we have already mentioned, in other cases consisted only of a symbolic (almost advertising) effort, which took shape in the simultaneous launch of a prosecution against 127 defendants of bankruptcy crimes (in all US states). The reality is that the hypotheses of bankruptcy frauds are prosecuted, in most cases, only when associated with other non-bankruptcy cases (tax fraud, mail fraud, wire fraud).

In an attempt to remedy the total inefficiency of the system, instead of foreseeing new, irrational, types of crime (the draconian prediction referred to in § 1519 introduced in 2002, as we have seen, gave rise to 39 complaints in 2012) in 2005 the Congress launched the Bankruptcy Abuse Prevention and Consumer Protection Act (BACPA)[626]. The new legislation sets, essentially, on the strengthening (in terms of economic resources and links with the other governmental structures involved, F.B.I. and Attorney General Office) of the US trustee office and

---

bankruptcy fraud. It occupies, however, the curious position of a statute which is often invoked, but seldom enforced (...)".

624On the contrary, today's numbers are particularly pleased with the Office of the U.S. Trustee considering that in 1995 (according to the Statistical Report of the US Attorney Offices, Fiscal Year 2005, cited by R.C. MCCULLOUGH II, Bankruptcy Fraud, cited above) on a total of 883,457 applications pursuant to Title 11, the complaints of a total of 158 were committed (and 75 in 1989).

625R.C. MCCULLOUGH II, Bankruptcy fraud: Crime without punishment II, op. cit., pp. 5ss.

626G.F. MUNITZ, Keynote address: Stories in the development of bankruptcy law, op. cit., pp. 546ss.

on the elaboration of new numerical/quantitative fraud detection parameters aimed at introducing presumptions of system abuse by natural persons.

Although no longer young, the new discipline would not seem, at least according to the data above, to be decisive. Time, as always, will offer more reliable judgments.

13.Concluding remarks: Attempts to build a dam at regressus ad infinitum.

The path undertaken has led us to analyze some of the main problems of criminal policy and dogmatic nature, present in the criminal subsystem of insolvency crimes. In doing so, particular attention has been paid to the cases of bankruptcy and, in particular, to those with the highest degree of affliction.

We were not surprised by the fact that, after more than seventy years from the systematic introduction of these cases in the bankruptcy law, and now more than a decade since the reform of the cases of improper bankruptcy, these problems have remained substantially the the same ones on which generations of scholars and masters have ventured.

It would be reductive, in the opinion of the writer, to believe that this is due, at least exclusively, to the substantial invariance of the normative data (at least with reference to the cases of bankruptcy, also applicable in the case of companies conducted in corporate form). On the contrary, more likely, the incapacity on the part of the legislator to engage in a serious intention to reform the crime of insolvency derives first of all from a cultural datum, which could also be defined as ideological.

A confirmation of this conclusion was given to us by the study of US system. The substantial benevolence, in the model taken as reference, granted by the bankruptcy regulatory apparatus towards the honest but unfortunate debtor, while not translating into a discipline of the crimes of the insolvency insolvency, differs, however, in a rather significant manner from that known in the national system.

This, in particular, if we refer to all those hypotheses of crime, we refer to the macro world of distractions, which in the interpreter raise the greatest perplexities about their compatibility with the constitutional principles of guilt and offensiveness in relation to the time of the conduct with respect to bankruptcy, the impact of the same on the damage of the protected legal asset, etc.

Let's be clear, not that similar problems can be seen even with reference to US criminal bankruptcy cases. On the contrary, a system that essentially involves abstract formal risk crimes whose configurability totally ignores the infringement of the patrimonial interests of social creditors, and is instead often entrusted to the intent of the agent, could be considered the maximum expression of violation of the offensive principle[627]. And yet, even if we find its limits true to the eyes of the interpreter and almost never discussed critically in US system we cannot underline the fact that, in that system, it is easier to trace the limits of relevance criminal conduct: Discerning between the lawful and the unlawful, to foresee criminal consequences of the own entrepreneurial choices (or personal in the case of the consumer bankruptcy).

By setting the deadline from which to ascertain the criminal relevance of any typical conduct at the time of signing the petition (so for most of the hypotheses described by 18 USC§152), and regardless of the final outcome of the bankruptcy proceedings, the debtor is placed in front of an all-in-one simple alternative act with the utmost transparency towards the organs of the procedure both with reference to documentary/declaratory obligations, with reference to the obligation to deliver the assets or subject to the punishment of any conduct knowingly, maliciously , deviant, regardless of the concrete effect of the same on the procedure for the division of any active assets[628].

With reference to the cases that we would define as pre-bankruptcy pre-petition, governed by 18 U.S.C. § 152 (7) which certainly raise the major problems in the national system, US regulatory framework is particularly effective in preparing a filter for the criminal relevance of the pipelines. The filter does not work on the objective plane (in etiological

---

[627]Confirmed also by the United States Supreme Court, U.S. Supreme Court, Marrama Vs. Citizens Bank of Mass., 2007, 430 F. 3d 474: "The principal purpose of the Bankruptcy Code is to" fresh start "to the" honest but unfortunate debtor (...)".

[628]Even the requirement of the materiality, even if required for the declarative cases governed by the 18 U.S.C. § 152 (2) (3), is interpreted in jurisprudence in a rather broad and punitive case.

terms), but subjective. As seen to be punished is a wide range of conduct of concealment/transfer of assets (even the personal ones of the administrator of a corporation), but only provided that a rigorous test is provided on the fact that these behaviors are put in place in contemplation of a bankruptcy.

A particularly meaningful psychological link is required between the conduct of the active subject and the signing of bankruptcy petition: In terms of representation and will in the case of voluntary bankruptcy (own bankruptcy); or, at least, of total representation in the cases of involuntary bankruptcy (bankruptcy on the instance of personal or social creditors). In the jurisprudential interpretation, a whole series of symptomatic elements (circumstantial evidence) from which to deduce the specific intent required, such as, first of all, the awareness about the condition of failure or pre-insolvency of the debtor are valued. An awareness to be ascertained when the pipelines are implemented, and not subsequently.

Even the case specifically defined bankruptcy fraud incriminates intrinsically fraudulent pre-bankruptcy behaviors, which see in the access to the bankruptcy system a further instrument of perpetration of the artificial design put in place to the detriment of the passive subjects of fraud (gaining on the application of the automatic stay), i.e. on the automatic suspension of all individual enforcement actions on the debtor's assets. In these hypotheses (only latently similar to those of bankruptcy properly understood), therefore, failure, not only falls within the focus of the prediction of the active subject, but is the result of a deliberate choice, which can be traced to a scheme of fraudulent use of the procedure competition.

At this point, in the American system, every question of causal efficiency of the conduct on the verification of instability immediately loses its meaning[629].

---

[629]With the paradox (certainly reserved for sporadic limit cases) to make typical conduct punishable regardless of the concrete start, after them, of a bankruptcy procedure. according to our opinion it would appear to reject proposals favorable to widen the sphere of operation of bankruptcy crimes allowing their application regardless of the bankruptcy of the company (or other insolvency procedure). This would be an excessively penalizing prospect, as well as not very reassuring for the entrepreneur, subjected to a pervasive

The access to the bankruptcy procedure is, in those cases, subject to the widest provision by the active subject and to be charged are carried out with reference to the patrimonial cases of concealment in a broad sense aimed not to subject (albeit potentially) to the organs of bankruptcy the entire assets of the debtor. In other words, they are fraudulent in themselves (regardless of the actual pecuniary damage) that do not pose problems, at least in the order of origin, of reprimanding.

The accent is placed on the part of some who propose to apply the theory of objective imputation of the event to the cases of pre-bankruptcy on the necessary verification of the exceeding, with the typical conduct, of an allowed risk, which translates into 'activation of an illicit risk (which must then turn into failure).

The intrinsic unlawfulness of the conduct, in terms of exceeding the allowed risk, should already be ascertained at the level of typicality of the conduct. If the conduct remains within the permitted risk threshold, it is no longer typical: That is, it does not correspond to that provided for by the criminal case; however it is legal.

This assessment should be carried out, not only in those cases in which the conduct of continuation of the business, even without saving it, has reduced the liabilities, but, in any case, even when the economic imbalance in its measurable component remains unchanged or even increased due to the continuation of management.

The need to verify the exceeding of a permitted risk parameter, as a condition of typical conduct, would derive from the analysis of the same positive right. We would therefore be in the presence, in these cases, of legislative instruments governing a risk (continuation of the business activity) allowed, in view of an advantage for the company and its creditors. A risk, however, albeit with a non-impeccable formulation that inhibits the punishability of payments made in the execution of these management paths, in continuity, of the crisis, even if, due to factors unknown or predictable, they are unsuccessful and prelude to failure[630].

---

criminal syndicate; and inappropriate for creditors, at least when the company's difficulties have been overcome by a favorable recovery of the economic cycle, revealing therefore not only unproductive but even inadvisable the use of penal sanctions.

[630]When the criminal law expressly exempts a from penalty some operations, therefore authorized this does not entail that the interpreter should assume the unlawfulness of what

Secondly, even in criminal law would be considered the possibility of considering lawful, and therefore not contrary to the duty of proper management of the company, offensive conduct (of the patrimony of the entrepreneurial subject in whose name the agent operates) implemented in the reasonable expectation of an adequate return (for other companies in the group and ultimately for the injured party).

It has been argued that from such a normative assumption an applicable principle should be abstracted also beyond the specific reference context (infra-group relations) according to which profit (and, therefore, harm) is not unjust if compensated by advantages achieved or fundamentally foreseeable for the administered company[631].

It would remain, so far, to dissolve the fundamental issue about the criteria for determining the extent of the risk allowed. That is, the problem of how to structure the case in order to avoid restricting too much or radically excluding a legitimate sphere of risk remains.

The most obvious danger, even in the eyes of the undersigned, is to open the field to assessments of "economic rationality" of the entrepreneurial

is not expressly authorized. It does not work, that is, the argument to the contrary. Rather, one is in the presence of the particular expression of a general principle: the law formally consecrates a field of criminal lawfulness, subordinating it to precise requirements, without excluding that the interpreter invests from the system further spaces of lawfulness in which the fact may fall, even without the aforementioned requirements.

[631] In any case, the profit of the associated company or of the group is not unjust, if compensated by advantages, achieved or fundamentally foreseeable, deriving from the connection or belonging to the group. The applicability of this clause of exclusion of anti-legalness even to the hypotheses of improper fraudulent bankruptcy for pre-Commission of patrimonial infidelity is subject to much caution in jurisprudence. We can thus affirm that in the matter of fraudulent bankruptcy due to intra-group distraction, the interest that can exclude the effectiveness of distraction can not be reduced to the fact of participation in the group, or identify itself in the advantage of the parent company, having to exclude the existence of a distraction only if the lack of consideration is merely apparent, in consideration of the concrete compensatory advantages, that the administrator has the duty to attach and prove; however, there are no applicative experiences. The operation between two companies belonging to the same group, one in good economic conditions and the other in a momentary liquidity crisis, through which the former stipulates a liquidity loan with a bank, does not constitute a significant distraction. the purpose of providing a loan to the latter to enable it to correct the arrears of a loan contracted with the same bank, considering the adequacy of the fees for the transaction, that the overcoming of the liquidity crisis allows the funded company to honor its debt without any loss to the lender and that there is an interest in the operation of the group as a whole and therefore of the same lending company.

choices made ex post (and, therefore, heavily vitiated by the empirical evidence of their failure resulted in failure) of the criminal trial.

On the other hand, such fear could make us smile in light of our country's application practice. Evaluations of "economic rationality" are now carried out in the courtrooms for the assessment of many types of crime, not just bankruptcy penalties: Think, for example, of the macro-sector of criminal tax evasion and of the abuse of right.

Therefore, it becomes important that the judicial review should be brought back to the moment in which the conduct takes place (ex ante) and, in judging the attempt to reorganize the company in difficulty or insolvent, aims to ascertain the sustainability of the initiatives undertaken, as a rational economic assessment, not condemned ab initio to failure. In light of this, they may be exorbitant to the lawful risk, and therefore, typical, the only conduct that, already at the time they were made, appeared (or should have appeared), based on a technical-managerial appraisal, economically irrational or unsustainable.

This type of verification, together with that relating to the permanence of the effects of the typical conduct in terms of injury (or endangerment) of the credit guarantee at the time of the opening of the bankruptcy procedure, and the existence of a psychological coefficient that embraces the two extremes of the objective imputation judgment, pending a long awaited reform of the pre-bankruptcy cases, could contribute to the emergence of the cases covered by this study from the condition of perennial specialties in which they are found and finally make them compatible with the constitutional provisions of guilt and offense.

PART 3

Analysis and interpretation of bankruptcy of financial banking groups between private international law and European Union law

1.Introduction.

Conducting a survey on the aspects of international private and procedural law of the insolvency of multinational banking groups is of primary interest in the light, on the one hand, of the evident relevance of the topic at the time of writing and, secondly, of the lack of a specific discipline that regulates the case, both at the level of individual States and at a supra-State, regional or international level.

The relevance of the theme derives from the fact that the group is one of the most frequently used forms for conducting business activity[632], as well as the fact that, in more or less recent times, there have been many cases of bankruptcy banking groups located in more than one jurisdiction. Consider, for example, the failure of Lehman Brothers[633], Kaupthing

---

[632]See, UNCITRAL, Legislative Guide on Insolvency Law, Part three: Treatment of enterprise groups in insolvency, 21 July 2010. The Commission of the House of Lords affirmed that "the most common form of business model". The Communication of European Union of 20 October 2009, par. 4.1, states that "(...) subsidiaries are the predominant form of cross-border banking business in Europe, holding assets of almost € 4 trillion (...)". Communication from the Commission to the European Parliament, the Council, the European Economic and Social Committee, the European Court of Justice and the European Central Bank-An EU Framework for Cross-Border Crisis Management in the Banking Sector, 20 October 2009, COM(2009) 561.

[633]In re Lehman Bros. Int'l (Eur.) [2011] EWHC (Ch) 2022, [2011] All ER 273 (Eng.). G. XINYI, To recognise or not to recognise? Comparative study of Lehman brothers cases in Mainland China and Taiwan, op. cit., pp. 240ss. J.L. WESTROOK, An empirical study of the implementation in the United States of the Model Law on cross border insolvency, op. cit., pp. 247ss P.L. DAVIES, Resolution of cross-border groups, in M. HAENTJENS, B. WESSELS, Research handbook on crisis management in the sector, op. cit., pp. 264ss, the author discussing how both the U.S. and the U.K. took unilateral action in the bailouts of non-national entities, including Lehman Brothers, in order to protect national interests. J.M. PECK, Cross-border observations derived from My Lehman Judicial Experience, op. cit., pp. 134ss., the author explaining that cross-border conflicts and self-interested behaviours in the context of the Lehman insolvencies were unavoidable). S.L. BUFFORD,

Bank, Dexia, the Fortis Group and the Bank of Credit and International Commerce (BCCI)[634].

The lack of a discipline in this area, we can define it as a cumbersome gap, which affects, in particular, if we consider that, starting from 1997, at both international and regional level, studies and enacted normative instruments have been carried out, questions of private international law and of procedural law or of substantive law relating to a situation bordering on the subject of this work. This lack was made dependent on: a) The rarity with which the banks in the past failed, or because they were largely owned by the States, or because the latter intervened, in emergency situations, giving financial aid;[635] b) the difficulty that the legislation, especially that in financial matters, it manages to update itself and renew itself as quickly as the evolution of its object; c) the reluctance of state systems to renounce their exclusive jurisdiction precisely in relation to a branch of law, such as the competition, by public definition and expression of sovereignty, to which

---

Coordination of insolvency cases for international enterprise groups: A proposal, op. cit., pp. 685ss.K.P. WOJCIK, Bail-in in the Banking Union, op. cit., pp. 124ss.

[634]For more analysis see: J.M. GARRIDO, No two snowflakes the same: The distributional question in international bankruptcies, in Texas International Law Journal, 46, 2011-2012, pp. 460ss. T. CAMACHO, A. NUNEZ-LAGOS BURGUERA, Secondary proceedings: Are cross-border insolvencies in the EU dealt with efficiently?, in International Insolvency Review, 2, 2013, pp. 142ss. S.J. ROTHMAN, Note, lessons from general growth properties: The future of the special purpose entity, in Fordham Journal of Corporate, Finance Law, 17, 2012, pp. 228ss. S.L. BUFFORD, Coordination of insolvency cases for international enterprise groups: A proposal, op. cit., pp. 689ss. M. HUEMER, Bailout in context: The true costs of government bailout, in Georgetown Journal of Law & Public Policy, 11, 2013, pp. 336ss. A. COLETON, Banking insolvency regimes and cross-border banks-complexities and conflicts: Is the current European insolvency framework efficient and robust enough to effectively resolve cross-border banks, can there be a one size fits all solution?, in Journal of International Business Law Review, 27 (2), 2012, pp. 64ss. B. REYNOLDS, E. TEO, Early Bank Recovery and Resolution Directive (BRRD) experiences: Lessons learned from Greece, in Journal of International Banking Law and Regulation, 31, 2016, pp. 360ss. F.J. GARCIMARTÍN, Resolution tools and derivatives, in M. HAENTJENS, B. WESSELS (eds), Bank recovery and resolution: A conference book, Den Haag: Boom Uitgevers 2014, pp. 184ss. C.THOLE, Gläubigerschutz in einem Sonderinsolvenzrecht für Banken, in P.S. KENADJIAN (ed.), Too big to fail-Brauchen wir ein Sonderinsolvenzrecht für Banken?, Walter de Gruyter, Berlin, 2012, pp. 220ss.

[635]E. HÜPKES, Insolvency-why a special regime for banks?, in IMF (ed.), Current Developments in Monetary and Financial Law, vol. 3, 2005.

must be added the "inherent peculiarity (...) in the "bank" matter[636] and; d) the complexity of the provision of bankruptcy regulations for banks, moreover in a transnational perspective[637].

The financial crisis recalled the necessity and importance of a coordinated crisis resolution mechanism for large financial conglomerates that the authorities of the States involved can use. In fact, a considerable expansion, according to unpublished methods, of the scope, scale and complexity of international financial transactions did not correspond to an evolution, according to an equal speed, of the tools and techniques prepared for the management of transnational financial crises, so that, if necessary, we have to adopt measures created ad hoc for each case, very limited because of the need to act promptly and mostly oriented towards the request for a massive public intervention[638].

The system of which various projects have been hoped for, specifically aimed at managing the crises of the large financial conglomerates, while also clearly aiming, ultimately, to maximize the value of the assets, for the benefit of all curators, should be, because of the particular nature of these entities, different and further, in many ways, compared to that expected for commercial companies. Within this framework the difficulties that could be encountered in trying to identify principles and rules regarding the insolvency of banking groups that can be widely shared internationally have been underlined, due to the frequent and substantial differences present in this matter in the national disciplines, for historical, cultural and structural reasons. In this regard we can point out that those who had dealt with the establishment of a discipline of

---

[636]We see in this peculiarity one of the reasons why the legislator of the European Union, as we shall see, to regulate the insolvency of credit institutions, chose the instrument of the directive and not that of the regulation, which had instead used for the international-private law insolvency of the trading companies. D. BLIESENER, Legal problems of bail-ins under the EU's proposed Recovery and Resolution Directive, in A. DOMBRET, P.S. KENADJAN (eds.), The Bank Recovery and Resolution Directive. Europe's solution for "too big to fail"?, Walter de Gruyter, Berlin, Boston, 2013, pp. 192ss L.JANSSEN, Bail-in from an insolvency law perspective, in Norton Journal of Bankruptcy Law & Practice, 26 (5) 2017, pp. 6ss.

[637]E. HÜPKES, Insolvency-why a special regime for banks?, op. cit.

[638]L. CHAN HO, R.M. LASTRA, International developments, in R.M. LASTRA (ed.), Cross-border bank insolvency, Oxford University Press, Oxford, New York, 2011, pp. 210ss.

insolvency of groups of commercial companies had met the same skepticism and the same parochialism encountered by those who began to deal with international cooperation on crisis management of financial conglomerates[639]. Even at UNCITRAL, despite the substantial cooperation between the various state components involved in the negotiations, there was widespread skepticism regarding the actual possibility of achieving some result. When an agreement in relation to the model law was reached and, moreover, in a very short time, many predicted that, in reality, this law would be adopted by a small number of States. When even this criticism had tried to discredit this instrument, underlining that the excessive vagueness of the provisions contained in it would have prevented a direct application by the judicial authorities of the States. Without a doubt, a new criticism would have been about to be advanced, having also been debunked last. Until that moment, every accusation of parochialism and lack of a global perception had, in reality, proved unfounded[640].

2.Spontaneous cooperation between curators and judges in the absence of a general and abstract discipline.

The current international lack of any kind of regulation for bankruptcy cases by multinational banking groups would seem to entail prima facie that they must be dealt with at the state level, in an independent and therefore necessarily fragmentary manner, by each of the legal systems involved, through the application of the respective national procedures and without the measures adopted having effect beyond the

639A. FLESSNER, Das Insolvenzrecht für Banken Europäischer Rundblick und grundsätzliche Überlegungen, in Österreichisches BankArchiv, 2010, pp. 657ss.

640L. WESTBROOK, The elements of coordination in international corporate insolvencies: What cross-border bank insolvency can learn from corporate insolvency, in R.M. LASTRA (ed.), Cross-border bank insolvency, Oxford University Press, Oxford, New York, 2011, pp. 186ss. B. WESSELS, A global approach to cross-border insolvency cases in a globalizing world, in The Dovenshmidt Quarterly, 2013, pp. 18ss. I. MEVORAH, The future of cross border insolvency: Overcoming biases and closing gaps, Oxford University Press, Oxford, 2018. S.N. GRÜNEWALD, The resolution of cross-border banking crises in the European Union: A legal study from the perspective of burden sharing, Kluwer Law International Alphen aan den Rijn, 2014.

borders of the state of adoption.

In fact, this is what happened in relation to the failures of the Fortis and Kaupthing groups[641]. Otherwise, in the failures of BCCI and Lehman Brothers, in an attempt to overcome the obstacle caused by the lack of a supranational bankruptcy regime, the curators charged with managing the crisis of the various companies in the multiple states involved have tried, as far as possible, to coordinate procedures in progress.

The spontaneous cooperation between curators and judges in the absence of a general and abstract discipline is the importance of a shared solution, at least between the central banks and the authorities of the States involved[642]. However, in addition to the fact that these agreements were concluded informally and therefore no documents relating to them are available, a bankruptcy proceeding against the Dexia group has never been opened and therefore the discussion of the case is outside the scope of this study.

Also with reference to the bankruptcy of commercial companies, some soft law documents[643] drawn up since the mid-1990s will also be analyzed. Regulation (CE) n. 1346/2000[644] dates back as the only hard law instrument that today provides for forms of cooperation between the curators of the main proceedings and those of secondary procedures. In more recent years Regulation n. 2015/848, which entered into force on 25 June 2017[645] establishes that the CJEU hearing the opening of the

[641] J. ADAMS KIRSHNER, International bankruptcy. The challenge of insolvency in a global economy, University of Chicago Press, Chicago, 2018.

[642] A. COLETON, Banking insolvency regimes and cross border banks-Complexities and conflicts: Is the current European insolvency framework efficient and robust enough to effectively resolve cross-border banks, can there be a one size fits all solution?, op. cit., pp. 69ss.

[643] C. BRUMMER, Soft law and the global financial system: Rule making in the 21st century, Cambridge University Press, Cambridge, 2012.

[644] See in particular the next cases: CJEU, C-641/16, Tünkers France and Tünkers Maschinenbau of 9 November 2017, ECLI:EU:C:2017:847, C-116/11, Bank Handlowy and Adamiak of 22 November 2012, ECLI:EU:C:2012:739, above the cited cases published in the electronic Reports of the cases. For further analysis see also: O.CACHARD, Droit international privè, ed. Larcier, Bruxelles, 2018

[645] Regulation (EU) 2015/848 of the European Parliament and of the Council of 20 May 2015 on insolvency proceedings. See also: C. LISANTI, L. SAUTONIE-LAGUIONIE, Règlement UE n. 2015/848 du 20 mai 2015 relatif aux procèdures d'insolvabilitè, in Societè de lègislation comparèe, Trans Europe experts, 2016.

insolvency proceedings[646] will verify its jurisdiction by its own jurisdiction by providing an area of harmonization in a difficult sector which precludes many rights which must be protected as those debtors, property, freedom of establishment, free movement, satisfaction of curators and so on[647].

The main features of Regulation 2015/848 include: (i) Broader scope; rules extended to "pre-insolvency" or "hybrid proceedings". Regulation 2015/848 does not contemplate only wind-up proceedings, but extends to pre-insolvency proceedings to promote the rescue of economically viable but distressed businesses. Other types of proceedings include public proceedings; interim proceedings (a temporary stay to allow negotiations with curators); and adjustment of debt, reorganization, or liquidation (including where the debtor maintains possession, but under the control or supervision by a court or the appointed insolvency practitioner). (ii)New rules on secondary proceedings. Secondary proceedings can be opened in a Member State other than the one where the debtor's COMI is located, provided the debtor has an "establishment" in that jurisdiction. Establishment is defined as any place of operations where a debtor carries out or has carried out-in the 3-month period prior to the request to open main insolvency proceedings-a non-transitory economic activity with human means and assets. Regulation 2015/848 limits the need to open secondary proceedings through the introduction of "synthetic" or "virtual" secondary proceedings, where a main proceedings practitioner provides that the distribution and priority rights of local curators of other Member States will betreated as if secondary proceedings had been opened. An insolvency practitioner may request that a competent court postpone or refuse to open secondary proceedings if such are not essential to protect local curators' interests. Such an undertaking must be submitted and approved by known local curators, according to rules that apply to restructuring plan adoption under the law of the Member State where secondary insolvency proceedings could have been opened. The

646B. WESSELS, International insolvency law. Part II. European insolvency law, Wolters Kluwer, The Hague, 2017.

647J.G. SRANKLING, The international law of property, Oxford University Press, Oxford, 2014.

undertaking will be subject to any other requirements relating to form and approval of the Member State where main insolvency proceedings were opened. In addition, Regulation 2015/848 provides for enhanced and expanded duties of communication and cooperation between insolvency practitioners in main proceedings and those in secondary proceedings. (iii) The creation of an EU-wide system of web-based insolvency registers. The Regulation introduces a new instrument in order to improve access to information for curators, any interested party, and courts, and prevents the opening of parallel insolvency proceedings by creating a central European database that is linked with a national electronically searchable database[648].

Regulation 2015/848 has introduced specific procedural rules on the coordination of the insolvency proceedings among a group of companies. Regulation 1346/2000 did not contain any provision on groups of companies, but issues on cross-border insolvency typically arise in the context of companies belonging to a same group and located in different countries across Europe. Therefore, it is reasonable to believe that Regulation 2015/848's new provisions on group insolvency proceedings constitute an important innovation and will likely become the backbone of cross-border insolvency proceedings. While Regulation 2015/848 does not introduce a common jurisdiction for the insolvency of a group of companies, it lays down a complex mechanism for the coordination of the various proceedings intended to facilitate communication and efficiency between processes in different Member States. However, it offers no exceptions to the general principle that each insolvent company be treated independently pursuant to the substantive law of its COMI.

The harmonization in that case according to the perception that legal culture: "(...) Has undergone (...) an evolution in the Member States, reflecting a range of influences. To confine such richness within the straight jacket of harmonization is to rob Europe of its past (...) and this dissenting vein is nurtured by the profound belief that Europe is strengthened by its diversity (...) according to the opinion of Weatherhill. In the new silence/omission of Regulation n. 2015/848 to locate the credit

---

[648]CJEU, C.430/17, Walbusch Walter Busch of 20 September 2019, ECLI:EU:C:2019:759, published in the electronic Reports of the cases.

law allows you to address the relevant conflict rules of the forum, in particular Rome Regulation I on the law applicable to contractual obligations[649]. In particular, pursuant to art. 2 of the Regulation the principles of uniqueness, universality and exclusivity of the procedure in coordination with art. 6 and 9 are essential for countering and avoiding the phenomenon of forum shopping[650], since in matters of bankruptcy jurisdictional jurisdiction[651] also implies the legislative competence of the lex fori by applying and identifying the objective and subjective assumptions of opening a competition procedure. The principle of unity and universality of the procedure such as prevention (art. 4.2 (c)) and safeguard (art. 5)[652] remain the necessary foundation for a system involving the coexistence of several protocols even in the case the Court of Justice of the European Union (CJEU) for the determination,

---

[649]G. LARDEUX, Droit international privè des obligations contractuelles, ed. Larcier, Bruxelles, 2016.

[650]S. RAMMELOO, From Rome to Rome. Cross-border employment contract. European private international law. Intertemporal law and foreign overriding mandatory laws, in Maastricht Journal of European and Comparative Law, 24, 2017.

[651]H. EDENMÜLLER, A new framework for business restructuring in Europe: The EU Commission's proposal for a reform of the European Insolvency Regulation and beyond, in Maastricht Journal of European and Comparative Law, 20, 2013, pp. 134ss. P. MANGANELLI, The modernization of European insolvency law: An ongoing process, in Journal of Business & Technology Law, 11, 2016, pp. 156ss. C. THOLE, Die Reform der Europäischen Insolvenzverordnung, Zeitschrift für europäisches Privatrecht, 22, 2014, pp. 42ss. R. BORK, K. VAN ZWEITEN (eds.), Commentary on the European Insolvency Regulation, Oxford University Press, Oxford, 2017. R. BORK, Principles of cross-border insolvency law, ed. Intersentia, Cambridge, 2017. M.T. EPEOGLOU, The recast European Insolvency Regulation: A missed opportunity for restructuring business in Europe, in UCL Journal of Law and Jurisprudence, 1 (6), 2017. A. KEAY, The harmonization of the avoidance rules in European Union insolvencies, in International and Comparative Law Quarterly, 67 (1), 2017, pp. 82ss. J.H. KLAUS, Groups of companies-A comparative study on the economics, law and regulation of corporate groups, in J. GORDON, G. RINGE, (eds) Oxford handbook of corporate law and governance, Oxford University Press, Oxford, 2015. S. MADAUS, Insolvency proceedings for corporate groups under the new insolvency regulation, in International Insolvency Law Review, 25 (2), 2016, pp. 237ss. G. MCCCORMACK, A. KEAY, S. BROWN, European insolvency law. Reform and harmonization, Edward Elgar Publishers, Cheltenham, 2017. A. MERLINI, Reorganisation and liquidation of groups of companies: Curators' protection vs. going concern maximisation, in International Insolvency Law Review, 25 (1), 2016, pp. 120ss.

[652]F. FERRARI, La loi applicables aux contrats conclus par les consommateurs (article 5 de la Convention de Rome), in Revue de Droit des Affaires Internationales, 2008, pp. 234ss. F. FERRARI, Rome I Regulation, Selier European Law Publishers, Münich, 2015.

continuation or suspension of the whole proceedings[653]. 47.In the material before the entry into force of Regulation n. 2015/848 the CJEU sought to define and reemphasize the notion of "core interests", which should be understood as "(...) the place where the debtor exercises in a habitual manner and therefore recognizable by third parties management of its interests (…), interpreting it in a strictly factual manner and by favoring the objective elements of stability and continuity over time. In particular, the Court has: "(...) the location of the COMI (Centre of Main Interests) should be ascertainable by third parties does not entirely prevent forum shopping at curators' expense[654]. Indeed, if a company transfers its registered office from one Member State to another, the "ascertainability" criterion protects only new curators whose debts were incurred after the debtor has relocated its headquarters. In contrast, pre-existing curators, whose debts were incurred before the transfer, are not protected if the company makes the new headquarters sufficiently public (...)". In particular the authors: Virgós and Garcimartín declared in relation of the CJEU judgments that: "(...) In the insolvency proceedings opened in Member State 1, the disputed claim would be accepted as a conditional or contingent claim (...) the creditor may bring his case to the Courts of Member State 2 and obtain a money judgment fixing the amount of his claim (...) This judgment cannot be directly enforced in State 2 because this state must recognize the insolvency proceedings opened in State 1 and the effects thereof, in particular the stay of executions by individual curators. However, pursuant to Regulation n. 44/2001 the money judgment has, in its turn, to be recognized in State 1, "(which means that this claim must be admitted in the insolvency proceedings opened in State (...)"[655].

After the proposal of Regulation n. 2015/848, noting in particular

---

[653]H. EIDENMÜLLER, E.M. KINENINGER (eds), The future of secured credit in Europe, in European Company and Financial Law Review, 5, 2008, pp. 4ss.

[654]P.K. BOOKMAN, The unsung virtues of global forum shopping, in Notre Dame Law Review, 92, 2016, pp. 582ss. According to the author: "(...) Principles of recognition and enforcement must balance many factors, including fairness to defendants and plaintiffs' need for Court access. A federal statute on foreign judgment recognition and enforcement, like the one proposed by the American Law Institute, should recognize and enforce foreign judgments arising out of proceedings that meet basic requirements of fairness (...)".

[655]M. VIRGÓS, F. GARCIMARTÍN, The European Insolvency Regulation: Law and practice, Kluwer Law International, The Hague, 2004, pp. 56ss.

the non inclusion of hybrid translation, but only an affirmative restriction according to recitals 33 and 34 that "the Court is not required to open the insolvency proceedings", the Court followed another path of thought through its case law[656] as in the case: C-310/14, Nike European Operations Netherlands BV v. Sportland Oy of 10 December 2015, where the CJEU states that: "(...) If a domestic Court's rules of evidence were not sufficiently rigorous, which led, effectively, to a shifting of the burden of proof to the defendant in an avoidance claim, it would not be regarded as being in line with the principle of effectiveness, for this principle, together with the principle of equivalence, must be taken into account in any case (...)"[657]. In this case the principle of effectiveness has been constructed under the effort to ensure that EU law actually takes effect in all Member States and domestic private law or civil procedure is not able to be applied in a relationship or might be interpreted differently from what the parties in the relationship expected[658].

---

[656]In particular see the next cases: CJEU: C-649/13, Comitè d'enterprise de Mortel networks SA and others v. Cosme Rogeau liquidator of Nortel networks SA and Cosme Rogeau liquidator of Nortel networks SA v. Alan Robeau Bokm and others of 11 June 2015, ECLI:EU:C:2015:384. C-212/15, ENEFI v. DGRF of 9 November 2016, ECLI:EU:C:2016:841. C-195/15, SCI Senior Home v. Gemeinde Wedemark & Hannoversche Volksbank EG of 9 December 2016, ECLI:EU:C:2016:804. C-327/13, Burgo Group Spa v. Illochvona SA and J. Theetten of 24 October 2014, ECLI:EU:C:2014:2158. C-328/12, R. Schmid v. L. Hertel of 16 January 2014, ECLI:EU:C:2014:6. C-527/10, ERSTE Bank Hungary Nyrt v. Magyar Állam and others of 4 July 2012, ECLI:EU:C:2012:417. C-213/10, F-TEX SIA v. Lietuvos-Anglijos UAB of 25 May 2012, ECLI:EU:C:2012:215. C-251/12, Van Buggenhout and Ilse van de Mierop v. Banque Internationale à Luxembourg SA of 16 January 2014, ECLI:EU:C:2014:566. C-557/13, H. v. H.K. C-295/13 of 16 April 2015; H. Lutz v. E. Bäuerle of 11 June 2015, ECLI:EU:C:2015:2410. C-116/11, Bank Handlowy y Adamiak w Warszawie SA and PPHU "ADAX"/Ryszard Adamiak v. Christianapol Sp. z.o.o. of 19 September 2013, ECLI:EU:C:2013:739, all the above cited cases published in the electronic Reports of the cases. C-444/07, MG Probud Gdynia sp. z.o.o., of 20 October 2011, ECLI:EU:C:2011:24, I-00417. C-396/09, Interedil Srl in liquidation v. Fallimento Interedil srl and Intesa gestione crediti SpA of 17 November 2011, ECLI:EU:C:2011:671, I-09915. C-112/10, Antwerpen Zaza Retail BV of 15 December 2011, ECLI:EU:C:2011:743, I-11525. C-191/10, D. Rastelli and C. Snc v. Jean-Charles Hidoux of 19 April 2012, ECLI:EU:C:2012:838, I-13209.

[657]A.VAN HOE, Enterprise groups and their insolvency: It's the (common) interest, stupid!, in European Company and Financial Law Review, 11 (2), 2014. B.WESSELS, A global approach to cross-border insolvency cases in a globalizing world, op. cit., pp. 17ss.

[658]In the same spirit see: CJEU, C-529/14, YARA Brunsbüttel GmbH v. Hauptzollamt Itzehoe of 17 December 2015, ECLI:EU:C:2015:836, not published. C-353/15,

In particular with the judgment C-157/13, Nickel & Goeldner spedition v. Kintra of 4 September 2014, the CJEU held: "(...) That the Regulation (...) must be interpreted in such a way as to avoid any overlap between the rules of law that those texts lay down and any legal vacuum. Accordingly, actions excluded, under article 1(2)(b) of Regulation n. 44/2001, from the application of that Regulation in so far as they come under bankruptcy, proceedings relating to the winding-up of insolvent companies or other legal persons, judicial arrangements, compositions and analogous proceedings fall within the scope of Regulation n. 1346/2000 (...)"[659]. The CJEU thus in the notion of "(...) action arising out of a procedure of insolvency and closely related to it", as elaborated by its previous case law, included an action where the insolvency administrator obtained the payment of a company's claim and declared insolvent on an international freight transport contract, from the moment that "that action found its foundation not in the insolvency of the undertaking, but in the contract previously concluded by the company itself with the defaulting counter party (...)". It referred to the concept of direct action against the administrator of a insolvent company with the ultimate aim of obtaining the repayment of payments made after the insolvency of the company itself. "(...) As such action, from the subject matter of the previous judgment, presupposes the debtor's insolvency status, even if the action in question could have been practiced, in principle, independently of the opening of insolvency proceedings (...)". The main objective is the limitations on the recognition and enforcement of competition decisions, as well as the reference to public policy objections considered in its narrowest sense of the term, which must only concern violations of the principles of the due process and include the protection of fundamental rights such as personal liberties.

The last cases cited allow us to take a stand on the topics dealt

---

Leonmobili Srl, Gennaro Leone/Homag Holzbearbeitungssysteme GmbH and others of 24 May 2016, ECLI:EU:C:2014:354, not published. C-85/12, LBI hf v. Kepler Capital Markets SA and Frédéric Giraux of 24 October 2013, ECLI:EU:C:2013:697, published in the electronic Reports of the cases. C-111/08, SCT Industri AB i likvidation v. Alpenblume AB of 2 July 2009, ECLI:EU:C:2009:419, I-05655.

[659]K. PAUNEN, European Insolvency Regulation. Commentary, De Gruyter, Hamburg, 2011.

with and resolved, such as the case of insolvency liquidator against the managers of a legal person to pay a certain sum into the assets of a company in insolvency (case Gourdain[660]); the case of insolvency by the liquidator against a third party (case Deko Marty[661]); the irrespective of the domicile or place of residence of the defendant (case Schmid)[662]; the validity of a transfer granted by the insolvency liquidator "on the ground that the liquidator had no power to dispose of the assets transferred" (case SCT Industri[663]), which the CJEU declared that: "(...) Article 4(2)(f) of the EIR, seems to restrict the scope of Article 4(2)(f) suggesting that that provision determines the effects of the insolvency proceedings on executions brought by individual curators, their suspension or prohibition after the opening of collective insolvency proceedings (...)"; the insolvency proceedings against the managing director of a company for reimbursement of payments "after the company became insolvent or after it had been established that the company's liabilities exceeded its assets" (case H. and Kornhaas[664]); the basis of a reservation title against an insolvent purchaser (case German Graphics[665]); the insolvency administrator for "the payment of a debt arising out of the provision of services implementing a contract (...)" (case Nickel[666]); an actio pauliana

---

[660]CJEU, C-133/78, Gourdain v. Nadler of 26 February 1979, ECLI:EU:C:1979:49, I-00733.

[661]CJEU, C-339/07, C. Seagon v. Deko Marty Belgium of 12 February 2009, ECLI:EU:C:2009:83, I-00767.

[662]CJEU, C-328/12, R. Schmid v. Lilly Hertel of 16 January 2014, ECLI:EU:C:2014:6, published in the electronic Reports of the cases.

[663]CJEU, C-111/08, SCT Industri AB i likvidation v. Alpenblume AB of 2 February 2009, ECLI:EU:C:2009:419, I-05655.

[664]CJEU, C-594/14, H. and Kornhaas of 10 December 2015, ECLI:EU:C:2015:804, published in the electronic Reports of the cases.

[665]CJEU, C-292/08, German Graphics Graphische Maschinen GmbH v. A. Van der Schee of 10 September 2009, ECLI:EU:C:2009:544, I-08421.

[666]CJEU, C-157/13, Nickel & Goeldner spedition v. Kintra of 4 September 2014, ECLI:EU:C.2014:2145, published in the electronic Reports of the cases. In particular the CJEU held: "(...) that the Regulation (...) must be interpreted in such a way as to avoid any overlap between the rules of law that those texts lay down and any legal vacuum. Accordingly, actions excluded, under article 1(2)(b) of Regulation n. 44/2001, from the application of that Regulation in so far as they come under bankruptcy, proceedings relating to the winding-up of insolvent companies or other legal persons, judicial arrangements, compositions and analogous proceedings' fall within the scope of Regulation n. 1346/2000. In the notion of "(...) action arising out of a procedure of insolvency and closely related to it", as elaborated by its previous case law, included an action where the insolvency administrator obtained the payment of a company's claim and declared insolvent on an

(case Reichert)[667], which the CJEU declared that: "(...) The de facto vis attractiva principle (thus the de facto exclusive jurisdiction of the insolvency forum) regarding the non-insolvency related actions one would necessarily violate the jurisdictional provisions (...)"[668]; an action to set aside a transaction brought by an applicant "(...) on the basis of an assignment of claims granted by the insolvency liquidator (...)" (case F-Tex SIA[669]). In that case cannot be qualified as insolvency actions, where the Court has held that: "(...) The main action is aimed at refunding the sums received by the defendant by a debtor prior to the opening of an insolvency proceeding against the latter (...)". It should be noted that the Court has tried to include only those actions that are related to the scope of Regulation to the insolvency procedure in accordance with the principle of vis attractiva concursus. The line and the basis of the spirit of the CJEU was based on the right or the obligation which form the basis of the action and find its source in the common rules of civil and commercial law or in the derogating rules specific to insolvency proceedings under the

international freight transport contract, from the moment that "that action found its foundation not in the insolvency of the undertaking, but in the contract previously concluded by the company itself with the defaulting counter party (...)". It referred to the concept of direct action against the administrator of a insolvent company with the ultimate aim of obtaining the repayment of payments made after the insolvency of the company itself: "(...) As such action, from the subject matter of the previous judgment, presupposes the debtor's insolvency status, even if the action in question could have been practiced, in principle, independently of the opening of insolvency proceedings (...)". The main objective is the limitations on the recognition and enforcement of competition decisions, as well as the reference to public policy objections considered in its narrowest sense of the term, which must only concern violations of the principles of the due process and include the protection of fundamental rights such as personal liberties. For more analysis see: D. LIAKOPOULOS, Interactions between European Court of Human Rights and private international law of European Union, in Cuadernos de Derecho Transnacional, 10 (1), 2018, pp. 254ss. D. LIAKOPOULOS, European integration and its relation with the jurisprudence of European Court of Human Rights and private international law of European Union, in Homa Publica. Revista Internacional de Direitos Humanos e Impresa, vol. 2, n. 2, 2018.

[667]CJEU, C-261/90, M. Reichert Hans-Heinz Reichert and Ingeborg Kockler v. Dresdner Bank AG of 26 March 1992, ECLI:EU:C:1992:149, I-02149.

[668]CJEU, C-261/90, M. Reichert Hans-Heinz Reichert and Ingeborg Kockler v. Dresdner Bank AG of 26 March 1992, op. cit.

[669]CJEU, C-213/10, F-Tex sia v. Lietyuvos-Anglijos UAB of 25 May 2012, ECLI:EU:C:2012:215, published in the electronic Reports of the cases.

Regulation[670].

---

[670]See ex multis: K. KERAMEUS, L'harmonisation procédurale dans le monde contemporain, in L. VOGEL, La procédure entre tradition et modernité, èd. Panthéon-Assas, Paris, 2010, pp. 10ss. D. MILMAN, Personal insolvency law. Regulation and policy, ed. Routledge, London & New York, 2017, pp. 2048ss. F. TOLMIE, Corporate and personal insolvency law, ed. Wolters, Kluwer, The Hague, 2013. G. MCCORMACK, Something old, something new: Recasting the European Insolvency Regulation, in The Modern Law Review, 79, 2016, pp. 122ss. M. REQUEJO ISIDRO, La cooperaciòn judicial en materia de insolvencia transfronteriza en la propuesta de Regulation del Parlamento europeo y del consejo por el que se modifica el Regulation (CE) n. 1346/2000 sobre procedimientos de insolvencia, in Anuario Español de Derecho Internacional Privado, 13, 2013, pp. 218ss. V. FINCH, D.MILMAN, Corporate insolvency law. Perspectives and principles, Cambridge University Press, Cambridge, 2017, pp. 486ss. S. GOPALAN, M. GUIHOT, Cross-border insolvency law and multinational enterprise groups. Judicial innovation as and international solution, in George Washington International Law Review, 49, 2016, pp 4ss. S. MOCK, Das geplante neue europäische Insolvenzrecht nach dem Vorschlag der Kommission zur Reform der EuInsVO, in Zeitschrift für Gemeinschaftsprivatrecht, 10, 2013, pp. 137ss. A. PIEKENBROCK, The future scope of the European Insolvency Regulation, in International Insolvency Law Review, 23 (3), 2014, pp. 434ss. C. THOLE, Die Reform der Europäischen Insolvenzverordnung, op. cit., pp. 40ss. B. WESSELS, What is an insolvency proceeding anyway?, in International Insolvency Law Review, 20 (4), 2011, pp. 492ss. G. MOSS, I. FLETCHER, S. ISAACS, The EC Regulation on Insolvency Proceedings, Oxford University Press, Oxford, 2009. T. RAUSCHER, Europäisches Zivilprozess-und Kollisionsrecht, Europäisches Zivilprozess-und Kollisionsrecht (EuZPR/EuIPR), ed. Verlag O. Schmidt, Heidelberg, 2010, Art. 1 paras. 2-4. C. THOLE, Sanierung mittels Scheme of Arrangement im Blickwinkel des Internationalen Privat-und Verfahrensrechts, in Zeitschrift für Unternehmens und Gesellschaftsrecht, 42, 2013, pp. 110ss. M. VEDER, The future of the European Insolvency Regulation-Applicable law, in particular security rights, in International Insolvency Law Review, 20 (2), 2011, pp. 286ss. A. J. BĚLOHLÁVEK, Effects of opening (commencement) of insolvency proceedings on pending lawsuits and similar proceedings under article 15 of Council Regulation (EC) No. 1346/2000 of 29 May 2000 on insolvency proceedings and under Article 18 of the European Parliament and Council Regulation (EU) No 2015/848, in Czech Yearbook of International Law, 7, 2016, pp. 69ss. S. BLOCK-LIEB, The UK and EU cross-border insolvency recognition: From empire to Europe to egoing it alone, in Fordham International Law Journal, 42, 2017, pp. 1374ss. F.M. MUCCIARELLI, The function of corporate law and the effects of reincorporations in the U.S. and the EU, in Tulane Journal of International and Comparative Law, 21, 2012, pp. 440ss. J. RODRÍGUEZ RODRIGO, El centro de intereses principales, como foro de competencia internacional en el Reglamento 1346/2000, en relación con empresas de un grupo de sociedades, in Anuario de Derecho Concursal, 2014, pp. 502ss. G. GARCÍA-ROSTÁN CALVIN, El proceso consurcal ante insolvencias conexas, Tirant Lo Blanch, Valencia, 2015. M. LLORENTE SÁNCHEZ-ARJONA, Tratamiento procesal de la insolvencia transfronteriza en la Unión Europea, Tirant Lo Blanch, Valencia, 2013, pp. 76ss. J. RODRÍGUEZ RODRIG, Bienes sujetos a un procedimiento secundario de insolvencia. Comentario a la sentencia del Tribunal de justicia de la Uniòn europea de 11 Junio 2015, Nortel, C-649/13, in Cuadernos de Derecho Transnacional, 9 (3), 2017, pp. 694ss. G. MCCORMACK, Reconciling European conflicts and insolvency law, in European

Business Organization Law Review, 15, 2014, pp. 335ss. I. LINNA, Actio pauliana and res judicata in European Union insolvency proceedings, in Journal of Private International Law, 14 (4), 2015, pp. 570ss. B. XIE, Comparative insolvency law: The pre-pack approach in corporate rescue, Edward Elgar Publishing, Cheltenham, 2016, pp. 272ss. A. JAKAB, D. KOCHENOV, The enforcement of European Union Law values: Ensuring Member States compliance, Oxford University Press, Oxford, 2017, pp. 208ss. A. KEAY, The harmonization of the avoidance rules in European Union insolvencies, op. cit., pp. 80ss. G. MCCORMACK, A. KEAY, S. BROWN, European insolvency law: Reform and harmonization, op. cit., pp. 174ss. M. BORN, Europäisches Kollisions Recht des Effektengiros: Intermediatisierte Wertpapiere im Schnittfeld Internationalem Sallen-Schuld und Insolvenzrecht, ed. M. Siebeck, 2014, pp. 189ss. A. KEAY, Security rights, the European Insolvency Regulation and Concerns about the non-application of avoidance rules, in European Law Review, 22, 2016, pp. 73ss. G. MOSS, I.F. FLETCHER, S. ISAACS (eds), The EC Regulation on Insolvency Proceedings: A commentary and annotated guide, op. cit., pp. 12ss. G. MCCORMACK, Secured credit and the harmonisation of law, Edward Elgar Publishing, Cheltenham, 2011, pp. 58ss. R.J. DE WEIJS, Towards an objective European rule on transaction avoidance in insolvencies, in International Insolvency Review, 21, 2011, pp. 220ss. J. GARRIDO, Two snowflakes the same: The distributional question in international bankruptcies, op. cit., pp. 462ss. S. LEVMORE, Harmonization, preferences, and the calculus of consent in commercial and other law, in Common Market Law Review, 50, 2013, pp. 250ss. L. CADIET, E. JEULAND, S. AMRANI-MEKKI, Droit processuel civil de l'Union européenne, ed. LexisNexis, Paris, 2011, pp. 350ss. E. FABRIES-LECEA, Le règlement "insolvabilité": Apport à la construction de l'ordre juridique de l'Union européenne, ed. Bruylant, Bruxelles, 2013, pp. 614ss. F. JAULT-SESEKE, D. ROBINE, Le droit européen des procédures d'insolvabilité à la croisée des chemins, ed. Lextenso, Paris, 2012, pp. 242ss. D. ROBINE, F. JAULT-SESEKE, Le droit européen des procédures d'insolvabilité à la croisée des chemins, ed. Montchrestien, Paris, 2012, pp. 243ss. L.S. SEALY, D. MILMAN, Annotated Guide to the Insolvency Legislation, ed. Sweet & Maxwell, London, 2014. T. ARONS, Recognition of debt restructuring and resolution measures under the European Union regulatory framework, in International Insolvency Review, 24, 2014, pp. 58ss. Y. BRULARD, Que penser de la proposition de la Commission sur les groupes de sociétés dans le projet de nouveau règlement insolvabilité?, in Revue des Procédures Collectives, 2013, pp. 68ss. R. DAMMANN, S. MILLET, L'action en revendication exercée au titre d'une clause de réserve de propriété relève-t-elle du champ d'application du règlement Bruxelles I?, in Revue Lamy Droit Civil, 2010, pp. 32ss. C. KESSEDJIAN, L'espace judiciaire civile et commercial européen: le règlement "Bruxelles I" refondu, in Revue Gènèrale de Droit International Public, 117, 2013, pp. 546ss. R. DAMMANN, Application du Règlement (CE) numéro 1346/2000 modifié aux groupes de sociétés, in Revue des Procédures Collectives, 2013, pp. 65ss. D. FASQUELLE, Raisons et contours d'une refonte nécessaire du règlement (CE) 1346/2000, in Bulletin Joly Entreprises en Difficulté, 2012, pp. 52ss. D. FASQUELLE, L'Europe: une opportunité pour les professions d'AJMJ et pour le mandat de justice?, in Revue des Procédures Collectives, 2013, pp. 50ss. G.C. GIORGINI, Le centre des intérêts principaux du débiteur insolvable en droit comparé, in Revue Internationale de Droit Comparé, 64, 2012, pp. 868ss. L.C. HENRY, Compétence internationale du Tribunal pour ouvrir une procédure d'insolvabilité en cas de transfert de siège statutaire, in Bulletin Joly Entreprises en Difficulté, 2012, pp. 35ss. L.C. HENRY, De l'art d'articuler la procédure principale et la procédure secondaire, in Revue des Sociétés,

3.The adoption of a territorial model for the failures of the Fortis and Kaupthing groups.

The Fortis group, formed by companies established in Belgium,

---

12, 2012, pp. 186ss. L.C. HENRY, Eclairage-Règlement insolvabilité européen et groupes de sociétés: je t'aime moi non plus!, in Bulletin Joly Entreprises en Difficulté, 2012, pp. 355ss. L.C. HENRY, Règlement insolvabilité européen et les groupes: bilan et perspectives. Une approche textuelle, in Revue des Procédures Collectives, 2013, pp. 59ss. L. IDOT, Un nouveau chantier pour les juristes: la révision du règlement "procédures d'insolvabilité, in La Semaine Juridique (Europe), 2013, pp. 4ss. V. LEGRAND, Quelle clôture pour la procédure européenne d'insolvabilité?, in Lettre d'Actualité des Procédures Collectives Civiles et Commerciales, 2013, pp. 112ss. A. LIENHARD, Procédure d'insolvabilité: Notion de "centre des intérêts principaux", in Recueil Dalloz Sirey, 2011, pp. 2916ss. R. LOWE, From client money rules to the EC Insolvency Regulation, legislative change beckons, in Insolvency Intelligence, 29, 2014, pp. 48ss. T. MASTRULLO, L'extension de procédure collective pour cause de confusion des patrimoines est-elle compatible avec le règlement numéro 1346/2000?, in Revue des Sociétés, 2010, pp. 594ss. T. MASTRULLO, Procédures d'insolvabilité transfrontalières: la reconnaissance mutuelle conditionnée par le respect du droit d'accès au juge, in Revue des Sociétés, 2011, pp. 8ss and 443-447. M. MENJUCQ, L'extension de procédure pour confusion de patrimoines passée au crible du règlement n° 1346/2000: une question à suspense!, in Revue des Procédures Collectives, 2010, pp. 2ss. M. MENJUCQ, La proposition de règlement modifiant le règlement (CE) n°1346/2000 sur les procédures d'insolvabilité: une évolution mais pas de révolution, in Revue des Procédures Collectives, 2013, pp. 20ss. I. MEROVACH, European insolvency law in a global context, in Journal of Business Law, 13, 2011, pp. 668ss. I. MEROVACH, The new proposed regime for EU corporate groups in insolvency: A critical note, in Corporate Rescue and Insolvency, 2013, pp. 90ss. C. MOILLE, Un point sur les conditions de la mise en oeuvre de la procédure intiale d'insolvabilité et son extension, in Revue Trimestrielle de Droit Européen, 50, 2013, pp. 28ss. P. NABET, Bref aperçu du projet de la commission pour la révision du règlement (CE) n° 1346/2000 sur l'insolvabilité, in Les Petites Affiches, 2013, pp. 6ss. J. PAYNE, Cross-border schemes of arrangement and forum shopping, in European Business Organization Law Review, 14, 2013, pp. 564ss. P. ROUSSEL-GALLE, La proposition de révision du règlement n° 1346/2000 sur les procédures d'insolvabilité, entre prudence et audace, in La Semaine Juridique (édition entreprise), 2013, pp. 14ss. J.L. VALLENS, Tourisme judiciaire et insolvabilité: les risques du forum shopping, in Revue des Procédures Collectives, 2012, pp. 10ss. G.F. SCHLAEFER, Forum shopping under the regime of the European Insolvency Regulation, in International Insolvency Institute, International Insolvency Studies, 2010, pp. 26ss. C. HONORATI, G. CORVO, A double lesson from Interedil: Higher Courts, lower Courts and preliminary ruling and further clarifications on COMI and establishment under EU insolvency Regulation, in International Insolvency Law Review, 21 (4), 2012, pp. 655ss. C.H. VAN RHEE, Harmonisation of civil procedure: An historical and comparative perspective, in X.E. KRAMER, C.H. VAN RHEE, Civil litigation in a globalizing World, T.M.C. Asser Press, The Hague, 2012, pp. 41ss. D. LIAKOPOULOS, Procedural harmonization, mutual recognition and multi-level protection of fundamental procedural rights, in Revista General de Derecho Procesal, 47, 2019.

the Netherlands and Luxembourg, came into crisis in 2008. However, the relative bankruptcy was avoided through a transaction in which the Netherlands bought the bank and insurance part of the group based in their territory, as well as the part of ABN Amro that the Fortis group had recently acquired. The Belgian government bought the Belgian part of the group, which was the largest, and, after overcoming some obstacles posed by the bank's shareholders[671], then sold 75% of the shares to BNP Paribas. The latter directly acquired the Belgian insurances of the group and the majority of the shares of the subsidiary companies of Luxemburg. Although the initial intention was to address the situation in a coordinated way[672], we ended up adopting a territorialist approach, with autonomous and independent solutions from one state to another. This is particularly striking when it is considered that the three States involved, namely Belgium, the Netherlands and Luxembourg, have a long tradition of cooperation, including between supervisors and financial regulators and in the mutual exchange of information, as well as highly harmonized legislative systems[673].

Kaupthing, on the other hand, was an Icelandic bank with branches and/or group companies in thirteen states. In October 2008, the Icelandic government took control, along with the other two largest Icelandic banks, Landesbanki and Glitnir, on the basis of an Emergency Act issued shortly before. These banks were subdivided into a “new bank”, containing all the accounts, assets and liabilities, exclusively domestic, and in an “old bank” to which all other reports were referred; the assets of companies established in countries other than Iceland have been sold off. Therefore the crisis of the Kaupthing group was also dealt with on the basis of a nationalistic approach according to a “ring-fencing” which prevented the maximization of the value of the assets.

---

[671]In fact, on 12 December 2008, the Court of Appeal of Brussels suspended the proceeding of selling the shares to BNP, accepting the request made by the shareholders in the sense that the sale was previously approved by them. Initially they did not approve the terms of sale which were then amended and finally approved on 12 May 2009.

[672]A. COLETON, Banking insolvency regimes and cross border banks-Complexities and conflicts: Is the current European insolvency framework efficient and robust enough to effectively resolve cross-border banks, can there be a one size fits all solution? op. cit.

[673]INTERNATIONAL MONETARY FUND (IMF), Resolution of Cross-Border Banks, op. cit., 13.

The adoption of a territorial model has not allowed to achieve satisfactorily those objectives traditionally pursued through a bankruptcy procedure. In general, it was stressed that this approach does not allow the conduct of the procedure to be fair, efficient and transparent, nor to predict costs and duration. It also makes it more difficult to save the group. In particular, then, it prevents the maximization of the asset value of the group.

The spontaneous cooperation between curators and judges in the absence of a general and abstract discipline should instead be pursued for the benefit of all the curators of the same. The cause is to be found in the high management costs, which are at least doubled compared to a situation in which the failure of the entire group is managed in a unitary manner. In turn, these costs derive from the high number of disputes that must be resolved in the bankruptcy proceedings and the way in which the assets of the group are sold. In relation to the first aspect, these are disputes relating to issues of private and procedural international law rather than merit, which entail an unpredictable outcome of the proceedings, in particular with regard to the rights and priorities of the group's curators, with the risk that not all of them will receive equal treatment. In relation to the second aspect, it was noted that a sale of the individual assets separately makes it possible to achieve a lower value compared to what could be obtained through a sale of the same within a "cross-border package"[674].

To these negative notes is added the fact that the management of a bankruptcy of a group of companies, whether banks or commercial companies, according to a pure territorialist model does not allow to respect even the real structure of the group, because the assets, responsibilities and the operations of the societies that compose it are rarely attributable exclusively within the boundaries of a single legal system and, moreover, often depend on intra-group transactions and guarantees, so that the courts of no State would be able to have a full and exclusive control of the situation[675]. The lack of adequate regulation to

[674]UNCITRAL, Practice Guide on Cross-Border Insolvency Cooperation, op. cit., 9.

[675]J.L. WESTBROOK, International Judicial Negotiation, in Texas International Law Journal, 38, 2018, pp. 572ss. In this sense see also: European COMMISSION, Commission Staff working document-Impact assessment Accompanying the document Revision of Regulation (EC) No 1346/2000 on insolvency proceedings, 12 December 2012,

efficiently manage the crises of multinational banking groups in itself creates a high cost. It is also true that the disciplines dictated by the individual national legal systems for internal bankruptcies are often inadequate, but in the cases of transnational insolvency the negative repercussions are much greater[676]: In the cases mentioned, the losses were substantial.

4.The characteristics of the cooperation agreements: Cross-Border Insolvency Protocols.

It is known that the term "cooperation", regarding transnational relationships, can indicate different phenomena. In a first and more common sense, it indicates that cooperation between states through which treaties are concluded or other instruments are created that regulate the typical questions of private international law and of trial. In a second sense, less widespread, it indicates a form of cooperation that is implemented in the absence of the first, according to spontaneous methods, by private subjects other than states, belonging to more than one system, wishing to achieve results that would not otherwise be possible, precisely because of the absence of intergovernmental forms of collaboration. This characteristic as a means to remedy a lack of discipline agreed at the level of the States is explicitly highlighted, for example, in the introduction to the Cross-Border Insolvency Concordat of the Committee, which qualifies the Concordat itself as an "interim measure", applicable until, in fact, treaties or other agreements will be adopted by the States. In a system like the current one, based on a territorial model, international cooperation can only happen on a case-by-case basis[677] and is an essential tool for the rapid development of appropriate solutions for each case.

These are forms of cooperation that are spreading in a growing number of areas of law. However, it is in the context of transnational insolvency that, on the one hand, everything has begun, in particular, and

---

SWD(2012) 416 final, par. 3.2.3.

676UNCITRAL, Practice Guide on Cross-Border Insolvency Cooperation, op. cit., 9.

677L.M. LOPUCKI, The case for cooperative territoriality in international bankruptcy, in Michigan Law Review, 18, 2000, pp. 2219.

especially at the beginning, between the United States and Canada[678] and that, on the other hand, the most significant developments are still found. The spontaneous cooperation between curators and judges in the absence of a general and abstract discipline every other area of law[679], even if there is still greater diffusion in the common law systems. In bankruptcy this cooperation leads to the creation, by some or all of the bankruptcy bodies, of documents commonly called "cross-border insolvency Protocols"[680] or, more simply, protocols, or "cross-border insolvency agreements", "insolvency administration contracts"[681], "cooperation and compromise

---

[678]See, Supreme Court of the United States, 3 June1895, Hilton et al. v. Guyot et al., 159 U.S. 113 (1895) and Supreme Court of the United States, 10 December 1883, Canadian Southern Ry. Co. v. Gebhard, 109 U.S. 527 (1883).

[679]B. LEONARD, The developing use of protocols in major cross-border filings, in American Bankruptcy Institute Journal, 18, 1999, pp. 12ss. E. WARREN, L. WESTBROOK, Court-to-court negotiation, in American Bankruptcy Institute Journal, 204, 2003, pp. 28ss.

[680]A. KAMALNATH, Cross border insolvency protocols-A success story, in International Journal of Legal Studies and Research, 2 (1), 2013, pp. 172-190.

[681]Old Drone Co. Inc, Tennessee Western Bankruptcy Court (tnwbke) of 11 January 2018, case n. 14-11077-JLC. In re Toft, 453 B.R. 186, 198 (Bankr. S.D.N.Y. 2011) (stating that the United States rarely denied recognition of foreign proceedings when manifestly contrary to the United States' public policy); In re ABC Learning Centres Ltd., 728 F.3d 301 (3d Cir. 2013) (recognizing foreign proceeding even when it allowed secured curators to retain all of the debtor's assets instead of providing for the administration of all creditor claims) 16 737 F.3d 14 (4th Cir. 2013); In re OAS S.A., 533 B.R. 83, 103 (Bankr. S.D.N.Y. 2015) ("courts are reluctant to proscribe an action a party merely finds inconvenient, unusual or even unjust in some way"); Re Taisoo Suk (as foreign representative of Hanjin Shipping Co Ltd) (2016) 5 SLR 787 (recognizing andproviding assistance to Korean proceedings); Re Opti-medix (in liquidation) (2016) SGHC 108 ("A consequence of a greater sensitivity to universalist notions in insolvency is a greater readiness to go beyond traditional bases for recognising foreign insolvency proceedings)". Companies (Winding Up and Miscellaneous Provisions) Ordinance (Cap 32) par. 264 (2016); Re Moulin Global Eyecare Trading Ltd [2007] HKCFI 747 23 Joint Administrators of African Minerals Ltd (in administration) v. Madison Pacific Trust Ltd & Shandong Steel Hong Kong Zengli Ltd (2015) HKEC 608 (stating that a court will apply stricter requirements for recognizing a foreign order as the foreign court could proscribe relief not allowed in Hong Kong)See Beluga Chartering GmBH (in liquidation) and others v Beluga Projects (Singapore) Pte Ltd (in liquidation and another (2014) 2 SLR 815); Re Opti-medix (in liquidation) (2016) SGHC 108. For details see: P. KINDLER, Hauptfragen der Reform des Europäischen Internationalen Insolvenzrechts, in Zeitschrift für Insolvenzenrecht, 75, 2014, pp. 28ss. G. MCCORMACK, Reforming the European Insolvency Regulation: A legal and policy perspective, in Journal of Private International Law, 10, 2014, pp. 42ss. W.F. EBKE, L. HUMPENÖDER, Europäisierung des Insolvenzrechts, in U. HOMMEL, T. KNECHT, H. WOHLENBERG (eds) Handbuch Unternehmensrestrukturierung, ed. Springer, Wiesbaden, 2016.

agreements" or "memoranda of understanding"[682]. Some of them are based on the models drawn up by international organizations or private associations, others are created spontaneously by the interested parties.

As regards the legal nature of these documents, no agreement has yet been reached in doctrine. According to some it is a sort of transnational bankruptcy law otherwise missing[683], according to others, of treaties of ad hoc bankruptcy international law ad hoc[684] and according to others, of contracts concluded between the various bodies of bankruptcy that, like any contract concluded after the opening of bankruptcy proceedings and which exceeds normal administration, must be approved by the judge[685]. Not even the UNCITRAL has taken a definitive position on the point, suggesting that it may be a lot of contracts and provisions/orders of the judge who is called to approve them[686].

According to the UNCITRAL Practice Guide[687], they may or may

---

[682]Depending on the content, finally, one can possibly speak of "operating protocols" and "distribution agreements".

[683]E. WARREN, L. WESTBROOK, Court-to-court negotiation, op. cit.

[684]E.D. FLASCHEN, R.J. SILVERMAN, Cross-border insolvency cooperation Protocols, in Texas International Law Journal, 33, 1998, pp. 590ss. E.D. FLASCHEN, R.J. SILVERMAN, The importance of comity and co-operation in resolving international insolvencies, in E.B. LEONARD, C. BESANT, Current issues in cross-border insolvency and reorganizations, Graham and Trotham International Bar Association, London, 1994, pp. 44.

[685]A. V. SEXTON, Current problems and trends in the administration of transnational insolvencies involving enterprise groups: The mixed record of protocols, the UNCITRAL Model Insolvency Law, and the EU insolvency regulation, in Chicago Journal of International Law, 17, 2012, pp. 818ss. The author in particular criticizes the position of Flaschen and Silverman (see above), believing that we can not speak of treaties for two reasons: (i) the protocols are not binding while they would be if they were treated; (ii) each bankruptcy body may refuse to become part of a protocol. In the same spirit see also: J.A. KIRSHNER, International bankruptcy. The challenge of insolvency in a global economy. University of Chicago Press, Chicago, 2018, pp. 146ss.

[686]UNCITRAL Legislative Guide, part three, cit., par. 50.

[687]See, UNCITRAL, Legislative Guide on Insolvency Law, Part three: Treatment of enterprise groups in insolvency, 21 July 2010. The Commission of the House of Lords affirmed that: "the most common form of business model". The Communication of European Union of 20 October 2009, par. 4.1, states that: "(...) Subsidiaries are the predominant form of cross-border banking business in Europe, holding assets of almost € 4 trillion (...)". Communication from the Commission to the European Parliament, the Council, the European Economic and Social Committee, the European Court of Justice and the European Central Bank-An EU Framework for Cross-Border Crisis Management in the Banking Sector, 20 October 2009, COM(2009) 561.

not be legally binding between the parties who sign them or may contain provisions that are and others that are not[688], but in practice they are basically always intended as binding agreements. The structure, which presents, for example, the premises[689] or definitions, and the effects produced recall those typical of a contract between individuals. In addition to the signature of the parties, in most cases, a formal approval order issued by the competent courts, which reinforces its effectiveness, in particular because it prevents any dissenting parties, such as curators, to undermine the positive effects linked to the protocol itself, contesting one or more aspects.

The minimum prerequisite is that the regulatory systems that from time to time come into play at least do not prevent administrative or judicial authorities from undertaking such forms of cooperation. In this respect, the difference in attitudes of civil law to those of common law towards the conclusion of these protocols deserves attention. Moreover, the protocols are always explicit in doing without prejudice to the mandatory provisions in force in the individual legal systems. Another assumption is a collaborative attitude on the part of the courts involved[690].

5.Spontaneous cooperation between curators and judges in the absence of a general and abstract discipline.

Since cross-border insolvency agreements are spontaneous agreements, there are no particular requirements concerning the form they must cover: They are generally written but can also be oral and, depending on the needs of the concrete situation, can be concluded at the beginning of the crisis, as mostly happens, that in the course of the same. Furthermore they are based and therefore guarantee the autonomy of all the parties involved. The type of cases in which they were used is large, ranging from

---

[688]UNCITRAL, Practice Guide on Cross-Border Insolvency Cooperation, op. cit., 38.

[689]See in particular: Loewen: Cross-Border Insolvency Protocol for the Loewen Group Inc. and its Affiliates between the United States Bankruptcy Court for the District of Delaware (Case No. 99-1244) and the Ontario Superior Court of Justice at Toronto (Case No. 99-Cl-3384). For further details see: J. ADAMS KIRSHNER, International bankruptcy. The challenge of insolvency in a global economy, op. cit., pp. 238ss.

[690]E. WARREN, L. WESTBROOK, Court-to-court negotiation, op. cit. pp. 29ss.

liquidation proceedings to reorganization procedures, from cases in which several main proceedings had been opened, to cases in which a main proceeding was flanked by one or more secondary proceedings, against one and the same debtor who is responsible for multiple debtors belonging to the same group of companies. The combination of the legal systems involved is equally varied, since they can be two or more common law or civil law systems or a combination of the two types.

Regarding the content, it can be, above all, both generic and specific. "Generic" cooperation agreements may have as their object the simple future projection of the need for cooperation between the parties with more specific contents or ways in which such cooperation will take place.

6.(Follows) Issues covered in protocols with specific content.

Initially there were frequent forms of cooperation aimed at a mutual exchange of information related to the different procedures in progress, in order to have an overall view, for example through an exchange of provisions or transcripts of the proceedings or informative unofficial writings. With regard to this first form of cooperation, a brief digression is needed, especially as regards the information relating to the law to be applied by foreign judges and the effects that could derive from it: They could also be requested directly to the parties but often this solution, as well as being rather expensive, it does not offer satisfactory results because the parties tend to present the information requested by them in ways that in some way, though subtle, may favor them. So a direct request to foreign courts seems to be a much more attractive solution[691].

A second, more advanced cooperation variant is aimed at negotiating shared measures and solutions[692]. For the most part, these are procedural in nature, since these protocols are intended to facilitate cooperation and coordination between two or more bankruptcy proceedings opened in different States against one and the same debtor or

[691]UNCITRAL, Practice Guide on Cross-Border Insolvency Cooperation, op. cit., pp. 37, 39.

[692]E. WARREN, L. WESTBROOK, Court-to-court negotiation, op. cit.

debtor belonging to the same group of companies and to assist in the management of these proceedings. It is not excluded, however, that sometimes issues of merit are also addressed.

Specifically, without claiming to be exhaustive, the contents may concern: a) Organizational/procedural aspects. The provision of a common procedure to be used before the courts of various states and the procedures for filing documents and other information, with the warning, however, that such coordination could be difficult to implement when there are differences in the rules that regulate domestic and international jurisdiction in individual States; suspension of proceedings; the prediction of terms of forfeiture; the determination of the methods of communication and execution of notifications; the setting of hearings and common meetings; the coordination and harmonization of the reorganization plans and the assistance provided in relation to them; the referral of matters from one judge to another; the methods of communication between the different courts; the appointment of a single bankruptcy trustee who is responsible, jointly or severally, for the procedures open to the various companies, or, if this is not possible, the coordination of the activities of the various curators; the applicable law. Other contents may include: b) The methods for managing group assets and, in particular, the recovery and distribution of the same in a unitary manner, when this allows to obtain a higher revenue than that deriving from a sale of the assets individually considered and independently in different jurisdictions or when the value of the assets present in a single system is not high enough to justify a separate management; c) with regard to curators, then, unified lists may be drawn up or the conclusion of agreements with them may be encouraged in the sense of not asserting their claim in a particular order, in order to avoid that some curators are, to example, satisfied twice, in two different systems; they will be given the opportunity to assert their claims and a right of direct access to the jurisdiction they deem most appropriate and, at the same time, procedures will be provided to take into account and resolve in real time, in all jurisdictions, the claims made by them; meetings between curators' committees will be encouraged, as it is unlikely that a single committee will be established to represent all curators, since the interests of the latter will probably differ according to whether they are curators of a company rather than a other; d) the protocols can then regulate the modalities according to which the group must be managed during the crisis, if it is expected a continuation of the activities of the same, therefore, for example, providing for the appointment of new directors. Finally, some provisions of closure, such as issues closely related to the agreement, such as the modification, extinction, interpretation and effectiveness of the same, the resolution of disputes arising from it, the allocation of costs and expenses; in addition to those already mentioned and which are always present, which exclude any derogation from the jurisdiction of the courts and public order, there may be clauses relating to the information that must be disclosed to the other parties and the protection of the rights of the parties who have not signed the protocol[693].

7.Subjects involved in cooperation.

As for the form of the protocols, also in relation to the nature of the subjects taking part in the same there are no defined rules, the protocols being forms of spontaneous collaboration. In principle, therefore, promoters and parts of the same can be all the subjects who, in various ways, are involved in a process of insolvency of a group: The curators, the judges, the bankrupt companies and the curators, organized or not in a committee. Taking the Maxwell case, for example, the US judge Tina Brozman, in the Final Supplemental Order Appointing Examiner and Approving Agreement between the Examiner and Joint Administrators, has explicitly indicated among the subjects involved a harmonization of the two proceedings in progress in the United States respectively and in the United Kingdom, the two courts, the Examiner, the Joint Administrators and the debtor company[694]. The initiative to conclude such agreements generally consists in encouraging the judges to other subjects, that is, in most cases the curators, through forms of direct communication

[693]L. LOPUCKI, Cooperation in international bankruptcy: A post-universalist approach, in Cornell Law Review, 84, 1999, pp. 750ss. UNCITRAL, Practice Guide on Cross-Border Insolvency Cooperation, op. cit., pp. 37, 39; UNCITRAL Legislative Guide, part three, op. cit., par. 23ss.

[694]United States Bankruptcy Court, Southern District of New York, In Re Maxwell Communication Corporation plc, Debtor. Chapter 11 Case No. 91 B 15741 (TLB), Final Supplemental Order Appointing Examiner and Approving Agreement between Examiner and Joint Administrators, in Annual Survey of Bankruptcy Law, 1994-1995, pp. 96ss.

and a mutual exchange of information, reach an agreement on some central points, limiting the courts to provide the necessary assistance. According to the UNCITRAL Practice Guide, the possibility that it comes from the courts, which would therefore be involved in a very anticipated moment, represents a guarantee of success of the conclusion of the agreement. Generally, such agreements are then approved by the judges, on the condition of reciprocal approval by the authorities of at least one other of the regulations involved. Westbrook, therefore, said that these mutual concessions can only be seen as the mechanism and result of a negotiation conducted between authorities, regardless of the role, probably of intermediaries, played by the parties[695]. On the one hand, the approval of the protocols by the courts is not always present, being more difficult to obtain than the mere conclusion of the same by the curators[696]. On the other hand, it is possible that the approval of the judges should be added to that of the curators or of the curators' committee[697]. The protocols so far concluded have seen a prevalent participation of curators and judges, according to variable combinations often, and above all in the civil law systems, also according to the applicable law and, in particular, to the powers conferred on the various bodies. The frequent absence of curators, with some exceptions represented by large curators or curators' committees, depends on the complexities that would result from negotiating an agreement between a large number of parties. However, it is generally possible for them to comment or oppose the content of the agreements[698].

They will have to assist in the management of a specific case, for example in the translation of the proceedings records, or by informing and updating the courts of any other proceedings that are taking place in foreign jurisdictions, or by keeping in continuous contact with the judges, if is the need to modify measures initially issued in an emergency situation

---

[695]E. WARREN, L. WESTBROOK, Court-to-court negotiation, op. cit.

[696]American LAW INSTITUTE, Transnational Insolvency: Cooperation among NAFTA Countries. Principles of Cooperation among the NAFTA Countries, Huntington, Juris Publishing, New York, 2003, pp. 65ss.

[697]UNCITRAL Legislative Guide, part three, cit., par. 48.

[698]UNCITRAL, Practice Guide on Cross-Border Insolvency Cooperation, op. cit., par. 32ss.

or for other similar events[699]. There are those who have even considered it opportune that the parties are not further involved in the process of concluding the protocols, since the disadvantages that would otherwise arise are known: The already mentioned difficulty in reaching any kind of agreement and the partiality of the information provided to the courts. For this reason, it was hoped that the courts themselves would assume a pre-eminent and active role in concluding protocols and in general in negotiations, in such a way as to render the role played by the parties superfluous[700].

In finis we can say that the harmonization system should have the following features: 1.There have to be an international supervisory body to supervise banks activities and regulate the banking sector which is recognized internationally. The recognition is important to ensure that the policy is applicable in various jurisdictions. This international body could cooperate with the domestic supervisory body in each jurisdiction to gain an effective supervisory coordination. The emergence of having this body is because the rapid growth of international bank which operates in multiple jurisdiction. This is the reason of having unified supervisory body to supervise and regulate this sector effectively, because further they would have the same measurement of insolvency. The supervisory body could also declare the insolvency if there is a finding from their examination; 2. The appropriate measurement of bank solvency has to be identified appropriately. It has to be started with having an appropriate disclosure. Further, the risk management and capital adequacy leverage measures have to be coherent between the supervisory policy and banking regulation; 3. A coherence regulation between supervisory policy and banking law. The emergence of this point is to gain confidence and certainty in financial system; 4. In the case of the declaration of insolvency, the COMI of a multinational bank has to be determined to ensure the security of the assets and creditor's protection. Moreover, any transactions which might be endangered and caused loses have to be blocked; 5. The regime should permit a common administrator for all of the cases

---

[699]J.M. FARLEY, A judicial perspective on international cooperation in insolvency cases, in American Bankruptcy Institute Journal, 44, 1998, pp. 13ss.
[700]E. WARREN, L. WESTBROOK, Court-to-court negotiation, op. cit.

commenced for the entire member of the multinational banks; 6. Cooperation and communication should be authorized and encourage to the maximum level of possibility between the courts, judges and office holders among all related cases[701].

We can also say that the benefits deriving from the conclusion of protocols have highlighted the disadvantages linked to the absence of cooperation. Therefore, on the contrary, it can now be recalled that cooperation guarantees a reduction in costs and therefore the maximization of the value of the assets that can then be distributed to the curators, through an orderly, effective and efficient management of the proceedings; the reduction, to the maximum extent possible, of conflicts of laws and jurisdictions; greater predictability of results; the resolution of infragroup claims according to transparent and efficient schemes; a sale of assets as a unitary rather than parcellized[702].

To this we must now add the benefit deriving from being the protocols flexible tools that allow us to outline ad hoc solutions for each case and to obtain, in substance, effects close to those that would be obtained if we adopted a universalist approach[703]. Flexibility is particularly important in terms of transnational insolvency because in this sector more than in others the situations that may arise, including the interests of the parties and the characteristics of each legal system (such as the applicable law) are so diverse as to make any rigid rule that is unsuitable for resolving all of them satisfactorily[704] or requiring the modification of some terms of the agreement during the procedure or the conclusion of a new protocol that is added to the previous one.

---

[701]P. PASCALIDIS, Freedom of establishment and private international law for corporations, Oxford University Press, Oxford, 2012, pp. 188ss. C.J. REDMOND, COMI: In search of predictability, in Norton Annual Review of International Insolvency, 2010, pp. 4ss.

[702]AMERICAN LAW INSTITUTE, Transnational Insolvency, op. cit., 23ss. C.J. LEONARD, The way ahead: Protocols in international insolvency cases, in American Bankruptcy Institute Journal, 12, 1998, pp. 12ss. E.D. FLASCHEN, R.J. SILVERMAN, Cross-border insolvency cooperation Protocols, op. cit. UNCITRAL, Model Law on Cross-Border Insolvency with Guide to Enactment, 30 May 1997, par. 173.

[703]S. DI SANO, The third road to deal with the insolvency of multinational enterprise groups, in Journal of International Banking Law and Regulation, 15, 2011, pp. 23ss.

[704]UNCITRAL, Practice Guide on Cross-Border Insolvency Cooperation, op. cit., par. 7.

8.Difficulties linked to cooperation...of a juridical and practical nature.

Legal difficulties, they depend primarily on the need to ensure that cooperation takes place in compliance with the constitutional principles of each legal system, including those of independence and impartiality of judges, due process and confidentiality of decisions or relating to the mandatory rules of the legal systems involved. For example, it may be necessary to inform the parties, with appropriate notification, of the operations that will take place in view of the conclusion of a cooperation agreement and to ensure that they can assist or take action on them. It is possible that legal frameworks set the necessary conditions, but in reality specific regulation is often lacking, or the margins of effectiveness are uncertain, or different states pose different conditions: This limits the possibility of developing such protocols, especially in civil law orders[705].

Secondly, there are difficulties related to the type of system to which the judges and other bodies belong, among which cooperation is established. In fact, in general, the latter is easier to implement when only common law systems are involved, within which the courts enjoy greater discretion in their work. In the civil law countries it seems that there must necessarily be a regulation of authorization for cooperation and this creates the risk that the lack of such legislation would undermine possible forms of cooperation. Moreover, as regards the practical modalities, in the common law systems it is generally possible to make use of all the modern means of communication available, while in those of civil law it is easier to place more stringent procedural requirements[706]. The major difficulties existing in the civil law systems have not prevented the conclusion of protocols even among bodies belonging exclusively to the latter. The first and most important protocol traditionally mentioned, also concluded between curators belonging to a civil law system, is that related to the

[705]UNCITRAL, Model Law, cit., parr. 38, 182; UNCITRAL, Practice Guide on Cross-Border Insolvency Cooperation, op. cit., par. 17. E. WARREN, L. WESTBROOK, Court-to-court negotiation, op. cit.

[706]L. LOPUCKI, Cooperation in international bankruptcy: A post-universalist approach, op. cit.

Nakash case[707], which then facilitated the solution of some issues that arose also in the Lehman case[708]. Another, recalled by the UNCITRAL Practice Guide on the Cross-Border Insolvency Cooperation[709], is the one related to the EMTEC case, which developed between Germany and France.

As far as practical problems are concerned, we must first recall those of a linguistic nature, deriving from the difficulties in translating technical terms, which, however, do not seem irresolvable, considering also the results that in this aspect are reaching some international organizations, among which the European Union stands out in particular[710]. Secondly, there may be some problems related to the attitude of reluctance or hesitancy that certainly still exists in several environments towards the adoption of new procedural forms, in particular, towards the direct communication between judges. For example, state authorities are not always willing to accept that a court is to negotiate with another court

---

[707]E. WARREN, L. WESTBROOK, Court-to-court negotiation, op. cit.

[708]In re Lehman Bros. Int'l (Eur.) [2011] EWHC (Ch) 2022, [2011] All ER 273 (Eng.). G. XINYI, To recognise or not to recognise? Comparative study of Lehman brothers cases in Mainland China and Taiwan, op. cit., pp. 240ss. J.L. WESTROOK, An empirical study of the implementation in the United States of the Model Law on cross border insolvency, op. cit., pp. 247ss P.L. DAVIES, Resolution of cross-border groups, in M. HAENTJENS, B. WESSELS, Research handbook on crisis management in the sector, op. cit., pp. 264ss, the author discussing how both the U.S. and the U.K. took unilateral action in the bailouts of non-national entities, including Lehman Brothers, in order to protect national interests. J.M. PECK, Cross-border observations derived from My Lehman Judicial Experience, op. cit., pp. 132ss., the author explaining that cross-border conflicts and self-interested behaviours in the context of the Lehman insolvencies were unavoidable). S.L. BUFFORD, Coordination of insolvency cases for international enterprise groups: A proposal, op. cit., pp. 685ss. K.P. WOJCIK, Bail-in in the Banking Union, op. cit., pp. 124ss.

[709]In re Betcorp Limited (in Liquidation) 400 BR 266 (Bankr D Nev 2009). In re Fairfield Sentry Ltd 440 BR 60 (2010 (July 22 2010). (Ackers v. Saad Investment Company [2010] FCA 1221 at 58. In re Millennium Global Emerging Credit Master Fund Limited [2011] 458 BR 63 Lehman Brothers Special Financing Inc. v BNY Corporate Trustee Services Ltd 422 BR 407 (Bankr SDNY 2010). P.J.F. BERNARDO, Cross-border insolvency and the challenges of the global corporation: Evaluating globalization and stakeholder predictability through the UNCITRAL Model Law on cross-border insolvency and the European Union insolvency regulation, in Ateneo Law Journal, 56, 2012, pp. 800ss. N.W.A. TOLLENAAR, Dealing with the insolvency of multinational groups under the European Insolvency Regulation, in Insolvency Intelligence, 23 (5), 2010, pp. 65ss.

[710]A. HATJE, J.P. TERHECHTE, P.C. MÜLLER-GRAFF, Europarechtswissenschaft, ed. Nomos, Baden-Baden, 2018. J. SCHWARZE, V. BECKER, A. HATJE, J. SCHOO, EU-Kommentar, ed. Nomos, Baden-Baden, 2019.

or with foreign bankruptcy trustees and even less with the parties, so much so that the negotiation process is rarely given. Furthermore, courts typically tend to focus on the issues that have been posed before them and may be reluctant to provide assistance in other proceedings when their own does not present elements of internationality[711]. This attitude can have the most varied causes, from ethical considerations to legal culture, to the same linguistic differences or to the lack of familiarity with foreign legal systems[712]. In this regard, in favor of cooperation, it has been argued that although it may seem a form of anomalous development compared to the traditional forms of administration of bankruptcy and justice in general, it still represents a form of "healthy" development. It is necessary, in a situation where there is no authority controlling or coordinating the conduct of equal procedures, for example, of the United States Supreme Court or the CJEU[713].

Some of the difficulties that have been taken into consideration have been taken into consideration and resolved in those soft law instruments, born precisely to favor, in various ways, precisely the cooperation between courts in cases of transnational insolvency. This of course does not exclude that other possible difficulties will have to be faced from time to time, as they arise in concrete cases[714].

9.Conclusion of Protocols and the principle of comity.

Deciding whether international cooperation in the matter of transnational insolvency is an expression of the principle of comity depends on the meaning given to the term itself. In this regard, one can firstly refer to a recent text by Adrian Briggs, dedicated to the principle of comity in private international law[715]. The concept of "comity", typical of common law, has played an important role in past centuries and, although

---

[711]UNCITRAL, Practice Guide on Cross-Border Insolvency Cooperation, op. cit., par. 35.
[712]UNCITRAL, Practice Guide on Cross-Border Insolvency Cooperation, op. cit., par. 21.
[713]UNCITRAL Legislative Guide, part three, op. cit., par. 72ss. UNCITRAL, Practice Guide on Cross-Border Insolvency Cooperation, op. cit., par. 20.
[714]E. WARREN, L. WESTBROOK, Court-to-court negotiation, op. cit.
[715]A. BRIGGS, The principle of comity in private international law, in Recueil des Cours, ed. Brill, The Hague, vol. 354, 2011, pp. 69ss.

no longer considered or criticized by some to be an indefinite concept and therefore usable as a kind of secret weapon, still covers a role in assisting the jurist who has to answer questions in relation to which there must be an answer but it does not yet exist. This is a means to address issues arising in areas of law where it is desirable to develop forms of international cooperation between judicial authorities but for which no international agreement or other suitable legislative mechanism is available. Comity means full mutual trust between judicial institutions of different States, not interference with the work of the same, full respect for the acts of the same and their definitiveness. Comity, on the other hand, is not a form of reciprocity[716] and therefore, according to the perspective of this author, cooperation in the matter of transnational insolvency can not be traced back to the concept of comity.

In the sense that the cooperation between courts, in the specific field of transnational insolvency, is not an expression of the principle of comity, Warren and Westbrook have already expressed that they understand this principle in a slightly different way from what Briggs[717] described. It would indicate only an attitude of deference of some courts towards others, dictated, basically, by courtesy reasons and therefore independently of any expectations in relation to future behavior of that same judge in similar cases, let alone in the same case[718]. Eventually, in deciding whether to behave according to comity, the judges will look at the past relations between the two courts. This insolvency principle would be obsolete because it is clearly not the kind of situation that occurs when the courts of several states work together to resolve a bankruptcy case of a group of multinational companies, where a "real-time reciprocity" is necessary. The latter is distinguished from traditional reciprocity, because it refers to the same case for which the courts have been invested more than one order and not, instead, a cooperation based on a kind of exchange of favors, perhaps in relation to previously occurred cases. Cooperation is explicitly subject to "conditionality", whereas a specific judge will act on

---

[716]E. WARREN, L. WESTBROOK, Court-to-court negotiation, op. cit.
[717]A. BRIGGS, The principle of comity in private international law, op. cit.
[718]E. WARREN, L. WESTBROOK, Court-to-court negotiation, op. cit. E.J. JANGER, Reciprocal comity, in Texas International Law Journal, 46, 2011, pp. 442ss: who suggests giving a greater role to local priorities in the context of modified universalist solutions.

the principle of comity only in the hope that in the future the other judge will act according to the same rules of behavior; but mere hope can certainly not be considered a condition of reciprocity. As an example, to explain how "conditionality" can work, Westbrook recalled the Blanco v. Banco Industrial de Venezuela S.A. case[719]. A Venezuelan company, had established, before the courts of New York, against the defendant bank, a proceeding which then, following the bankruptcy of the Venezuelan company itself, the bankruptcy trustee, charged with the management of insolvency in the state of origin, he requested cancellation. The shareholders of the company intervened by requesting the rejection of the bankruptcy receiver's request, complaining that they could not obtain any satisfaction in the bankruptcy proceedings under way in Venezuela. The US courts felt they had to stop the process in favor of the Venezuelan bankruptcy courts, based on the principle of the forum non conveniens, but explicitly placing the condition that they should appoint a co-curator. The perspective that, instead, the use of protocols in the field of transnational insolvency is an expression of the principle of comity has been adopted in UNCITRAL. On closer inspection, this conclusion was reached by referring to "comity" as an attitude of respect for the equality and absolute independence of the subjects involved in the conclusion of the protocols and towards the sovereignty of the States concerned, without taking a specific position in relation to the question of reciprocity[720].

10.Soft law initiatives to support cooperation. The Cross-Border Insolvency Concordat.

The importance of the use of protocols is increasingly recognized by international organizations and professional associations of the utmost importance, which encourage their use and/or assist in their negotiation[721],

[719]United States Court of Appeals, Second Circuit, 30 April 1993, Pedro Pablo Blanco, F. and Jesus Vasquez Mancera, as Trustees for Proyecfin de Venezuela, S.A., Plaintiffs-Appellees, Inversiones Eufrates, S.A., Inversiones Gusanca, C.A., Plaintiffs-Intervenors-Appellants, v. Banco Industrial De Venezuela, S.A., Defendant-Appellee, 997 F.2d 974 bankruptcy that could guarantee shareholders adequate protection. If this condition had not been met, the proceeding could have been reopened in the United States.

[720]UNCITRAL, Model Law, cit., par. 175. UNCITRAL, Practice Guide on Cross-Border Insolvency Cooperation, op. cit., par. 38.

[721]S. DI SANO, The third road to deal, op. cit., par. 22; UNCITRAL, Practice Guide on

mostly through soft law, a feature that, at seeing well, it should not prevent them from achieving their purpose. In fact, in recent years, the so-called "non-binding", such as recommendations, documents published by private bodies or self-help codes, to which the market players and their legal and financial advisors have paid the utmost attention.

One of the first documents that must be remembered for having foreseen the possibility, for the parties and the judges involved in an international bankruptcy, to conclude protocols when several main proceedings were opened in different jurisdictions is the Cross-Border Insolvency Concordat, drawn up in 1995 by the Committee J of the Section on Business Law of the International Bar Association. Work had begun following the case involving the Canadian company Olympia & York in the early 1990s[722]. It contains principles that have the advantage of being flexible and therefore of being able to be adapted, by the lawyers of the parties, to the needs of the specific case and to any mandatory rules in force in the States concerned.

In principle, on the basis of what had already been done with the Model International Insolvency Cooperation Act, the Concordat would have ideally favored the opening of a single main proceeding, a solution that was however unattainable. Therefore, opting for a middle ground approach, it provides, in the event that several main proceedings are opened, more or less simultaneously, in multiple jurisdictions, on the one hand, principles aimed at facilitating the coordination of the same and the claims of curators and on the other hand, useful principles for the identification of the applicable law, the latter valid both in the case in which only one main proceedings is open, as in the case where more than one is open.

The first principle that interests us here is n. 3, which provides for certain rights due to the trustees and curators and some provisions relating to the exchange of information. First of all, if several main proceedings are opened in parallel, it is envisaged that the bankruptcy trustees

---

Cross-Border Insolvency Cooperation, op. cit., par. 27.

[722]J. ALTMAN, A test case in international bankruptcy in international bankruptcy protocols: The Lehman Brothers insolvency, in San Diego International Law Journal, 12, 2011, pp. 477.

appointed in each of them will receive notifications of the measures taken also in the other proceedings and may appear in them. If necessary, it will be possible to resort to an exequatur procedure to recognize the powers of the curators in different systems from the one to which they belong. The trustee thus remains subject to the jurisdiction of the judge before whom he appears. In order to guarantee that, at least in principle, none of the curators are subject to discrimination, the right to appear before the judges of all the legal systems involved is also guaranteed, regardless of whether or not they have filed a claim before the themselves, without becoming, by the mere fact of having appeared, subject to the jurisdiction of these. In case they want to be heard on matters related to their claims, then they will be subject to the jurisdiction of the judge concerned, but only in relation to those specific issues. The curators must also be guaranteed the possibility of requesting, even if only for a limited period of time, a review of the merits of any provision (including provisional measures) adopted by the courts of other jurisdictions than those to which they are subject. The reasons linked to the need for such a mechanism derive from the complexity of the situations that generally occur in the transnational insolvency proceedings and from the opportunity that the parties damaged by the measures referred to above may request their revision when the situation has stabilized and the facts have been clarified. Finally, the principle under consideration provides that the information made public in a forum is also in the other forums and that the information held in the possession of one or more curators is also made available to the other curators.

Principle n. 4 deals with the procedures for managing curators' claims and underlines the need for each judge to coordinate with others, where necessary through a protocol. Claims for damages must, in principle, be filed before a single judge and, in the event that they are filed before more than one judge, care should be taken to prevent the parties from receiving more than due. Tendentially, each creditor must be allowed to choose the most appropriate forum, so that everyone, as noted above, is treated fairly. This choice will not affect the law applicable to the claim itself because, pursuant to the Concordat, for this aspect a single system of conflict rules must be used in all proceedings; however, it is possible that one court is considered more attractive than another or that a preferential creditor receives better treatment under a distribution system than under another. In fact, in each proceeding the assets will be distributed according to the order of precedence established by each order. On the other hand, the classification of the various claims of curators must be made in a coordinated manner by the judges of the various states involved, so that classes of comparable curators can be assessed comparatively. The revenues of the properties must be distributed among the different jurisdictions in proportion to the rights of the curators, while the proceeds resulting from revocation actions will be, optionally, distributed proportionally between the different jurisdictions or entrusted to the judge who ordered the revocation, which then he will deal with distributing them to curators.

Principles n. 6 and 7 provide that the trustees of each forum can make use of the rules present in each of the jurisdictions involved, even if no identical or similar rules are available in their own, including those governing revocatory actions. For example, if in one of the states in which the group operates, there is a rule that allows the cancellation of a periodic or continuous execution contract that is particularly burdensome, any concerned trustee can use it for the benefit of all curators, regardless of the fact that there is a rule of this kind in the order of belonging. However, to protect the safety of commercial traffic, these rules can not be used unpredictably. This is probably to be understood as a reference to principle n. 8, expressly made subject to the rules just analyzed, which provides that even if the parties are subject to a specific jurisdiction, the rules governing the revocation action in that forum do not apply to transactions that do not have any significant connection with the same forum.

Furthermore, the same principle establishes that the validity and admissibility of the claims of curators, including those relating to any related or compensated contracts, must be decided in each forum on the basis of a law identified through the rules of private international law.

Finally, it concerns principle n. 9, pursuant to which the conclusion of a bankruptcy agreement is not precluded by the mere fact of not being provided for by the laws of some jurisdictions, provided that however the execution of the same does not involve any discrimination for the parties.

Finally, as a general rule, the Concordat requires that the parties' expectations should not be frustrated by unexpectedly adopted accepacies following the opening of insolvency proceedings. Among the protocols that have used the Concordat as a model we traditionally recall those relating to the cases Everfresh[723], AIOC[724], and, indirectly, Livent[725], which entirely takes over the former.

11.The UNCITRAL model law.

On the basis of a chronological order, the UNCITRAL Model Law of 1997[726], must now be mentioned, and in particular its chapter IV (articles 25-27), entitled "Cooperation with foreign courts and foreign representatives" and indicated by the guide to enactment of the UNCITRAL Model Law, as the "core element" of the Law itself[727]. According to the doctrine, the express prediction with which courts and curators of the different states are authorized to communicate directly with each other represents the most radical innovation contained in Model Law.

The proposed rules take account of what emerged during the second Multinational Judicial Colloquium on Cross-Border Insolvency, organized in New Orleans in 1997, under the aegis of UNCITRAL and INSOL. The aim is to favor the development of cooperation, especially in those systems in which judges have a very limited possibility of acting outside of express regulatory provisions; in any case, the Guide noted that, even in those jurisdictions in which an explicit legislative authorization for

---

723Orders Approving Cross-Border Insolvency Protocol between Canada and the United States in Re Everfresh Beverages Inc., Ontario Court of Justice, Toronto (Mr. Justice J.M. Farley), Case No. 32-077978, (December 20, 1995) and United States Bankruptcy Court for the Southern District of New York. (Hon. Burton R. Lifland), Case No. 95 B 45405, (December 20, 1995).

724Cross-Border Liquidation Protocol in Re AIOC Corporation and AIOC Resources AG, between United States and Switzerland: United States Bankruptcy Court for Southern District Court of New York (Chief Judge Tina L. Brozman), Case Nos. 96 B 41895 and 96 B 41896, (April 3, 1998).

725Cross-Border Insolvency Protocol in Re Livent Inc. between United States Bankruptcy Court for the Southern District of New York (Hon. Arthur Gonzales), Case No. 98-B-48312, and Ontario Superior Court of Justice, Toronto (Mr. Justice J.D. Ground), Case No. 98-CL-3162, (June 11, 1999).

726E. WARREN, L. WESTBROOK, Court-to-court negotiation, op. cit.

727See in particular: E. WARREN, Bankruptcy and article 9: 2017 statutory supplement, Wolters Kluwer Law & Business, New York, 2017.

cooperation is not in principle necessary, the presence of a legislative framework within which such cooperation can be placed represents a useful element supporting the same[728]. In the systems in which the implementation of cooperation is based on the principle of comity, the Model Law can serve to concretize this principle and adapt it to the particular characteristics of transnational insolvency; in the jurisdictions where, on the other hand, the legal basis of the cooperation is represented by an ad hoc agreement between the parties, the Model Law can serve as a model for the elaboration of such an agreement.

Coming now to individual forecasts, articles 25 and 26 encourage cooperation and direct communications between courts and curators at transnational level through the use of the verb "shall" and the phrase "to the possible maximum extent"[729]. These bodies can communicate with each other and request information directly, with a certain degree of autonomy and freedom of initiative, without the need for intermediaries or other formalities, which would be in contrast with the policy to which the rules are based and with the objective to facilitate the dispatch of operations. In particular, on the one hand, we want to avoid the use of procedures, such as rogatoria, which are very expensive in terms, first of all, of time; on the other hand, prior formal recognition of the insolvency proceedings opened in the foreign state is not required for the purpose of implementing the cooperation.

Article 27 non-exhaustively enumerates six possible forms of cooperation, through which implementation of the provisions of articles 25 and 26. The contents of art. 27 of the Model Law was then further specified by the UNCITRAL Practice Guide on the Cross-Border Insolvency Cooperation[730] and therefore, the analysis that follows will take into account both the precise provisions of the Law, as well as that specified in the Practice Guide[731].

The first method of cooperation provided for by art. 27 consists in

[728]J.L WESTBROOK, A global solution to multinational default, in Michigan Law Review, 7, 2000, pp. 2279s.
[729]E. WARREN, Bankruptcy and article 9: 2017 statutory supplement, op. cit.
[730]UNCITRAL, Practice Guide on Cross-Border Insolvency Cooperation, op. cit., parr. 17ss.
[731]UNCITRAL, Practice Guide on Cross-Border Insolvency Cooperation, op. cit., par. 17.

the appointment of a person, physical or juridical, who acts under the direction of a judge, covering a wide variety of functions, among which, by way of example, the intermediary between the different courts involved, in particular where they are obstacles given by linguistic differences, or that of promoter of the conclusion of a bankruptcy agreement or of an agreement between the parties on some nodal issues of the procedure. It is also envisaged that the appointment may specify the conditions for carrying out the assignment and may request that a report on the activities carried out be prepared.

The second method considered essential for the purpose of implementing the cooperation referred to in articles 25 and 26 of the Model Law is the exchange of information, which can take place through any means of communication considered appropriate and in both written and oral form. The Practice Guide dedicates a long part of in-depth study to this mode of cooperation. Firstly, it is emphasized that the establishment of a communication channel in cases of transnational insolvency can benefit the related procedures in various aspects. For example, it can help the parties to better understand the implications or the methods of application of foreign law, in particular regarding differences or overlaps with the local law, which could determine the emergence of further controversies; it can then facilitate the resolution of issues in relation to which there are conflicting visions; it can help the parties to exchange reliable information, avoiding the prejudices and distortions inevitably present when the same, each within their own legal system, become the bearers of their own interests. Communications can also benefit, more in general, the interests of international community, facilitating a better understanding between the different actors of the same and therefore indirectly favoring the development of global economy, preserving a value that could otherwise be lost if the insolvency was dealt with according to a territorialist model. Other possible advantages may not be easily identifiable ex ante but may become evident once the aforementioned communications are undertaken: For example, they could help to stimulate, in a long-term perspective, legislative reforms. The parties involved in communications can be, according to the Practical Guide, both judges and bailiffs or intermediaries appointed by the courts, as well as bankruptcy trustees. In carrying out the communications, transparency, effectiveness and credibility must be guaranteed and, in general, the protection of both procedural and substantive interests of the parties, for example through guidelines, which will eventually be incorporated into specific "insolvency agreements".

For example, an appropriate notification system should be provided, in order to allow interested parties to watch or oppose communications, and a registration system, with a view to filing in the files of proceedings, with the possible provision of measures to protect their confidentiality. Furthermore, it will be necessary to establish whether the communications constitute the rule or only an exception that can be used in case of absolute necessity; if only procedural issues are to be dealt with within the same or if aspects of merit can also be addressed; if a judge can claim that a certain process is followed in conducting the same; which language should be used and any consequent need for translation[732].

The third mode of cooperation envisaged by art. 27 of the Model Law consists in coordinating the management and supervision of the assets and activities of the debtor. For example, research or joint actions could be conducted jointly[733]. It will be possible to determine, inter alia, the law regulating the substantial relationships to which the assets refer, the parties in charge of establishing the arrangements for their disposal, the possible need for authorizations, the possibility of dividing the various related to them and, finally, the modalities for the exchange of information necessary to ensure coordination and cooperation. This can help to avoid the occurrence of any disputes and to ensure that the main objective pursued, especially in the reorganization procedures, is the safeguarding of the interests of all the parties involved.

The fourth modality, foreseen in letter d), consists in the approval and execution, by the involved courts, of the so-called "cross-border insolvency agreements"-essentially the protocols-relating to the coordination of proceedings, the conclusion of which seems to be particularly appropriate in the presence of certain circumstances identified by the Practice Guide itself. Among these, the presence, in this case, of a

---

[732]D.D. CARON, L.M. CAPLA, The UNCITRAL arbitration rules. A commentary, Oxford University Press, Oxford, 2013, pp. 572ss.
[733]D.D. CARON, L.M. CAPLA, The UNCITRAL arbitration rules. A commentary, op. cit.

large number of elements of internationality; a complex structure of the debtor; the opening, in the various States concerned, of different types of bankruptcy proceedings; the presence of sufficient assets to cover the costs of preparing the agreement; the availability of time to conduct the necessary negotiations; the similarity of contents of the substantive legal provisions; uncertainty regarding issues of applicable law and choice of court; the uncoordinated suspension of proceedings in the various jurisdictions; the availability of a centralized active mass management system; the appointment of bankruptcy trustees for the various jurisdictions by the same company, active internationally[734].

Letter e) of art. 27 provides for the possibility of coordinating the proceedings opened against the same debtor and art. 29 contains some indications, addressed to the courts, to facilitate such coordination, which may also take place through simultaneous hearings or, in the case of reorganization proceedings, through the negotiation, drafting, approval and/or joint execution of the related plans, also with the involvement of curators of all the relevant legal systems.

Finally, letter f) grants states that adopt Model Law the right to indicate further forms or examples of cooperation. The Practice Guide provides two possible contents: a) Issues of jurisdiction and allocation of management of the various claims of curators among the courts, which are presumed to cooperate anyway; b) the coordination of the claims, of the evaluation and of the order of satisfaction of the curators. In relation to the first possibility, the Practice Guide observes that the determination of a forum suitable for the treatment of a particular claim could imply the need for a judge to postpone a dispute initially submitted to another judge, but this operation may not always be possible, since that some subjects must necessarily be subject to jurisdiction or at least to the control of a given system. Furthermore, especially in civil law systems, there may be procedural limitations to the possibility for judges to refer the proceedings to other judges. A solution suggested by the Practice Guide consists in the abstention, by a specific curator, from subjecting the matter to the local judge, leaving everything in the hands of the trustee in charge of the appropriate arrangement.

---

[734]UNCITRAL, Practice Guide on Cross-Border Insolvency Cooperation, op. cit., par. 30.

12.The study of G-30 "International Insolvency in the Financial Sector".

Shortly after the UNCITRAL Model Law is the study published by the Group of Thirty on international bankruptcies in the financial sector. Following the failure of the English bank Barings, which took place in 1995, a study group was set up to investigate the relevant aspects of the failures of financial institutions operating globally. The interim results of the research contained in a report and in some recommendations were then the subject, between the end of 1996 and the beginning of 1997, of comments and observations from fourteen states[735], of the then European Community and of two international organizations: UNCITRAL and the International Monetary Fund (IMF). Subsequently, in May 1997 the draft of the study and the comments collected were discussed at a conference in London and the final version of the Report and Recommendations was then published by the Group of Thirty in 1998. These recommendations were already seen at the time as a short-term solution, awaiting an initiative aimed at standardizing the bankruptcy disciplines of individual States[736].

Coming to the content, they point out first of all those addressed to the supervisory authorities, who are advised, in order to prepare for any crises, to identify ex ante possible ways of communication that can be used to cooperate not only with colleagues but also with lawyers, curators and judges of other States and to find internationally an agreement on the organization, timing and type of assistance that they and the other subjects mentioned will provide each other. Three other relevant recommendations are addressed to the legislators of the individual states, which should allow the recognition of foreign bankruptcy proceedings with the aim of facilitating international cooperation, authorizing the exchange of information between the various actors of bankruptcy proceedings and identifying a

---

[735]Australia, Canada, Czech Republic, Germany, Hong Kong, Indonesia, Italy, Japan, Luxembourg, Mexico, Netherlands, Netherlands Antilles and United States. See GROUP OF THIRTY, International Insolvencies in the Financial Sector. A study group Report, Washington, 1998, pp. 65ss.

[736]For details see: P. OMAR, International insolvency law. Themes and perspectives, ed. Routledge, London & New York, 2017.

judge or otherwise a single center of reference for each international failure. Finally, he notes a recommendation to lawyers, who are invited to agree with the supervisory authorities on measures to facilitate cooperation and recognition of foreign bankruptcy proceedings.

13.Principles of cooperation among the NAFTA Countries of the American Law Institute.

A pioneering role in the field of inter-state cooperation between bodies of bankruptcy proceedings was held by the American Law Institute with the Transnational Insolvency Project of 2003. This project establishes a procedure, which has received the support of both judges and practical, both of common law that of civil law[737], for the conduct of communications between the various bodies. Even the doctrine was enthusiastic: In particular, Jay Westbrook in 2000 described the project as the best answer to the problems posed by the phenomenon of transactional failures, through a model that defines "modified universalism", on the one hand because it was a a flexible tool that could adapt pragmatically to the various problems posed by the presence of numerous systems, each with its own rules and on the other hand, because it would have allowed a rapid and non-problematic transition to a desired universally universalist model. Here are some general principles contained in Section III of the Project, some procedural principles contained in Section IV and the guidelines applicable to communications between courts, contained in Appendix B to the Project itself.

Beginning with the general principles, the first of these requires judges and curators to cooperate in cases of transnational insolvency, pursuing the dual objective of maximizing the total value of all the debtor's assets and ensuring that the process is administered fairly. The third principle indicates the need, of utmost importance according to the curators of the principles themselves, to suspend as quickly as possible, in order to favor cooperation, any activity related to the bankrupt company. The fourth principle, however, concerns the information that must or can be exchanged to implement the cooperation and to prevent the commission

---

[737]J.L. WESTBROOK, The transnational insolvency project of the American Law Institute, in Connecticut Journal of International Law, 17, 2001, pp. 99ss.

of any wrongdoing by the bankrupt or curators, among which are certainly those relating to the assets recovered and the claims made by curators in each order. The principle states that in order to obtain this information foreign trustees can make use of all the means provided for by the applicable law, also according to what was later reiterated by the ninth procedural principle.

Turning to procedural principles, it concerns first of all the eighth principle, which deepens the fourth general principle, just mentioned. It provides that the trustee, the debtor or a creditor, who requests the court of a State to open insolvency proceedings or to recognize an open procedure abroad, must provide the same court with all the necessary information concerning the existence and progress of any other bankruptcy proceedings or similar procedures already opened abroad against the same debtor or a debtor connected to it. In fact, according to what we read in the commentary on the principle itself, cooperation can not take place in the absence of such information and therefore a rule must be provided for the provision of the same in all the systems within a reasonable time. However, two problems may arise in relation to the rule now under consideration: The first relating to the extent of the obligation to provide information, which will be regulated by the law of the place where the information is to be made available, and the second relating to confidentiality, a question which instead will be regulated by the law of legal order. Furthermore, it is emphasized that any incompatibility between the provisions of the two laws, unless an agreed solution is found, could undermine the objectives pursued in both proceedings.

The tenth procedural principle provides that the courts before which insolvency proceedings have been opened or those requiring assistance from foreign bankruptcy courts communicate with each other directly or through the curators, to the maximum extent possible, within the limits of what is permitted from the applicable legal provisions, both through an exchange of written documents and through telematic means of communication.

They also note, with regard to the cooperation between bodies of bankruptcy, the procedural principles from 14 to 22, relating to cases of the opening of several parallel proceedings. First of all it is envisaged that the curators must cooperate on every aspect of the procedure and that the instrument which is the main prerogative for this purpose is an agreement or, if you prefer, protocol, referred to as a "superior method of cooperation". In it, the decision-making mechanisms must be defined, at least in the salient features, while also making it possible to make decisions on an informal basis. In particular, methods for the approval by the courts in a coordinated manner and for the communication between curators, when required by the applicable law, must be envisaged. Furthermore, mechanisms should be provided to avoid unnecessary and costly hearings or other proceedings.

The fifteenth principle establishes that each trustee should obtain from the competent judge the approval of any action that may affect the assets or operations of one of the companies of the group established in another legal system, when this is required by the laws of order to which the court belongs, except as provided for by a protocol approved (also) by the judge himself. Furthermore, each trustee, unless there are circumstances of particular urgency, must try to obtain in advance the consent of the other curators, in relation to matters concerning the assets that are found or the proceedings that take place in the systems of such other trustees. The sixteenth principle governs the methods for notifying the trustees of the hearings or of the measures adopted by the judges. The commentary on the principle also provides that any activity in relation to which the approval of the competent judge is also required must be notified, constituting this requirement an index of importance such as to make a notification necessary. The seventeenth principle provides that the trustees of each proceeding must try to sell the assets in a coordinated manner, in order to maximize their value, and that each local judge must approve those sales that effectively allow the achievement of this result. To this end, it may be advantageous for the trustees to appoint a qualified, third party and neutral, for example a banker or a financial intermediary, who deals with the sale of assets according to certain criteria approved by the curators and judges. Another possibility, if this is permitted by local laws, consists in entrusting the determination of the methods for distributing assets to arbitrators. The eighteenth principle states that if one of the group's companies is reorganized in one of the three NAFTA states, the courts of the other two states must cooperate in order to make the respective proceedings compatible with the reorganization objectives pursued in the first. It is also envisaged in the following three principles that cooperation between judges must also be aimed at obtaining the necessary bankruptcy financing and that the trustees must reach a common position on the rules applicable to revocation actions. Each trustee must undertake to make available to foreign colleagues in a timely manner all information relating to claims made by curators, including the degree of certainty of the same. The twenty-second principle establishes that the claims admitted in one of the bankruptcy procedures must also be in the other procedures opened in the NAFTA countries, unless the same facts must be interpreted differently according to the local distribution rules[738].

The groups of societies are taken into consideration only from the twenty-third and twenty-fourth principle, wanting the project to devote themselves to such realities only in a small part[739]. The first of these provides that the possibility of opening a bankruptcy procedure against a subsidiary company in the same order in which a bankruptcy procedure is already open against its parent company and to coordinate these proceedings, both from a procedural point of view and from a substantial point of view, in the event that a proceeding is not already opened in the State in which the subsidiary has the center of its interests. In the latter case, this procedure will have to be coordinated with the first, realizing, where possible, substantial consolidation. The second of the aforementioned principles provides that in parallel proceedings against several companies in a group, coordination and cooperation must, as a general rule, work in a similar way to cases where several parallel proceedings are open against the same debtor, even if some issues, such as the distribution of assets, may need to be resolved differently, due to peculiarities inherent in the group structure[740].

---

[738]R. BORK, Principles of cross-border insolvency law, op. cit.

[739]AMERICAN LAW INSTITUTE, Transnational Insolvency, op. cit., 23, n. 42.

[740]J.L. WESTBROOK, The duty to seek cooperation in multinational insolvency cases, in Annual Review of Insolvency Law, 2004, pp. 364. In particular, there are many protocols that refer to the guidelines: of the forty-five published on the website of the International Insolvency Institute, nineteen incorporate the guidelines. The first case was Matlack System, Inc. between Canadian courts and US courts (Cross-Border Insolvency Protocol in Re Matlack Inc. between Ontario Superior Court of Justice, Toronto (Mr. Justice J.M.

14.(Follows): Guidelines applicable to court-to-court communications in cross-border cases.

Particularly important is the appendix B of Principles, containing seventeen guidelines applicable to communications between judges, considered, also by the American Law Institute, one of the fundamental elements for cooperation in transnational insolvency. They provide a sort of procedural guide for the coordination of communications between the parties involved in insolvency proceedings and specify which are the appropriate means of communication. Due to their particular importance, they have been translated into several languages, thus spreading their knowledge also outside the NAFTA countries.

The application of the guidelines must be in compliance with the local procedural provisions and with any relevant uses or practices, also to ensure that the proceedings are carried out fairly. In particular, judges wishing to use them must first adopt them in a formal manner and such adoption must be notified to the parties and their counsel, who may also possibly oppose them.

Judges are expected to communicate with each other and with foreign curators or with representatives of foreign courts, to coordinate and harmonize the related proceedings. As far as concerns the curators in particular, with the prior authorization of the judge from whom they were appointed, they will be able to communicate directly, as appropriate, with the judges, the foreign curators or the authorized representatives of judges. In principle, judges will have to respond directly to requests received, in particular when they come from another (foreign) judge; and only exceptionally can they avail themselves, in their reply, of authorized representatives or curators. As for the media, there is the greatest freedom of choice: Documents can be exchanged or they can use means of immediate communication. No obstacle to communication derives from the type of procedure open to each judge, provided that there is a commonality of the issues dealt with and/or of the parties involved: The

---

Farley), Case No. 01-CL-4109, (April 19, 2001) and United States Bankruptcy Court for the District of Delaware (Hon. Mary F. Walrath), Case No. 01-01114 (MFW), (May 24, 2001) including approval and adoption of the American Law Institute Guidelines for Court-to-Court Communications in Cross-Border Cases).

main objective to which communications must be inspired is the interest in justice[741].

Whether contacts between judges or between a judge and a curator, or even between a judge and a representative of a foreign judge, the seventh and eighth guidelines guarantee the lawyers of the parties the right to attend communications and to be notified of the same with a special notification, performed according to local procedural rules. In addition, communications must be recorded, may be transcribed and a copy of the registration and any transcription must be filed in the files of the proceedings and made available to the lawyers of the parties, with the necessary precautions to protect the confidentiality of information. Finally, the agreements relating to time and place of communication will be concluded having regard, in principle, exclusively to the needs of the judges. The possibility of conducting simultaneous hearings is foreseen, during which, in each of the hearing rooms, it is possible to watch in real time what is happening in the others. In view of the hearing, the documents deposited with each judge must be made available, either physically or by electronic means, also of the other judges, without however this determining the purchase of the quality of part in more than one jurisdiction[742].

The representatives of the parties must, unless special permits in the opposite direction, file their requests or defenses only before the court of belonging, and also in the exceptional case where a party is authorized to appear and be heard before a foreign judge, not for this reason it will only be subject to the jurisdiction of the latter. The judges will have to establish guidelines for an orderly filing of claims, for the issuing of decisions in a coordinated manner and for joint resolution of any preliminary, procedural or administrative matter. Any suspension of the proceedings before a judge, with reference to a part or to a particular request of the same, must not have effect on the requests made by that party before another judge and the two judges must commit to communicating with each other in order to resolve any problems of

[741]H. HANNAN, Cross-border insolvency: The enactment and interpretation of the UNCITRAL Model law, ed. Springer, Berlin, 2017, pp. 9ss.

[742]R. BORK, Principles of cross-border insolvency law, op. cit.

overlap between the claims made before them. The laws or regulations applied before foreign judges and the provisions issued by them must be recognized and accepted as valid, unless one of the parties object. Finally, a list of subjects must be drawn up, the so-called "non-resident parties"[743], which will also receive notifications regarding proceedings before foreign courts.

The provisions that the courts adopt according to the guidelines may be modified over time if this is necessary to achieve the goals set out in the guidelines or to adapt them to changes and developments in the proceedings. The changes will take effect following a joint approval of the courts involved and, in the event that the initiative comes from a single judge, this must notify the other judges involved of their intention in this regard. Finally, it is expected that no action taken under the guidelines should be understood as a compromise or an exception to the powers, responsibilities or authority of the courts, nor as the resolution on the merits of any controversial issue, or as the renunciation of the parties to any substantial right or to any claim or waiver of the effects produced by the judges' orders.

The guidelines are not designed to be static but to be adapted and modified according to the needs of the concrete case and to change and evolve in parallel with the change and evolution of reality. This feature makes it easy to insert them into the protocols, which in turn are flexible and adaptable to the relevant characteristics from time to time[744].

15.Cooperation between trustees in Regulation (CE) n. 1346/2000 and the European Communication and Cooperation Guidelines for Cross-border Insolvency.

Also in Regulation CE n. 1346/2000 it is possible to find provisions on cooperation in insolvency proceedings. This Regulation does not apply to the insolvency of groups of companies, nor to the insolvency of banking groups, but it deserves to be remembered as the

---

743R. BORK, Principles of cross-border insolvency law, op. cit.

744On the other hand, as regards Directive 2001/24/EC, no question arises about cooperation since it is based on the universalist model.

only "hard law" instrument currently in force, containing provisions on the matter of cooperation. In any case, it is worth pointing out that the Regulation's approach is different from the typical one of cooperation because it is based on the supremacy of the judge and the main proceedings, compared to the judge and the adjudicator of the secondary procedure, whereas be the equality between the subjects of the various States involved.

The recital n. 20 of the aforementioned Regulation provides that "primary and secondary insolvency proceedings may (...) contribute to an effective liquidation of assets only if all the pending procedures are coordinated collaboration between the various curators, which must involve in particular a sufficient exchange of information"[745]. Article 31 therefore envisages a "duty of collaboration and information" between the administrator of the main proceedings and the curators of the secondary procedures, without prejudice to the provisions limiting the transmissibility of information. The standard in question does not further specify the methods through which communications must take place, so that, from time to time, the curators should take action to adopt ad hoc measures. Therefore, the "Core Group" of the Academic Wing of INSOL Europe, in its second congress held in Prague in October 2004, assessed the possibility of defining a set of non-binding standards to facilitate communication and cooperation in the foreseen cases from Regulation 1346. According to the Core Group, this could have benefited in many ways: First of all, it would have facilitated the achievement of those objectives typically pursued in bankruptcy procedures, starting from the maximization of the value of assets; it would also have contributed to increasing the professionalism of bankruptcy experts; finally it would have been a support to possible measures issued by the judges in bankruptcy proceedings or related procedures. It was thus sent to a "Task Force", chaired by professors Bob Wessels and Miguel Virgós, who initially prepared a draft of a document subject to multiple moments of confrontation between experts of the raw material in Scottsdale (USA), in May 2006 , on the occasion of the Congress of INSOL International Academics, then in Bucharest, in September of the same year, at the annual

[745]R. BORK, Principles of cross-border insolvency law, op. cit.

Conference of INSOL Europe, in Oxford in March 2007 at the annual Conference of the Insolvency Lawyers Association and finally in Cape Town, always in March 2007, at a further congress of INSOL International Academics.

Published with the name of the European Communication and Cooperation Guidelines for Cross-border Insolvency Cooperation[746], the document contains eighteen guidelines and a related commentary, primarily designed to function as the first step towards the creation of a framework within which curators and judges involved in an insolvency procedure falling within the scope of Regulation 1346, they can operate efficiently and effectively. Furthermore, it should be pointed out immediately that even subjects operating in bankruptcy procedures other than the latter are encouraged, where possible, to make use of the guidelines. The guidelines strongly encourage the conclusion of collaboration agreements or protocols[747], as a means of co-ordinating insolvency proceedings open in more than one state, setting minimum requirements that may need to be complemented by other measures specifically designed for particular situations. While not offering an absolute guarantee of success, they should in any case inspire the activity of every active subject in the framework of a bankruptcy procedure, acting as the first point of reference.

Coming to specific forecasts, first of all it is clarified that the general objective of the same, consisting in allowing judges and curators to operate efficiently and effectively, must be pursued by targeting the pre-eminent interests of curators. The immediate aim is to facilitate the coordination of bankruptcy procedures concerning the same creditor. In particular, the guidelines aim to promote an orderly, effective, efficient and rapid management of these procedures; maximizing on a global scale the value of the assets, subject to identification and securement of the same; the exchange of information; the elimination or reduction of disputes, costs

[746]European Communication and Cooperation Guidelines for Cross-border Insolvency Developed under the aegis of the Academic Wing of INSOL Europe by Professor Bob Wessels and Professor Miguel Virgós, July 2007.

[747]Literally the text of the introduction of the guidelines speaks of agreements concerning cooperation or "protocols". European Communication and Cooperation Guidelines, op. cit., 24.

and inconveniences. It is further specified that the guidelines were not intended to prejudice the independent exercise of jurisdiction by any national court, nor to interfere with the procedural rules or ethical principles applicable to the curators in the various states, nor to grant substantial rights or to interfere with any function or duty imposed on the different actors by Regulation 1346 or by national regulations.

A series of guidelines for curators follows. First of all it is foreseen that they must be allowed to appeal to any foreign judge for the exercise of any equal rights of an internal curator. In addition, they must ("are required to") communicate with each other directly and from the moment they receive the appointment, at the initiative of the appointed trustee in the main proceedings, and respond promptly to any requests for information, as well as keep an updated record of the communications made. The language of communications is decided by the curators themselves on the basis of considerations of convenience and cost containment. As regards in particular the exchange of information, it is expected that they must provide each other quickly and completely with any relevant information, periodically updated, in particular concerning the existence and progress of the insolvency proceedings for which they were appointed, possibly after the conclusion of specific agreements to protect confidentiality where sensitive data are involved. Furthermore, they must inform the judges, within the limits of what is permitted or required by their national laws, of any considerable development relating to foreign proceedings. Foreign administrators must be empowered to use all lawful means to obtain all the information that would be available to a creditor or a trustee in any national proceeding. The cooperation between the curators is also necessary in order to reduce the possible incompatibility between the proceedings and increase the chances of a successful outcome, whether one has opted for a reorganization of the activity of the insolvent company, or whether it has come to a liquidation of the same, in which case the sale of the assets must take place in a single solution. In this regard, it is also foreseen that the curators of the secondary proceedings must indicate to the administrator of the main proceedings which, in their opinion, is the best way to proceed with regard to the branch in relation to which they were appointed and that the final decision it will then be taken in concert by all of them. As a means to implement cooperation, the conclusion of agreements or protocols ("agreements or protocols") is suggested and if these protocols contain no provision for a specific case, the curators will have to act bearing in mind the general objective referred to above. In principle, that is to guarantee an effective and efficient management of the procedure. All the curators must be informed in good time of any hearing or any provision that concerns them. When a trustee can not appear personally before the judge, the judge must, before taking any action, invite the first to send his observations.

Another group of guidelines is dedicated to issues in a broader sense of the process. It is expected that procedures are established in each order for the authentication of documents and the transmission of the same; that the judges are encouraged, if necessary, to authorize in the course of the proceeding the use of a language other than the national one, provided that this does not cause prejudice to any of the parties and to accept the documents relating to communications in the language decided and used by the curators, without requesting a translation; or at least that the provisions issued in the framework of bankruptcy proceedings are, within the limits of what is permitted by national procedural rules, also published in a language other than that of the trial.

Finally, the sixteenth guideline which, despite the silence of the Regulation on the matter, contains provisions concerning the cooperation between courts deserves attention. This particularity is justified in the comment to the guidelines on the one hand through the reference to some judgments of state bodies that have considered that even the judges should comply with the provisions of article 31 of Regulation[748] as well as to some states in which the cooperation between judges in cases of international bankruptcy was effectively implemented; on the other hand, through the consideration that cooperation between judges would be implicit in the system of Regulation[749], expression of judicial cooperation in civil

---

[748]In particular, the decision of the Oberlandesgericht in Vienna of 9 November 2004 concerning the Stojevic case (28 R 225/04w), in Neue Zeitschrift für das Recht der Insolvenz und Sanierung, 2005, pp. 56ss. The Austrian courts have expressed themselves in the sense that according to the prevailing opinion and also in accordance with the UNCITRAL Model Law the judges are also required to cooperate with each other.

[749]Recital 22 in particular states that: "This Regulation should provide for the immediate

matters, as well as in the principles of mutual assistance and loyal collaboration between Member States referred to in art. 10 TCE[750]. The guideline in question provides that the judges must allow the achievement of the general objective of ensuring the conduct of the proceedings in an effective and efficient manner; to seek a shared solution to any doubts concerning the application of the guidelines or other agreements or protocols concluded in accordance with the guidelines themselves; evaluate the possibility of appointing the same person as a trustee in the various open procedures or appointing the curator or co-curator of the secondary procedure a representative (literally "agent") of the trustee appointed in the main proceedings; in general cooperate with each other

---

recognition of decisions relating to the opening, conduct and closure of an insolvency proceedings falling within its scope, as well as decisions closely linked to this insolvency procedure. The automatic recognition should therefore have as a consequence that the effects that the law of the State of opening of the procedure involves for it extend to the remaining Member States. The recognition of decisions by the courts of the Member States should be based on the principle of mutual trust. In this respect, the reasons for non-recognition should be reduced to the minimum necessary. According to this principle, the conflict which arises when the courts of two Member States consider themselves competent to open a main insolvency procedure should also be resolved. The decision of the judge who is the first to open the procedure should be recognized in the other Member States, without the latter having the right to review the decision of the first judge". For further details and analysis see: L. ATHANASSIOU, Maritime cross-border insolvency: Under the European insolvency, ed. Routledge, London & New York, 2017. C. TOKATLIDES, Retails depositor and retail investor protection under European Union law. In the event of financial institution failure, ed. Routledge, London & New York, 2017, pp. 56ss. R. MILES GOODE, Principles of corporate insolvency law, Sweet & Maxwell, London, 2011.

[750]For more analysis and details see: A. HARTKAMP, C. SIBURGH, W. DEVROE, Cases, materials and text on European Union law and private law, hart Publishing, Oxford & Oregon, Portland, 2017, pp. 282ss. K. LENAERTS, I. MASELIS, K. GUTMAN, European Union procedural law, Oxford University Press, Oxford, 2014, pp. 133ss. M. WIERZBOWSKI, A. GUBRYNOWICZ, International investment law for the 21st century, Oxford University Press, Oxford, 2015. A.H. TÜRK, Judicial review in European Union law, Edward Elgar Publishers, Cheltenham, 2010. L. WOODS, P. WATSON, Steiner & Woods European Union law, Oxford University Press, Oxford, 2017, pp. 37ss. C. BARNARD, S. PEERS, European Union law, Oxford University Press, Oxford, 2017, pp. 788ss. E. BERRY, M.Y. HOMEWOOD, B. BOGUSZ, Complete European Union law. Texts, cases and materislas, Oxford University Press, Oxford, 2013. G. CONWAY, European Union law, ed. Routledge, London & New York, 2015. F. NICOLA, B. DAVIES, European Union law stories, Cambridge University Press, Cambridge, 2017. J. USHERWOOD, S. PINDER, The European Union. A very short introduction, Oxford University Press, Oxford, 2018. J.L. DA CRUZ VILAÇA, European Union law and integration. Twenty years of judicial application of European Union law, Hart Publishing, Oxford & Oregon, Portland, 2014.

directly or through the curators or other body appointed for this purpose; urge the trustees to periodically report on the ways in which the guidelines themselves and any protocols concluded are applied as well as on any practical problems encountered.

16.The relevant protocols related to the bankruptcy of commercial companies.

The protocols concluded in relation to the failures of commercial companies are quite numerous: About forty-five are published on the website of the International Insolvency Institute. Previously, a list had been drawn up by the American Law Institute for the preparation of the Transnational Insolvency Project, updated in April 1998, reproduced in an appendix to an article by Leonard published in the American Bankruptcy Institute Journal[751]. Some of these are particularly relevant for the present study, representing, as already pointed out, of the "leading cases" and having provided a starting point for the solution of numerous critical issues presented above all on the occasion of the failure of the Lehman Brothers group[752].

17.The first protocol concluded: The Maxwell Communication Corporation case.

In many respects, the Maxwell Communication Corporation case was a novelty in terms of transnational insolvency. First of all, the related protocol was the first global successful distribution plan that has ever been concluded on a worldwide basis, thus contributing to the diffusion of a form of transnational cooperation, formalized and approved by the judges, between curators operating in the of two main bankruptcy procedures open, in two different jurisdictions, with respect to the same company[753]. Furthermore, it was the first case in which a British company subject to an administration procedure in the United Kingdom was simultaneously

[751]LEONARD, The way ahead, cit., 12 ss.

[752]J. ALTMAN, A test case in international bankruptcy in international bankruptcy protocols: The Lehman Brothers insolvency, op. cit.

[753]E. WARREN, L. WESTBROOK, Court-to-court negotiation, op. cit. J.ALTMAN, A test case in international bankruptcy in international bankruptcy protocols: The Lehman Brothers insolvency, op. cit.

subjected to a proceeding under the terms of Chapter 11 in the United States[754].

Maxwell Communication Corporation plc (MCC) was a parent company, as we said, English, controlling more than 400 companies worldwide. Following some substantial financial difficulties, which arose immediately after the death of the group owner, Ian Robert Maxwell, which occurred in November 1991, the MCC began a voluntary procedure in New York on 16 December 1991, pursuant to Chapter 11, the next day, he requested and obtained the opening in London of a "administration" procedure under the UK Insolvency Act. On the one hand, US-based subsidiaries accounted for around 75% of the group's assets, and administrators hoped that the US bankruptcy favor towards reorganization plans would offer a good chance of getting out of a crisis situation. On the other hand, the initiative before the British courts had been undertaken in order to protect the group from the claims of local curators. The situation that was created was therefore that of the same parent company simultaneously subject to two main insolvency proceedings and therefore also hypothetically, the subject of conflicting provisions issued by the judges of one or the other state.

Considering that the conduct of two parallel proceedings in relation to the same company would entail innumerable disputes and very high costs, in order to avoid the emergence of any possible conflict and to facilitate and speed up the reorganization procedure of the MCC, the US bankruptcy, Tina L. Brozman, appointed a "Special Examiner", giving him the CDs "Expanded powers" under sections 1104 and 1106 of Bankruptcy Code and instructing it to engage in order to harmonize the proceedings. Similarly, the English court Hoffmann authorized the local administrators in the same direction [755].

After extensive negotiations between New York and London, the directors appointed by the English courts (the Joint Administrators) and the American Examiner signed a protocol[756], approved by the British

---

[754]E.D. FLASCHEN, R.J. SILVERMAN, Cross-border insolvency cooperation Protocols, op. cit.

[755]For further details see: G.W. NEWTON, Bankruptcy and insolvency accounting, ed. Wiley & Sons, New York, 2010, pp. 180ss.

[756]Cross-Border Insolvency Protocol and Order Approving Protocol in Re Maxwell

courts on 31 December 1991[757] and by the United States on 15 January 1992[758], thus gaining strength of law within the specific Maxwell case. It was decided to pursue stage-by-stage coordination: The initial protocol should have dealt with stabilizing the situation and securing the existing assets, while questions relating to the way the procedure was concluded, the possibility of exit and the methods of distribution of the remaining assets to the curators would have been defined later, except for some general indication. Beyond the specific content, the protocol became the basis for future coordination and future co-operation between the parties.

In the protocol the group companies were divided into two groups: "The M & O Group" and "the Other Subsidiaries", depending on the type of activity carried out. These two groups were joined by the debtor company controlling the entire group, i.e. the MCC. David Shaffer, the group's director already in the period before the crisis, was guaranteed the possibility to continue to supervise the trend and maintain some of the previously held positions, but the Examiner and the Joint Administrators still reserved the right to appeal the bankruptcy judge, if they encounter difficulties in achieving the objectives set in the protocol itself. The remaining composition of the boards of directors of some of the group companies was determined on the basis of an agreement between the Joint Administrators and the Examiner, and an opinion of the parent company. It was also established that, in relation to the subsidiaries of the MCC and controlling the M & O Group, the Joint Administrators could, in case of necessity, initiate an insolvency procedure or other similar procedures, but giving prior notice to the Examiner. On the one hand, the US judge consented that the directors appointed by the English judge assume the

---

Communication plc between the United States and the United Kingdom. United States Bankruptcy Court for the Southern District of New York (Hon. Tina L. Brozman), Case No. 91 B 15741, (January 15, 1992) and the High Court of Justice, Chancery Division, Companies Court, Case No. 0014001 of 1991, (December 31, 1991). For further details see: M. BODE, Le groupe international de sociètès: Le système de conflit de lois en droit comparè français et allemand, ed. Peter Lang, Bruxelles, 2010, pp. 542ss.

[757] High Court of Justice, Chancery Division, Companies Court, Case No. 0014001 of 1991.

[758] United States Bankruptcy Court, Southern District of New York, In Re Maxwell Communication Corporation plc, Debtor. Chapter 11 Case No. 91 B 15741 (TLB), Final Supplemental Order Appointing Examiner and Approving Agreement between Examiner and Joint Administrators, in Annual Survey of Bankruptcy Law, 1994-1995, pp. 96ss.

function of directors of the MCC and, on the other hand, the English judge granted the American Examiner the right to be heard before the English courts themselves[759]. Depending on the company or category of companies involved, and depending on the economic-financial relevance of the operation to be undertaken, the protocol then set up specific procedural rules for the approval of a series of ordinary and extraordinary administrative acts, which involved the parties and provided for different advertising mechanisms, from time to time. In principle, a primary role was assigned to the Joint Administrators, who sometimes had to obtain prior consent from, or make a timely notification, the Examiner or, secondly, to the US bankruptcy court. Lastly, the protocol reiterated that the ultimate goal pursued by all parties was to ensure that the plan proposed before the US Court pursuant to Chapter 11 in relation to the parent company and the proposals of the Joint Administrators provided substantially the same solution for all the companies of the M & O Group.

On the basis of the frame constituted by the first protocol, two documents formally separated and distinct were concluded in February 1993: A reorganization plan and a scheme of arrangement, which defined, in an interdependent way, the aspects previously left unresolved, that is, the methods of distribution of assets to curators and of final conclusion of proceedings, harmonizing in many ways the implementation of the relevant provisions contained in the British and US bankruptcy laws. These documents were then approved by the two judges. A single mass of assets was created from which one could draw for the satisfaction of the claims of all curators, wherever localized, who were informed of the possibility of asserting their claims with, save what is said, equal results,

[759]See, United States Bankruptcy Court, S.D. New York, 5 August 1994, In re Maxwell Communication Corporation plc, et al., Debtors. Maxwell Communication Corporation plc, by Andrew Mark Homan, Colin Graham Bird, Jonathan Guy Anthony Phillips, and Alan Rae Jamieson, its Joint Administrators, Plaintiffs, and Richard A. Gitlin, Examiner, Intervenor Plaintiff, v. Barclays Bank plc, Defendant. Maxwell Communication Corporation plc, by Andrew Mark Homan, Colin Graham Bird, Jonathan Guy Anthony Phillips, and Alan Rae Dalziel Jamieson, its Joint Administrators, and Richard A. Gitlin, Examiner, Plaintiffs, v. National Westminster Bank plc, Defendant. Maxwell Communication Corporation plc, by Andrew Mark Homan, Colin Graham Bird, Jonathan Anthony Guy Phillips, and Alan Rae Dalziel Jamieson, its Joint Administrators, Plaintiffs, v. Société Génèrale, Defendant, 170 B.R. 800, 802.

so much ahead of them to the English courts that in front of the US courts, determining case by case the appropriate forum to deal with each situation. However, curators were given the opportunity to request, in any case, opinions of experts in relation to possible differences that the management of the questions they asked, although without substantially influencing the application of substantial legal principles, could have suffer in the two holes, going to affect the amount that they could get to satisfy their claim.

The conclusion of the protocol and of the other two agreements mentioned above allowed, in the Maxwell case, to maximize the value of the assets, while at the same time satisfying the interests and expectations of both the judges and therefore of both the regulations involved. Despite the existence of a crisis situation in which the liabilities amounted substantially to double the assets, the British and US administrators found an agreement on each issue, so that no conflict arose between them that would then be resolved in giudizial way[760].

18.A protocol concluded in a liquidation case: The Inverworld case.

The Inverworld group had its head office in Texas, owned many assets in New York and concluded contracts through its subsidiaries based in the United Kingdom and the Cayman Islands[761]. Following a crisis situation, insolvency proceedings were opened against both the parent company and many subsidiaries. Also in this case, a separate insolvency management for each company would have been highly expensive, could have resulted in different solutions and would have left little active mass for curators' satisfaction. In order to avoid such inconveniences, the representatives of the various companies signed a protocol then accepted by each of the judges involved. Through it, the parties agreed to close the procedure that had been opened in the United Kingdom, however,

---

[760]Except for a question concerning the possible applicability of the US law to certain transfers made in favor of non-US banks, in the period immediately preceding the request to open insolvency proceedings.

[761]See, Cross-Border Insolvency Protocol in Re Inverworld, Inc. between United States District Court for the Western District of Texas (Hon. Frederick Biery), Case No. SA99-C0822FB, (October 22, 1999) and U.K. High Court of Justice, Chancery Division, (1999) and the Grand Court of the Cayman Island, (1999).

providing for certain conditions of treatment of the curators that had crept into it, and to entrust the resolution of the related issues to the competent courts in relation to the other two proceedings, one open in the United States, in Texas, and the other in the Cayman Islands. In particular, the US courts should have resolved all the pending issues, both in fact and in law, relating to the order of satisfaction of the various classes of curators, while the courts of the Cayman Islands should have monitored the distribution of assets to the various curators. Furthermore, each judge should have considered himself bound by the decisions of the other, so as to avoid parallel proceedings and decisions on the same question. This mechanism has allowed to solve the whole affair with costs much lower than those that would have had to be sustained if three proceedings were carried out in a parallel and independent way from one another in the different jurisdictions involved.

19.The first protocol that involved a civil law system: The Nakash case.

Joseph Nakash was a US citizen who was doing business internationally in various sectors of the economy. As part of the bankruptcy proceeding of the North American Bank, on 27 December 1993, the Jerusalem District Court recognized him as a debtor of $ 160 million, due to his role as a member of the bank's board of directors. Following this ruling, a bankruptcy proceeding against him was opened in Israel and the Israeli bankruptcy trustee initially obtained an order in the United States allowing forced execution of the assets therein. A bankruptcy procedure was then opened in the United States, in which, on 7 February 1995, Richard Gitlin was appointed Examiner and charged with drafting a protocol to harmonize and coordinate the two proceedings. This protocol was then signed by the Examiner and the Israeli curator and approved by the US judge. The Israeli judges, although without officially approving it, abided by the provisions of the same[762].

[762]Cross-Border Insolvency Protocol between the United States and Israel in Re Nakash, United States Bankruptcy Court for the Southern District of New York, Case No. 94 B 44840, (May 23, 1996) and District Court of Jerusalem, Case No. 1595/87, (May 23, 1996).

20.International cooperation in bank group failures. The liquidation of BCCI group.

The BCCI group was founded in 1972 by the Pakistani Agha Hasan Abedi, based in Luxembourg and two main offices in London and Karachi. Between 1982 and 1988 it reached the maximum expansion with a total of 417 offices in 73 States. On 5 July 1991, the formal date of the collapse of the group, the latter operated in 71 States with a structure that saw BCCI Holdings, headquartered in Luxembourg and headed by BCCI SA, one of its larger subsidiaries, also established in Luxembourg, of BCCI Overseas, based in the Cayman Islands and numerous other smaller companies and branches in the rest of the world. BCCI was then joined by the ICIC group, controlled by the first and closely connected to it for the type of activity carried out. The center of operations was initially placed in Abu Dhabi but after a short time it was transferred to London. In addition to the size and dispersion of the group companies in more than 70 States, other characteristic features related to the conduct of the transactions and the circumstances from which the bankruptcy originated must be immediately reported to have led to a significant increase in the uncertainties that normally arise they place in any bankruptcy proceedings, unpublished issues and a prospect of long and costly disputes not only against third parties but also between the different companies of the group. First of all the activities were carried out on an international scale and according to highly integrated schemes, without the possibility of distinguishing the various companies of the group in relation to the various operations undertaken; moreover, the inadequacy in the keeping of the accounting records, the widespread frauds and the numerous irregularities found in the company management made the determination of the financial situation of the group uncertain.

21.(Follows) Cooperation between the curators.

The cooperation between the subjects involved in the various bankruptcies and the coordination of the activities undertaken in relation to each company of the group were immediately felt as fundamental especially in order to protect and maximize assets and prevent an increase in liabilities. The beginning of the story must be traced back to 5 July 1991, when the Bank of England, the Institut Monétaire Luxembourgeois and the Cayman Islands supervisory authorities, following various reports received from rating agencies, coordinated the cessation of activities of the group companies established in the respective jurisdictions. In response to this, the authorities of the other States in which the group owned subsidiaries also took steps as far as they were responsible. Between 5 and 22 July 1991 in Luxembourg, England and the Cayman Islands some professionals of the Deloitte group were appointed curators, so as to facilitate cooperation between them. The British curators were charged with recovering the assets of BCCI SA in any state they were in; similarly, the curators of BCCI Overseas should have done the same with the assets of this and the other affiliated companies within their competence. As for Luxembourg, the Commissaires de Surveillance were responsible for protecting the assets of BCCI Holdings and BCCI SA wherever they are located.

The cooperation initially took place informally, facilitated, as mentioned, by the fact that many of the curators were members of the same company, Deloitte. The circumstance that was mentioned last also prevented the emergence of conflicts of interest between the British and the Luxembourg curators on the assets of BCCI SA. From the beginning, the liquidation commissioners in the Cayman Islands, Luxembourg and England worked closely together, despite the obstacle of the rules on bank secrecy in the individual states[763] that prevented a free flow of information. Contacts were made with the local curators responsible for the various subsidiaries and affiliates and branches.

In principle, monthly meetings were held between the curators and some expert groups of particular subjects were formed, most of them initially active at the Abu Dhabi headquarters, where the greatest amount of information on the group companies was present, together with the headquarters London. Among these groups, it is worth mentioning that one who favors the coordination of, and planning, the different activities to be conducted on a global scale and the one charged with determining the group's liabilities and ensuring that all curators, regardless of jurisdiction in which they were found, were treated in a just and fair manner and that,

---

[763]R. ANAT ADMANTI, M. HELLWIG, The bankers' new clothes: What's wrong with banking and what to do about it, Princeton University Press, Princeton, 2013.

at the same time, they did not make the same claims in more than one order. This task was particularly complicated due to the difficulties mentioned above with regard to the possibility of exchanging information, the widespread practice of intra-group loans and the high number of claims made by curators.

It soon became clear that liquidation on a global scale would be the best solution from the point of view of the interests of the curators of the group companies. To this end, the cooperation agreement was formalized in the "BCCI and ICIC Pooling Agreements" and in other minor agreements[764], then approved by the judges of the main states involved. They remained open to the membership of the liquidators' commissioners of all the other states in which the BCCI group operated and, in fact, over time, the initial participants joined the curators of Bahrain, China, Cyprus and Japan. Subsequently, the UAE trustees also participated in the agreements after wider agreements were undertaken with the Abu Dhabi government. On the other hand, less formal agreements were occasionally concluded with the curators of other jurisdictions, such as Gibraltar and Hong Kong.

However, there were also numerous jurisdictions whose curators decided to operate independently, among which the United States in particular were reported to have taken a strong attitude of "ring fencing"[765]. This naturally created some difficulties in the coordination between "cooperating" failures on the one hand and "non-cooperating" failures on the other. By way of example, the possibility of offsetting debit and credit relationships belonging to a specific natural or legal person towards the group was undermined by the possibility that it had relations with several companies or branches thereof, some of which "cooperating"; to allow curators to assert their claim directly in bankruptcy proceedings opened in England, in Luxembourg or in the Cayman Islands towards BCCI SA or BCCI Overseas, despite the fact that they had dealings with another company or branch, entailed difficulties in ascertaining the

---

[764]"Company/Branch Pooling Agreements; Global Cost and Recovery Sharing Agreement; Paying agency Agreement". It is interesting to note that the term "protocol" is never used in the context of the liquidation of the BCCI group.

[765]E. WARREN, L. WESTBROOK, Court-to-court negotiation, op. cit.

goodness of the claim itself, having to access information not immediately available; moreover, in the context of the cooperating procedures, the amount of the amount due to each creditor was difficult to determine if they had already been partially satisfied in the context of independent proceedings; finally, it was necessary to reject the claims made by the trustees of some companies not taking part in the agreements against the British, Luxemburgish or Cayman Islands bankruptcies.

Ex post it can be said that the cooperation in the case of bankruptcy BCCI has allowed to determine the overall financial situation of the group, the entity of the assets of each of the companies that composed it and to manage satisfactorily the mutual claims of the latter; to define a common position towards majority shareholders; to find and share evidence to support claims against third parties; to coordinate and share resources, including human resources; to plan a global liquidation.

22.(Follows) Some special agreements.

The "BCCI Pooling Agreements" was concluded on 20 February 1992 by the curators of the Cayman Islands competent in relation to the BCCI Overseas, the British and the competent banks of BCCI in relation to BCCI SA. The agreement provided that the assets of all the participating companies and branches were channeled into a single fund; that all curators were satisfied in an equal percentage; that the participating companies renounce to assert their claims against the others; that any company in the BCCI group could decide to take part.

The ICIC Pooling Agreement was concluded and approved by the courts of Luxembourg, the British and the Cayman Islands three years later, in January 1995, due to the close integration of the activities of the BCCI and ICIC groups.

Another agreement to remember is the "Company/Branch Pooling Agreements"[766] which was attended by several companies of the group based in ten different countries. Under this agreement, the curators of each of the participating companies were authorized to assert their claim in any of the jurisdictions in which these companies were established, regardless

---

[766]W. GRANT, K. GRAHAM WILSON (ed.). The consequences of the global financial crisis-The rhetoric of reform and regulation, Oxford University Press, Oxford,2014.

of the state in which the claim arose, and would be satisfied in the same percentage, except what has already been received in other proceedings not participating in the agreement.

Finally, the "Board of Liquidators", an informal structure that gathers the curators of all the companies of the group for the accomplishment of various activities, includes the conclusion of an agreement on global projects, the definition of objectives and strategies; liquidation and the assessment of any progress with respect to the objectives set; the definition of a spending plan and the evaluation of actual costs compared to the pre-set ones; cross-examination of the financial information relating to the BCCI and ICIC companies; finding solutions to the various problems and coordinating the activities to be undertaken in the numerous jurisdictions concerned. I would like to point out that the decisions taken by the Board of Liquidators did not bind the dissenting curators and that this, like all the agreements mentioned above, also worked on a voluntary basis.

23.The failure of the Lehman Brothers group.

Before addressing in detail the events that concerned the bankruptcy of the Lehman Brothers group, it must first clarify whether this company can be considered a bank. The doubt arises, if nothing else, following a decree issued on 17 December 2009 by the court of Milan[767], in the context of a dispute initiated by the E.C., M.G., G.P., F.R., P.S., D.S. and S.S., requesting the satisfaction of a work credit accrued towards the Lehman Brothers International Italian Branch, a branch company of Lehman Brothers International-(Europe) which was subject to an administration procedure in England. In particular, the plaintiffs requested the opening in Italy of a secondary insolvency proceeding pursuant to art. 27 of Regulation (CE) n. 1346/2000. The court of Milan declared the appeal inadmissible, considering this regulation to be inapplicable, pursuant to art. 1, second paragraph, of the same which defines its scope. According to the Court, "in this case, the relevant exemption is the one

[767]Tribunal of Milan, decree of 17 December 2009, E.C., M.G., G.P., F.R., P.S., D.S. e S.S. c. Lehman Brothers International Italian Branch e Lehman Brothers International-(Europe), in Rivista di Diritto Internazionale Privato e Processuale, 2010, pp. 987ss.

referred to investment companies"[768] and therefore not the one referred to credit institutions. Therefore, the question posed in principle can be reformulated as follows: In the common language, the term "banks" refers only to credit institutions or even "investment firms that provide services that involve the holding of funds or third party securities"? The same doubt exists if instead of the Italian terminology we refer to the English one: Both the "credit institutions" and the "investment firms" can be generically indicated by the term "banks"?

The answer is positive, that is to say that the term banks is generally used to refer both to credit institutions and investment firms and therefore also to Lehman Brothers, which inter alia the Court of Milan has qualified as an investment, can be considered a "bank". This conclusion derives from an analysis of linguistic praxis developed in the sector. First of all, many documents that in the title declare to deal with the insolvency of banking groups, such as for example that of IMF entitled: "Resolution of Cross-Border Banks-A proposed Framework for enhanced coordination"[769] or that of the Basel Committee entitled "Report and Recommendations of the Cross-border Bank Resolution Group "also deal with the Lehman Brothers case. Likewise, the proposed Directive "establishing a framework for the reorganization and resolution of crises by credit institutions and investment firms"[770], distinguishes, however, already in the title, between "credit institutions" and "investment firms" but then indicates both generically with the term "banks".

24.(Follows) The structure of the group and the beginning of the crisis.

The Lehman Brothers group, before the crisis that hit it at the end of 2008, was, by size, the fourth largest investment bank in the United States, and one of the largest financial services companies in the world[771].

---

[768] J.H. BINDER, D. SINGH, Bank resolution. The European regime, Oxford University Press, Oxford, 2016.

[769]J.H. BINDER, Resolution: Concepts, requirements and tools, in J.H. BINDER, D. SINGH, Bank resolution. The European regime, op. cit.

[770]J.H. BINDER, Resolution: Concepts, requirements and tools, in J.H. BINDER, D. SINGH, Bank resolution. The European regime, op. cit.

[771]Official representatives and other participating affiliates pursuant to the cross-border insolvency protocol for the Lehman Brothers group of companies, Report of Activities

It had a headquarter in New York and regional offices in London (LBIE) and Tokyo, and operated in at least 40 states around the world, through over 900 entities. The entire group was centrally managed by the parent company, Lehman Brothers Holding Inc. ("LBHI"), which exercised a control over the overall financial resources, through a system that allowed the collection and consolidation of revenues deriving from activities of the various group companies and then use them in fulfilling the obligations contracted in the performance of the overall activity. This system guaranteed the parent company control over the financial resources of the entire conglomerate, the possibility of formulating forecasts on the economic performance of the same, and to draw up truthful reports, in compliance with the legislative requirements of the various states concerned. This type of management determined numerous interdependencies and connections, also internationally, among the multiple companies of the group, which were in constant contact to exchange information and work together.

After a US part of the group (the LBI) was bought by Barclays, the LBHI and some of its subsidiaries, on 15 September 2008, depositing in a crisis situation, voluntarily deposited before the United States Bankruptcy Court an application to open a insolvency proceedings pursuant to Chapter 11. The inability of LBHI to fulfill the obligations assumed by the group companies, its subsidiaries or affiliates, then determined, in the days and weeks immediately following, the opening of a plurality of insolvency proceedings, both main and secondary to many group companies in the rest of the world. At 15 January 2010, the total number of cases opened was 80, with 16 different companies in charge of managing the entities involved, so much so that it was repeatedly observed that never before had the failure of a group of such dimensions occurred.

At least at first and, in particular, until the protocol referred to in the following paragraph had been concluded, this phenomenon had occurred, as discussed in Chap. I, for which the management of the crisis

---

through January 15, 2010. United States Bankruptcy Court, Southern District of New York, In re Lehman Brothers Holdings Inc., et al., Debtors, Chapter 11 Case No.08-13555 (JMP) (Jointly Administered), Order Approving the Proposed Cross-Border Insolvency Protocol for the Lehman Brothers Group of Companies, 17 June 2009.

of a multinational group having the characteristics seen above on the basis of the principle of territoriality could not but lead to an upheaval of the structure with which the group worked before the crisis, fragmenting it into many small entities that do not they had never operated independently from each other and subjected them to so many bankruptcy laws as were the legal systems involved[772].

25.(Follows) Negotiations and conclusion of the protocol.

Through meetings and exchanges of ideas that took place in the month of October 2008 among the various curators of the companies, it was recognized, by some of the latter, the need to cooperate with each other in the management of the crisis, at least on some central and common issues, as well as promoting a form of cooperation between the various judges involved, in order to allow, even on the part of these, effective management of the matter and the adoption of compliant decisions. For at least three months, delicate negotiations were conducted and various difficulties were faced, given the fact, already highlighted, that never before had a protocol been signed in relation to a group of companies of this size and involving such a large number of jurisdictions. The Lehman case extended over sixteen different jurisdictions, both common law and civil law, among which there were also many Asian, foreign, until then, the practice of concluding protocols or other similar instruments. In addition to reasons linked to cultural differences, even legal obstacles prevented all the bankruptcy trustees from being able to participate quietly in negotiations, probably having some of them the fear of incurring any sanctions or responsibilities related to the public nature of the office held. Thus, the Trustee company SIPA[773], a member of the United States in the management of Lehman Brothers Inc., declared itself prepared to participate in the conclusion of a protocol, but only in order to exchange information and data; for the United Kingdom, PricewaterhouseCoopers

---

[772]In the United States, all proceedings opened pursuant to Chapter 11 had been merged into one proceeding, pursuant to Rule 1015 (b) of the Federal Rules of Bankruptcy Procedure.

[773]M.L. COOK, Bankruptcy litigation manual, op. cit.

(PwC) was reluctant to create a precedent and worried about a hypothetical incompatibility between such action and the official role it played; for companies in Asia, Australia and other UK companies other than those operated by PwC, KPMG and PPB Advisory declared themselves fully available to cooperate; finally, for Japan, Oh-Ebashi expressed his desire not to conclude the protocol. Particularly negative effects resulted from the failure to participate in the PwC protocol, for the United Kingdom, since Lehman Brothers International Europe was essentially the driving force of all the companies of the group based in Europe. As of 15 January 2010, ten of the sixteen restructuring companies had signed the protocol. Two others, in charge of the management of the companies in Japan (the Oh-Ebashi just mentioned) and Bermuda, although they had not signed it, took part in some meetings in which they discussed the methods for implementing the objectives identified in it.

A version of the protocol was circulated on the afternoon of February 10, 2009 among the curators who controlled most of the group's assets outside the United States. The following day, 11 February 2009, Alvarez & Marsal presented and presented to the United States Bankruptcy Court-Southern District of New York a protocol proposal, a report of the negotiations that had led to it and some general data on the situation of the companies of the group. From the presentation it transpires that, according to Alvarez & Marsal, the ideal protocol should have been inspired by the principle of universality, for reasons related to the benefits, proper to the same. According to it, the entire failure of the Lehman group would have been managed in a unitary way, trying to coordinate the different situations arising from the simultaneous filing of a very high number of claims in front of as many courts. However, this result seemed unattainable even in the eyes of Alvarez & Marsal, aware of the fact that states traditionally want to maintain their own sphere of independence, sovereignty and authority, in order to protect local interests[774]. In the protocol proposal, among the forecasts that require foreign judges and curators to cooperate and exchange information with each other, the provisions of articles 25 and 26 of the Model Law UNCITRAL and sections 1525 and 1526 of the U.S. Bankruptcy Code, which, moreover,

[774]M.L. COOK, Bankruptcy litigation manual, op. cit.

take over the former[775] almost entirely and formed the basis for the Bankruptcy Court's approval of the Lehman protocol. Finally, we note the difficulties that could have arisen in the approval and implementation of the protocol by the judges of civil law, since they are not expressly authorized to operate in this sense by law; in this regard, however, two cases are mentioned, Nakash and United Pan-Europe Communications NV, in which the judges of both Israel and the Netherlands, and therefore two civil law systems, had acted in accordance with the provisions of a protocol that had been concluded by the curators, even without ever officially approving it.

The first comments to the version circulated on February 10th were received, in the following weeks, by the curators of Hong Kong, Singapore and Australia. On 11 March 2009, the group companies subject to the ex Chapter 11 procedure and the parent company discussed the contents of the protocol with the German and Dutch trustees. Other curators still then sent their impressions.

The legal obstacles that were identified initially appeared insurmountable. However, gradually, through negotiations, an agreement was reached on some broad issues of principle. Numerous versions were circulated with the aim of reaching a compromise result and finally reached an agreement on the protocol, in the version which is published today, dated 12 May 2009 and entitled "Cross-Border Insolvency Protocol for the Lehman Brothers Group of Companies ", and the immediate subsequent execution of the same by a first group of curators.

26.(Follows) The request for approval of the Protocol to the U.S. Bankruptcy Court.

On May 26, 2009, LBHI and other affiliated companies that had been subjected to a proceeding pursuant to Chapter 11, represented by Richard Krasnow of Weil's law firm, Gotshal & Manges LLP, filed a formal request ("motion") to the judge James Peck of the United States Bankruptcy Court-Southern District of New York to approve the protocol and adopt the guidelines attached thereto, or the applicable Guidelines to court-to-court communications in ALI cross-border cases.

---

[775]As well as the section 1527 resumes the art. 27 of the Model Law.

Already in the request it was made clear that, on the one hand, the expectations in the protocol were numerous and that, on the other hand, it was not a legally binding document, but a declaration of intent and guidelines. Therefore, the same did not create any obligation or burden on the parties nor was it intended as if it were to be executed against any of them. The protocol, rather, we read in the request, provided a framework to facilitate cooperation, in a scenario in which there was no international treaty on bankruptcy that could itself serve as a framework. The hope was that, thanks to the context created by the protocol, further agreements could be reached on more specific issues, in order to avoid the passage of years between expensive intragroup disputes on the one hand and insolvency management on the other. In this regard, the objective was to organize, once the curators had signed the protocol and obtained the approval of the same by the judges and/or the Committee of curators, a series of meetings and teleconferences in order to reach an agreement on further issues. From this point of view, when the request for the approval of the protocol was presented to the US court, a meeting was scheduled for mid-July of that same year, aimed at highlighting the major differences, both procedural that of a substantial nature, existing between the different procedures and to analyze in detail the intra-group economic and financial relations. The protocol remained open for further subscriptions and, in any case, any company in the Lehman group could take part, either directly or through its insolvency administrator, in the meetings organized within the framework of the same, without being a signatory, thus participating substantially, at least on an informal basis, to the coordination efforts promoted by the same. The request for approval, after having offered an overview of the contents of the protocol, closed by underlining the broad economic justifications, traditionally adduced, connected to the acceptance of the same. The U.S. Bankruptcy Court for the Southern District of New York upheld the request on June 17, 2009[776].

27.(Follows) The content of the protocol.

It must first be noted that the validity of all the provisions of the

[776]United States Bankruptcy Court, Southern District of New York, In re Lehman Brothers Holdings Inc., op. cit.

protocol was expressly subject to the condition of compatibility of the same with the laws applicable from time to time. In particular, nothing in the protocol had to be interpreted in such a way as to interfere with the fulfillment of the duties and obligations of the curators or with the exercise of the powers attributed to them by the law. This provision is of utmost importance given the large number of parties involved and the nature of the protocol's private instrument: Without it, the parties would have been reluctant to sign it[777].

The Protocol preliminarily specified its nature of declaration of intent and contain guidelines aimed at minimizing costs and maximizing revenues, for the benefit of all curators. Therefore it is not meant to be performed in a binding way towards the parties, nor to impose on them any burden or obligation in contrast with the provisions of the applicable rules or with the objective of preservation of the active mass of the debtor. The overall aim pursued by the protocol, clarified at the outset, was to facilitate the coordination of the various open bankruptcy procedures and to create a basis for legitimizing judges, curators and curators' committees to cooperate and communicate with each other in the administration. proceedings, in the interest of curators of the entire group. All the curators would have to coordinate and cooperate in a reciprocal way, eventually concluding further bilateral protocols, to facilitate communication between them, the judges and the committees of the curators. Other bilateral agreements could then be concluded in relation to matters concerning only a part of the debtors, with the commitment, however, to keep the other parties informed of this, especially in cases where similar aims were pursued with those of the protocol itself. The legal basis for these further agreements would have been established, as already mentioned, by the main protocol. The parties undertook to behave in good faith in order to achieve the ultimate goal of maximizing total capital. The proceedings should have been managed in an orderly, effective and efficient manner in order to reduce the costs associated with them and thus maximize returns for curators. The protocol also aimed to promote the exchange, between the parties, of all necessary or relevant information and

---

[777]J. ALTMAN, A test case in international bankruptcy in international bankruptcy protocols: The Lehman Brothers insolvency, op. cit.

the international coordination of the activities of the same, in order to avoid a multiplication of efforts and initiatives. At the same time, the interests of the various curators should have been safeguarded, the fact that each proceeding remained regulated by the lex fori and the independence, sovereignty and autonomy of each of the judges involved, in the name of the principle of comity. Further aims of the protocol were to identify, reorganize, preserve and maximize the value of the assets of the group companies; coordinating the various claims made by curators in an efficient and transparent manner and, in particular, in defining a coherent and weighted method for the calculation and assignment of infragroup claims, so as to avoid the arising of disputes relating to them. Even if mentioned at the end, it is precisely the latter central question, due to its importance; in this sense, in addition to the protocol, the defenders of the US companies expressed themselves in the request for approval presented to the U.S. Bankruptcy Court.

Bankruptcy trustees and curators, according to the protocol, had locus standi in every open procedure in relation to the insolvency of the group, both in front of the judges and in official meetings organized according to the applicable law. However, they would have been subject to the jurisdiction of a specific judge only in relation to the matter for which they had appeared before it, unless the protocol provided otherwise or that the editor specifically specified the opposite. This provision is fundamental because it is aimed at protecting the sovereignty of the various States[778]. In the event that a trustee could not appear, personally or represented by a lawyer, the signing parties of the protocol should have consented that he could in any case send his observations in good time, provided that he used written communication means and that a copy of these communications should be made available to all interested parties.

Entering in detail the specific provisions related to communications, we must first clarify that there are three types of provisions: Those between curators, those between judges and those between committees of curators. The curators should have kept each other informed of any relevant information or development concerning debtors

[778]J.ALTMAN, A test case in international bankruptcy in international bankruptcy protocols: The Lehman Brothers insolvency, op. cit.

or proceedings, and consent, where possible, to an exchange of information. This in the context of what they are authorized to divulge from the law that regulates the work, even if the protocol was in any case concerned to protect the confidentiality of the information disseminated and even if it was expected that interested parties could sign special agreements of confidentiality. Any confidential information could not be passed on to third parties, unless there was consent from the party from whom the information came or was not required by law or by a judge. The approval of the protocol by the judges would constitute a further formal confirmation of the fact that any information exchanged would maintain its nature of qualified information. Always in a spirit of collaboration, the curators, if they were in possession of documents concerning a company of the group managed by another curator, would have to work to ensure that they were transmitted to it. Furthermore, they should have coordinated each other in relation to the investigative activities. As for the communications between the judges, they should have occurred, as already mentioned, on the basis of the guidelines drawn up by the American Law Institute and attached to the protocol, where the same were applicable, recognized and approved by the judges themselves. In the event of a discrepancy between the provisions of the protocol and the provisions of the guidelines, the former would prevail. Finally, as regards the communications between the curators' committees, the protocol merely provided that confidential information could be exchanged between them, after the conclusion of appropriate confidentiality agreements.

The next part of the protocol is dedicated to the methods of asset management. If the trustee of a group company was aware, because it was informed by another trustee, that it had the material availability of an asset of substantial interest to another group company, it should consult that other trustee before selling or otherwise dispose of it; make any decision about the employees involved in it or start any judicial or out-of-court proceedings that may affect it. In the event that a trustee deems that a specific good, transferred to another company of the group, was of particular importance, from an economic or juridical point of view, for the company of which he is engaged, or in the case in which he believed that between the assets that are administered there is one that actually belongs to another mass of assets, this curator should cooperate with the other parties in determining who actually owns that property and in providing all relevant information; once the property of the property is ascertained, it should cooperate to transfer it to its rightful owner. The cooperation between curators should also have been aimed at maximizing the value of a relevant asset for several companies in the group. If then a trustee had a particular interest in an asset belonging to a company administered by another trustee, he could, with the agreement of the same, grant a loan in order to preserve this asset and maximize its value. If the asset was later sold and it derives a revenue, the trustee who financed the maintenance should receive a portion of the proceeds. All the foregoing forecasts, concerning the methods of asset management, should have been, where appropriate, approved by the competent court or by the curators' Committee, according to the provisions of local laws.

Then we move on to the regulation of the methods according to which the curators could have asserted their claims. It is envisaged that, if several proceedings were opened against the same debtor, the competent receiver indicated in which procedure a specific request should have been filed. Without prejudice to privileged claims or to real rights of curators, the trustees would have to organize the distribution of assets in such a way as to ensure that a creditor, whose claim had already been satisfied in a proceeding, was not again satisfied in a second procedure. The curators would have had to worry about fixing, as far as possible, identical terms for the filing of applications by curators and, in general, for the entire process of management of the same.

28.(Follows) The management of infragroup claims.

In this way we arrive at the clearly more important part of the protocol, that is the one relating to the management of infragroup claims. The curators of the various companies had been invited to seek an agreement, aimed at establishing a single accounting register, which could form the basis for the management of the various infragroup claims. The data contained in that register should have been considered prima facie valid until proven otherwise. The trustees would then have to conduct negotiations in good faith between them in order to reach an agreement on any differences originally existing in the respective registers in relation to infragroup claims and, if they could not reach such agreement, only after the issuance of a formal declaration in this sense, they could have submitted their dispute to the competent court.

It was then necessary to establish, in agreement between the various trustees, committees of curators and tribunals, a committee that supervised the proceedings and tried to find a consensual solution to settle the differences existing in the accounting records of the various companies of the group, as concerns precisely the claims between them. To this end, already in the request for approval of the protocol the debtors had asked Bankruptcy Court to validate the appointment of one or more members of the Committee, which should have indicated the procedural rules, the calculation criteria and the evidence that it would have intended to use in order to reach the consensual solution referred to above. Special provisions are envisaged for the intragroup claims deriving from the possible signing of derivative contracts: The amount of the compensable damages would have been determined by the Committee, on the basis of a calculation method previously established by the same. The procedures and criteria defined in this way, both for ordinary claims and for derivative contracts, should have been submitted by each director to their respective courts and, if this had been requested, also to the curators' committees, so that they could use them to resolve any infragroup claims. The curators would also have undertaken to submit to the respective courts the results of the investigations carried out by the Committee. Finally, any objections raised by the parties in relation to the calculation criteria established by the Committee or to the results obtained by the latter should have been examined by all the curators.

29.(Follows) Transitional provisions.

Among the closing forecasts, particular mention is made of the one entitled “comity”, which reiterates the independence of each of the courts involved and the exclusive competence of the same in relation to each issue submitted to them and the work of the curator: No provision of the protocol should have been perceived as an element of interference with the jurisdiction of the various judges involved or with the rules governing the work of the curators.

Each trustee should have made sure that the liquidation or reorganization plans presented by it were compatible with those presented by the other curators, but this did not entail the automatic approval of such plans or a waiver of any objections to them. The curators would also have to cooperate in good faith in carrying out all the necessary and appropriate actions and efforts to implement and implement the protocol. Any request for provision contrary to the provisions of the protocol should have been notified by the receiver of origin to the other trustees and to the committees of curators or shareholders.

The protocol would have been effective when it was signed by all parties originally contracting and approved, where necessary, by the competent courts or by the various and any committees. It would remain in force with respect to each trustee until: a) The conclusion of the procedure in which he operates; b) the issue of a provision by the competent court in relation to that provision, or, where required, the approval of the extinction of the protocol by the committees, after it has been established that, within that specific procedure , all the objectives set in the protocol had been achieved.

The protocol remained open for the signature of any other curators who wanted it, according to a procedure established in the same, which should have also applied in the case of modification of the content. Even the trustees who had not signed it would have been able to comply with what is provided for, but this did not give rise to the same rights, since the protocol produces effects only against the parties that have signed and exclusively in the relationships between them.

30.(Follows) Recent developments.

The economic and financial crisis of the last few years has contributed to reinforce the awareness among states, professionals and scholars of the necessity to equip itself with a general instrument to prevent, administer and resolve the crises of multinational banking groups, avoiding the related uncertainties adoption of ad hoc solutions. In November 2008, the G-20 leaders meeting in Washington called for a review of the resolution regimes and bankruptcy laws in light of recent experience to ensure an orderly liquidation or resolution of large financial conglomerates. The following year, the same leaders, assembled in Pittsburgh, undertook to undertake joint action to implement the most effective tools to take into account the actual risks inherent in large financial institutions and, more particularly, to develop effective instruments and resolution frameworks of financial conglomerates to mitigate the effects of crises and the likelihood of their occurrence[779]. It is in this context that initiatives have flourished in many international organizations for the preparation of guidelines, principles, model laws or, in some cases, binding legislative instruments. Among these initiatives, the proposal for a Directive of the Parliament and of the Council of the European Union establishing a crisis and resolution framework for credit institutions and investment firms, which modifies, inter alia, Directive 2001/24/EC[780]. The Report and Recommendations of the cross-border Bank Resolution Group of the Basel Committee, the Framework for Enhanced Coordination of IMF, the Principles for Cross-border Cooperation on Crisis Management of the Financial Stability Forum and the Key Attributes of the Financial Stability Board. Finally, even within UNCITRAL, this issue was discussed and the Secretariat was asked to undertake some studies on the issue.

In parallel, there have also been developments in the commercial

---

[779]V. European COMMISSION, 6 June 2012, Bank recovery and resolution proposal: Frequently Asked Questions.

[780]The Directive 2014/59/EU covers credit institutions established in EU Member States, parent companies, (mixed) financial holding companies, investment firms, and other financial institutions established in the EU and subject to consolidated banking supervision. It provides for resolution powers, including rules relating to the early intervention and restructuring power as well as tools for the sale of an institution's business; transfer of assets and liabilities to a bridge institution; separation of assets for transfer to an asset management vehicle; and treatment of shareholder rights (bail-in), as well as curators' rights and obligations, avoidance powers, treatment of intra-group claims, rights to set-off and netting, and the treatment of financial contracts. Directive 2014/59/EU of the European Parliament and of the Council of 15 May 2014 establishing a framework for the recovery and resolution of credit institutions and investment firms and amending Council Directive 82/891/EEC, and Directives 2001/24/EC, 2002/47/EC, 2004/25/EC, 2005/56/EC, 2007/36/EC, 2011/35/EU, 2012/30/EU and 2013/36/EU, and Regulations (EU) No 1093/2010 and (EU) No 648/2012, of the European Parliament and of the Council Text, OJ L 173, 12.6.2014, pp. 190-348.

sector. As is known, even the insolvency of multinational groups of commercial companies is not regulated by any legislative instrument adopted at international or at least regional level; in relation to this case the inconveniences deriving from this lack of discipline are, if possible, even better known than those of groups of banks. Thus, also in this field the European Union has been activated, with a proposal for the modification of Regulation CE n. 1346/2000, UNCITRAL with the third part of the Legislative Guide entitled "Treatment of enterprise groups in insolvency", the American Law Institute and the International Insolvency Institute with the Global Principles Project, again the International Insolvency Institute with the Guidelines for coordination of multi-national enterprise group insolvencies and finally the World Bank with Principles for Effective Insolvency and Creditor/Debtor Regimes. These initiatives are of some interest and offer possible ideas for the present work, which focuses on a specific case, that of multinational banking groups, with characteristics very close to that of commercial groups, being first of all the group structure to pose, regardless of the nature of the activity carried out, problems that must be faced before any other aspect.

Lastly, it must be remembered that some states have already taken legislative reform initiatives to adapt to the new socio-economic scenarios[781].

In fact, for example, the Basel Committee Report explicitly states that it was inspired by the drafting of the Recommendations from the recent financial crisis and in particular by an analysis of the concrete cases that took place[782]. The only exception to this time criterion is the Practice Guide on Cross-Border Insolvency Cooperation which, although it was published in 2009.

---

[781]UNCITRAL: "Insolvency of large and complex financial institutions-Note by the Secretariat", op. cit.

[782]BASEL COMMITTEE ON BANKING SUPERVISION, Report and Recommendations, op. cit., 10.

31.Initiatives in the banking sector. The proposal of the Directive of European Commission of June 2012.

On 6 June 2012 a proposal for a Directive establishing a framework for the reorganization and resolution of credit institutions and investment firms was published and which modifies Council Directives 77/91/EEC and 82/891/EC, the Directives 2001/24/EC, 2002/47/EC, 2004/25/EC, 2005/56/EC, 2007/36/EC and 2011/35/EU and Regulation (EU) n. 1093/2010[783].

The changes are aimed at strengthening financial stability, reducing risks and protecting depositors and core banking services, while preserving public money and the internal market. Furthermore, it is considered that it can have a positive social impact, on the one hand reducing the probability of a systemic banking crisis and on the other hand reducing losses to tax payers to a minimum, to the point that in a document accompanying the proposal it is stated that "(...) had these powers and tools in the recent cases (...), we would have seen more cooperation and preventive actions in cross-border banking groups"[784].

The proposal is of fundamental importance for this work as it introduces provisions aimed at regulating the disruption of multinational banking groups. In particular, this is primarily art. 7, 8, 11, 12 and 15, which regulate the drafting of a group's reorganization and resolution

---

[783]Proposal for a Directive of the European Parliament and of the Council establishing a framework for the recovery and resolution of credit institutions and investment firms and amending Council Directives 77/91/EEC and 82/891/EC, Directives 2001/24/EC, 2002/47/EC, 2004/25/EC, 2005/56/EC, 2007/36/EC and 2011/35/EC and Regulation (EU) No 1093/2010, SWD(2012) 166 final, COM82012)280 final, 2012/0150 (COD). For further details see: P.S. KENADJIAN, A. DOMBRET, The bank recovery and resolution directive: Europe's solution for "too big to fail"?, De Gruyter, Hamburg, 2013, pp. 91ss. G.J. BRANDSMA, J. BLOM-HANSEN, Controlling the European Union executive? The politics of delegation in the European Union, Oxford University Press, Oxford, 2017, pp. 171ss.

[784]European COMMISSION, 6 June 2012, Bank recovery and resolution proposal, op. cit., FAQ n. 32 ("If we had had this proposal already in place, would this have saved banks like Dexia, Lehman Brothers, or BayernLB?, in European COMMISSION, 6 June 2012, Bank recovery and resolution proposal: Frequently Asked Questions, cit., FAQ n. 32 ("If we had had this proposal already in place, would this have saved banks like Dexia, Lehman Brothers, or BayernLB?").

plans, as well as the powers to address or eliminate impediments to crisis resolution. Then they note articles from 16 to 22, dedicated to intragroup financial support and art. 25 which provides for the coordination of early intervention measures and regulates the appointment of an extraordinary director. Finally, the provisions contained in articles from 80 to 83, which together form Title V of the Directive proposal, entirely dedicated to the resolution of group crises, art. 98 on the "pooling of national financing mechanisms in case of group resolution" and articles 84, 88 and 89, relating to relations with third countries.

The above mentioned standards are based on the consideration that an efficient and rapid resolution of the crisis and that allows to minimize the losses can be ensured by assigning a pre-eminent role to the so-called "group resolution authority", while still granting the necessary guarantees to the Member States in which the group's smaller institutions are located, in particular through: The establishment of special colleges within which all the authorities can cooperate resolution of the crisis; an assessment of the financial stability of all Member States in which the group operates before taking any decision concerning the group; the definition of a clear decision-making process that offers all the authorities involved the possibility of being able to make their prospects known, while at the same time guaranteeing the possibility of reaching a common resolution position; the establishment of mechanisms for the settlement of conflicts between resolution authorities, also by making use of the role of obligatory mediator that Regulation UE n. 1093/2010 assigns to the European Banking Authority ("the ABE")[785].

In the last months of 2013 there was a close development of the legislative process concerning the proposal for a Directive. On 27 June 2013 the ECOFIN adopted a common position on the Directive proposal and asked the Presidency of the Council to undertake negotiations with the European Parliament in order to adopt the Directive at first reading by the end of the year[786]; on 12 December the European Commission (EC), the

---

[785]Regulation (EU) No 1093/2010 of the European Parliament and of the Council of 24 November 2010 establishing a European Supervisory Authority (European Banking Authority), amending Decision No 716/2009/EC and repealing Commission Decision 2009/78/EC, OJ L 331, 15.12.2010, p. 12-47.

[786]European COMMISSION, 27 June 2013, Statement of Commissioner Barnier following

European Parliament and the Member States reached agreement on the Directive, which is also subject to technical completion and formal approval by the Parliament and the Council[787]; finally (for now) on December 19th ECOFIN reached the final agreement.

32.(Follows) The preparation and content of group resolution plans.

First of all, we need to spend a few words on group resolution plans. Article 11 (1), first sentence, of the proposal provides that Member States shall ensure that resolution authorities draw up group resolution plans. In this preparatory phase, as well as in the updating of the plans themselves[788], the main role is played by the group-level resolution authorities, who must collaborate with the resolution authorities of all the other bodies of a given group, within the framework of cooperation represented by the colleges[789] and by consulting "the relevant competent authorities". Group-level resolution authorities may involve in the preparation and maintenance of these resolution plans the resolution authorities of third States where the group owns "subsidiaries"[790] or significant financial holding companies or branches within the meaning of art. 42 bis of Directive 2006/48/EC (article 12 (2) of the proposal)[791].

Member States must give group resolution authorities the power

---

agreement in ECOFIN on bank recovery and resolution. COUNCIL OF THE European UNION, 27 June 2013, Council agrees position on bank resolution.

[787]European COMMISSION, 12 December 2013, Commissioner Barnier welcomes trilogue agreement on the framework for bank recovery and resolution.

[788]The art. 12 (3) provides that updates should take place at least once a year and following any change in the legal or organizational structure of the institution or group, in its activity or in its financial situation that may substantially affect the plans or make them change required.

[789]Thus, literally, the proposal for a directive, indicating subsidiaries: See art. 2 no.5 according to which a subsidiary is defined as a subsidiary company as defined in Article 4, point 13, of Directive 2006/48/EC.

[790]That is what seems to be inferred from the combined provisions of Articles 11 (2), 10 (1) and 12 (1) of the Proposal. The list in Section B of the Annex, to which we refer, is a long one. It concerns all the information that allows us to get to know a group, especially regarding the structure, the management.

[791]In this regard, see, for example, the definition of a credit institution that gives directive 2006/48/EC "concerning access to the activity of credit institutions and its exercise (recast)", in art. 4 (1): "(a) An undertaking whose business consists of receiving deposits or other repayable funds from the public and granting credit for its own account, or b) an electronic money institution within the meaning of Directive 2000/46/EC (1).

to impose on parent companies and institutions subject to supervision on a consolidated basis pursuant to arts. 125 and 126 of Directive 2006/48/EC to provide them with all the necessary information, relating to them, to all legal entities belonging to the group and to the companies referred to in art. 1, lett. c) or d), for the drafting and implementation of the group resolution plans, in particular with reference to the information and analyzes indicated in section B of the annex to the proposal[792]. In order to facilitate the retrieval and transmission of such information, art. 10 (2) provides that the competent authorities in the different Member States work together with the resolution authorities to verify the availability of such information and, if so, to transmit them to the authorities themselves. The information will be communicated on the basis of standard forms, models and procedures developed by the European Banking Authority, presented to the EC within twelve months of the entry into force of the Directive and adopted by the latter in compliance with art. 15 of Regulation (EU) no. 1093/2010[793].

The group-level resolution authority, in turn, transmits the information received to the EBA, to the institution-resolution crisis authorities, to the relevant competent authorities referred to in articles 130 and 131 bis of Directive 2006/48/EC and to the resolution authorities of the Member States in which the companies referred to in art. 1, lett. c) or d). Within four months of this broadcast, group resolution plans must be adopted by a joint decision of all the resolution authorities involved. The European Banking Authority may, on its own initiative, assist the competent authorities in reaching an agreement pursuant to art. 19 of Regulation (EU) no. 1093/2010[794]. If the resolution authorities do not share any element of the resolution plan, they may, before the four-month deadline or before a joint decision is reached, refer the matter to the EBA

---

[792]Pursuant to art. 2 (20) of the Proposal, the competent authorities are the competent authorities as defined in art. 4, point 4, of the directive 2006/48/CE or to art. 3 (3) (c) of Directive 2006/49/EC, i.e. national authorities authorized by law or regulation to supervise credit institutions or investment firms.

[793]For further details see: C. HARLOW, R. RAWLINGS, Process and procedure in European Union administration, Bloomsbury Publishing, New York, 2014.

[794]C. HARLOW, R. RAWLINGS, Process and procedure in European Union administration, op. cit.

in accordance with art. 19 of Regulation (EU) no. 1093/2010[795]. In this case, the group-level resolution authority is obliged to postpone its decision pending the decision of the EBA, which must be received within one month[796], and the subsequent resolution of the resolution authority to group level will have to comply with the EBA decision. If, on the other hand, after the four-month period, a joint decision can not be reached, the group-level resolution authority can decide on its own, explaining the reasons and taking into account the opinions and reservations expressed by the other competent authorities during the four months. The decision is transmitted to the parent companies or the institution subject to supervision on a consolidated basis, as well as to the other resolution authorities.

Group resolution plans include a) a resolution plan at the level of the parent company or of the entity subject to supervision on a consolidated basis pursuant to art. 125 and 126 of Directive 2006/48/EC, b) resolution plans for individual institutions set up in compliance with art. 9 of the proposal, c) plans of the company's crisis resolution in art. 1, letters (c) or (d) of the proposal and (iv) resolution plans of institutions having branches in other Member States, in accordance with Directive 2001/24/EC[797].

Group resolution resolution plans, pursuant to art. 11 (3) of the proposal, indicate the resolution actions to be initiated concerning the group as a whole or part of it, including the individual subsidiaries, and through resolution actions against the companies referred to in art. 1 (d) -"parent financial holding companies in a Member State, financial holding companies in the Union, mixed financial holding companies in a Member State, mixed financial holding companies in the Union"-, of parent company and subsidiaries, both through coordinated resolution actions against institutions, in the scenarios referred to in art. 9 (2), ie in cases where the failure is specific or occurs at a time of wider financial instability or system-level events; examine to what extent the resolution

[795]See also from the CJEU: C-88/18, Schyns of 06 June 2019, ECLI:EU:C:2019:467, published in the electronic Reports of the cases.

[796]The four-month period is instead assimilated, pursuant to art. 12 (6) of the Proposal, to the conciliation period referred to in Regulation (EU) no. 1093/2010.

[797]C. HARLOW, R. RAWLINGS, Process and procedure in European Union administration, op. cit.

tools and powers can be applied and exercised in a coordinated manner towards group entities located in the Union, including measures to facilitate the acquisition by a third party of the group as a whole or separate activity areas or activities carried out by a number of group entities or by certain group entities, and identifies potential barriers to coordinated crisis resolution; in the case of a group comprising entities established in third countries, they establish agreements for cooperation and coordination with the relevant authorities of these third countries; indicate the measures, including the legal and economic separation of particular functions or areas of activity, necessary to facilitate the resolution of group crises when the conditions are met; they indicate how to finance group resolution actions and, where appropriate, set out principles for sharing responsibility for funding between sources in different Member States. The plans do not require any extraordinary public financial support in addition to the use of the financing mechanisms established pursuant to art. 91[798]. These principles are established on the basis of fair and balanced criteria and take into account, in particular, the economic impact of the resolution of the crises in the Member States concerned and the division of supervisory powers among the various competent authorities.

33.Evaluation of the possibility of resolving group crises and removing impediments.

Article 15 establishes a procedure-in fact quite complex and sometimes obscure-to reach a shared decision on the identification of impediments to the resolution of the groups and the measures suitable to eliminate them. This procedure would seem to start when, pursuant to art. 14, a resolution authority ascertains, in relation to a particular group company, the existence of such impediments and notifies the entity concerned. The latter may indicate the measures it deems appropriate to deal with this problem and then the authority will notify the institution itself of its opinion on the suitability of these measures. Moreover, according to what is foreseen (or, at least, it seems to provide) art. 15 (1),

[798]Article 91 provides the Member States with the obligation to set up financing mechanisms, with adequate financial resources, in order to enable the resolution authority to apply or effectively implement resolution tools and powers.

group-level resolution authorities and crisis resolution authorities of the subsidiaries should make a reasonable effort to make a joint decision on the application of these measures.

Furthermore, par. (2) of art. 15 of the proposal provides that the group-level resolution authority, in collaboration with the consolidated supervisor and the European Banking Authority and in consultation with the competent authorities, shall prepare a report, pursuant to art. 25 (1) of Regulation (EU) no. 1093/2010, on impediments to the resolution of the crises and on the measures necessary to eliminate them, which is then transmitted to the parent companies or to the institution subject to supervision on a consolidated basis and to the crisis resolution authorities of the subsidiaries[799].

Regarding the nature of the measures that may be proposed, the recital 19 and 20 provide that they may also consist of imposing changes to the structure and organization of the institution or group. However, in order to respect the freedom of enterprise established by art. 16 of the Charter of Fundamental Rights, these amendments must be limited to the strict minimum. Furthermore, it is envisaged that the measures imposed must comply with European Union law, in particular by not discriminating, directly or indirectly, on grounds of nationality, without violating the rights inherent to fundamental freedoms, including those relating to freedom of establishment, and pursuing only the public interest in financial stability.

Within four months of the notification (it would appear to be that referred to in article 14), the parent undertaking or the institution subject to supervision on a consolidated basis may submit observations and/or propose alternative measures to which the resolution authority at group reports to the supervisory authority on a consolidated basis, to the European Banking Authority and to the crisis resolution authority of the subsidiaries.

Finally, it is envisaged that, within the college, the group-level resolution authorities and the crisis resolution authorities of the subsidiaries commit themselves to the highest possible degree in order to

[799]C. HARLOW, R. RAWLINGS, Process and procedure in European Union administration, op. cit.

reach a joint decision in consultation with the competent authorities identifying impediments and evaluating the measures proposed to circumvent them. This decision must be taken, possibly with the help provided by the EBA on a voluntary basis, within four months of the submission of the report. In the event that a decision can not be reached within that time frame, the group-level resolution authority can decide for itself in relation to the whole group. In both cases the decision must be motivated, with any indication of the opinions and reservations expressed by the participants in the decision-making process, and transmitted by the group-level resolution authority to the parent companies or the supervised institution. on a consolidated basis. The decision must now be recognized as definitive and applied by the competent authorities in the Member States concerned. If, however, no later than the four months referred to above, one of the resolution authorities concerned has referred the matter to the EBA pursuant to art. 19 of Regulation (EU) n. 1093/2010, the group-level resolution authority, is obliged to suspend the decision pending a position on the EBA, which must be expressed within one month and the four months are treated as equivalent to the conciliation period pursuant to Regulation itself. The group-level resolution authority will comply with the EBA decision.

34.Resolution colleges.

First of all, spend a few words on the so-called "resolution colleges", provided for by art. 80 of the proposal. These are entities, clearly conceived in parallel with the supervisory colleges, which must be established by the group resolution authority, that is, pursuant to art. 2 (38) of the proposal, the resolution authority operating in the Member State in which the supervisor is established on a consolidated basis. In turn, the latter is, pursuant to art. 3 (3) of the Proposal, "the competent supervisory authorities may be resolution authorities for the purposes of Directives 2006/48/EC and 2006/49/EC, central banks, competent ministries or other public administrative authorities, provided that Member States shall adopt the rules and provisions necessary to avoid conflicts of interest between the supervisory functions pursuant to art. 2 (31) of the proposal, the competent authority of supervision on a consolidated basis as defined in art. 4, point 48, of the Directive 2006/48/EC. The only case in which the group-level resolution authority is not obliged to set up resolution colleges is that in which, in relation to a specific group, an entity with exactly the same characteristics already exists that art. 80 provides for colleges. In this case, any reference to the resolution colleges contained in the proposal must be understood as a reference to this entity[800].

Members of the boards in question are first and foremost the group level resolution authorities. To these are added, as permanent members, pursuant to art. 80 (2), the other resolution authorities of each Member State in which a subsidiary of a consolidated supervisor and the European Banking Authority is established. Furthermore, in the event that resolution authorities are not identifiable with the "competent ministries", i.e. "the finance ministries or other ministries responsible for economic, financial and budgetary decisions"[801], the latter will also be members of the resolution colleges and will be able to participate in meetings, in particular those which may have repercussions on state public funds.

With regard to the European Banking Authority, pursuant to par. 4, it may participate, if it deems it appropriate, to specific meetings or activities, but without the right to vote, in order to help promote and monitor the efficient, effective and uniform functioning of the colleges. It must immediately be noted, however, that this seems in some way contrary to what has been seen to be provided by par. 2 of the same standard, which, providing that "are members (...)" seems to indicate, among others, the European Banking Authority as a member of Directives 2006/48/EC and 2006/49/CE[802], or the other functions of the authority in question, and the functions of resolution authorities under this Directive. In particular, Member States shall ensure that, within the competent authorities, central banks, competent ministries or other public administrative authorities, the resolution function is separate from the supervisory function or other

[800]C. HARLOW, R. RAWLINGS, Process and procedure in European Union administration, op. cit.

[801]R. KATTEL, J. KREGEL, M. TONVERONACHI, Financial regulation in the European Union, ed. Routledge, London & New York, 2015.

[802]Directive 2006/49/EC of the European Parliament and of the Council of 14 June 2006 on the capital adequacy of investment firms and credit institutions (recast), OJ L 177, 30.6.2006, p. 201-255. For further details see: R. KATTEL, J. KREGEL, M. TONVERONACHI, Financial regulation in the European Union, op. cit.

functions of the authority in question"[803]. There may then be additional members, under certain circumstances or for the achievement of particular objectives. First of all, the resolution authority of the Member State in which a company referred to in article 1 (d) is established, when such company is the parent company of one or more institutions. In addition, where a parent undertaking or an institution established in the Union has subsidiaries in non-member States, the resolution authorities of those states may be invited, at the request of the group-level resolution authority, to participate to the resolution college as an observer, provided that they are subject to confidentiality obligations equivalent to those established in art. 76. In order to decide about the necessity to draw up a group resolution program in accordance with art. 83, par. (6) of art. 80 provides for participation in the meetings or activities of the resolution colleges of the authority or resolution authorities of each Member State in which a subsidiary is established. Finally, to reach an agreement on the group resolution programs proposed pursuant to art. 83 and to coordinate the use of funding mechanisms referred to in Title VII of the proposal, par. (7) of art. 80 provides for participation in the meetings or activities of the colleges of the resolution authority (ies) of each Member State in which a subsidiary is established which meets the conditions for resolution of the crisis.

Finally, to reach an agreement on the group resolution programs proposed pursuant to art. 83 and to coordinate the use of funding mechanisms referred to in Title VII of the proposal, par. (7) of art. 80 provides for participation in the meetings or activities of the colleges of the resolution authority (i.e.) of each Member State in which a subsidiary is established which meets the conditions for resolution of the crisis. The rule in question, in the first sentence of par. (3), recommends to all public bodies participating in the activities of the colleges[804] to implement close mutual cooperation.

The group-level resolution authority is not only responsible for setting up the college, but also for coordinating its activities and for

[803] R. KATTEL, J. KREGEL, M. TONVERONACHI, Financial regulation in the European Union, op. cit.
[804] C. HARLOW, R. RAWLINGS, Process and procedure in European Union administration, op. cit.

convening and presiding over its meetings. In particular, ex ante, it must inform all the members of the college and the EBA of the meetings that will be held and of the topics that will be discussed at the same time. Furthermore, he/she may decide from time to time which authorities and/or ministers invite, taking into account, according to the provisions of art. 80 (3), the importance of the issues to be discussed, the activities to be planned or coordinated and the decisions to be taken, in particular with reference to their possible impact on the stability of the financial systems of the Member States involved. Ex post, the group-level resolution authority must inform all board members of all decisions taken and of all actions taken during the meetings.

The functioning of the colleges is governed by two sets of rules. A first group, which regulates the operating procedures, consists of draft regulatory technical standards developed by the ABE for each college, according to the provisions of art. 80 (9). Within twelve months of the entry into force of the Directive, the EBA must submit the above technical standards to the EC which, in turn, will adopt them in accordance with the procedure set out in articles 10 to 14 of Regulation (EU) no. 1093/2010[805]. A second group of rules, subordinated to the first, consists of written rules, established by the resolution authority at group level, after consultation with the other resolution authorities, which define ad hoc procedures and procedures for each college for each college of the same.

Coming to the nature of the colleges and the purpose for which they are created, must first clarify that it is not about new decision-making bodies with autonomous powers created by the Directive: Rather, they are intangible entities that act as a frame within which the several members can fulfill the provisions of art. 80 (1). This provision, in the first paragraph, refers to articles 11, 15 and 83 of the proposal relating to the preparation of group resolution plans, to addressing and eliminating impediments to the possibility of resolving crises and resolving a group. The same paragraph also establishes that colleges must serve as means to facilitate cooperation and coordination with the resolution authorities of

[805]C. HARLOW, R. RAWLINGS, Process and procedure in European Union administration, op. cit.

non-EU Member States[806]. The second sub-paragraph of art. 80 (1) further specifies the tasks whose realization should be facilitated by the colleges: In addition to referring again to the aforementioned articles 11, 15 and 83, it also includes the exchange of information, which is the necessary basis for carrying out all the other tasks, the assessment of the possibility of resolving the groups' crises, the coordination of public communications of strategies and programs. resolution and finally the coordination of the use of funding mechanisms established under Title VII[807].

35.The European resolution colleges.

Alongside the crisis resolution colleges described above, art. 81 discipline the "European resolution colleges", which must be established in the event that (a) an institution of a third state or a parent undertaking of a third state has two or more institutions established in the Union and b) have not been concluded agreements with the authorities of third states regarding the exchange of confidential information. The task of setting up such colleges is the resolution authorities of the Member States in which the parent institutions are established and it is to them that the activity of the colleges is addressed exclusively. They work in the same way and perform the same tasks as the resolution colleges provided for by art. 80, except for a particularity, contained in art. 81 (3), concerning the authority delegated to preside over them. In principle, the president is appointed and appointed by the members of the college itself. However, if the parent companies are held by a financial holding company established in the Union pursuant to art. 143 (3), 3rd paragraph, of Directive 2006/48/EC[808],

---

[806]So it seems to have to deduce from the art. 80 (9), where it is specified that the regulatory technical standards are aimed at specifying the operating procedures of the colleges.

[807]C. HARLOW, R. RAWLINGS, Process and procedure in European Union administration, op. cit.

[808]The referenced standard refers to the case of a credit institution, the parent company of which is a credit institution or a financial holding company with its head office in a third state, not subject to supervision on a consolidated basis in accordance with articles 125 and 126 of the same directive, nor to a supervision on a consolidated basis in the equivalent substance by a competent authority of a third state. In these circumstances, the rule provides that the competent authority may, inter alia, in particular provide for the establishment of a financial holding company with headquarters in the Community and apply the provisions relating to supervision on a consolidated basis to the consolidated position of that company. financial holding company.

the panel is chaired by the resolution authority of the Member State in which the supervisory authority is located on a consolidated basis pursuant to said Directive[809].

36.(Follows) The exchange of information.

Article 82 is entirely dedicated to the exchange of information between the resolution authorities of a particular college. According to the general rule, resolution authorities must spontaneously exchange one another, or communicate following a specific request, all the information relevant to the exercise of their respective activities. The group-level resolution authorities, in particular, have the duty to provide all the other resolution authorities with the relevant information in a short time, in order to facilitate them carrying out the tasks referred to in art. 80 (1), second sub-paragraph, letters from (b) to (h). It is also expected that the information thus exchanged may also be made available to the competent ministries.

37.(Follows) The resolution of group crises.

Article 83, entitled "resolution of group crises", can be divided into two parts dedicated to (probable) failure of one parent institution and the other of a parent company of the Union.

With regard to the parent company, art. 83 (1) provides that when a resolution authority deems or is informed by a national authority empowered to supervise credit institutions[810] that a parent institution of a group is failing or likely to fail, it shall immediately communicate to the group-level resolution authorities and other resolution authorities in the resolution college for the group concerned its decision to do so and resolution actions or other insolvency measures which it considers appropriate to adopt. The group-level resolution authority must assess, together with the other members of the resolution college of the group in question, what the impact of the bankruptcy or of the actions or measures proposed on the whole group or on affiliated institutions with established

---

[809]For more analysis see: J. KILPONEN, Sovereign risk European crisis-resolution policies and bond spreads, in International Journal of Central Banking, 11 (2), 2015, pp. 287ss.
[810]See the articles 74 (3) and 2 (20) of the Proposal and art. 4 (4) of Directive 2006/48/EC

in other Member States, with two possible consequences. In the event that a negative impact is not expected, the competent resolution authority in relation to the failing subsidiary may take the actions or adopt the notified measures and must periodically inform the resolution college fully of these actions or measures and their progress. In the event that a negative impact is expected, the group resolution authority must propose, within 24 hours of the notification referred to above, a group resolution program and present it to the college. If a member of the latter disagrees with the program, preferring, for reasons of financial stability, autonomously to initiate, in relation to a given entity or entity of the group, actions or measures other than those proposed, within 24 hours issue to the European Banking Authority, according to the procedure set out in art. 19 Regulation (EU) n. 1093/2010, to which, within the next 24 hours, it will have to take a decision on the point that will bind the resolution authority[811].

Regarding the possible failure of a parent company of the Union, art. 83 (8) of the proposal provides that when the group-level resolution authority decides or is informed by a national authority empowered to supervise credit institutions[812] that a parent company of the Union in relation to which it is the competent authority is failing or likely to fail, it communicates to the other resolution authorities part of the resolution committee of the group in question its decision and the actions or measures it deems necessary. Only in this case, but not in the hypothesis examined above, one of the actions proposed by the group-level resolution authority may already consist of a group resolution program.

Pursuant to par. 9 of the standard in question, all the steps of the procedures described above must be implemented in a short time, taking into account "the urgency of the situation"[813].

The content of group resolution programs is indicated in art. 83 (5): They outline the resolution actions that the relevant resolution authorities have to initiate, in relation to the parent company in the Union or to particular group entities, in order to preserve the value of the group

---

[811]C. HARLOW, R. RAWLINGS, Process and procedure in European Union administration, op. cit.

[812]See the articles 74 (3) and 2 (20) of the Proposal and art. 4 (4) of Directive 2006/48/EC

[813]R. KATTEL, J. KREGEL, M. TONVERONACHI, Financial regulation in the European Union, op. cit.

as a whole, to reduce at least the impact on financial stability in the Member States in which the group is active and to minimize the use of extraordinary public financial support; specify the methods for coordinating resolution actions; establish a financing plan that takes into account the principles on the division of responsibilities established in accordance with art. 11 (3) (e) of the proposal.

In the event that no group resolution program is implemented and therefore actions are taken solely against each institution failing individually considered, the competent authorities are in any case required to cooperate closely with each other within the framework of resolution colleges in order to reach a coordinated solution for all failing entities.

Lastly, recital 63 deserves attention, in that it provides that "(...) the resolution actions proposed by the group-level resolution authority should be prepared and discussed among the different national resolution authorities crises within the corresponding group-level plans"[814]. In fact this seems to be the only indication of the relationship existing between the programs referred to in art. 83 and the resolution plans pursuant to art. 11 of the proposal[815].

38.(Follows) The financing of the resolution of group crises.

Article 98 of the proposal provides for the obligation of Member States to ensure that each national funding mechanism contributes to the financing of the resolution of a possible group crisis. The financing plan is established by the group-level resolution authority, in consultation with the other resolution authorities, and forms an integral part of the resolution plan referred to in art. 83. Member States must ensure that the respective national funding mechanism pays the contribution to the financing plan as soon as the resolution authority of the state concerned has received a request to that effect from the resolution authority at group. Group financing mechanisms may require loans or other forms of support as

---

[814] R. KATTEL, J. KREGEL, M. TONVERONACHI, Financial regulation in the European Union, op. cit.

[815] C. HARLOW, R. RAWLINGS, Process and procedure in European Union administration, op. cit.

necessary to finance the resolution of the group crisis. These loans will be guaranteed by national funding mechanisms in proportion to their respective share of the financing plan itself. Likewise, income or profits from the use of financing mechanisms benefit all national funding mechanisms depending on the contribution made by each of them. The last paragraph of art. 98 provides that the EC may adopt delegated acts, pursuant to art. 103 of the proposal, to specify further details related to the financing plans[816].

39.Groups partially outside the European Union.

Title VI, dedicated to "relations with third countries", includes articles from 84 to 89. Not all of these norms seem to be relevant to groups: In particular, art. 85, 86 and 87[817] would seem to regulate only cases of companies established in third countries but having branches in the Union.

Starting from art. 84, it provides for the possibility for the Union to conclude agreements with one or more third states concerning the arrangements for cooperation at the planning and implementation stages of the resolution procedure of institutions present both in the Union and in third states. In particular, it is expected that the EC will submit to the Council, on its own initiative or at the request of a Member State, proposals relating to the negotiation. The standard indicates some situations in which "in particular" this procedure can be activated; the assumptions referred to in letters a) and (c) concern groups, ie the case in which a subsidiary of the group is located in a Member State and the case in which a parent company or one of the companies referred to in art. 1, letters (c) or (d)[818], established in one Member State, has one or more

[816]C. HARLOW, R. RAWLINGS, Process and procedure in European Union administration, op. cit.

[817]Regarding the art. 87 is certainly so, having already been clarified in the column. Article. 85 and consequently the connected art. 86, are not clear in this regard but in this sense it seems to have to understand the letter (b) of par. (2).

[818]Financial holding company, mixed financial holding company, mixed holding company; parent financial holding companies in a Member State, parent financial holding companies in the Union, mixed financial holding companies mothers in one Member State, mixed financial holding company mothers in the Union.

significant branches[819] in one or more third states. Par. (2) of art. 84, partly repeats what had already been stated in par. (1) and in part ago (an obscure) reference to art. 89[820].

Article 88 instead provides some provisions relating to cooperation with the authorities of third countries that are applicable until it is concluded with the third country from time to time relevant to an agreement ex art. 84 or 53 to the extent that the subject is not governed by this agreement. Article 88 provides for two successive steps. Initially, the European Banking Authority may conclude non-binding framework agreements for cooperation with the "relevant" authorities of third States[821].

40.Thoughts and observations on the model introduced by the proposal of Directive and Regulation.

There are three models proposed to deal with the phenomenon of bankruptcy of multinational companies (not necessarily of a banking type). The least evolved consists in a cooperation between the bankruptcy curators and the competent courts in the different jurisdictions involved. The second model adds to the first the presence of an authority (judge or bankruptcy trustee) who is entrusted with the necessary powers to guide and coordinate cooperation activities. The third model, on the other hand, moves away from the first two and envisages the opening of a single procedure in respect of all members of the group, as if the latter were a single entity[822]. The Directive proposal just analyzed has adopted the second type of model mentioned here, entrusting the group resolution

---

[819]See art. 42-bis of Directive 2006/48/EC.

[820]The norm says "and" instead of "or" but it would make no sense. That is, if the agreement pursuant to art. 84 is not concluded, then art. 88. If an agreement pursuant to art. 84 is concluded, it will be able to continue to apply art. 88 for matters not covered by the agreement pursuant to art. 84.

[821]C. HARLOW, R. RAWLINGS, Process and procedure in European Union administration, op. cit.

[822]B. WESSELS, The future European Union legislative framework on cross-border crisis management in the banking sector: A legal stress test, in B. WESSELS, P. OMAR, Cross-border management in the banking sector, Wolters, Kluwer, Nottingham-Paris, 2011, pp. 59ss.

authority with a prominent role in the various activities necessary to resolve the crises. Moreover, the provision of the European Banking Authority seems to be of some importance, also in light of the powers conferred upon it by the articles from 23 to 27 of Regulation (CE) n. 1093/2010[823]. At first glance, the solution proposed must certainly be welcomed, firstly because, unlike the regulatory instruments currently in force in the Union, it has identified the existence of the problem of the failure of multinational groups and has sought to find a how to solve it; furthermore, due to its binding nature, it is the only example on an international scene studded with soft law instruments; finally because it is the result of a particularly strengthened cooperation, without precedents outside the European Union.

The framework established through the resolution colleges seems to be a suitable environment for overcoming the difficulties linked to cooperation: In fact it is precise and flexible at the same time, thus combining the benefits deriving from a well-defined rules system with those linked to the adaptability of these rules according to the needs of the different cases from time to time relevant[824]. According to the EC, the system of the proposal also ensures that the various authorities involved can act quickly and effectively when the situation requires it[825].

However, at a closer look, the proposed rules do nothing more than ratify and make binding a practice that, as we have seen, had already been widely adopted, albeit on a purely voluntary basis and therefore according to less structured schemes, by numerous curators bankruptcy and courts, especially in the United States and in the European Union, responsible for resolving cases of cross-border insolvency. Furthermore,

---

[823]European COMMISSION, Commission Staff Working Document, Impact Assessment Accompanying the document Proposal for a Directive of the European Parliament and of the Council establishing a framework for the recovery and resolution of credit institutions and investment firms and amending Council Directives 77/91/EEC and 82/891/EC, Directives 2001/24/EC, 2002/47/EC, 2004/25/EC, 2005/56/EC, 2007/36/EC and 2011/35/EC and Regulation (EU) No 1093/2010, parr. 55ss.

[824]European COMMISSION, Communication from the Commission to the European Parliament, the Council, the European Economic and Social Committee, the Committee of the Regions and the European Central Bank, An EU Framework for Crisis Management in the Financial Sector, cit., 13.

[825]Communication from the Commission, COM(2009) 561, cit., 13.

over the years many soft law tools have been published to encourage the conclusion of agreements between authorities and courts in different jurisdictions. Indeed, the EC itself recognized that tackling the problem of the insolvency of transnational groups through the coordination of the various actions undertaken at the level of individual states would only represent a strengthening of existing agreements and would not necessarily imply the most effective reorganization. However, the EC continues, a positive aspect can also be seen in a system like the one proposed, namely that an orderly resolution of a failing transnational bank is highly likely in the presence of a structured and legally binding European framework that strengthens the agreements of cooperation during a crisis. Although this is certainly correct, a real step forward would have been the adoption of a global solution, as has been invoked in doctrine, both at European and international level[826]. For example, during the preparatory work, the possibility of setting up a European authority to independently manage the international crises of banking groups was evaluated[827]. Many reasons have been used to justify the failure to adopt this model. The official one, coming from the EC, depends on the fact that it would have been difficult to establish an integrated European resolution model in the absence of a uniform bankruptcy law in all the Member States and of a single supervisory authority[828]. Similarly, the non-uniformity of

---

[826]M. ČIHÁK, E. NIER, The need for special resolution regimes for financial institutions- The case of the European Union, IMF Working Paper, 26, September 2009. E. HÜPKES, Rivalry in resolution. How to reconcile local responsibilities and global interests?, in European Company and Financial Law Review, 7, 2010, pp. 240ss. C. CUMMING, R.A. EISENBEIS, Resolving troubled systemically important cross-border financial Institutions: Is a new corporate organizational form required?, in Federal Reserve Bank of New York Staff Reports, July 2010, 39. B. WESSELS, Towards a European bank company law?, op. cit., pp. 18ss. G.G.H. GARCIA, R.M. LASTRA, M.J. NIETO, Bankruptcy and reorganization procedures for cross-border banks in the EU: Towards an integrated approach to the reform of the EU safety net, in LSE Financial Markets Group Paper Series, 25, May 2009.

[827]European COMMISSION, Commission staff working document impact assessment accompanying the document proposal for a Directive of the European Parliament and of the Council establishing a framework for the recovery and resolution of credit institutions and investment firms and amending Council Directives 77/91/EEC and 82/891/EC, Directives 2001/24/EC, 2002/47/EC, 2004/25/EC, 2005/56/EC, 2007/36/EC and 2011/35/EC and Regulation (EU) No 1093/2010, cit., 54ss.

[828]European COMMISSION, Communication from the Commission to the European Parliament, the Council, the European Economic and Social Committee, the Committee of

the solutions adopted by the Member States in some branches of law which directly affect bankruptcy proceedings has been mentioned. The second reason is political: It is considered that the Member States are not yet ready to surrender their sovereignty in this matter to the extent that would have been necessary to provide for a global regime[829].

41.The Report and Recommendations of the Cross-border Bank Resolution Group of the Basel Committee.

The Basel Committee, in its document of March 2010 entitled "Report and Recommendations of the Cross-border Bank Resolution Group"[830], proposes, as a solution for the regulation of the crises of multinational banking groups, the adoption of a middle-ground approach since if, according to the Committee, the time does not seem to be ripe yet for a universalist system, a strictly territorialist approach would end up hindering the achievement of the objectives typically pursued in a bankruptcy procedure. According to the proposed model, in principle supervisory authorities and resolution authorities are authorized to adopt, in relation to the bodies subject to them, measures independent from those possibly taken by other foreign authorities, with the sole objective of allowing everyone the legal systems involved the continuation of essential services. However, the possibility of implementing a certain level of cooperation is envisaged through the approximation of the various relevant national legal provisions.

With the aim of giving life to the model just described, the Committee has formulated ten recommendations of which, for the purposes of this study, concern the n. 3, which indirectly refers to n. 1 and 2, and n. 4, 5 and 7[831]. The first of the mentioned recommendations urges the legislative authorities of the states to pursue a convergence of the

---

the Regions and the European Central Bank, An EU Framework for Crisis Management in the Financial Sector, p. 12.

[829]E. HÜPKES, Rivalry in resolution. How to reconcile, op. cit.

[830]BASEL COMMITTEE ON BANKING SUPERVISION, Report and Recommendations, op. cit., par. 6.4.

[831]BASEL COMMITTEE ON BANKING SUPERVISION, Report and Recommendations, op. cit.

instruments and measures provided for by the respective legal systems, in particular by using the provisions of Recommendations n. 1 and 2, so, as we said, to facilitate a coordinated resolution of the crises while allowing the continuation of essential services. Based on recommendation n. 1, States must make available to their authorities the necessary tools to cope with the difficulties of any type of financial institution and that can minimize the impact of the crisis or its resolution on the financial system and promote the continuity of functions systematically relevant. Recommendation n. 2 instead prescribes the adoption, within each national system, of procedural rules that allow to deal with the crisis of the various bodies that form an (internal) group in a unitary way.

Going to the recommendation n. 4, indicates as a useful means of coordination the adoption of procedures that facilitate the mutual recognition of procedures and resolution or crisis management measures, while respecting the limit of public order, in particular with reference to financial stability of the system. Recommendation n. 7, then, indicates the need to coordinate the various national procedures open against companies belonging to the same group. To this end, it requires national authorities to comply, in accordance with the laws and policies in force in their laws, in order to ensure a reciprocal exchange of information that is efficient in terms of time, both during periods of normal economic situation of a group as during crisis periods. In particular, the agreement will have to define which information can be exchanged, at what time and according to what modalities, with particular regard to the confidentiality, security, relief and accessibility of each information[832].

Recommendation n.5, proposes the adoption of a measure of a different nature from those traditionally proposed, placing itself from a point of view not of international bankruptcy law but of substantive law. Supervisors are encouraged to implement close cooperation with the resolution authorities in order to assess how the crisis of a particular group or its component entities can be resolved. If they believe that the group in question has a structure too complex to allow an orderly and cost-effective resolution, they should consider whether to offer incentives to simplify their structure, in order to ensure-eventually-a resolution effective. The

[832]E. HÜPKES, Rivalry in resolution. How to reconcile, op. cit.

IMF has criticized this proposal considering that it would result in a significant loss of efficiency and would hinder the access of emerging economies to the capital market and the expansion of international trade. In fact, if it is true that reducing the size of a group could help to ensure greater economic stability, it is also true that the presence of large banking groups in emerging economies has often strengthened their capacity for recovery.

42.The Framework for Enhanced Coordination of International Monetary Fund.

It is now necessary to take into account a document drawn up by IMF, in response to the stimulus of the G-20, entitled "Resolution of Cross-Border Banks-A Proposed Framework for Enhanced Coordination". It is based on the work of the Cross-border Bank Resolution Group of the Basel Committee. The scope of application is quite broad. In fact, on the one hand, the term "resolution" is used to indicate any type of reorganization or resolution operation that involves the intervention of third parties, both private and public bodies[833]. On the other hand, it deals not only with multinational groups but also with companies with only branches present abroad.

According to the Framework, the most realistic solution in the immediate future to regulate the insolvency of multinational banking groups is to strengthen the coordination between national authorities through the adoption of a non-binding agreement between those states that are able to respect the requirements set by the agreement itself, to guarantee reciprocal availability and ability to take effective action. To this end, the respective disciplines of supervision and resolution of the crisis must be, at least minimally, convergent. The document, therefore, indicates and analyzes the "core-coordination standards", minimum necessary requirements that states must possess to take part in the "core coordination framework". The implementation of this form of cooperation would represent a significant step forward because the states that meet these requirements, although they are not numerous, represent the largest

[833]INTERNATIONAL MONETARY FUND (IMF), Resolution of Cross-Border Banks, pages: 3, 15.

financial centers in the world.

First of all, the document prescribes, in order to implement an "enhanced coordination framework", that the internal regulations of the States be amended to require the authorities to coordinate in dealing with crisis situations. In fact, the rules currently in force in some jurisdictions in some cases hinder the coordination between authorities at international level, for example by preventing them from exchanging information or, more generally, by adopting a ring-fencing. In any case, the authorities must always target the interests of curators and the financial stability of their respective legal system, up to the point that they can disregard coordinated action, if this is necessary in order to protect the two values indicated last. Beyond cooperation, it is then required that, in any case, measures to deal with crisis situations are taken as quickly as possible and have extraterritorial effectiveness.

Regarding the "core coordination standards", three are identified. Firstly, a certain degree of convergence of the respective bankruptcy regulations, in particular on certain aspects such as: a) Non-discrimination of curators of other jurisdictions; b) the availability of effective means of intervention, that is, that above all guarantee the possibility to act quickly without interrupting the provision of essential services and avoid the contagion of other institutions[834]; c) appropriate protection of curators, in particular with regard to guarantees related to the recognition of the right to property; d) the order of satisfaction of the various categories of curators, the recognition of the "insured depositors" and "deposit guarantee schemes"[835]. Secondly, an adequate and efficient system of preventive supervision, which is also subject to other financial institutions and insurance companies. Finally, the ability to adopt solutions at an international level, in terms of adequacy of the structure and preparation of personnel.

The competent authorities will also have to identify, before the onset of a crisis, possibly guided by principles defined in the Framework,

---

[834]INTERNATIONAL MONETARY FUND (IMF), Resolution of Cross-Border Banks, p. 20.

[835]INTERNATIONAL MONETARY FUND (IMF), Resolution of Cross-Border Banks, op. cit.,

the criteria and parameters on which to base the burden of losses, although one of the objectives is and still remains to minimize the use of funding from the public.

The coordination procedures that can be used by the States that adhere to the Framework must then be specified. In fact, the availability of a "pre-packaged" procedure increases the chances of a rapid and effective coordination. Taking as a starting point the UNCITRAL's work on groups of commercial companies, the IMF indicates the need to identify the authority that will take the initiative and will lead the procedure and the modalities of communication and consultation. As regards the groups in particular, the competent authority must be identified for each of the bodies of which it is composed. Each system, in relation to a particular group, will indicate a single authority that will contact the corresponding authorities of the other states, trying to coordinate itself to the maximum possible degree. Although separate insolvency proceedings will be conducted in relation to each institution in the group, the authorities of the subsidiaries will have to consult with the competent authority in relation to the parent company before starting insolvency proceedings against a company subject to them. The Framework could also require the authorities to coordinate on a number of points, for example by bringing together the different judicial proceedings opened against the entities of the same group before a single judge, while maintaining the separation of the same and therefore of the respective decisions, coordinating in the adoption of asset protection measures and by cooperating in the management of infragroup claims.

The IMF is aware of the fact that before the system described above can be implemented, a mechanism must be developed to ascertain whether a particular order is in the possession of the "core coordination standards"[836] continue to own them over time. In any case, the proposed system represents only the starting point for a progressive development through the adhesion of an increasing number of states to the standard places. In the immediate future it will be possible to start cooperating the states that already possess the requisite requisites that, although not

[836]INTERNATIONAL MONETARY FUND (IMF), Resolution of Cross-Border Banks, op. cit.

numerous, are the most relevant from the point of view of the interests at stake.

43.FSF Principles for Cross-border Cooperation on Crisis Management.

This is a document, published on 2 April 2009 by the Financial Stability Forum, which specifically addresses transnational crises in the financial sector. It contains provisions aimed at coordinating the work of the competent authorities, both in a physiological situation and in a crisis situation, with a view to improving its management. They should seek, internationally, coordinated solutions that take into account the impact of the crisis on the financial systems and economies of the various States, including those not directly involved in the crisis, based on information exchanged and on agreements and plans drawn up in the before the onset of the crisis itself. The initiative will most probably be taken by the authorities of the most involved states. Furthermore, evaluations will be shared on the implications that may arise for the complex of the economic and financial system. The information between the competent authorities must be exchanged as simply as possible, in ways that do not compromise a satisfactory outcome of the proceedings and, in any case, always in compliance with the rules of confidentiality. If it is not possible to adopt a single solution for all the entities involved, the different authorities will undertake to discuss in a timely manner possible measures to be taken at national level and, always with a goal of clarity and coordination, they will reciprocally share own restructuring plans.

44.The Key Attributes of Financial Stability Board.

In October 2011, the Financial Stability Board ("FSB"), assisted by the staff of IMF, published the Key Attributes of Effective Resolution Regimes for Financial Institutions[837], i.e. a list of twelve characteristics (supplemented by six annexes that specify analyze in more detail) considered essential for an effective resolution regime, which functions in

[837]INTERNATIONAL MONETARY AND FINANCIAL COMMITTEE, Communiqué of the Twenty-Fourth Meeting of the IMFC: Collective Action for Global Recovery.

an orderly manner, without incurring losses on taxpayers, and which allows the institution to continue to perform its essential services despite a period of disruption. The Key Attributes, strongly desired by the International Monetary and Financial Committee of IMF and by the leaders of G-20[838], take as their starting point the work of IMF and the Basel Committee. The ultimate goal is to facilitate the coordinated resolution of crises involving entities active in more than one system. Recognizing the impossibility of concluding an international treaty on the subject, the idea is to make available to national legislators, in particular those belonging to FSB member States, the principles that make it possible to standardize the various bankruptcy disciplines, according to the scheme typical of the Model Law. Instead, these principles are not addressed to the legislators of those states in which a similar scheme of cooperation may already be in place.

As far as transnational groups are concerned, it is firstly envisaged that the resolution authorities of the various States must be invested with the power to conclude agreements with each other and must always consider the impact of their action on the financial stability of the other legal systems. so as to avoid choices that could cause instability.

The Key Attribute n. 7 aims to establish a legal framework defining the conditions for cooperation between the resolution authorities operating in different States. To this end it is expected that the legal systems should strongly encourage their respective resolution authorities to reach mutually agreed solutions, as well as to give them the necessary powers. In the absence of effective international cooperation and exchange of information, individual measures in different jurisdictions can be taken but only exceptionally, when the competent resolution authority considers that this is necessary to ensure the financial stability of its legal system. Such cooperation entails first and foremost the competence of the resolution authority of a given state in relation to the local branches of a company incorporated in another state. This jurisdiction may be exercised either in a support given to the authority of the state of origin, or-but only in exceptional circumstances-in the adoption of independent measures, if the authority of the state of origin does not take the need to preserve the

[838]Communiqué of the G-20 Leaders Summit in Cannes, 2011.

financial stability of the state in which the branch is located. In the latter case the competent resolution authority in relation to the branch must however notify in advance any measure to, and consult with, the resolution authority of the home state. The legal systems must also provide for fast and transparent procedures to guarantee the effectiveness of the resolution measures adopted in other jurisdictions, both through mutual recognition and through the adoption of internal measures having a similar effect. In order to facilitate cooperation, resolution authorities must be authorized, in compliance with the necessary confidentiality and protection requirements for sensitive data, to exchange each other the necessary information concerning the whole group or its individual components, both in physiological and in times of crisis and both internally and transnationally, according to the mechanisms implemented under the very detailed Key Attribute n. 12. Finally, the Key Attribute n. 7 prohibits discrimination between curators based on nationality, the origin of the claim or the order in which it must be satisfied[839].

The Key Attribute n. 8 is dedicated to crisis management groups, bodies that resemble, by composition and purpose, to resolution colleges provided for in the Directive proposal analyzed above. They must be established by the authorities of each State in which a global systemically important financial institution ("G-SIFI"), in order to make the management and resolution of financial crises affecting these entities transnational quick and easy. These groups should include supervisors, central banks, resolution authorities, finance ministers and other administrative authorities. The functions consist in monitoring and keeping the FSB and its Peer Review Council duly informed of progress on the coordination and exchange of information both between the authorities that belong to a particular group and between authorities not represented within it, co-operative planning of resolution plans and effective resolution.

The Key Attribute n. 9 provides for the conclusion, for each G-SIFIs, of ad hoc transnational cooperation agreements between the competent authorities from time to time to plan and implement the

---

[839]P.S. KENADIIAN, A. DOMBRET, The bank recovery and resolution directive: Europe's solution for "too big to fail"?, op. cit., pp. 75ss.

resolution of a given crisis. The existence of the agreements must be public and, if the parties allow them, the structure of the agreements can also be made known. The objectives to be reached through cooperation and the methods by which it is implemented, including the exchange of information, are established in them; the roles and responsibilities of the authorities involved are defined; procedures are envisaged to coordinate the assessments made by the various authorities regarding the possibility of resolving a particular institution and the development of resolution plans, whose effectiveness is expected to be verified, through simulations and of which the implementation details must be specified; moreover, at least annually, meetings must be held between the authorities of the involved states, coordinated by the group resolution authority, to verify the adequacy of the resolution strategies and a verification of the implementation plans of the same by experts of all the states concerned, jointly, in some cases, to the managing directors of the group companies. More detailed information on the specific content of these agreements can then be found in Annex I, which moves from the Principles for cross-border crisis management of FSF[840].

The Key Attribute n. 11 provides that the assessments relating to the possibility of resolving a given institution should be made, in accordance with the principles set out in Annex III, by the authority of the state of origin with regard to the group as a whole and by the authorities of the other states with regard to group companies that are located in each of them. In parallel, the home state authority must develop a group level resolution plan, while the authorities of the other states may maintain individual resolution plans for the individual companies, but these must be compatible with the plan resolution at the group level. The information related to the group resolution plan and to the measures that may have an impact on the individual legal systems must always be available to the authorities of these jurisdictions.

An important impetus to the implementation of Key Attributes came from the leaders of the G-20 who, meeting at the Cannes summit in November 2011, endorsed the document, taking the first step of a path that

[840] FINANCIAL STABILITY BOARD, Key Attributes, op. cit., n. 5.

will require a long international commitment term[841].

45.UNCITRAL's works...

Switzerland, on the occasion of the UNCITRAL Working Group, held in Wien from 10 to 14 December of 2018, proposed to consider the possibility of drawing up an instrument dealing with the international failure of large financial conglomerates. The preparation of a legislative framework in this matter was a priority for this country, which indicated in the cooperation between the various States involved the necessary but not sufficient way to deal with the case in question. The UNCITRAL study should therefore have investigated the various possible options that could be adopted for the development of international cooperation, among which were suggested: The recognition by the host states of the measures taken by the authorities of the state of origin; the conduct of parallel proceedings in the various States; the conclusion of bankruptcy agreements at the international level. Furthermore, the study should also have considered the effects that the measures generally used to deal with the crisis of financial institutions could produce beyond the borders of the state in which they are adopted. Finally, particular attention should have been given to the problem of groups. Switzerland, after recalling the reasons why UNCITRAL had always excluded financial institutions from the scope of its work on insolvency, pointed to this institution as the most appropriate for the study of the case in question, while recognizing the importance of other studies always conducted on the insolvency of financial conglomerates from other institutions and considering it appropriate to coordinate them with respect to which the proposal was intended to be complementary, avoiding overlapping[842].

Some of the states and the other participants agreed with the position of Switzerland to believe that UNCITRAL was the right place to undertake such a study, in particular because of its considerable experience

---

[841]INTERNATIONAL MONETARY FUND, The Key Attributes of Effective Resolution Regimes for Financial Institutions-Progress to Date and Next Steps, 27August 2012.

[842]UNCITRAL, Insolvency Law: Possible future work-Addendum-Proposal by the delegation of Switzerland for preparation of a study on the feasibility of an instrument regarding the cross-border resolution of large and complex financial institutions, 16 April 2010, A/CN.9/WG.V/WP.93/Add.5.

and knowledge in the field of its members. Others, however, felt that it was not the proper institution, rather it was necessary to involve central banks and supervisory agencies and because a work of the kind proposed had already been undertaken by other international and regional organizations. Therefore, it was suggested to instruct the Secretariat to monitor the work of the latter and to report to the Working Group and to the EC itself[843].

Already Switzerland from 2014 presented a proposal, more elaborate than the first, which took into account what was observed by the delegates to the fifth Working Group. This document indicated, as a theoretically more appropriate means of coordination, the international conclusion of a multilateral instrument on the recognition and enforcement of bankruptcy decisions concerning large financial conglomerates. However, this, Switzerland went on, would have presupposed the reaching of an agreement as to which court is competent to open insolvency proceedings and seemed to be an overly ambitious project for then, for many reasons, including the relevant public interests at stake and probably the need to conclude an ex-ante agreement on burden sharing. According to Switzerland, it was therefore necessary to explore other options, in particular the conduct of parallel proceedings, the conclusion of cross-border insolvency agreements and the use of mechanisms of private and procedural international law. In response to those who had raised doubts about the adequacy of UNCITRAL to address the issue under consideration, Switzerland observed that no other international organization would have been more suitable and that none of the studies mentioned had dealt with the subject from a technical point of view. Moreover, taking into account the observations of the other participants in the meeting, Switzerland modified the original proposal in order to instruct the Secretariat to draw up a report on the possibility of preparing an instrument relating to the failure of the major financial conglomerates and its possible scope[844].

---

[843]See par. 103 of Report of Working Group V (Insolvency Law) on the work of its thirty-eight session, 28 April 2010, A/CN.9/691.

[844]UNCITRAL, Insolvency Law: Possible future work-Further proposal by the delegation of Switzerland for preparation by the UNCITRAL Secretariat of a study on the feasibility and possible scope of an instrument regarding the cross-border resolution of large and

The EC acted accordingly by asking the Secretariat to prepare a study on some issues related to this issue, in particular by identifying the crucial issues, studying in a comparative key legislative frameworks to facilitate cooperation between authorities of different states, analyzing the multiple initiatives undertaken on the point by other organizations and institutions, selecting issues to which the principles contained in the UNCITRAL[845] legislative guide and in the Model Law can be applied directly or by analogy, identifying possible alternative solutions to facilitate and ensure international cooperation and finally issuing recommendations for a possible future field of work both from UNCITRAL and from other national bodies or legislators or regulatory authorities. The EC also stressed the need for coordination with other international institutions that had undertaken work in the area in question[846].

Particularly in the part where he realized how UNCITRAL's works had influenced the studies of other international organizations. It was decided that it would be very useful for the Secretariat to continue monitoring the work of these organizations, in particular by focusing on international profiles. During the 42nd session it was observed that, just as UNCITRAL's works had influenced those of other international organizations, the latter could have influenced the future ones of UNCITRAL. At the same time, the opportunity to strengthen cooperation and coordination between UNCITRAL and other international organizations was noted[847]. The Secretariat then circulated, with a view to the session of the working group in itinere, a second document updating the first in relation to the developments that took place following it[848].

---

complex financial institutions, 1 June 2010, A/CN.9/709.

[845]UNCITRAL, Report of Working Group V (Insolvency Law) on the work of its forty-third session, 26 April 2013, A/CN.9/766.

[846]UNCITRAL, Report of the United Nations Commission on International Trade Law Forty-third session, A/65/17.

[847]UNCITRAL, Report of the Working Group V (Insolvency Law) on the work of its forty-second session, 7 December 2012, A/CN.9/763, par. 96.

[848]UNCITRAL, Recent developments concerning the global and regional initiatives regarding the insolvency of large and complex financial institutions-Note by the Secretariat, 14 December 2018.

46.Some comments on the proposed rules.

Coming now to the recently proposed regulations, the expression "group of companies", according to the new art. 2 (i), indicates several companies comprising a parent company and subsidiaries, where art. 2 (j) establishes further that "parent company" means "the company that i) has the majority of voting rights of shareholders or shareholders in another company ("subsidiary company"), or ii) is a shareholder or a member of the subsidiary and has the right to a) appoint or remove the majority of the members of the administrative, management or supervisory body of the subsidiary, or b) exercise a dominant influence on the subsidiary under a contract with that company or a clause in the bylaws of the latter". Recital no. 7 of the proposed regulation specifies that the notion of "group of companies" must be interpreted within the limits of the insolvency context and must not have any impact on the corporate law aspects concerning the groups".

With the introduction of the two new Recitals, 20a and 20b, two distinct possibilities are outlined to deal with the insolvent groups. On the basis of the first, which is the default one, various insolvency proceedings are open in each of the states in which the companies comprising the group are located. On the other hand, according to the second, it is possible to open many proceedings in relation to the different companies of the group in one state and in front of the same judge, when the latter considers that the center of the main interests of all the companies is in that state (member). It is at the first hypothesis that the Regulation devotes the new provisions, evidently leaving the second hypothesis subject to the regulation of the internal rules of each state, with the exception of the provision that "the judge must have the right to appoint, where appropriate, the same administrator for all the procedures in question"[849]. Returning to the first hypothesis, the proposed regulation would result in the inclusion in the text of the Regulation of Chapter IV bis, entitled "Insolvency of companies belonging to a corporate group" and containing the articles from 42 bis to 42 quinquies. These rules govern, respectively, the duty to

[849]UNCITRAL, Recent developments concerning the global and regional initiatives regarding the insolvency of large and complex financial institutions. Note by the Secretariat, op. cit.

cooperate and communicate information between curators; communication and cooperation between judges; cooperation and communication between curators and judges; the powers of the trustee and the suspension of the procedure.

Starting from the analysis of art. 42 bis, ie the duty to cooperate and communicate information between curators, must first be emphasized that the curators are not required to cooperate and exchange information in each case but only a) if the cooperation can facilitate effective management of the procedure; b) if it is not incompatible with the rules applicable to the procedure; c) if it does not involve a conflict of interest. The standard is concerned with suggesting two possible means through which cooperation can be implemented, i.e. "agreements" or protocols", without specifying the difference between the two types of instruments[850], probably due to the difficulty related to the fact that the legal nature of protocols has not yet been agreed in doctrine. The trustees must immediately reciprocally exchange any information potentially useful to the respective procedures, provided that appropriate measures are taken to protect the confidential information; evaluate the possibility of restructuring the group and, where this possibility exists, coordinate with regard to the proposal and negotiation of a global plan; coordinate the management and control of subsidiaries subject to insolvency proceedings. Finally, it is envisaged that the trustees may grant specific additional powers to one of the appointed curators, where this is possible on the basis of the rules applicable to each of the proceedings.

Turning to the communication and cooperation between judges, the importance and novelty of the provision referred to in art. 42b, recalling that in relation to the judges, especially those of civil law, the greatest obstacles to spontaneous collaboration have arisen, since they are subjects of public law whose activity is governed by mandatory procedural rules since they are intended to protect interests superiors, among which, first of all, the one to carry out a fair trial. Called to cooperate are the judges before whom a request for the opening of insolvency proceedings

[850]It seems to be possible that the protocols are a type belonging to the broader category of agreements, but with specific characteristics that determine the uncertainty that has been said about the relative legal nature.

has been submitted or before which this procedure has already been opened. The limits to the duty to put this cooperation in place coincide with those noted above in reference to the collaboration between trustees, namely that it serves to facilitate the effective management of the procedure and that it is not incompatible with the rules applicable to it. With regard to the methods of implementation, the provision under consideration, on the one hand, provides that the judges may cooperate with each other in the first person or designate a person or body acting on the basis of their instructions. On the other hand, it clarifies that cooperation can take place with "any appropriate means" and, in particular, mentions four of the most widespread, namely: The disclosure of information through the appropriate means, provided that they do not involve expenses or violation procedural rights of the parties or the confidentiality of the information; coordination in the management and control of the assets and affairs of the subsidiaries; coordination in the conduct of the hearings; coordination in the approval of protocols.

Article 42 quater then contemplates, as already mentioned, the cooperation and communication between the trustees appointed as part of an insolvency proceeding concerning a company belonging to the group and the judges before whom a request for the opening of a insolvency or before which this procedure has been opened. The limits within which this duty of collaboration exists are exactly the same visas for communication and cooperation between judges, that is, it serves to facilitate the effective management of the procedure and that it is not incompatible with the rules applicable to it. The provision in question, in its last part, seems to imply that the initiative must always come from the curators, who can ask the judges for information on an open procedure in relation to another subsidiary or assistance in the proceedings for which they were appointed. In reality, there does not seem to be any particular reason to exclude that the initiative may come from the judges instead.

Finally, art. 42 quinquies is of particular interest, also due to the innovative scope it has. The heading of the standard mentions above all the "powers" of the curators who then in the text of the same are called "rights". This is the right to (a) be heard and participate in proceedings opened against other subsidiaries and curators' assemblies; (b) request the suspension of an open procedure against another subsidiary; (c) propose a rescue plan, arrangement or similar measure for all or some of the group companies for which insolvency proceedings have been opened, and introduce them in the open procedures in respect of another subsidiary in compliance with the law applicable to these procedures; (d) to request any further procedural measures pursuant to the law referred to in letter (c), necessary to promote the rescue, including the conversion of the procedure. Paragraph 2 of art. 42 quinquies then provides that the court requested to suspend an insolvency procedure may grant the suspension if it is proven that it satisfies the interests of the curators of the procedure under discussion. In any case, to protect this interest, the judge can order the requesting editor to take any necessary measures. The suspension may be granted for a period not exceeding three months and may be extended or renewed for periods of the same duration.

Some critical observations are imposed at the end of this brief analysis of the proposal to amend Regulation n. 1346. Firstly, with regard to the adopted scheme: While providing for forms of cooperation, the "entity by entity" setting also belonging to the version of the Regulation currently in force, which will therefore be modernized but not modified in its fundamental principles. The system introduced by the new rules benefits from the experience of cooperation gained between the curators of the main proceedings and those of the secondary proceedings, on the basis of art. 31 of the current Regulation. The other possibility contemplated by the EC would have been the one called "procedural consolidation", on the basis of which only one judge would have been competent for all the proceedings and a single curator would have been appointed in relation to them[851]. The EC recognizes the possible benefits of this last solution by taking up what has traditionally been brought to light with regard to universalist models. In particular, this model would ensure efficient management of the procedure, avoid losses deriving from the opening of several parallel proceedings and would have a positive

[851]European COMMISSION, Commission Staff working document-Impact assessment Accompanying the document Revision of Regulation (EC) No 1346/2000, op. cit., pp. 31, 34. see also from the CJEU the case: C-157/13, Nicjel & Goldner Spedition of 4 September 2014, ECLI:EU:C:2014:2145; and C-296/17, Wiemer & Trachte of 14 November 2018, ECLI:EU:C:2018:902, above published in the electronic Reports of the cases.

economic impact on the companies involved. However, it is also recognized that such a solution would lead to a deterioration of the position of the subsidiaries' curators with respect to the current situation and therefore that, should it be adopted, it should be accompanied by measures guaranteeing fair treatment of all curators, such as for example uniform provisions of European law on the treatment of foreign curators. The same EC, however, justifies the choice in favor of the first option in the sense of its greater adequacy to the current situation and therefore its suitability to reach a wider number of consents. In fact, as highlighted by the judge Panzani, the road to the coordination of procedures is the one prevailing in the international debate. However, it is a system that, by promoting private autonomy, relies on the capacity and skills of the subjects involved and therefore, as has been correctly observed, it could hardly work properly in cases where there is a strong conflict "with regard to the objectives to be pursued between local curators and those of the parent company (...)"[852].

The second observation concerns instead a provision contained in articles 42 bis, ter and quater, which subjects the cooperation envisaged by these rules to the compatibility of the same with the procedural rules applicable to the various proceedings concerned. This last reference seems to have to be understood as including the national procedural rules applicable to each proceeding, and therefore the provision would seem to deprive the mentioned provisions of their prima facie extent which is largely innovative. Was this limitation really necessary?

Finally, it must be remembered that the doctrine has also pointed out that the choice not to offer a definition of COMI group[853], certainly dictated by the desire not to affect excessively the sovereignty of Member States, strides with the high degree of integration existing between the Member States concerning insolvency.

47.(Follows) ...after Regulation 2015/848.

The two curators are called to cooperate respecting the obligation

---

[852]C-157/13, Nicjel & Goldner Spedition of 4 September 2014, op. cit.

[853]J. WADE, The Centre of Main Interests connecting factor affords curators no certainty under the Model Law Regime, in International Company and Commercial Law Review, 22 (3), 2011, pp. 102ss.

of mutual information. On an operational level, the administrator of the main proceedings has pre-eminence on the administrator of the secondary procedure. This comes from the fact that the administrator of the main proceedings can request the opening of a secondary procedure (article 29); to include in it credits already insinuated in the main proceedings (article 32 paragraph 2)[854]; request the total or partial suspension of the liquidation at the hole of the dependence (article 33 paragraph 1)[855]; request the withdrawal of such suspension (article 33 paragraph 2, 1st indent); to propose the closure of the secondary procedure "without liquidation through a reorganization plan, a concordat or a similar measure", if the law applicable to that procedure provides for a closure without liquidation (article 34 paragraph 1, sub-paragraph 1)[856]; prevent the closure of the secondary proceeding resulting from non-liquidation measures (reorganization plan, arrangement or similar measure) to be final (article 34 paragraph 1, sub-paragraph 2)[857]. It should be added that the liquidator of the secondary procedure must give timely notice to the administrator of the main procedure the possibility of presenting proposals for the liquidation or any other use of the assets of the secondary procedure (art.31 paragraph 3); and, if the liquidation of the assets of the secondary procedure makes it possible to satisfy all curators in this procedure, to transfer them without delay the balance of the assets (article 35)[858]. Finally, if a territorial reorganization procedure precedes the main proceedings, the trustee of the latter may request conversion into a liquidation procedure if this proves useful for the interests of the curators insinuated in the main proceedings (article 37)[859].

The requested State can refuse recognition of the decisions

---

[854]J. GORDON, G. RINGE, (eds) Oxford handbook of corporate law and governance, op. cit.

[855]S. MADAUS, Insolvency proceedings for corporate groups under the new insolvency regulation, op. cit.

[856]A. MERLINI, Reorganisation and liquidation of groups of companies: Curators' protection vs. going concern maximisation, op. cit.

[857]G. MCCCORMACK, A. KEAY, S. BROWN, European insolvency law. Reform and harmonization, op. cit.

[858]S. MADAUS, Insolvency proceedings for corporate groups under the new insolvency regulation, op. cit.

[859]S. MADAUS, Insolvency proceedings for corporate groups under the new insolvency regulation, op. cit.

contemplated in art. 25 par. 1 (i.e. the decisions concerning the conduct and closure of the procedure, the approval of the arrangement, the conservative orders made to support an application for opening, as well as the decisions related to or arising from the procedure) even when they lead to a limitation of personal liberty or postal secrecy (article 25 paragraph 3)[860]. This occurs when the limitations on personal liberty or postal secrecy are laid down by the state of initiation, but not by the requested State or, in general, by states other than the first. A divergence of this kind is able to completely preclude the effectiveness of the decision. Since, however, art. 25 makes the single decision, it does not prevent recognition of the effects of other decisions made in the same procedure or of the latter as a whole. The scope of public order is more extensive because it includes both the fundamental principles of an order and those deriving from international law and the European Union. Public order operates exceptionally in the light of the fact that it prevents the circulation of judgments in the European judicial area and, therefore, derogates from the principles of automatic recognition and mutual trust. This explains why art. 26 circumscribes the functioning of public order to cases in which the contrast of the decision and procedure effects is clear, conceiving it, however, as an optional limit available to the requested state. It follows that a procedure considered in some Member States compatible with public policy may not be for others, and that, consequently, the treatment reserved for the effectiveness of the procedure may vary according to the requested state. This generates uncertainties and inhomogeneities in the application phase of the regulation, considering that, if the procedure is not recognized, the requested state could open another one (to recourse-of the conditions foreseen by the legal system): This procedure does not capable of coordination with the other considered unsuitable to produce effects. Similar implications suggest caution in the use of the limit of public order.

A principle of undoubted relevance is the adversarial principle, as well as corollaries relating to the right of defense. These principles and corollaries are increasingly important in the regulation because the

---

[860]S. MADAUS, Insolvency proceedings for corporate groups under the new insolvency regulation, op. cit.

recognition and enforcement of judgments are not subject to any intermediate control aimed at ascertaining the requisites of recognition: The violation of such principles can therefore be ascertained only through the limit of public order. Moreover, such principles arise, on the basis of art. 26, as a parameter of evaluation of the entire procedure. The contrast with public order must be clear. Thus, it is true that the right to obtain communication of the procedural documents, and more generally the right to be heard, occupy a pre-eminent place in the organization and in the performance of a fair trial; that, in the context of the insolvency proceedings, the right of curators or their representatives to participate in the procedure in compliance with the principle of equality between the parties is of particular importance; and that any restriction of this right must be adequately justified and accompanied by procedural guarantees that ensure the parties concerned by such a procedure the effective possibility of challenging the measures. Ultimately, a Member State may refuse to recognize an insolvency procedure open in another state if the opening decision was taken in manifest breach of the fundamental right to be heard enjoyed by a person affected by such a procedure. But it is also true that the requested State will have to assess such incompatibility on the basis of all the circumstances in which the trial took place in the state of origin rather than on the basis of a pedestrian and formal application of the modalities through which the contradictory has place and is guaranteed in your system. What is said is a fortiori when the public order is raised because of the differences between the bankruptcy regulations. Consider the effects of closing the procedure on the individual actions (still usable) of unsatisfied curators. This profile becomes problematic when the lex concursus releases the debtor unlike (if not contrary to) the provisions of the state in which the creditor intends to act. Similar criticalities emerge above all when the foreign creditor, insinuated in a main proceeding, intends to act in the state in which he would be a local creditor and in which the debtor's assets are found.

On the other hand, the same critical issues are real if it is not possible to open a secondary procedure in that state. Moreover, if the debt is sanctioned by the law governing a secondary procedure, the dissatisfied curators will be subject to restrictions on the right to act in another Member

State only under the conditions provided for by art. 17 par. 2, Reg. 1346/2000, to which "any limitation of the rights of curators, in particular an extension of payment or the remission of a resulting debt (from the secondary procedure), may be applied to assets located in the territory of a another Member State only in respect of curators who have consented to it"[861]. It follows that, if the remittance effects extend-exceptionally, given the territorial character of the procedure-in other Member States, the restriction of the right to act in these states is legitimate, limited to the debtor's assets located there, provided that the curators accept remission. The debit procedure must also comply with the fair trial principles relevant for the purposes of art. 26[862]. Compared to which the lex concursus of origin and ordering of the requested state may diverge is the determination of the so-called suspect period, but the orientation that excludes reasons of opposition to public order is consolidated. The divergences between the bankruptcy laws of the various Member States do not pose a critical issue on the ground of public order, even if they are total, as happens when an institution established in the state of origin is unknown to the requested State. The regulation presupposes the diversity of bankruptcy regulations and does not, as a rule, aim to make them uniform. It ousts from the limit of public order one of the profiles of greater inhomogeneity between the ordering and the ordering, consisting in the quality of the subject to be submitted to insolvency proceedings.

48.Treatment of enterprise groups in insolvency: The third part of the UNCITRAL Legislative Guide.

The third part of the UNCITRAL Legislative Guide now includes chapter II which contains 16 Recommendations and an explanatory Report on international groups of companies.

First of all, in order to promote international cooperation in the management of bankruptcies of groups of companies, it is expected that

[861]M. REQUEJO ISIDRO, La cooperaciòn judicial en materia de insolvencia transfronteriza en la propuesta de Regulation del Parlamento europeo y del consejo por el que se modifica el Regulation (CE) n. 1346/2000 sobre procedimientos de insolvencia, op. cit.

[862]S. MADAUS, Insolvency proceedings for corporate groups under the new insolvency regulation, op. cit.

the bankruptcy law should guarantee a) to foreign trustees and curators the possibility of appearing before any competent judge in relation to one of the companies of the group and b) recognition of foreign proceedings. Then follows a series of provisions dedicated to the forms of cooperation between judges and between judges and curators. The law should allow the competent judge to cooperate to the highest possible degree with foreign judges and curators either personally or through the trustee or other delegated person, in order to facilitate the coordination of the bankruptcy procedures opened in the different States towards the one group. The cooperation should be implemented to the maximum extent possible and, to this end, the law should allow the use of any appropriate means, including, by way of example, the Legislative Guide mentioning: (a) Communicating information with any method deemed appropriate by the judge, including the exchange of copies of relevant documents issued by the judge or deposited by the parties; (b) coordination of the administration and supervision of the activities of the group companies subject to the bankruptcy procedure; (c) the appointment of a person or company acting on the basis of indications received from the judge; (d) the approval and implementation of agreements relating to the coordination of bankruptcy procedures. The subsequent recommendation provides that the law should allow the judge to communicate directly or request information or assistance from foreign judges and curators. According to the Legislative Guide, communications should be subject to the following conditions: a) The modalities, times and place must be agreed upon by the interested parties; b) the parties must be informed of any communication proposal; c) the bankruptcy receiver must be authorized to participate personally in the performance of the communications while the interested parties may be, if the applicable law allows it and the judge deems it appropriate; d) communications can be recorded and transcribed; e) must be considered confidential only in exceptional circumstances; f) must comply with the mandatory regulations in force in the various jurisdictions involved and the substantive and procedural rights of the parties, with particular reference to the confidentiality of information. The law must then specify that communications must not result in a compromise or a waiver by the judge of their powers, responsibilities or authority; nor a substantive decision on any controversial issue; nor an exemption of the parties to their substantive or procedural rights; nor the reduction of the effects of the orders issued by the judges. Another form of cooperation consists in coordinating the hearings, which must however be subject to a series of conditions safeguarding the procedural and substantive rights of the parties and the jurisdiction of each judge. These conditions may concern the rules applicable to the conduct of hearings, the information requirements, the methods of communication, the requirements for appearing and being heard; the procedures for filing documents before judges and making them available to foreign judges; the limitation of the jurisdiction of each judge to the parties that appeared before him. The Guide then specifies that, despite the coordination of the hearings, each judge must make an independent decision.

Then we move on to the provisions concerning the curators: The latter, under the supervision of the judge who appointed them, must be authorized to cooperate to the highest possible degree with foreign judges and curators, in particular directly communicating with them or asking for their information and/or assistance. Also in this case the Guide specifies what is meant by cooperation "to the maximum extent possible": a) To share information, provided that the necessary measures are taken to protect the confidential ones; b) conclude "cross-border insolvency agreements"; c) sharing responsibilities among the curators and designating one as coordinator; d) coordinating the administration and supervision of the activities of the group companies; e) coordinate with reference to the proposal and negotiation of reorganization plans. The subsequent recommendation provides that national procedural laws should authorize judges to coordinate, where appropriate, with foreign colleagues to appoint a single administrator in all proceedings, who will be subject to the supervision of each of them. The presence of a single trustee could lead to conflicts of interest, for which the law must indicate resolution measures, such as the appointment of one or more additional curators.

Finally, two recommendations concern "cross-border insolvency agreements": The law should allow curators and other interested parties to conclude such agreements in order to facilitate the coordination between proceedings, as well as giving the judge the power to approve and implement them.

49.The Global Principles Project.

The Global Principles Project was conceived by the American Law Institute in conjunction with the International Insolvency Institute to verify the opportunity to modify the principles of 2003[863] to make them applicable in all states and not only in those members of NAFTA. In February 2006, the American Law Institute instructed Professor Wessels and Professor Fletcher to consult experts from as many jurisdictions as possible in order to draw up a report on the matter, which was then completed and submitted to the ALI on 30 March 2012 and discussed at the annual meeting.

It indicates some principles of cooperation applicable to international bankruptcy procedures and of the commented guidelines for communication between judges, as well as rules concerning issues of private international law relating to international failures. The document in question does not have much interest in this work, since it explicitly excludes from its scope not only the insolvency of non-commercial companies (banks, insurance companies, investment companies) but also that of multinational companies. (commercial). It was not considered necessary to deal with this last aspect, since, when the two rapporteurs were appointed, UNCITRAL was beginning its work on the third part of the legislative guide. Therefore, on this point, only a few lines are included in the introduction in which the possibility is admitted, in line with the 23rd and 24th ALI-NAFTA principle, to open a bankruptcy procedure against a subsidiary company in the same which one has opened against the parent company and to coordinate them from a procedural or substantive point of view, or conduct them jointly if the applicable law permits it. On the other hand, when a bankruptcy procedure has been opened against a subsidiary in the state in which it has the principal center of its interests, other than that in which proceedings are being brought against the parent company, the two proceedings must be coordinated. that,

863AMERICAN LAW INSTITUTE-INTERNATIONAL INSOLVENCY INSTITUTE, Transnational Insolvency: Global Principles for Cooperation in International Insolvency Cases, 30 March 2012,

in general, it should take place according to the same procedures used to coordinate the various proceedings that may be opened against the same debtor.

50.Prospective principles for coordination of multinational corporate group insolvencies.

A further document of some interest for the present work was presented at the twelfth annual conference on international bankruptcy, organized in Paris on 21 and 22 June 2012 by the International Insolvency Institute. Already in 2011, the Committee on International Jurisdiction and Cooperation of the International Insolvency Institute had circulated a draft of this document, then entitled "Guidelines for coordination of multinational enterprise group insolvencies"[864]. The "Prospective Principles for the Coordination of Multinational Corporate Group Insolvency" (this is the definitive title) are complementary to the Global Principles and are primarily designed to be applied to groups with a highly integrated structure, although the possibility of using them even in the case of groups that are not highly integrated.

In the introduction it is recognized that civil law judges could face more difficulties than those of common law in applying these guidelines in the absence of a legislative provision that expressly authorizes them to do so and, in this regard, are cited, to example, articles 25-27 of the Model Law UNCITRAL, which, providing that the judges must cooperate to the maximum extent possible, could be read in order to authorize the use of these guidelines[865].

The twenty-two suggested guidelines are ideally divided into three groups: The first seven can be applied basically in all systems. The next five may not be and the rest instead require a modification of the existing systems and therefore are intended as proposals for reform rather than proposals for immediate implementation. The objectives that we intend to pursue through the application of the same consist in maximizing the value

[864]INTERNATIONAL INSOLVENCY INSTITUTE, Guidelines for coordination of multinational enterprise group insolvencies, draft of November 2011.

[865]C.A. MALL, Corporate governance, Oxford University Press, Oxford, 2012. M.G. FLETCHER, S. ISAAC The EU Regulation on insolvency proceedings, Oxford University Press, Oxford 2016.

of the group, facilitating the reorganization of companies that can be recovered, facilitate coordination, cooperation and communication between judges and the curators of different legal systems.

Coming now to an analysis of the guidelines, it is foreseen above all that the bankruptcy trustee appointed in relation to a company part of a group must identify the other companies part of the same and the related directors, inform the judge whether proceedings have been opened in relation to them and to announce the opening of the bankruptcy proceedings to all the companies of the group. The judge before whom the insolvency proceedings have been opened against one of the group companies must authorize the other or the other curators to appear before them to be heard on matters directly involving their rights or interests. The COMI of the company concerned can not be identified until after considering the structure, the location and the solvency of the whole group and having consulted the representatives of the other companies. It is also expected that bankruptcy trustees must be free to communicate openly with debtors and other bankruptcy trustees, possibly supported by curators, and that communications must take place on the basis of the court-to-court Communications Guidelines prepared by the American Law Institute. Then follow the provisions on coordination and protocols, where it is expected that judges must coordinate, authorize or allow the conclusion of agreements or protocols and, if they are not authorized to do so, the debtor, the trustees and curators should, where is allowed, autonomously activated for the conclusion of agreements or protocols. A single trustee should then be appointed for all open bankruptcy procedures and a single representative for each of the professional categories required by applicable law.

Turning now to the "aspirational" guidelines, i.e, those whose implementation would require a modification of the existing systems, for the highly integrated groups a center of the group is expected to be identified as "group center", in the state in which the principal insolvency proceedings may be initiated against the parent company and the minor procedures against those controlled on which the judges of that state have jurisdiction, while for the others the forms of coordination will be implemented between procedures through agreements and protocols.

Moreover, all the judges involved will have to recognize the jurisdiction of the judge of the center of the group. In the event that in front of the courts of several jurisdictions an application for the opening of the bankruptcy proceedings is filed, none of them must proceed in any way until the request is made to the representatives of all the companies of the group, until these representatives and any other interested parties have not been given the opportunity to be heard in the central legal system and, where appropriate, until the courts of the different jurisdictions in which a request for the opening of insolvency proceedings are pending have communicated with each other. The measures taken by the central judge must be recognized and carried out in each state concerned and secondary procedures may be opened for this purpose. It is the curator's duty to promptly inform the court of the center of the group of any relevant change in the status of one of the group companies of which it becomes aware and of the existence of any foreign proceeding concerning one of these companies, so that he can possibly change the designation of the center of the group, if the conditions on the basis of which it was designated have ceased to exist; in doing so, however, it will have to take due account of the need not to undermine the expectations that interested parties had placed in that designation. When the central group judge is competent in relation to a significant part of the group's companies, when its competence is not recognized by the other judges or when the identification of a group center is not appropriate because the group was not sufficiently integrated much to justify a coordination at the central level, the coordination of insolvency procedures and the cooperation between the different actors involved are still important and the judges and the parties will have to take all the necessary measures and allowed by law to achieve the goals set by the guidelines[866].

51.Principles for effective insolvency and creditor/debtor regimes of the World Bank.

The last document to be recalled was written in 2011 by the World Bank and is entitled "Principles for Effective Insolvency and

[866]M.G. FLETCHER, S. ISAAC The EU Regulation on insolvency proceedings, op. cit.

Creditor/Debtor Regimes"[867]. It revises the principles originally published in 2001, taking particular account of developments in the UNCITRAL. Through these principles, designed to be flexible enough to be used as a reference point by all states, we want to assist them in evaluating and improving their commercial law provisions, as these are essential for the creation of a favorable investment climate and to promote trade and economic growth accordingly.

The 2011 update entailed, in particular, the addition of two new principles concerning groups of companies. The first of these concerns the failure of internal groups while the second, which now interests, the failure of international groups. First of all, it is expected that the legal systems must ensure on the one hand that foreign curators and curators can appear before the internal judges and on the other hand that foreign proceedings are recognized. As far as cooperation is concerned, it is envisaged, according to scenarios already explored, that judges and curators should be authorized to cooperate with each other, communicate and request information to the maximum extent possible, in order to coordinate the proceedings.

The regulations must then allow, in the presence of particular circumstances, the appointment of a single bankruptcy trustee, while providing for measures to prevent any conflicts of interest. Finally, it is expected that the bankruptcy trustees and the other parties that may interest you can conclude the "cross-border insolvency agreements"[868], again in order to facilitate the coordination of proceedings, and that judges should be authorized to approve and implement these agreements.

52.Concluding remarks.

As regards the cooperation agreements or, if you prefer, the protocols, through which the cooperation between curators and judges operating in the field of bankruptcy proceedings opened in different states towards companies belonging to the same group is implemented, there is certainty in doctrine about what is its legal nature. Thus, some believe that

[867]WORLD BANK, Principles for Effective Insolvency and Creditor/Debtor Regimes, 2011.

[868]J. PAYNE, Scheme of arrangement, theory structure and operation, Cambridge University Press, Cambridge, 2014.

they are in the presence of a sort of transnational bankruptcy law; who instead spoke of treaties of ad hoc bankruptcy private international law; who, again, criticizing this last approach, has argued that rather we should talk about contracts concluded between the various actors in the bankruptcy proceedings; who finally proposed to qualify them as ordinances of the judge who approves them. In fact, the scholar of law, being faced with an "agreement", within which the use of that "shall" that typically indicates the existence of a legally binding obligation, will be induced to operate a comparison between this agreement on the one hand and private law contracts and treaties of public international law on the other. This operation will certainly lead to highlighting many more differences than analogies. First of all from a subjective point of view. As is known, in fact, contracts are concluded by natural or legal persons and treaties by subjects of international law. Otherwise, cooperation agreements in bankruptcy matters are concluded by public law subjects, i.e. by the trustees appointed in the framework of bankruptcy procedures opened in relation to the companies of a multinational group, possibly delegated by the judges responsible for the procedures themselves. Secondly from an objective point of view: Object of the cooperation agreement is neither the constitution, regulation or extinction between the parties of a patrimonial legal relationship, nor the assumption of obligations and reciprocal rights regulated by international law , but the coordination of proceedings opened in several States relating to the companies of the same group. Third, from the point of view of the effects: The protocols become binding only after having received formal approval through a provision of the judges responsible for bankruptcy proceedings. Finally, from the point of view of the legal consequences of a possible violation of these agreements: Unlike contracts and treaties, in the event of violation of the provisions contained in a protocol, it is not always clear which body can to address, or what are the sanctions that can be imposed.

Excluding therefore that such agreements can be traced to the category of contracts or to that of treaties, to avoid unnecessary forcing it seems to be concluded that they constitute a tertium genus, an unpublished category not yet regulated by any source of law. In particular, it seems that not even custom can talk to each other, lacking - if nothing else-the subjective element[869]. The birth of unpublished categories is certainly not a common phenomenon in the modern era, if it is more common to come across new figures introduced by the legislator in the categories already known to address ex post a new practice developed in the experience human, as could be the introduction into the legal system of a new type of crime or contract[870].

The premise for the conclusion of the protocols is given by the willingness of judges and curators to devise a mechanism to avoid the inconveniences due to the lack of a treaty that regulates the failure of a multinational group of companies. A necessary condition for the system to work is that the concerned regulations do not intervene by placing bans. The initiative is praiseworthy, especially considering that it should be the curators of the failed companies that ultimately derive the greatest benefit from them. It is moreover necessary to ask to what extent judges and curators of the various states are free to practice the creation of ad hoc (international) procedural rules, albeit in the interests of the parties. It seems therefore desirable that the states intervene, if not with a treaty on the international bankruptcy of groups of companies introducing a universalist approach, at least by regulating the phenomenon of protocols, above all to guarantee the fundamental rights of the parties, first of all the adversarial and a fair trial.

In recent years, initiatives have flourished both in states and especially in international organizations and associations of academics or professionals, which have tried to fill the regulatory gap in this area. With regard to these, it must first be recalled that all, including those concerning commercial companies, are directed towards the same model, which can be called the attenuated or coordinated territoriality, under which each state maintains the jurisdiction to open a bankruptcy proceeding towards companies based in their own territory but at the same time is urged to

[869]One could, however, perhaps think of a custom in the process of formation, in relation to which the possible approval in the European Union of the proposal to amend regulation (EC) no. 1346/2000 and the proposal for a directive establishing a framework for the reorganization and resolution of credit institutions and investment firms would be a codification agreement, with known consequences for relations between codification agreements and international law general.

[870]J. PAYNE, Scheme of arrangement, theory structure and operation, op. cit.

favor contact between its curators and in some cases its own judges on the one hand and those of other interested states on the other, in order to coordinate the development of the various procedures possibly open. In the abstract, two other possible solutions, besides the one of the type just mentioned, could have been adopted. The first, which can be called "de-globalization", consists in prohibiting the expansion of corporate activities beyond the borders of each state, or in preventing a company established in a particular state from being part of a larger group formed by companies with offices in other states. It is not necessary to spend too many words to criticize this solution and justify its refusal, since it would imply a downturn with respect to the current situation, not so much in terms of crisis management as from an economic point of view. The second, instead, which would have represented a real step forward, would consist in the adoption of that global or universalist approach that has been seen to have been variously desired by the doctrine. Even the reasons for not adopting this second option, in a sense opposed to those valid for the previous one, are well known: On the one hand it would require an excessive effort on the part of the states, not yet ready-even from a point of view emotional-to surrender sovereignty in a matter, such as the bankruptcy, having connotations of publicism, in which still lives a strong parochial attitude and the desire to control the business activity that takes place in the State; on the other hand, the profound difference existing between the bankruptcy regulations in force in the states poses a further obstacle to the possibility of orienting oneself in the indicated sense.

Having said this, the first consideration to be made regarding the soft law initiatives that has been considered concerns the existence or not of a possibility of mutual coordination of the same, since the respective scope ratione materiae often coincides. As far as the banks are concerned, the Report and Recommendations of the Cross-border Bank Resolution Group of the Basel Committee, the Framework for Enhanced Coordination of IMF, the Principles for Cross-border Cooperation on Crisis Management of the Financial Stability Forum and the Key Attributes of the Financial Stability Board; as regards commercial companies, the third part of the UNCITRAL Legislative Guide dedicated to the "treatment of enterprise groups in insolvency", of the Global Principles Project jointly prepared by the American Law Institute and the International Insolvency Institute, of the Prospective Principles for coordination of multinational corporate group insolvencies of the International Insolvency Institute and the Principles for Effective Insolvency and Creditor/Debtor Regimes of the World Bank. The doubt also arises from the fact that it is frequent to find cross-references[871] within the relevant documents, but without specifying if and how they should be coordinated. There is no answer, and this could lead one to think that it would have been more efficient to combine the efforts of the various international organizations and associations of scholars and to devise a single study on the subject or more studies on different coordinated aspects. Instead, one must rather consider that the wide range of soft law tools to be inspired in implementing international bankruptcy cooperation is certainly positive, because it leaves users free to choose the instrument that best suits their needs. At the same time promoting a race to the top in which there is a continuous attempt to improve the offer in order to attract an increasing number of "followers". And indeed, by following the protocols concluded over the last twenty years, we realize that, among the various models available, a major choice was made in favor of the Guidelines applicable to court-to-court communications in cross-border cases drawn up from the American Law Institute, which therefore proved to be suitable for achieving the objectives for which they were created.

The second consideration concerns the fact that all the documents just mentioned, as well as the modification of Regulation (CE) n. 1346/2000[872], do not seem to add much to what was already spontaneously the parties did before and therefore in the absence of the same initiatives. This is particularly striking when it comes to proposals from international organizations and in particular from the European Union, which, given the high level of integration existing between Member States, could have been the only actress able to at least try to to reach that global solution- that is,

[871]European COMMISSION, 6 June 2012, Bank recovery and resolution proposal: Frequently Asked Questions, op. cit., FAQ n. 6.

[872]Therefore we want to refer to all the documents, both of hard law and of soft law, analyzed in the third Chapter, with the exception perhaps of the proposal of the European Commission's Directive of 6 June 2012 which establishes a framework for rehabilitation and resolution of credit institutions and investment firms.

universalist-of which it was said. Evidently, for the aforementioned reasons also common to non-Member States, not even at the European level the time is still ripe for this. On the other hand, the added value deriving from an endorsement of the practice of documents and studies published by private associations of scholars and professionals is linked to the particular influence they have on the governments of the states, despite the lack of stricto power legislative sensu. In this perspective, the results achieved do not seem to be so disappointing, however, the need not to stop and continue in the search for a discipline that adapts over time to developments in economic reality.

BIBLIOGRAPHY

ADAMS KIRSHNER, J., International bankruptcy. The challenge of insolvency in a global economy, University of Chicago Press, Chicago, 2018.

ADAMS, E.S., BAILLIE, J.L., A privatization solution to the legitimacy of prepetition waivers of the automatic stay, in Arizona Law Review 38, 1996, pp. 9ss.

ADLER, B., CAPKUN, V., WEISS, L. Value destruction in the new era of Chapter 11, The Journal of Law, Economics, and Organization, 29 (2), 2013, pp. 462ss.

AHART, A.M., The inefficacy of the new eviction exceptions to the automatic stay, in American Bankruptcy Law Journal, 80, 2006, pp. 126ss.

ALTMAN, J., A test case in international bankruptcy in international bankruptcy protocols: The Lehman Brothers insolvency, in San Diego International Law Journal, 12, 2011, pp. 477.

AMERICAN LAW INSTITUTE, Transnational Insolvency: Cooperation among NAFTA Countries. Principles of Cooperation among the NAFTA Countries, Huntington, Juris Publishing, New York, 2003, pp. 65ss.

ANAT ADMANTI, R., HELLWIG, M., The bankers' new clothes: What's wrong with banking and what to do about it, Princeton University Press, Princeton, 2013.

ARONS, T., Recognition of debt restructuring and resolution measures under the European Union regulatory framework, in International Insolvency Review, 24, 2014, pp. 58ss.

ATHANASSIOU, L., Maritime cross-border insolvency: Under the European insolvency, ed. Routledge, London & New York, 2017.

AUSTIN, D.A., PARSONS, S.P., Business bankruptcy law in focus, Wolters Kluwer, New York, 2016.

AVRON, P.A., Does automatic stay apply to appeals being prosecuted by debtor of adverse order?, in ABI Journal, 31, 2012, pp. 22ss.

AYOTTE, D., SKEEL, D.A., Bankruptcy law as a liquidity provider, University of Chicago Law Review, 80, 2013, pp. 1560ss.

BAIRD, D.G., The elements of bankruptcy, Foundation Press, New York, 2010, pp. 195ss.

BARETZ, S.Z., Combating the Chapter 13 serial filer: An argument for orders containing prospective relief from the automatic stay provision, in Hofstra Law Review, 25, 1997, pp. 1316ss.

BARNARD, C., PEERS, S., European Union law, Oxford University Press, Oxford, 2017, pp. 788ss.

BARNES, T.A., The plain meaning of automatic stay in bankruptcy: the void/voidable distinction revisited, in Ohio State Law Journal, 57, 1996, pp. 315ss.

BARTELL, L.B., Staying the serial filer interpreting the new exploding stay provisions of § 362(c)(3) of the Bankruptcy Code, in American Bankruptcy Law Journal, 82, 2008, pp. 224ss.

BARTELL, L.B., Visualizing bankruptcy, Lexis Nexis, New York, 2011, pp. 76ss.

BASSIN, W., Why courts should refuse to enforce prepetition agreements that waive bankruptcy's automatic stay provision, in Indiana Law Review, 70, 1994, pp. 9ss.

BĚLOHLÁVEK, A.J., Effects of opening (commencement) of insolvency proceedings on pending lawsuits and similar proceedings under article 15 of Council Regulation (EC) No. 1346/2000 of 29 May 2000 on insolvency proceedings and under Article 18 of the European Parliament and Council Regulation (EU) No 2015/848, in Czech Yearbook of International Law, 7, 2016, pp. 69ss.

BERNARDO, P.J.F., Cross-border insolvency and the challenges of the global corporation: Evaluating globalization and stakeholder predictability through the UNCITRAL Model Law on cross-border insolvency and the European Union insolvency regulation, in Ateneo Law Journal, 56, 2012, pp. 800ss.

BERRY, B., HOMEWOOD, M.Y., BOGUSZ, B., Complete European Union law. Texts, cases and materials, Oxford University Press, Oxford, 2013.

BERTRAND, O., LUMINEAU, G., Partners in crime. The effects of diversity on the longevity of cartels, in Academy of Management Journal, 59 (3), 2015.

BINDER, J.H., SINGH, D., Bank resolution. The European regime, Oxford University Press, Oxford, 2016.

BLIESENER, D., Legal problems of bail-ins under the EU's proposed Recovery and Resolution Directive, in A. DOMBRET, P.S. KENADJAN (eds.), The Bank Recovery and Resolution Directive. Europe's solution for "too big to fail"?, Walter de Gruyter, Berlin, Boston, 2013, pp. 192ss.

BLOCK-LIEB, S., The UK and EU cross-border insolvency recognition: From empire to Europe to egoing it alone, in Fordham International Law Journal, 42, 2017, pp. 1374ss.

BLUM, B.A., Bankruptcy and debtor/creditor, Aspen Publishers, The Hague, 2010, pp. 292ss.

BODE, M., Le groupe international de sociètès: Le système de conflit de lois en droit comparè français et allemand, ed. Peter Lang, Bruxelles, 2010, pp. 542ss.

BOLES, R., Easing the tension between Statutes of limitations and the continuing offense doctrine, Nothwestern Journal of Law & Social Politics, 7, 2012, pp. 219ss.

BOOKMAN, P.K., The unsung virtues of global forum shopping, in Notre Dame Law Review, 92, 2016, pp. 582ss.

BORK, R., Principles of cross-border insolvency law, ed. Intersentia, Cambridge, 2017.

BORK, R., VAN ZWEITEN, K., (eds.), Commentary on the European Insolvency Regulation, Oxford University Press, Oxford, 2017.

BORN, M., Europäisches Kollisions Recht des Effektengiros: Intermediatisierte Wertpapiere im Schnittfeld Internationalem Sallen-Schuld und Insolvenzrecht,

ed. M. Siebeck, 2014, pp. 189ss.
BRANDSMA, G.J., BLOM-HANSEN, J., Controlling the European Union executive? The politics of delegation in the European Union, Oxford University Press, Oxford, 2017, pp. 171ss.
BRAUCHER, J., A guide to interpretation of the 2005 bankruptcy law, in American Bankruptcy Institute Law Review, 16, 2008, pp. 376ss.
BRAY, S.L., Preventive adjudication, in University of Chicago Law Review, 77, 2010, pp. 1276ss.
BRICKE, K.F., TAUB, J., Corporate and white collar crime: Cases and materials, Wolters Kluwer, The Hague, 2013.
BRIGGS, A., The principle of comity in private international law, in Recueil des Cours, ed. Brill, The Hague, vol. 354, 2011, pp. 69ss.
BROWNING WEBB, D., RICO conspiracy law and the Pinkerton doctrine, Xlibris Corporation, US, 2013.
BRUDE, R.F., Reorganizations under Chapter 11 of the bankruptcy code, Law Journal Press, New York, 2018.
BRULARD, Y., Que penser de la proposition de la Commission sur les groupes de sociétés dans le projet de nouveau règlement insolvabilité?, in Revue des Procédures Collectives, 2013, pp. 68ss.
BRUMMER, C., Soft law and the global financial system: Rule making in the 21st century, Cambridge University Press, Cambridge, 2012.
BUFFORD, S.L., Coordination of insolvency cases for international enterprise groups: A proposal, in American Bankruptcy Law Journal, 86, 2012, pp. 685ss.
BUTLER III, J.B., Section 362(d)(3): A singular provision of the Bankruptcy Code, in De Paul Business & Commercial Law Journal, 6, 2008, pp. 208ss.
CACHARD, O., Droit international privè, ed. Larcier, Bruxelles, 2018.
CADIET, L., JEULAND, E., AMRANI-MEKKI, S., Droit processuel civil de l'Union européenne, ed. LexisNexis, Paris, 2011, pp. 350ss.
CAMACHO, T., NUNEZ-LAGOS BURGUERA, A., Secondary proceedings: Are cross-border insolvencies in the EU dealt with efficiently?, in International Insolvency Review, 2, 2013, pp. 142ss.
CARLSON, T.E., FRASER HAYES, J., The small business provisions of the 2005 bankruptcy amendments, in American Bankruptcy Law Journal, 79, 2005, pp. 679ss.
CARON, D.D., CAPLA, L.M., The UNCITRAL arbitration rules. A commentary, Oxford University Press, Oxford, 2013, pp. 572ss.
CASE, D.K., ALDERFER, J.R., BAPCPA and the new provisions relating to small businesses, in Widener Law Journal, 15, 2006, pp. 587ss.
CASTLE, J.A. and others, Bankruptcy crime Statutes governing debtors, in Bankruptcy Strategist, 15, 1998, pp. 6ss.
CHAN HO, L., LASTRA, R.M., International developments, in R.M. LASTRA (ed.), Cross-border bank insolvency, Oxford University Press, Oxford, New York, 2011, pp. 210ss.
CHAVES, L.F., In rem bankruptcy refiling bars: Will they stop abuse of the automatic stay against mortages?, California Bankruptcy Journal, 24, 1998, pp. 3ss.

CHIRCOP, J., The impact of bankruptcy abuse prevention and consumer protection act of 2005 repo "safe harbor" provisions in investors, in The European Journal of Finance, 24, 2018, pp. 18ss.

COLEMAN, L.A., Individual consumer "chapter 20" cases after Johnson: An introduction to non business serial filings under Chapter 7 and Chapter 13 of the Bankruptcy Code, in Bankruptcy Developments Journal, 9, 1992, pp. 357ss.

COLETON, A., Banking insolvency regimes and cross border banks-Complexities and conflicts: Is the current European insolvency framework efficient and robust enough to effectively resolve cross-border banks, can there be a one size fits all solution?, in Banking Insolvency Regimes and Cross Border Banks, 27, 2012, pp. 69ss.

CONWAY, G., European Union law, ed. Routledge, London & New York, 2015.

COOK, M.L., Bankruptcy litigation manual, Wolters Kluwer Law & Business, New York, 2015.

COWANS, D.R., Cowans bankruptcy law and practice, West Group, Minnesota, 1989, pp. 469ss.

DA CRUZ VILAÇA, J.L., European Union law and integration. Twenty years of judicial application of European Union law, Hart Publishing, Oxford & Oregon, Portland, 2014.

DAMMANN, R., Application du Règlement (CE) numéro 1346/2000 modifié aux groupes de sociétés, in Revue des Procédures Collectives, 2013, pp. 65ss.

DAMMANN, R., MILLET, S., L'action en revendication exercée au titre d'une clause de réserve de propriété relève-t-elle du champ d'application du règlement Bruxelles I?, in Revue Lamy Droit Civil, 2010, pp. 32ss.

DAVIES, P.L., Resolution of cross-border groups, in M. HAENTJENS, B. WESSELS, Research handbook on crisis management in the sector, Edward Elgar Publishers, 2015, pp. 264ss.

DE WEIJS, R.J., Towards an objective European rule on transaction avoidance in insolvencies, in International Insolvency Review, 21, 2011, pp. 220ss.

DELANEY, K.J., Strategic bankruptcy, University of California Press, Berkeley and Los Angeles, 1992, pp. 60ss.

DERR, K.J., LAYDEN, A.K., The automatic stay: What are proceedings "against the debtor"?, in ABI Journal 13, 1994, pp. 27ss.

DI SANO, S., The third road to deal with the insolvency of multinational enterprise groups, in Journal of International Banking Law and Regulation, 15, 2011, pp. 23ss.

DUBERSTEIN, S., Are bankruptcy criminals?, St. John's Law Review, 25 (2), 1951, pp. 234ss.

DURRER II, V.C., JAIMEZ, K.D., Competing bankruptcies: What defenses survive the automatic stay?, in ABI Journal, 30, 2011, pp. 52, 74ss.

EBKE, W.F., HUMPENÖDER, L., Europäisierung des Insolvenzrechts, in U. HOMMEL, T. KNECHT, H. WOHLENBERG (eds) Handbuch Unternehmensrestrukturierung, ed. Springer, Wiesbaden, 2016.

EDENMÜLLER, H., A new framework for business restructuring in Europe: The EU Commission's proposal for a reform of the European Insolvency

Regulation and beyond, in Maastricht Journal of European and Comparative Law, 20, 2013, pp. 134ss.

EIDENMÜLLER, H., KINENINGER, E.M., (eds), The future of secured credit in Europe, in European Company and Financial Law Review, 5, 2008, pp. 4ss.

EPEOGLOU, M.T., The recast European Insolvency Regulation: A missed opportunity for restructuring business in Europe, in UCL Journal of Law and Jurisprudence, 1 (6), 2017.

EPSTEIN, D.G., Bankruptcy and related law in a nutshell, West Academic Publishibng, Minnesota, 2013, pp. 47.

FABRIES-LECEA, E., Le règlement "insolvabilité": Apport à la construction de l'ordre juridique de l'Union européenne, ed. Bruylant, Bruxelles, 2013, pp. 614ss.

FARLEY, J.M., A judicial perspective on international cooperation in insolvency cases, in American Bankruptcy Institute Journal, 44, 1998, pp. 13ss.

FASQUELLE, D., L'Europe: une opportunité pour les professions d'AJMJ et pour le mandat de justice?, in Revue des Procédures Collectives, 2013, pp. 50ss.

FASQUELLE, D., Raisons et contours d'une refonte nécessaire du règlement (CE) 1346/2000, in Bulletin Joly Entreprises en Difficulté, 2012, pp. 52ss.

FERRARI, F., La loi applicables aux contrats conclus par les consommateurs (article 5 de la Convention de Rome), in Revue de Droit des Affaires Internationales, 2008, pp. 234ss.

FERRARI, F., Rome I Regulation, Selier European Law Publishers, Münich, 2015.

FERRIELL, J., JANGER, E.J., Undestanding bankrutptcy, LexisNexis, New York, 2013.

FINCH, V., MILMAN, D., Corporate insolvency law. Perspectives and principles, Cambridge University Press, Cambridge, 2017, pp. 486ss.

FLASCHEN, E.D., SILVERMAN, R.J., Cross-border insolvency cooperation Protocols, in Texas International Law Journal, 33, 1998, pp. 590ss.

FLASCHEN, E.D., SILVERMAN, R.J., The importance of comity and co-operation in resolving international insolvencies, in E.B. LEONARD, C. BESANT, Current issues in cross-border insolvency and reorganizations, Graham and Trotham International Bar Association, London, 1994, pp. 44.A.

FLESSNER, A., Das Insolvenzrecht für Banken Europäischer Rundblick und grundsätzliche Überlegungen, in Österreichisches BankArchiv, 2010, pp. 657ss.

FLETCHER, M.G., ISAAC, S., The EU Regulation on insolvency proceedings, Oxford University Press, Oxford 2016.

FREY, M.A., SWINSON, S.K., Introduction to bankruptcy law, Cengage Learning, New York, 2013, pp. 395.

GARCÍA-ROSTÁN CALVIN, G., El proceso consurcal ante insolvencias conexas, Tirant Lo Blanch, Valencia, 2015.

GARCIMARTÍN, F.J., Resolution tools and derivatives, in M. HAENTJENS, B. WESSELS (eds), Bank recovery and resolution: A conference book, Den Haag: Boom Uitgevers 2014, pp. 184ss.

GARRIDO, J., Two snowflakes the same: The distributional question in international bankruptcies, in Texas International Law Journal, 47, 2011-212, pp. 460ss.

GAUMER, P., Operation total disclosure, American Bankruptcy Institute Journal, 15 (10), 1996, pp. 10ss.

GEBBIA, K., Debt and crime: Inevitable Bedfellows, Golden Gate University Law Review, 42, 2012, pp. 532ss.

GEWERTZ, N.M., Act or assets: Multiplicitous indictments under the bankruptcy fraud statute: 18 U.S.C. 152, The University of Chicago Law Review, 76 (2), 2009, pp. 927ss.

GIESER, S.C., Property of the estate: Section 541(a)(1), in Bankrupty Development Journal, 4, 1987.

GIORGINI, G.C., Le centre des intérêts principaux du débiteur insolvable en droit comparé, in Revue Internationale de Droit Comparé, 64, 2012, pp. 868ss.

GOPALAN, S., GUIHOT, M., Cross-border insolvency law and multinational enterprise groups. Judicial innovation as and international solution, in George Washington International Law Review, 49, 2016, pp 4ss.

GRANT, W,. GRAHAM WILSON, K., (ed.). The consequences of the global financial crisis-The rhetoric of reform and regulation, Oxford University Press, Oxford, 2014.

GROUP OF THIRTY, International Insolvencies in the Financial Sector. A study group Report, Washington, 1998, pp. 65ss.

GRÜNEWALD, S.N., The resolution of cross-border banking crises in the European Union: A legal study from the perspective of burden sharing, Kluwer Law International Alphen aan den Rijn, 2014.

HAHN, P.B., Bankruptcy Code section 362(e): Its application and effect, in Commercial Law Journal, 88, 1983, 195ss.

HANNAN, H., Cross-border insolvency: The enactment and interpretation of the UNCITRAL Model law, ed. Springer, Berlin, 2017, pp. 9ss.

HARLOW, C., RAWLINGS, R., Process and procedure in European Union administration, Bloomsbury Publishing, New York, 2014.

HARTKAMP, A., SIBURGH, C., DEVROE, W., Cases, materials and text on European Union law and private law, hart Publishing, Oxford & Oregon, Portland, 2017, pp. 282ss.

HATJE, A., TERHECHTE, J.P., MÜLLER-GRAFF, P.C., Europarechtswissenschaft, ed. Nomos, Baden-Baden, 2018.

HAZARD JR., G.V., TARUFFO, M., Civil procedure, Foundation Press, New York, 2011, pp. 240ss.

HENRY, L.C., Compétence internationale du Tribunal pour ouvrir une procédure d'insolvabilité en cas de transfert de siège statutaire, in Bulletin Joly Entreprises en Difficulté, 2012, pp. 35ss.

HENRY, L.C., De l'art d'articuler la procédure principale et la procédure secondaire, in Revue des Sociétés, 12, 2012, pp. 186ss.

HENRY, L.C., Eclairage-Règlement insolvabilité européen et groupes de sociétés: je t'aime moi non plus!, in Bulletin Joly Entreprises en Difficulté, 2012, pp. 355ss.

HENRY, L.C., Règlement insolvabilité européen et les groupes: bilan et perspectives. Une approche textuelle, in Revue des Procédures Collectives, 2013, pp. 59ss.

HONORATI, C., CORVO, G., A double lesson from Interedil: Higher Courts, lower Courts and preliminary ruling and further clarifications on COMI and establishment under EU insolvency Regulation, in International Insolvency Law Review, 21 (4), 2012, pp. 655ss.

HUEMER, M., Bailout in context: The true costs of government bailout, in Georgetown Journal of Law & Public Policy, 11, 2013, pp. 336ss.

HÜPKES, E., Insolvency-why a special regime for banks?, in IMF (ed.), Current Developments in Monetary and Financial Law, 3, 2005.

HUTCHINSON, R.M., Automatic stay exceptions: Section 362(b), in Bankruptcy Developments Journal, 4, 1987, pp. 44ss.

IDOT, L., Un nouveau chantier pour les juristes: la révision du règlement "procédures d'insolvabilité, in La Semaine Juridique (Europe), 2013, pp. 4ss.

JACOBY, M.B. JANGER, E.J., Ice cube bonds: Allocating the price of process in Chapter 11 bankruptcy, The Yale Law Journal, 123 (4), 2014, pp. 870ss.

JAKAB, A., KOCHENOV, D., The enforcement of European Union Law values: Ensuring Member States compliance, Oxford University Press, Oxford, 2017, pp. 208ss.

JANGER, E.J., Reciprocal comity, in Texas International Law Journal, 46, 2011, pp. 442ss.

JANSSEN, L., Bail-in from an insolvency law perspective, in Norton Journal of Bankruptcy Law & Practice, 26 (5) 2017, pp. 6ss.

JAULT-SESEKE, F., ROBINE, D., Le droit européen des procédures d'insolvabilité à la croisée des chemins, ed. Lextenso, Paris, 2012, pp. 242ss.

JOHNSON, R.A., O'LEARY, M.C., Automatic stay provisions of the bankruptcy act of 1978, in New Mexico Law Review, 13, 1983, pp. 604ss.

KADENS, E., The Pitkin affair: A study of fraud in early english bankruptcy, American Bankruptcy Law Journal, 84 (2), 2010, pag. 483ss.

KAMALNATH, A., Cross border insolvency protocols-A success story, in International Journal of Legal Studies and Research, 2 (1), 2013, pp. 172-190.

KATTEL, R., KREGEL, J., TONVERONACHI, M., Financial regulation in the European Union, ed. Routledge, London & New York, 2015.

KAVENY, C., Ethics at the edges of law: Christian moralists and American legal thought, Oxford University Press, Oxford, 2017.

KEAY, A., Security rights, the European Insolvency Regulation and Concerns about the non-application of avoidance rules, in European Law Review, 22, 2016, pp. 73ss.

KEAY, A., The harmonization of the avoidance rules in European Union insolvencies, in The International and Comparative Law Quarterly, 67, 2017, pp. 80ss.

KELLERBAUER, M., KLAMERT, M., TOMKIN, J., Commentary on the European Union treaties and the Charter of fundamental rights, Oxford University Press, Oxford, 2019.

KELLEY, S.V., Ginsberg & Martin on bankruptcy, Wolters Kluwer, New York, 2018, § 3.03(B).

KENADJIAN, P.S., DOMBRET, A., The bank recovery and resolution directive: Europe's solution for "too big to fail"?, De Gruyter, Hamburg, 2013, pp. 91ss.

KENNEDY, F.R., Automatic stays under the new bankruptcy law, in Michigan Journal of Law Reform, 12, 1978, pp. 12ss.

KENNEDY, J.E., Counterclaims under Federal rule 13, in Houston Law Review, 11, 1974, pp. 255ss.

KERAMEUS, K., L'harmonisation procédurale dans le monde contemporain, in L. VOGEL, La procédure entre tradition et modernité, èd. Panthéon-Assas, Paris, 2010, pp. 10ss.

KESSEDJIAN, C., L'espace judiciaire civile et commercial européen: le règlement "Bruxelles I" refondu, in Revue Gènèrale de Droit International Public, 117, 2013, pp. 546ss.

KEY, J.D., The advent of the serial Chapter 11 filing and its implications, in Bankruptcy Developments Journal, 8, 1991, pp. 245ss.

KILPONEN, J., Sovereign risk European crisis-resolution policies and bond spreads, in International Journal of Central Banking, 11 (2), 2015, pp. 287ss.

KINDLER, P., Hauptfragen der Reform des Europäischen Internationalen Insolvenzrechts, in Zeitschrift für Insolvenzenrecht, 75, 2014, pp. 28ss.

KING, L.P. (eds.), Collier on Bankruptcy, Matthew Bender, New York, 1997, §7-201.

KING, L.P., Jurisdiction and procedure under the bankruptcy amendments of 1984, in Vanderbilt Law Review, 38, 1985, pp. 676ss.

KIRSHNER, J.A., International bankruptcy. The challenge of insolvency in a global economy. University of Chicago Press, Chicago, 2018, pp. 146ss.

KLAUS, J.H., Groups of companies-A comparative study on the economics, law and regulation of corporate groups, in J. GORDON, G. RINGE, (eds) Oxford handbook of corporate law and governance, Oxford University Press, Oxford, 2015.

LANGEHENNIG, D.B., MANZ, S., To infinity and beyond: Exploring the reach of the automatic stay, in ABI Journal, 30, 2011, pp. 36ss.

LARDEUX, G., Droit international privè des obligations contractuelles, ed. Larcier, Bruxelles, 2016.

LARSEN, S., Understanding the new semiautomatic stay, in ABI Journal, 25, 2006, pp. 75ss.

LAWLESS, R.M., Small business and the 2005 bankruptcy law: Should mom and apple pie be worried?, in Southern Illinois University Law Journal, 31, 2007, pp. 588ss.

LEFKOWITZ, R., The filing of a bankruptcy petition in violation of 11 U.S.C. § 109(g): Does it invoke the automatic stay?, in 26 Cardozo Law Review, 26, 2004, pp. 326ss.

LEGRAND, V., Quelle clôture pour la procédure européenne d'insolvabilité?, in Lettre d'Actualité des Procédures Collectives Civiles et Commerciales, 2013, pp. 112ss.

LENAERTS, K., MASELIS, I., GUTMAN, K., European Union procedural law, Oxford University Press, Oxford, 2014, pp. 133ss.

LEONARD, B., The developing use of protocols in major cross-border filings, in American Bankruptcy Institute Journal, 18, 1999, pp. 12ss.

LEONARD, C.J., The way ahead: Protocols in international insolvency cases, in American Bankruptcy Institute Journal, 12, 1998, pp. 12ss.

LEVMORE, S., Harmonization, preferences, and the calculus of consent in commercial and other law, in Common Market Law Review, 50, 2013, pp. 250ss.

LIAKOPOULOS D., European integration and its relation with the jurisprudence of European Court of Human Rights and private international law of European Union, in Homa Publica. Revista Internacional de Direitos Humanos e Impresa, vol. 2, n. 2, 2018.

LIAKOPOULOS, D., Interactions between European Court of Human Rights and private international law of European Union, in Cuadernos de Derecho Transnacional, 10 (1), 2018, pp. 254ss.

LIAKOPOULOS, D., Procedural harmonization, mutual recognition and multi-level protection of fundamental procedural rights, in Revista General de Derecho Procesal, 47, 2019.

LIENHARD, A., Procédure d'insolvabilité: Notion de "centre des intérêts principaux", in Recueil Dalloz Sirey, 2011, pp. 2916ss.

LINNA, I., Actio pauliana and res judicata in European Union insolvency proceedings, in Journal of Private International Law, 14 (4), 2015, pp. 570ss.

LISANTI, C.C., SAUTONIE-LAGUIONIE, L., Règlement UE n. 2015/848 du 20 mai 2015 relatif aux procèdures d'insolvabilitè, in Societè de lègislation comparèe, Trans Europe experts, 2016.

LLORENTE SÁNCHEZ-ARJONA, M., Tratamiento procesal de la insolvencia transfronteriza en la Unión Europea, Tirant Lo Blanch, Valencia, 2013, pp. 76ss.

LOPUCKI, L., Cooperation in international bankruptcy: A post-universalist approach, in Cornell Law Review, 84, 1999, pp. 750ss.

LOPUCKI, L.M., The case for cooperative territoriality in international bankruptcy, in Michigan Law Review, 18, 2000, pp. 2219.

LOWE, R., From client money rules to the EC Insolvency Regulation, legislative change beckons, in Insolvency Intelligence, 29, 2014, pp. 48ss.

LUBBEN, S.J., A new understanding of the bankruptcy clause, in Case Western Reserve Law Review, 64, 2013, pp. 326ss.

LYNCH, G.E., RICO: The crime of being a criminal parts I&II, in Columbia University Law Review, 87, 1987, pp. 661ss.

MADAUS, S., Insolvency proceedings for corporate groups under the new insolvency regulation, in International Insolvency Law Review, 25 (2), 2016, pp. 237ss.

MALL, C.A., Corporate governance, Oxford University Press, Oxford, 2012.

MANGANELLI, P., The modernization of European insolvency law: An ongoing process, in Journal of Business & Technology Law, 11, 2016, pp. 156ss.

MARKAM LESTER, B., Victorian insolvency: Bankruptcy, imprisonment for debt, and company winding-up, in Nineteenth Century England, Oxford University Press, Oxford, 1995.

MARKER, R., When is a governmental unit's action to enforce its police or regulatory power exempt from the automatic stay provisions of section 362?, in Florida State University Law Review, 9, 1981, pp. 369ss.

MARTIN, J.E., Hanbury & Martin modern equity, Sweet & Maxwell, London, 2001, pp. 799ss.

MARTIN, R.M., Creditor alternatives to obtain relief from automatic stays in bankruptcy, in Banking Law Journal, 98, 1981, pp. 536ss.

MASTRULLO, T., L'extension de procédure collective pour cause de confusion des patrimoines est-elle compatible avec le règlement numéro 1346/2000?, in Revue des Sociétés, 2010, pp. 594ss.

MASTRULLO, T., Procédures d'insolvabilité transfrontalières: la reconnaissance mutuelle conditionnée par le respect du droit d'accès au juge, in Revue des Sociétés, 2011, pp. 8ss and 443-447.

MCCORMACK, G., KEAY, A., BROWN, S., European insolvency law: Reform and harmonization, Edward Elgar Publishing, Cheltenham, 2017, pp. 174ss.

MCCORMACK, G., Reconciling European conflicts and insolvency law, in European Business Organization Law Review, 15, 2014, pp. 335ss.

MCCORMACK, G., Reforming the European Insolvency Regulation: A legal and policy perspective, in Journal of Private International Law, 10, 2014, pp. 42ss.

MCCORMACK, G., Secured credit and the harmonisation of law, Edward Elgar Publishing, Cheltenham, 2011, pp. 58ss.

MCCORMACK, G., Something old, something new: Recasting the European Insolvency Regulation, in The Modern Law Review, 79, 2016, pp. 122ss.

MCCOY, D.R., The elusive Republic: Political economy in Jeffersonian America, University of North Carolina Press, North Carolina, 1980, pp. 179ss.

MCCULLOGH II, G.P., Bankruptcy fraud: Crime without punishment II, in Commercial Law Journal, 102, 1997, pp. 15.

MENJUCQ, M., L'extension de procédure pour confusion de patrimoines passée au crible du règlement n° 1346/2000: une question à suspense!, in Revue des Procédures Collectives, 2010, pp. 2ss.

MENJUCQ, M., La proposition de règlement modifiant le règlement (CE) n°1346/2000 sur les procédures d'insolvabilité: une évolution mais pas de révolution, in Revue des Procédures Collectives, 2013, pp. 20ss.

MERLINI, A., Reorganisation and liquidation of groups of companies: Curators' protection vs. going concern maximisation, in International Insolvency Law Review, 25 (1), 2016, pp. 120ss.

MEROVACH, I., European insolvency law in a global context, in Journal of Business Law, 13, 2011, pp. 668ss.

MEROVACH, I., The new proposed regime for EU corporate groups in insolvency: A critical note, in Corporate Rescue and Insolvency, 2013, pp. 90ss.

MEVORAH, I., The future of cross border insolvency: Overcoming biases and closing gaps, Oxford University Press, Oxford, 2018.

MICHAEL, S.L., White collar crime: Law, procedure, theory and practice, Kluwer Wolters, New York, 2014.

MILES GOODE, R., Principles of corporate insolvency law, Sweet & Maxwell, London, 2011.

MILMAN, D., Personal insolvency law. Regulation and policy, ed. Routledge, London & New York, 2017, pp. 2048ss.

MOCK, S., Das geplante neue europäische Insolvenzrecht nach dem Vorschlag der Kommission zur Reform der EuInsVO, in Zeitschrift für Gemeinschaftsprivatrecht, 10, 2013, pp. 137ss.

MOILLE, C., Un point sur les conditions de la mise en oeuvre de la procédure intiale d'insolvabilité et son extension, in Revue Trimestrielle de Droit Européen, 50, 2013, pp. 28ss.

MORGAN, E.M., How to approach burden of proof and presumptions, in Harvard Law Review 44, 1931, pp. 36ss.

MOSS, G., FLETCHER, I.F., ISAACS, S., (eds), The EC Regulation on Insolvency Proceedings: A commentary and annotated guide, (2nd ed), Oxford University Press, Oxford, 2009, pp. 12ss.

MUCCIARELLI, F.M., The function of corporate law and the effects of reincorporations in the U.S. and the EU, in Tulane Journal of International and Comparative Law, 21, 2012, pp. 440ss.

MUELLER, C.B. KIPKPATRICK, C.J., RICHTER, L., Aspen treatise for evidence, Wolters & Kluwer Law & Business, New York, 2018.

MUNITZ, G.F., Keynote address: Stories in the development of bankruptcy law, Golden Gate University Law Review, 42, 2012, pp. 4ss.

MURPHY, J.F., The automatic stay in bankruptcy, in Cleveland State Law Review, 1986, 34, 1986, pp. 569ss.

MURPHY, P.A., SAGERMAN, E.E., NEIER, D., Creditor's rights in bankruptcy, ed. Thomson Reuters, New York, 2017.

NABET, P., Bref aperçu du projet de la commission pour la révision du règlement (CE) n° 1346/2000 sur l'insolvabilité, in Les Petites Affiches, 2013, pp. 6ss.

NAPOLI, L.A., Reaffirmation after the Bankruptcy Abuse Prevention and Consumer Protection Act of 2005: Many questions, some answers, in American Bankruptcy Law Journal, 81, 2007, pp. 284ss.

NAPOLI, L.A., The not-so-automatic stay: Legislative changes to the automatic stay in a case filed by or against an individual debtor, in American Bankruptcy Law Journal, 79, 2005, pp. 755ss.

NELSON, K.L., Abusive filings: Can courts stop the abuse within the confines of the Bankruptcy Code?, in Bankruptcy Developments Journal, 17, 2000, pp. 331, 336ss.

NEWTON, G.W., Bankruptcy and insolvency accounting, ed. Wiley & Sons, New York, 2010, pp. 180ss.

NEWTON, G.W., LIGUERMAN, R., Bankruptcy and insolvency taxation, Wiley & Sons, New York, 2012, pp. 528ss.

NICCOLINIA, R.R., The voidability of actions taken in violation of the automatic stay: Application of the information forcing paradigm, in Vanderbilt Law

Review, 45, 1992, pp. 1679ss.
NICKELS, S.H., WHITE, J.J., Bankruptcy, West Group, Minnesota, 1993.
NICOLA, F., DAVIES, B., European Union law stories, Cambridge University Press, Cambridge, 2017.
NORTON, JR., W.R., Norton bankruptcy law and practice, Thomson Reuters, New York, 2018 § 36:4.
NORTON, W.L. (eds.), Bankruptcy law and practice, Thomson Reuters, New York, 1997, § 49.2, 49-4.
OGIER, T., WILLIAMS, J.D., Bankruptcy crimes and bankruptcy practice, American Bankruptcy Institute Law Review, 6 (2), 1998.
OMAR, P., International insolvency law. Themes and perspectives, ed. Routledge, London & New York, 2017.
ORLANDI, G., Property of the estate: Section 541, in Bankruptcy Developments Journal, 3, 1986, pp. 342ss.
PARKINSON, W.S., The contempt power of the bankruptcy court fact or fiction: The debate continues, in American Bankruptcy Law Journal, 65, 1991, pp. 592ss.
PASCALIDIS, P., Freedom of establishment and private international law for corporations, Oxford University Press, Oxford, 2012, pp. 188ss.
PATERSON, S., Bargaining in financial restructuring-market norms, legal rights and regulatory standards, Journal of Corporate Law Studies, 14 (2), 2014, pp. 336ss.
PAUNEN, K., European Insolvency Regulation. Commentary, De Gruyter, Hamburg, 2011.
PAYNE, J., Cross-border schemes of arrangement and forum shopping, in European Business Organization Law Review, 14, 2013, pp. 564ss.
PAYNE, J., Scheme of arrangement, theory structure and operation, Cambridge University Press,Cambridge, 2014.
PECK, J.M., Cross-border observations derived from My Lehman Judicial Experience, in Butterworths Journal of International Banking & Finance Law, 30, 2015, pp. 132ss.
PEITZMAN, L., SMITH, M.S., The secured creditor's complaint: Relief from the automatic stays in bankruptcy proceedings, in California Law Review, 1977, pp. 1216ss.
PERINO, M.A., Enron's legislative aftermath: Some reflections on the deterrence aspects off the Serbanes-Oxley Act of 2002, Columbia Law School, 2012, working paper n. 212.
PHELPS, K.B., Handling claims in Ponzi scheme bankruptcy and receivership cases, Golden Gate University Law Review, 42, 2012, pp. 567ss.
PICKARD, H.B., The new bankruptcy code, part II: The interests of secured creditors under the new bankruptcy code, in Memphis State University Law Review, 10, 1980, pp. 210, 220ss.
PIEKENBROCK, A., The future scope of the European Insolvency Regulation, in International Insolvency Law Review, 23 (3), 2014, pp. 434ss.
POLASKY, A.N., Collateral estoppel-effects of prior litigation, in Iowa Law

Review, 39, 1954, pp. 218ss.
PONTANI, M., Pre-bankruptcy crimes and entrepreneural behaviour. Some insights from American and italian bankruptcy laws, German Working Papers in Law and Economics, Berkeley Electronic Press, 2004, paper 14.
RAMMELOO, S., From Rome to Rome. Cross-border employment contract. European private international law. Intertemporal law and foreign overriding mandatory laws, in Maastricht Journal of European and Comparative Law, 24, 2017.
RAUSCHER, T., Europäisches Zivilprozess-und Kollisionsrecht, Europäisches Zivilprozess-und Kollisionsrecht (EuZPR/EuIPR), ed. Verlag O. Schmidt, Heidelberg, 2010, Art. 1 paras. 2-4.
RAY, T.W., Postpetition claims and the automatic stay in chapter 13, in ABI Journal 19, 2000, pp. 12ss.
REDMOND, C.J., COMI: In search of predictability, in Norton Annual Review of International Insolvency, 2010, pp. 4ss.
REQUEJO ISIDRO, M., La cooperaciòn judicial en materia de insolvencia transfronteriza en la propuesta de Regulation del Parlamento europeo y del consejo por el que se modifica el Regulation (CE) n. 1346/2000 sobre procedimientos de insolvencia, in Anuario Español de Derecho Internacional Privado, 13, 2013, pp. 218ss.
RESNICK, A.N., Bankruptcy law manual, West Press, Minnesota, 2002, pp. 67ss
RESNICK, A.N., SOMMER, H.J., Collier on bankruptcy, ed. Mathew Bender, New York, 2013 § 362.02.
RESNIK, A.N., SOMMER H.J., Collier guide to chapter 11: Key topics selected industries, Lexis Nexis, New York, 2016.
REYNOLDS, B., TEO, E., Early Bank Recovery and Resolution Directive (BRRD) experiences: Lessons learned from Greece, in Journal of International Banking Law and Regulation, 31, 2016, pp. 360ss.
RIDER, B., Research handbook on international financial crime, Edward Elgar Publishers, Cheltenham, 2015, pp. 210ss.
RIEHL, R.W., Property of the estate, in Bankruptcy Developments Journal, 1, 1984, pp. 332ss.
ROBINE, D., JAULT-SESEKE, F., Le droit européen des procédures d'insolvabilité à la croisée des chemins, ed. Montchrestien, Paris, 2012, pp. 243ss.
RODRÍGUEZ RODRIG, J., Bienes sujetos a un procedimiento secundario de insolvencia. Comentario a la sentencia del Tribunal de justicia de la Uniòn europea de 11 Junio 2015, Nortel, C-649/13, in Cuadernos de Derecho Transnacional, 9 (3), 2017, pp. 694ss.
RODRÍGUEZ RODRIGO, J., El centro de intereses principales, como foro de competencia internacional en el Reglamento 1346/2000, en relación con empresas de un grupo de sociedades, in Anuario de Derecho Concursal, 2014, pp. 502ss.
ROE, M.J., Strong managers, weak owners. The political roots of American Corporate Finance, Princeton University Press, Princeton, 1966, Chapter 10.

ROTHMAN, S.J., Note, lessons from general growth properties: The future of the special purpose entity, in Fordham Journal of Corporate, Finance Law, 17, 2012, pp. 228ss.

ROUSSEL-GALLE, P., La proposition de révision du règlement n° 1346/2000 sur les procédures d'insolvabilité, entre prudence et audace, in La Semaine Juridique (édition entreprise), 2013, pp. 14ss.

RRIS, J., BATTILOSSI, S., State and financial systems in Europe and the USA. Historical perspectives on regulation and supervision in the nineteenth and twenthieth century, Routledge, London & New York, 2010.

SACK, J.R., Adequate protection, in Bankruptcy Developments Journal, 2, 1985, pp. 21ss.

SCHEB II, J.M., Criminal Law, Cengage learning, U.S., 2014, pp. 255ss.

SCHLAEFER, G.F., Forum shopping under the regime of the European Insolvency Regulation, in International Insolvency Institute, International Insolvency Studies, 2010, pp. 26ss.

SCHUSTER, M., Die Regulierung von Invetsment Crowdfunding in den USA: Der USA amerikanishce Crowdfund Act im Spannungsfeld von Anlegenschutz und Kapitalzugang, Nomos Verlag, Baden-Baden, 2018.

SCHWARZE, J., BECKER, V., HATJE, A., SCHOO, J., EU-Kommentar, ed. Nomos, Baden-Baden, 2019.

SCOTT, A.W., Collateral estoppel by judgment, in Harvard Law Review, 56, 1942.

SEALY, L.S., MILMAN, D., Annotated Guide to the Insolvency Legislation, ed. Sweet & Maxwell, London, 2014.

SEXTON, V., Current problems and trends in the administration of transnational insolvencies involving enterprise groups: The mixed record of protocols, the UNCITRAL Model Insolvency Law, and the EU insolvency regulation, in Chicago Journal of International Law, 17, 2012, pp. 818ss.

SHAIN, A.W., The effect of bankruptcy on State tax enforcement and proceedings, in Tax Analysts, 2012, pp. 948ss.

SKEEL, D., Debt's dominion. A history of bankruptcy law in America, Princeton University Press, Princeton and Oxford, 2014, pp. 6ss.

SPENCER, G.P., A simple solution for stub rent? How proposed changes to the treatment of stub rent could lead to unforeseen consequences, Review of Banking & Financial Law, 26, 2017, pp. 926ss.

SRANKLING, J.G., The international law of property, Oxford University Press, Oxford, 2014.

STRADER J.K., Understanding white collar crime, LexisNexis, New York, 2006, pp. 306ss.

SULLIVAN, J.R., STEWART, D.P., International and transnational criminal law, Wolters Kluwer, New York, 2018.

SULLIVAN, M.A., When the bezzle bursts: Restitutionary distribution of assets after Ponzi schemes enter bankruptcy, Washington & Lee Law Review, 68, 2011, pp. 1589ss.

TABB, C.J., Credit bidding, security and the obsolescence of Chapter 11,

University of Illinois Law Review, 2013, 103, pp. 104ss.
TABB, C.J., The bankruptcy clause, the fifth amendment and the limited rights of secured creditors in bankruptcy, University of Illinois Law Review, 2015, pp. 766ss.
TABB, C.J., The historical evolution of the bankruptcy discharge, American Bankruptcy Law Journal, 65, 1991, pag. 325.
TARVIN, T., The privilege against self-incrimination in bankruptcy and the plight of the debtor, Seton Hall Law Review, 44, 2014, pp. 78ss.
THAYER, J.B., The burden of proof, in Harvard Law Review 4, 1890, pp. 48ss.
THOLE, C., Die Reform der Europäischen Insolvenzverordnung, in Zeitschrift für Europäisches Privatrecht, 22, 2014, pp. 40ss.
THOLE, C., Gläubigerschutz in einem Sonderinsolvenzrecht für Banken, in P.S. KENADJIAN (ed.), Too big to fail-Brauchen wir ein Sonderinsolvenzrecht für Banken?, Walter de Gruyter, Berlin, 2012, pp. 220ss.
THOLE, C., Sanierung mittels Scheme of Arrangement im Blickwinkel des Internationalen Privat-und Verfahrensrechts, in Zeitschrift für Unternehmens und Gesellschaftsrecht, 42, 2013, pp. 110ss.
TIGHE, M.A. Calo, R.R., Congress, the Courts, and the feds agree-bankruptcy crime does not pay, in Annual Survey of Bankruptcy Law, sess. 1, 2004, pp. 355ss.
TIGHE, M.A., A guide to making a criminal bankruptcy fraud referral, American Bankruptcy Institute Law Review, 6, 1998, § 409.
TOBAR, D.R., The need for a uniform void ab initio standard for violations of the automatic stay, in Whittier Law Review, 24, 2002, pp. 24ss.
TOKATLIDES, C., Retails depositor and retail investor protection under European Union law. In the event of financial institution failure, ed. Routledge, London & New York, 2017, pp. 56ss.
TOLLENAAR, N.W.A., Dealing with the insolvency of multinational groups under the European Insolvency Regulation, in Insolvency Intelligence, 23 (5), 2010, pp. 65ss.
TOLMIE, F., Corporate and personal insolvency law, ed. Wolters, Kluwer, The Hague, 2013.
TRACHT, M.E., Contractual bankruptcy waivers: Reconciling theory, practice, and law, in Cornell Law Review, 82, 1997, pp. 312ss.
TÜRK, A.H., Judicial review in European Union law, Edward Elgar Publishers, Cheltenham, 2010.
USHERWOOD, J., PINDER, S., The European Union. A very short introduction, Oxford University Press, Oxford, 2018.
VALLENS, J.L., Tourisme judiciaire et insolvabilité: les risques du forum shopping, in Revue des Procédures Collectives, 2012, pp. 10ss.
VAN HOE, A., Enterprise groups and their insolvency: It's the (common) interest, stupid!, in European Company and Financial Law Review, 11 (2), 2014.
VAN RHEE, C.V., Harmonisation of civil procedure: An historical and comparative perspective, in X.E. KRAMER, C.H. VAN RHEE, Civil litigation in a globalizing World, T.M.C. Asser Press, The Hague, 2012, pp. 41ss.

VAZQUEZ, F., Modification of automatic stay to permit litigation to proceed remains possible, in ABI Journal, 27, 2008, pp. 34ss.

VEDER, M., The future of the European Insolvency Regulation-Applicable law, in particular security rights, in International Insolvency Law Review, 20 (2), 2011, pp. 286ss.

VIRGÓS, M., GARCIMARTÍN, F., The European Insolvency Regulation: Law and practice, Kluwer Law International, The Hague, 2004, pp. 56ss.

WADE, J., The Centre of Main Interests connecting factor affords curators no certainty under the Model Law Regime, in International Company and Commercial Law Review, 22 (3), 2011, pp. 102ss.

WARREN, D.J., Relief from the automatic stay: Section 362(d), in Bankruptcy Developments Journal, 3, 1986, pp. 199ss.

WARREN, E., Bankruptcy and article 9: 2017 statutory supplement, Wolters Kluwer Law & Business, New York, 2017.

WARREN, E., WESTBROOK, L., Court-to-court negotiation, in American Bankruptcy Institute Journal, 204, 2003, pp. 28ss.

WARREN, W.D., BUSSEL, D. J., SKEEL, JR., A., Bankruptcy, Foundation Press, New York, 2015, pp. 178ss.

WEBB, D.,K. TARUN, R.W., MORO, S.F., Corporate international investigations, Law Journal Press, New York, 2018.

WEISS, R., Contempt power of the bankruptcy court, in Bankruptcy Developments Journal, 6, 1989, pp. 212ss.

WESSELS, B., A global approach to cross-border insolvency cases in a globalizing world, in The Dovenschmidt Quarterly , 2013, pp. 17ss.

WESSELS, B., International insolvency law. Part II. European insolvency law, Wolters Kluwer, The Hague, 2017.

WESSELS, B., The future European Union legislative framework on cross-border crisis management in the banking sector: A legal stress test, in B. WESSELS, P. OMAR, Cross-border management in the banking sector, Wolters, Kluwer, Nottingham-Paris, 2011, pp. 59ss.

WESSELS, B., What is an insolvency proceeding anyway?, in International Insolvency Law Review, 20 (4), 2011, pp. 492ss.

WESTBROOK, J.L., A global solution to multinational default, in Michigan Law Review, 7, 2000, pp. 2279ss.

WESTBROOK, J.L., International Judicial Negotiation, in Texas International Law Journal, 38, 2018, pp. 572ss.

WESTBROOK, J.L., The duty to seek cooperation in multinational insolvency cases, in Annual Review of Insolvency Law, 2004, pp. 364.

WESTBROOK, J.L., The transnational insolvency project of the American Law Institute, in Connecticut Journal of International Law, 17, 2001, pp. 99ss.

WESTBROOK, L., The elements of coordination in international corporate insolvencies: What cross-border bank insolvency can learn from corporate insolvency, in R.M. LASTRA (ed.), Cross-border bank insolvency, Oxford University Press, Oxford, New York, 2011, pp. 186ss.

WESTROOK, J.L., An empirical study of the implementation in the United States of the Model Law on cross border insolvency, in American Bankruptcy Law Journal, 87, 2013, pp. 247ss.

WIERZBOWSKI, M., GUBRYNOWICZ, A., International investment law for the 21st century, Oxford University Press, Oxford, 2015.

WIGMORE, J.H., A treatise on the anglo-American system of evidence, Little Brown, Boston, 1940, pp. 266, 278ss.

WOJCIK, K.P., Bail-in in the Banking Union, in Common Markets Law Review, 53 (1), 2016, pp. 124ss.

WOODS, L., WATSON, P., Steiner & Woods European Union law, Oxford University Press, Oxford, 2017, pp. 37ss.

XIE, B., Comparative insolvency law: The pre-pack approach in corporate rescue, Edward Elgar Publishing, Cheltenham, 2016, pp. 272ss.

XINYI, G., To recognise or not to recognise? Comparative study of Lehman brothers cases in Mainland China and Taiwan, in International Corporative Rescue, 10, 2013, pp. 240ss.

ZARETSKY, B.L., Codebtor stays in chapter 11 bankruptcy, in Cornell Law Review. 73, 1988, pp. 214ss.

www.ingramcontent.com/pod-product-compliance
Lightning Source LLC
LaVergne TN
LVHW070743240926
848802LV00001B/1